Daring Dynasty

Daring Dynasty:

Custom, Conflict and Control in Early-Tudor England

By

Mark R. Horowitz

Cambridge
Scholars
Publishing

Daring Dynasty: Custom, Conflict and Control in Early-Tudor England

By Mark R. Horowitz

This book first published 2018

Cambridge Scholars Publishing

Lady Stephenson Library, Newcastle upon Tyne, NE6 2PA, UK

British Library Cataloguing in Publication Data
A catalogue record for this book is available from the British Library

ISBN (10): 1-5275-0378-X
ISBN (13): 978-1-5275-0378-6

For my father

A NOTE TO THE READER

This book came about from two different but related directions. For one, over time colleagues suggested that I pull together some of my articles, unpublished conference papers and essays into one volume for easy access. More recently, for four years I taught an upper-level course entitled The Tudor Kings at the University of Illinois at Chicago as a Visiting Professor. Students made a similar proposition with the addition of asking me to include "mini-Introductions" with anecdotes concerning how each piece materialized. I had assigned them several of my articles and essays to read as part of the class and they often asked about the process, the relationships between historians and how a project even came into being—interesting tidbits that usually never see the light of day.

I endeavor to do these things. Books of collected scholarship are usually just that, and they are meant for a specific academic readership. My hope is to reach broader audiences. While the scholarly articles are, predictably, scholarly in nature, I tried to write them using an explanatory narrative for those unfamiliar with the topics. That did not eliminate the "language" historians use in discussing their research, euphemistically called jargon. The papers were for audiences that included those with limited knowledge of English history or the research; hence, less jargon.

The result, hopefully, appeals not only to scholars and students of the period but also to those interested in the Tudors or English history. Indeed, I begin with a paper on the "war of words" between Richard III and Henry VII that cost the former his crown at the expense of the latter who seized it. Even the Bard was enticed to learn about them and pen a play. I put the chapters in a particular order to provide an overview of Henry and England and how people conducted every day affairs, working up from minister and citizen and town to the government and the king, along with a view of his son, Henry VIII. The addenda include two approaches to the historical method and how well-researched historical novels can be an enticing entry point to the real thing.

Finally, I pay tribute to graduate students, disclosing the trials and "fibrillations" of what they encounter when attempting to pass the dreaded Oral Exam for a PhD. It is the least I could do for these brave souls.

NOTE. The reader can continue this early-Tudor exploration at: www.daringdynasty.net or send an email to daringdynasty@aol.com.

TABLE OF CONTENTS

PREFACE

"The king is dead! Long live the king!" Thus the son and heir ascended the throne of England on 22 August 1485 as King Henry VII. He did so amid the cheers of well-wishers vocalizing the eight words of an age-old English tradition—or rather a "borrowed" tradition begun by their arch-enemy the French more than a half century earlier. Those words illuminated a seamless succession ordained by God. They proclaimed the new king on the very day the old king met his earthly demise and heavenly reward. It was followed by a magnificent royal burial of respect and pageantry. Order endured. Life continued. And the immutable world held forth its hope of a good reign and a good king amid peace and prosperity.

That is not how it happened. In fact, what actually occurred boggles the mind and shatters the fairy tale of succession and kingship. Uncovering the real story of what transpired in the reign of the first Tudor king would capture both my imagination and a desire to come as close as possible to figuring it all out after the passing of half a millennium. I could not speak with the man who would become king on that fateful August day. I could not talk to those who served him, supported him, revolted against him or feared him. But I could seek out contemporary writings and records that might divulge what ensued with the hope of trying to sort out what those remnants of the past were truly saying, and maybe what it all meant.

Henry Tudor was not the heir to the throne. In reality, he had perhaps the most anemic claim to the English monarchy since William the Conqueror in 1066. Prior to defeating Richard III in battle on 22 August at Bosworth Field, this twenty-eight year old fugitive spent the last fourteen years of his life in exile. When he invaded England with the aid of foreign soldiers, he claimed he was already king. As if to dare those supporters of Richard to renounce their allegiance to him, the new king, now Henry VII, claimed he was the rightful ruler of England on 21 August, the day *before* the battle. That made all those who fought for Richard at Bosworth Field traitors to the true monarch on that day! They now had to make a choice.

Henry was telling the courts of Europe, the Pope and his own people that he did not usurp the throne by killing the king—he reclaimed his throne from an imposter who rebelled against King Henry VII of England.

Far from the dead king being laid to rest in majesty, Richard III's naked body was tied to a horse and taken to the city of Leicester where it was displayed in public as proof of his death. His burial place there in Greyfriars church was eventually lost to memory, only coming to light in 2012 under a parking lot. After the battle, Henry VII could not even celebrate his victory in London for very long—a disease called the sweating sickness soon began to ravage the city, killing thousands.

Many of Richard's followers and relatives did not go gentle into that good night. They fomented revolts and spawned "pretenders" to the throne for much of the reign in the guise of Richard III's two nephews, whom he purportedly murdered to seize the throne for himself. Moreover, Henry was well aware that of the nine previous English kings, five had been murdered so they could be replaced. He was responsible for the death of the last one. His fanciful claim of descent from King Arthur or his joining of the red and white roses of Lancaster and York did little to quell dissent or danger for his dynasty.

And yet, when the first Tudor king died in 1509 he left behind a very different England than the one he found in 1485. He transformed the realm from an insolvent, often divided country in the waning years of the so-called Wars of the Roses into a stable, emerging modern state, a legacy inherited by his larger-than-life heir, Henry VIII. How did this happen?

Much of my research, and many of the publications and papers based on it over several decades and found in this book, involves my attempt to answer this question. These endeavors represent an ongoing immersion into national and local archives and secondary sources, as well as enjoying innumerable discussions over the years with fellow historians and students regarding different points of view and various paths of inquiry.

One outcome of this pursuit was being named Guest Editor for a special volume of the peer-reviewed journal *Historical Research* devoted to Henry VII to celebrate the 500th anniversary of his death (1509-2009). I contributed the Introduction and two articles, chose the scholars and gave it the enigmatic title "Who was Henry VII?" I thought it fitting since it offered a query about a monarch who was nothing if not enigmatic.

The results of my sojourn to date into the first Tudor's reign suggest a few emerging themes that have made things clearer to me about Henry VII and early-Tudor England. For one, through sheer tenacity and force of will, as well as a pragmatic approach to kingship, Henry discovered how to be king and what succeeded and what failed. He fortuitously received guidance and support from a cadre of financial and legal professionals connected to his mother, Lady Margaret Beaufort, countess of Richmond and Derby. She was a formidable force who used all means to protect and promote her only son, including marrying three husbands (possibly four) for political advantage and outliving them all.

After the first few years of learning and doing, Henry then took over the reins of his reign personally. He came to comprehend how English men and women functioned peacefully in everyday life at the local level, and then imprinted those important lessons on a national scale of royal administration and royal policy.

At the center of his policy was an understanding of the transactional lifestyle of English men and women founded on the customs and laws of the land since "time out of mind". This included entering obligations (in effect, contracts) to buy and sell goods and land, borrow money, keep the peace, appear in a court of law or make promises for future good behavior. Henry was blessed with ministers well-versed in how this way of life worked, and they established a bottom-up approach to ruling the realm based on it. It was therefore the law, in my view, that helped create the nation of England—a national law and the evolving institutions to promote it and serve it. Henry VII made customary and statutory law the cornerstone of his monarchy to mitigate conflict and to control the political winds.

However, there was a dark side to his policy of law and enforcement, one that would tarnish his reputation and forfeit the lives of two of the ministers who followed his lead. Being a master politician like his mother, Henry was the true exemplar of politics, which I define as the pursuit of self-interest and self-preservation through the use of power. Such pursuits could become abusive and harmful, and they did.

Nevertheless, the fact that young Henry VIII retained many of the policies and procedures of his father while resolving some of its defects attested to the success of the dynasty's progenitor. Respect for the law, if not always adherence to it, advanced the melding of the populace and its political players into a modern state. I explain how this came about through the actions of Henry VII and his government, which resulted in the founding of a most daring dynasty.

FOREWORD

SIR JOHN BAKER
Q.C., LL.D., F.B.A.
DOWNING PROFESSOR EMERITUS OF THE LAWS OF ENGLAND
UNIVERSITY OF CAMBRIDGE

Tudor history has never been more popular than it is at present, thanks to a flood of historical novels and plays, both on television and at the cinema. The dynastic aspect of the story, beginning with the "Wars of the Roses", and enlivened by the bloodthirsty disposal of queens and princes who found themselves in the way, have all the stuff of soap operas, combined with the fascination of knowing (as in Madame Tussaud's Chamber of Horrors) that much of it actually happened. It is more difficult to make the public, or even the average history student, interested in how countries actually functioned over the longer term.

No doubt to ponder whether modern England began with the Battle of Bosworth on 22 August 1485—which is when Englishmen traditionally believed the Middle Ages to have ended—is a futile exercise, since any conclusion would require some arbitrary definition of modernity. But there is no doubt that the Tudor period feels increasingly different from what went before, or that—for all its horrors—its features are more readily recognizable and accessible to the modern observer. Nor is there much dispute that some kind of transformation either began or accelerated rapidly under the remarkable monarch who, at the age of only twenty-eight and with the flimsiest of titles to the throne, defeated the last of the Yorkist kings at Bosworth.

In the following articles and essays Mark Horowitz sets out to identify and explain the nature of those changes. The story is largely about money, that is, about Henry VII's financial achievements in restoring the royal fortune while at the same time making his subjects generally feel that they were better off. And it is also about law. England had long been a constitutional monarchy, and the king's ordinary courts of law in Westminster Hall had gone about their daily business, with the same judges, throughout the upheavals of the fifteenth century. The feudal revenue of the crown was based on a sophisticated law of real property, fossilised from an earlier world. Henry VII made sure that the old system worked even better than before.

But he also harnessed the processes of the common law to the establishment of effective government in a new way, through the use of bonds and recognizances (with monetary penalties) to bring counties, towns, officials, and all people of substance, into line. In place of aristocrats and clergy, he filled the government offices with lawyers, men like Thomas Lovell of Lincoln's Inn, Richard Empson of the Middle Temple and Edmund Dudley of Gray's Inn. They proved very good at augmenting the revenue, and they made the mistake of overdoing it.

The king acquired in his own time a reputation for avarice, and after his death Empson and Dudley lost their lives for an imaginary treason—the first horror of Henry VIII's reign, intended no doubt to reassure the public that the new king would be less oppressive. How Henry VIII proceeded to deal with his legacy, and to what extent he introduced his own revolution in government through Thomas Cromwell (another Gray's Inn man who ended a career of royal service on the scaffold), is the other big story tackled here. And there both the author and I share a deep respect for the work of the late Sir Geoffrey Elton, even if we may disagree with some of it.

I do not suppose these stories will be turned into another film script, since their essence resides in the ingenuity of the main actors, the detail of their schemes, and the doggedness with which they were pursued, rather than in dramatic events and set-piece scenes for which riveting dialogue can be invented. But they are at the core of any understanding of the transition from medieval to modern England—whenever that may be thought to have happened.

ABOUT THE STRUCTURE OF THE BOOK

Introductions

As explained earlier in A Note to the Reader, I have written short Introductions to each chapter and addendum. They are anecdotal as opposed to discussions of the historiography of a topic. Nonetheless, I offer explanations for where the topic fit into the scheme of historical scholarship.

Spellings/Abbreviations

Most of the articles in the book appeared in British journals. Therefore, I preserved the British spelling (behaviour, skilful). The remaining articles, papers and reviews retain their original American spelling (behavior, skillful). Abbreviations for the two major document repositories in the UK varied by journal or by time frame when published. I have settled on Brit. Libr. (British Library) and T.N.A.: P.R.O. (The National Archives: Public Record Office). L&P is short for Letters and Papers, Foreign and Domestic of the Reign of Henry VIII. J.P. is a justice of the peace; M.P. is a member of parliament.

Late-medieval English

In most cases, I retained the original spelling found in the documents being quoted: "to cause my wyeff to be brentt & I to be hangyd" (to cause my wife to be burned and I to be hanged). I believe that keeping the spelling intact allows scholars a closer view of what the writer was communicating and even the possibility of discovering different meanings from what is being discussed. C.J. Harrison's critically-important article and transcription of a 17th century copy of Edmund Dudley's "confession" suggested a question to me from one entry that led to a different interpretation simply based on spelling. (Chapter Five). Contractions were common at the time and are mostly retained; for example, c^{r}ten (certain), y^t (that), matt^r (matter), y^e (the), w^t (with), ov^r (over), o^r (our).

Footnotes

Many footnotes seem to go on forever. My sincerest apologies. They were often constructed to provide scholars with expanded or tangential information that might prove useful for their own research, or for greater clarity of an argument. The reader may peruse or pirouette over the footnotes as befitting one's interests. I have also updated certain information where relevant, always with the thought of maintaining the original footnote text throughout the book.

Currency

Currency (species, coin) was in pounds (L or £), shillings (s) and pence (d). These were borrowed loosely from the Roman currencies and symbols of libra (which actually meant "weight" in Latin), solidus and denarius. There were 20 shillings to a pound, 12 pence to a shilling and 240 pence to a pound: £8 11s 3d is eight pounds, eleven shillings, three pence. A mark was two-thirds of a pound: 60 marks equaled 40 pounds (60m, £40). Often unhurried in changing customs and traditions, the British did not "go decimal" with their currency until Decimal Day on 15 February 1971. The shilling disappeared and 100 pence (or pennies) now equaled one pound.

Formats

Some publications and papers originally had spaces or sub-headings or asterisks between sections. I have retained the original format for each work. Quotation marks were a big challenge, whether for quotes, titles or emphasis. The British usually put them inside a comma or period. Americans do not! I have retained what was published by each source. Numbers one through ninety-nine are spelled out; percentages and monetary amounts always use numbers. Other things were modified for continuity and consistency.

Original work

These articles and papers were written over the course of more than three decades except the essay on the PhD Oral Exam, which I view as painfully timeless! Hence, they are reflective of secondary sources and scholarship available and used when they were written. The text is as it appeared in the years noted.

LIST OF TABLES, PHOTOGRAPHS AND ILLUSTRATION

Tables*

Photographs

Illustration

*   Tables 8.1-4 were tabulated by Mark R. Horowitz from data found in all the printed entries in the *Calendars of Close Rolls 1468-1509*.

CHAPTER ONE

RICHARD III AND HENRY VII: A CASE OF ROYAL PROPAGANDA[*]

Introduction

Today we are learning what many believe are new and disturbing concepts related to mass communication such as "fake news" and so-called "alternative facts". To the historian, of course, such notions are anathema to the discipline of seeking the truth, even though history is replete with fake news and alternative facts! With technological advances over the last century, it is easier to deceive enormous numbers of people in a short amount of time. Governments are just now experiencing the consequences of being on both the sending and receiving ends. One can only wonder if 20th century dictators would have been more successful had they possessed "weapons" such as Facebook, Twitter and email.

The goals for targeting large numbers of people with propaganda for political purposes are nonetheless the same regardless of the modes of dissemination. It can be to curry favor for a particular cause, action or belief. Conversely, it can be used to tarnish or harm a reputation or even the functioning of a government. Truth often takes a back seat because it is perception *that becomes the current reality.*

This was the case more than half a millennium ago when Richard III seized the throne of England from his nephew, the uncrowned Edward V,

---

[*] Paper presented at *The Mid-America Conference on History*, 21-22 Sept. 1984, University of Kansas, Lawrence, Kansas. A subsequent paper on a variation of the theme was read at the *29th Irish Conference of Historian*s, 12-14 June 2009, Centre for Historical Research, University of Limerick and Mary Immaculate College, Limerick, Ireland. Finally, a related paper on the use of Arthurian legend and creative genealogy as propaganda to justify the legitimacy of rule by Henry VII and Henry VIII—"The heir of King Arthur: Henry VII's 'historical' claims of kingship and their influence on Henry VIII"—was presented at *The Royal Body Conference*, 2-4 Apr. 2012, Royal Holloway College, University of London.

in 1483. That violence against a rightful king alone gave pretext for a rebellion led by an unlikely rival, Henry Tudor. However, in the context of what was written, spoken and circulated to large numbers of English citizens, it is instructive to explore how messages were crafted and perceived during the short reign of the last Plantagenet king, Richard III.

Because of my background in a parallel life as a marketing communications executive, I have always been curious about how Henry Tudor "pulled off" his revolution. Most scholarship up to the early-1980s centered on the events of 1483-85, usually with a venture into that most famous of mysteries: the murders of the Two Princes in the Tower. I thought it might be interesting to focus on what information Richard and Henry were providing to both their followers and enemies, and how they went about reaching those audiences. That was the basis for this paper.

Those messages did not cease after Richard III's demise. Henry VII continued to marginalize Richard in documents. He also dated his reign the day before *the 22 August battle at Bosworth Field, thereby making himself the rightful king on the battlefield and Richard an imposter. Some historians believe the 21 August dating denoted a means to seize legally the lands of traitors. But Henry could have done that with parliamentary attainders or simply declaring his enemies outlaws: he created a ministerial position to pursue outlaws late in his reign. I think he was communicating his right to the throne because, in truth, he barely had one.*

There is absolutely no way to quantify the effect of their messages or how many people they reached. I would argue we still have the same problem today. Internet traffic is measured in "clicks", which tells us nothing about how many people actually read or paid attention to what was on a web page, let alone if it encouraged them to act or react a certain way. This was already true for measuring "impressions" in newspapers: just because one million people obtained a publication does not mean they read a particular advertisement or article on a specific page, let alone remembered it or responded to it. It is the same with television, where on demand *viewing and storage force advertisers to embed ads despite the fact that viewers easily ignore them.*

In 15th century England, the sheriff read a proclamation in the village; the parish priest informed his flock of something he read, since few were literate; the traveling merchant told people in a northern tavern what he had seen or heard in London—three weeks earlier. In the drama leading to Bosworth Field, all we can do is learn what the participants hoped people were hearing and perhaps believing. The two rivals to the throne of England were purposefully using propaganda to win adherents and dishearten their enemies. It seems to have worked well for one of them.

The reign of Richard III has been scrutinized by historians, poets and dramatists alike since its abrupt ending almost 500 years ago on 22 August 1485. The Tudor dynasty—which supplanted this last Yorkist king—made good use of Richard's ill fortune to discredit his reign, his claim and practically everything connected with his twenty-six months as king of England. Not only is it true that to the victor go the spoils, but also the last word.

And it is precisely words that helped undo Richard's swift usurpation and reign, in part from his actions—imagined or real—in part from the enterprises of an alternative to his throne: Henry Tudor. How this was accomplished is instructive to historians not only for understanding the events of 1483 to 1485, but the subsequent special kind of paranoia that plagued the first two Tudor monarchs: Henry VII and Henry VIII. Moreover, while propaganda was clearly not new to English history or English politics by 1483, the first Tudor king employed a unique posture for rallying support: that of a rival king, as opposed to a rival to the throne per se. Ironically, it was this very ploy that was to cause Henry Tudor so much grief—and almost cost him his throne—after Richard was dead and Henry began his nearly twenty-four year reign as Henry VII.

By the time Richard III assumed the throne of his young nephew, Edward V, in 1483, England had witnessed several usurpations. Henry Bolingbroke began his unwitting march to the throne in 1399 as a persecuted lord seeking redress from an unjust king, his cousin Richard II. But what started out as a quest for justice ended with the overthrow and subsequent murder of the rightful ruler, with Bolingbroke seizing the throne as Henry IV. A half century later, Henry IV's grandson, Henry VI, would face the prospect of losing his throne to another wronged lord, Richard, duke of York, the father of two future kings, Edward IV and Richard III.

In the cases of both Henry IV and Henry VI, however, there was a great reluctance to put forth a rival claimant to the throne, despite the various possibilities emerging from the descendants of the numerous sons of Edward III, who died in 1377. Monarchy was above all sacrosanct in England; one need only recall the angry magnates who forced King John to sign Magna Carta, rather than simply overthrowing him. Attempting to mend the king's ways was an action that the lords—and the politically emerging House of Commons—could live with regardless of the situation.

Even when Richard, duke of York was appointed protector to the enfeebled Henry VI in March 1454, the lords were disinclined to be part of his council because it smacked of royal pretensions.[1] It was only when the Duke saw his power and life threatened by the ruling regime that rebellion became the last resort. Yet even after the Duke's supporters captured Henry VI at Northampton in June 1460, the plan was to call parliament for the reversal of the rebels' attainders. Henry VI was to be left on the throne.

It was Richard, duke of York who perhaps planted the seeds for how successful usurpations might take root in the turbulent 15th century. On 16 October 1460, he decided to claim the throne. He had been protector of the king twice, a forced exile and a man with a bleak future so long as Henry VI's supporters remained in power. Richard claimed descent through one of Edward III's sons, Lionel of Clarence. Lionel was an elder brother of John of Gaunt, the great-grandfather of Henry VI and founder of the Lancastrian line of nobility. Duke Richard also adopted the surname Plantagenet to emphasis his "royal" ancestry.[2] This all was undoubtedly news to many people, since the Duke bore the arms of the founder of the Yorkist line of nobility, Edmund of Langley, the first duke of York. Edmund in fact was a younger—and lesser—royal brother of Lionel of Clarence and John of Gaunt. Richard was clearly changing his lineage and public relations program in mid-air to gain a hereditary advantage.

The Duke may have thought of this move at an earlier date. He was already supporting a steady stream of propaganda by sending letters all over England recounting the grievances suffered through the inept rule of Henry VI.[3] Before invading England from Calais, Richard, his son Edward and other supporters issued a manifesto on the failures of the government and the greed of those Lancastrian lords who seized the rebels' lands after their attainders—this latter lamentation similar to that of Henry Bolingbroke fifty years earlier.

Richard hardly needed to manufacture problems for Henry VI. There was Cade's Rebellion in 1450; the constant rivalry and fighting among roving bands of soldiers; bellicose magnates, with the Percys and the Nevilles slugging it out for the control of Northern England; the disastrous ending of the Hundred Years War for England in the 1450s, losing all of France except for the port of Calais; and the temporary insanity of Henry VI in 1453. The Duke also obtained a useful propagandist in Francisco Coppini, bishop of Terni, who was on a papal mission to sign up Henry VI

---

[1] See R.A. Griffith, "The King's Council and the first Protectorate of the Duke of York, 1453-54," *Eng. Hist. Rev.*, Vol. XCIX, no. 390 (Jan. 1984), pp. 67-82.
[2] Charles Ross, *Edward IV* (1974), p. 16; J.R. Lander, *Conflict and Stability in Fifteenth Century England* (1969), p. 73.
[3] Ross, *Edward IV*, pp. 16ff.

for a Crusade. His ambition got the better of him, and he threw in with the Yorkists and wrote letters to Pope Pius II, telling of the impolitic rule of Henry VI and the just cause of the Yorkists, led by the duke of York. The ending to the Duke's story marks the full-blown internal strife of what much later generations referred to as the Wars of the Roses. He was killed at Wakefield in December, 1460, and a year later, after several battles, his claim was reiterated in parliament, casting the Lancastrians as usurpers and declaring the rightful king as Edward IV, eldest son and heir of the Duke. Proclamations went out to tell the people of this change in the monarchy and to warn against aiding any of Edward IV's enemies, notably the deposed Henry VI and his entrepreneurial wife, Margaret of Anjou. Edward IV thus began a reign lasting from 1461 to 1483, with an interruption in 1470-71 when Henry VI temporarily regained his throne. Henry would to lose it again along with his life and that of his only heir, Edward, Prince of Wales. The lesson of the danger of keeping a "past king" around would not be lost to Edward IV or to his younger brother, Richard, duke of Gloucester and the future Richard III.

It is difficult for any historian to view this period without coming to grips with those undocumented, intangible attributes that crop up in history time and again: fate and luck. That Henry Tudor was fated to become king of England can be dismissed with certainty, despite Polydore Vergil's apocryphal story of young Henry meeting Henry VI for a session on Tudor destiny.[4] Tudor's bloodline was anemic at best, and there were other potential claimants with closer links to the crown.

Luck is another story, and perhaps a bit too unpalatable for the tastes of sober historians. If nothing else, we can say quite comfortably that Henry Tudor's ability to survive, to be supported by cunning relatives and friends, and to take advantage of the prevailing political winds constituted a fortitude that stood the best chance of that most daring of political gambles we call usurpation: the seizure of the crown and rule from the current monarch. And since most usurpers publicly point to Divine Will as the source of their success, we can only guess at what Henry felt when he looked back at the first twenty-eight years of his life that took him from hostage to fugitive to conqueror and king.

We know very little about Henry Tudor from his birth in 1457 to the accession of Richard III in 1483.[5] These were the years of battles between

---

[4] *The Anglica Historia of Polydore Vergil*, ed. and trans. by Denys Hay (1950), p. 5.

[5] See S.B. Chrimes, *Henry VII* (1972), Chapter 1.

the supporters of York and Lancaster, and Henry was little more than a noticeable pawn because of two facts about his parentage: 1) His mother, Margaret Beaufort, was the great-great granddaughter of that prolific progenitor, Edward III, through one of his sons, John of Gaunt, thus occupying a branch on the tree royal, if a gnarled one since her great grandmother, Gaunt's third wife, was his mistress; 2) His father, Edmund Tudor, was the son of a liaison and probable marriage between Henry V's widow, Queen Catherine of Valois, and Owen Tudor, a page and keeper of the queen's wardrobe in the royal household. This latter lineage made Owen's sons, Edmund Tudor and his brother Jasper, half-brothers to Henry VI, and young Henry Tudor a half-nephew of that unfortunate king.

Before Edward IV's usurpation in 1461, things were looking up for these Tudor parvenus. In 1452, both Edmund and Jasper were created earls of Richmond and Pembroke respectively, and three years later Edmund married the intrepid Margaret Beaufort. But on 3 November 1456, Edmund died of natural causes in his mid-twenties; not three months later—on 28 January 1457—his son Henry was born at Pembroke Castle to the thirteen-year-old Margaret. Further disaster befell the Tudors four years later when, at Mortimers Cross, the Lancastrians were routed, Owen Tudor was beheaded and William Lord Herbert took Pembroke Castle, keeping young Henry Tudor and his mother in ward. Jasper Tudor escaped his father Owen's fate and became a fugitive in Brittany and France, where he skillfully made alliances and friends for what was to prove welcome, if precarious, havens for Lancastrian exiles.

The next year, Lord Herbert purchased the wardship and marriage of five-year-old Henry, and it was probably expected that the young Tudor would one day become a Yorkist peer if he behaved himself. The new king, Edward IV, was still not taking any chances. That summer, Henry was deprived of the lands and honor of Richmond, held by right of his father. What the king did with the title is something Shakespeare would have relished had he done a little homework: it was eventually bestowed upon Edward IV's younger brother, Richard, duke of Gloucester, the future Richard III, who would die at the hands of Henry Tudor's armies. Henry, however, continued to use the title "Richmond" for most of his life before becoming king, and there is evidence that this began within three years after losing his earldom.[6]

---

[6] Westminster Abbey Muniments, MS. 6660, document naming Margaret Beaufort, her (second) husband Lord Henry Stafford, and "Henry Dominus de Rychemonde."

During Henry VI's Readeption ("recovery") in 1470 and 1471 when he obtained the throne again, Jasper Tudor was back in England. He supposedly brought his nephew Henry, then fourteen and residing at Raglan Castle, to London to meet the hapless king. By this time, many of the nobility descended from Edward III's offspring had died or had been killed in combat. The battle of Barnet in 1471 and subsequent events dealt the final Lancastrian blow with the murder of Henry VI and the death of his only heir, Edward. Jasper was once again forced to flee, and this time he took Henry with him, probably because by the numbers alone Henry was now a "slight possibility" for the throne should Edward IV do something foolish, or the surviving Lancastrians something enterprising. Their destination was apparently France but a storm blew them into the hands of that moderate political chess player, Duke Francis II of Brittany, where they were to remain as polite prisoners for the next thirteen years. It was perhaps at this time that Jasper, and his former sister-in-law Margaret Beaufort, realized that any future Lancastrian uprising should necessarily put forth young Henry as a possible rival to Edward IV.

This possibility was warily noticed by Edward IV. In a letter dated 28 September 1471, Sir John Paston noted the following:

> It is seyde that the Erle of Pembroke [Jasper Tudor] is taken on to Brettayn; and men saye that the Kynge schall have delyvere off hym hastely, and som seye that the Kynge off France woll se hym saffe, and schall sett hym at lybertie ageyn.[7]

Although Henry Tudor is not mentioned, it is likely that the rumors focused on his uncle Jasper because of Jasper's known adherence to the Lancastrians and his involvement in trying to overthrow the Yorkists. Since, however, this seems to be the first interest in him expressed by Edward IV—the word "hastely" is telling—it is not unlikely that the king was now concerned about a viable rival in place of the deceased Henry VI, namely that of the former king's half-nephew.

Edward IV's final victory over the Lancastrians left him a more cautious monarch. He had been shocked by losing his throne after ten years of rule, and the defeat of his enemies at Barnet could easily have been followed by another attempt to overthrow him if he could not dissipate the ambitions of Lancastrian dissidents. In a proclamation on 27 April 1471, after Barnet, Edward declared that he was the rightful king by judgment given in parliaments past and by God giving him victories

---

[7] *The Paston Letters*, ed. James Gairdner (1875), III, p. 17.

against Henry VI in battle. Yet in a strange elaboration of his title by battle in an otherwise commonplace declaration of legitimacy for a usurper, he went on to say "in such controversy moved between princes upon the high sovereign power more evident proof of truth will not be had than by the said means, that is reason, authority and victory battles."[8] Edward in effect denigrated his father's hereditary claim in favor of a divine de facto rule, and this was to be emulated by the eventual destroyer of his dynasty, Henry Tudor.[9]

If Henry and Jasper were prizes to be had, Edward IV now seems to have made little effort to obtain them. We are told that Edward sought their return from Duke Francis, but this came to nothing.[10] So long as he knew where they were and he could maintain power and authority at home, there was no reason to risk a political conflict by trying to take them prisoner. France, under the wily Louis XI, was longing for an annexation of Brittany, the last independent duchy in his sphere of influence. Duke Francis II of Brittany hoped for aid from England to keep France in check, but not at the expense of forcing Louis XI's hand against the duchy. This situation changed little until the sudden and unexpected death of Edward IV on 9 April 1483, when one of the most famous—and infamous—chapters in English history commenced.

There is always a danger in getting stuck in the problematical murk that stretches across the reign of Richard III. If I may mix metaphors, it also requires us to temporarily tread into the historical firestorm involving the disappearance and likely murders of the Two Princes in the Tower. Few historians have emerged unscathed once they declared whether Richard III extinguished his nephews, or someone else did at his behest or without it—or if Henry VII directed the dastardly deed once he became king. I will attempt to stay on the fringes of the flames although it should be said that the truth in this matter, as in much of history, is often secondary to what people perceived to be the truth at the time. What contemporary or near-contemporary histories and documents we have can be interpreted in a variety of ways, adding to the mystery. Still, when one asks a few basic questions in the sober voice of reason—or at least reasonableness—an avenue or two emerges that can help explain why Richard III lost a throne and Henry VII gained one.

---

[8] *Calendar of Close Rolls 1468-76*, no. 703.
[9] See note 14.
[10] *Paston Letters*, III, pp. 58-60.

We need to ask ourselves how a young exile, who spent half of his first twenty-eight years of life abroad, could become king of England. We must also explore the fragility of Richard's rule and ask what he did to secure it, jeopardize it and what he possibly could have done to avoid his demise. One illuminating observation does surface when looking at the years 1483-1485: Henry Tudor, either through his own devices or from the machinations of his mother and uncle and loyal supporters, chose a role to play which he performed all the way to Bosworth Field, and it seems to have worked. And unlike his usurping predecessors who feared talking of royal claims until the eleventh hour, Henry Tudor decided to wear the purple early and openly. If he would be king, he would be king before God decided the battle, and his rival would be deemed an impostor.

When exactly Henry styled himself king is not known. Nor can we ascertain what lifestyle he led while a virtual prisoner in Brittany. That it at least bordered on one of a special guest may be gleaned from a grant given to John Williams by Henry as king some six weeks after Bosworth Field. Williams is referred to as "grome [for] oure mouth, in our seller . . . unto us hertofore, aswele in the parties beyonde the see as within oure royaume."[11] Henry apparently had his own taster and a kitchen at his disposal, and given Duke Francis' use of Henry as a potential Lancastrian rival to the house of York, we can believe that the young exile was treated with great dignity, royal or otherwise.

Henry's decision to change his stance to one of royalty was undoubtedly influenced by what was happening in England. Surely he kept close watch on the events of the spring of 1483 after the death of Edward IV, when young King Edward V and his brother became the captives of their uncle, Richard of Gloucester, only to disappear from view while Richard declared himself King Richard III. These events—and rumors about Richard's behavior—encouraged Henry Tudor to assume a rival position to Richard III. There is evidence that the transformation from earl of Richmond to legitimate king was complete by the fall of 1483.

In October of that year during Buckingham's futile rebellion against Richard, Henry signed a debt of 10,000 crowns owed to Duke Francis of Brittany to provision an invasion force. Henry signed his name "henry of Richemont", and though there are suggestions that he also signed documents "H R" for Henricus Rex while abroad, this debt should therefore not be construed as vacillating between reality and wishful

---

[11] *Materials for a History of the Reign of Henry VII*, ed. William Campbell, 2 vols. (1873-77), I, p. 76.

thinking. Not only would it have been impractical to sign a legal debt as King Henry—one that couldn't be repaid until he won the realm—it was clear that he was writing the name the world had recognized since he was born. Moreover, his uncle Jasper co-signed the debt, showing a need for validity more than propaganda. Yet a suggestion of Henry's overt claim to the throne appears within the language of the debt, where he promises to repay Duke Francis "on the word of a prince."[12] From now on, Henry Tudor would be king de jure (by right), with the hope of one day becoming king de facto (in fact).[13] This was a complete break from the past century of those who would be king.

Why Henry made this deliberate change can be understood in light of the events and rumors of the spring and summer of 1483. They involved not only Richard, duke of Gloucester's actions and usurpation of the throne but also Henry's own hand at the propaganda game. After Edward IV's death on 9 April, the royal family, represented by the Woodvilles, hoped to run the minority government in the name of the twelve-year-old son and heir of the late king and his wife, Elizabeth Woodville: Edward V. The dead king's brother, Richard of Gloucester, had no intention of allowing this to happen, most likely for fear of isolation, loss of power and lands, and even the loss of his life. Since the king's will provided for Richard to act as protector during his nephew's minority, he decided to test the waters and ask for total control of Edward V in a letter, which was made public. The Italian traveler and monk Dominic Mancini, in England until July 1483 and familiar with the letter, noted:

> This letter had a great effect on the mind of the people, who, as they had previously favored the duke [of Gloucester] in their hearts from a belief in his probity, now began to support him openly and aloud; so that it was commonly said by all that the duke deserved the government.[14]

But the lords in the council, including the Woodville supporters, feared the consolidation of power in the Duke's hands. They therefore set a coronation date for Edward V to make a speedy end to the protectorate.

---

[12] *Brit. Libr.*, Add. MS. 19398 fo. 33.

[13] In essence, "in fact" or "in reality" or "by deed". A de facto king is in actuality king because he is king, without need for further explanation.

[14] Dominic Mancini, *The Usurpation of Richard III*, trans. by C.A.J. Armstrong (1936), p. 89. His writings were first discovered by Armstrong in 1934 in the library in Lille, France.

This letter, and a previous circular letter telling of the Duke's intentions to support his nephew, Edward V, seems to have put him in good light with the people: a propaganda ploy to allay fears.[15] If he hoped that the people—and especially the vitally important city of London— would support him against the council, he never waited long enough to play politics with the Woodvilles. He in effect canceled the good will he achieved by these propaganda letters because of his next actions.

By 30 April, news arrived in London that Richard and his then-ally the duke of Buckingham seized Edward V and arrested Woodville adherents, including the queen's brother, Anthony Woodville (Earl Rivers) and the earl's nephew, Sir Richard Grey, who was also the young king's half-brother. According to Mancini, rumors now spread through London that Richard apprehended Edward V to gain the throne, rather than to protect his nephew. Richard heard of these rumors before entering London and tried to quash them in a letter to the mayor justifying his actions. The damage, however, had been done, exacerbated by the queen, Elizabeth Woodville. She now fled quickly to sanctuary in Westminster with her daughters and second son, Richard, duke of York, Edward V's younger brother.

In a last ditch effort to ameliorate the negative perceptions of his seizure of the king and, in Mancini's words, "to arouse hatred against the queen's kin, and to estrange public opinion from her relatives", Richard sent wagons to London filled with weapons to show that the Woodvilles planned to overthrow him and his allies. The people, however, knew that these weapons were part of a store against the Scots, and Richard's damage control effort turned against him. (One might ask how they knew: did a rumor spread from Henry Tudor's supporters that Richard lied about the weapons?) On 4 May, Richard, Buckingham and the young Edward V with a retinue entered London, and a week later Richard was declared protector by the council. The young king's coronation date was now postponed to 22 June, and the duke of Gloucester retained custody of Edward V in the Tower of London.

Richard's capture of the king was the beginning of a series of mistakes that were to fuel the propaganda engines of his detractors and Henry Tudor's supporters. While it is true that inaction by Richard may have meant his doom at the hands of the Woodvilles, his violence upon his

---

[15] Mancini, pp. 71-73; Charles Ross, *Richard III* (1981), p. 68 and n.18. Richard took no chances and had troops with him. (*Letters of the Kings of England*, ed. J. Halliwell, 2 vols. (1848), I, p. 150.)

nephew the king was something that could not be tolerated by even his most staunch adherents. Although historians have doubted that Lord Hastings, Thomas Rotherham, John Morton and Thomas Lord Stanley were plotting against Richard, duke of Gloucester once the young king was in custody, it was quite probable that these allies of Richard felt that he went too far too quickly. He may have sensed their hesitancy and questioned their loyalty. Morton was a political opportunist who had Lancastrian inclinations, and Lord Stanley, now married to Henry Tudor's mother, Margaret Beaufort, could not be seen as an unwavering supporter. Richard and Stanley had at least one falling out before the events of April and May 1483, and Richard now could ill afford counsel from a man related by marriage to a rival claimant, should Henry Tudor become one.[16]

With rumors of Richard's scheme for the throne in the air and the queen and her children in sanctuary in fear of their lives, the protector now decided the die was cast and there was no going back. His next move was more violent than the incarceration of his nephew, the uncrowned king. On 13 June—and some have argued for 20 June—Hastings was arrested and summarily executed. Rotherham, Morton and Stanley were imprisoned. Richard became the master of his destiny in the ensuing days. He convinced Queen Elizabeth to give up Edward V's younger brother, the duke of York, from sanctuary to attend the coronation, and once in custody Richard quickly canceled it.

Dr. Ralph Shaw then preached Richard's claim to the throne at St. Paul's Cross—which was tantamount to a broadcast to the realm—and Edward IV's children, the two princes and four daughters, were declared bastards because of a pre-contract agreement for marriage between the late king and Elizabeth Butler. On 25 June, Earl Rivers and Richard Grey were executed. The next day, 26 June, Richard, duke of Gloucester was proclaimed King Richard III; he was crowned at Westminster on 6 July.

News spread rapidly of the arrests, executions and subsequent events. In a strange list of memoranda among the Cely letters, written in June of 1483 about the purported deaths of some of Richard's councilors, there is perhaps the earliest mention of the fate of Edward V: "If the King, god save his life, were deceased."[17] This was more definitively declared in an annual list of mayors in the town of Lincoln, where for the year 1483 it was recorded "This yere the kynge sons were put to silence." Beneath this

---

[16] For the falling out, see *Cal. Close Rolls 1468-76*, no. 535.
[17] *The Cely Papers*, ed. H.E. Malden (1900), no. 200.

entry it was noted that now began the first year of the reign of Richard III, which would have been 26 June.[18]

Rumors began to swell in July that both brothers, Edward V and the duke of York, were dead. Mancini, who left England in July 1483, wrote that the two princes lived in the inner apartments of the Tower, "and day by day began to be seen more rarely behind the bars and windows, till at length they ceased to appear altogether."[19] The diplomat and French chronicler Philip de Commines recorded that Louis XI of France was not pleased with Richard III because of the murder of the princes and the breach of oath Richard swore to Edward V.[20] Since Louis died on 30 August, he probably heard the rumors in July or early August. The *Croyland Chronicle* noted that stories of the murders were around by October 1483.[21] Worse for Richard III, everyone believed he was responsible for their deaths. These rumors would not be lost to Henry Tudor.

Richard's immediate concern, it seems, was to establish his authority and protect his newly-acquired throne. To that end he issued a proclamation for the ships under Sir Edward Woodville, a potentially less-than-loyal person to Richard and a member of the royal clan, to return to England. Richard viewed this fleet under Woodville as a threat to his security. Furthermore, he was well aware that Henry Tudor remained abroad in Brittany, and a fleet in his hands could become a formidable invasion force. Fortunately for Richard, his proclamation worked since the captains were Genoese and feared endangering their fellow merchants. Only two ships, one with Woodville aboard, failed to return to England.[22]

Richard also turned to the problem of Henry Tudor, and here we can merely wonder how both felt about their individual situations. The only two people standing in Richard's way to the throne had been his nephews, and at least the public believed that those obstacles had been removed

---

[18] *Anno regni Regis Ricardi tercij primo*. (J.W.F. Hill, "Three Lists of the Mayors, Bailiffs and Sheriffs of the City of Lincoln", *Reports and Papers of The Architectural Societies of the county of Lincoln, county of York, archdeaconries of Northampton and Oakham, and county of Leicester"*, Vol. XXXIX (1927-29), p. 238.) Richard apparently visited Lincoln on 11 Oct. where he received word of Buckingham's rebellion.

[19] Mancini, p.113.

[20] *The Memoirs of Philip de Commines*, ed. Andrew R. Scoble, 2 vols. (1880-82), II, p. 63.

[21] *Croyland Chronicles*, p. 568.

[22] Mancini, p. 105.

forever. The same can be said for Henry Tudor, who would have needed to overthrow not only Edward V but secure the next heir in line, his brother, Richard, duke of York. This Richard III did for him, and it may have been the single event that decided Henry's course of action for the next two years.

Something must have been brewing in Brittany for Richard to instruct his ambassador, Dr. Thomas Hatton, in July 1483, to find out what Sir Edward Woodville was doing, and the inference is that Woodville was in or off the coast of Brittany. A further instruction does not mention Henry Tudor by name, but we cannot doubt that the fugitive is who Richard had in mind: "[find out] if ther be entended eny enterprise out of land upon any part of this realme, certifieng with all diligence all the newes and disposicion ther from tyme to tyme".[23]

Instructions from Duke Francis to his own ambassador to England one month later suggest that, indeed, Henry was on Richard's mind. Francis observed that ever since Edward IV's death, Louis XI tried on several occasions to get the Duke to deliver the "lord of Richmond" to him, with the promise of large payments. The duke of Brittany, however, had refused, probably believing that he could use Henry to gain support from England against France. Francis therefore instructed his ambassador to ask for what amounted to a small army from Richard to defend Brittany. Whether Henry Tudor was the price for this army was vaguely inferred but not definitively stated.[24]

Buckingham's rebellion and its failure in October 1483, and Henry's abortive landing in England at the same time, is more instructive for how it came about than for its consequences. It also shows that Henry Tudor was a real threat to the throne for the first time in his life and that, after the death of Buckingham—who had his own claims to the kingship—Henry had become the major viable claimant for the Lancastrian dynasty.

Our main source for the insurrection is the rolls of parliament, written several months after the rebellion, which recounted the uprising, the conspirators and the punishments.[25] It began by stating that the "greate and singler movers, sterers, and doers" of the rebellion were the duke of Buckingham and John Morton, bishop of Ely, who had escaped imprisonment. The roll stated that besides armed rebellion, the rebel leaders were responsible for "diverse false and traiterous proclamacions

---

[23] *L&P*, I, pp. 22-3.
[24] *Letters . . . Richard III and Henry VII*, I, pp. 37-43.
[25] *Rotuli Parliamentorum*, VI, pp. 244-50.

ayenst oure said Soveraigne Lorde," which helped them acquire supporters.

Buckingham was also accused of sending messages to various people for the same purpose, including communications before the October rebellion. Since the next sentence mentioned Richard's ultimate nemesis— Henry Tudor—we can believe that the conspiracy had been going on for some time if letters were being exchanged and answered across the Channel to Brittany. The accusation from the rolls of parliament read as follows:

[The duke of Buckingham], to execute and accomplish the same his false traiterouse purpos and entent, conspiraction, ymaginacion and compassying, by his severall writyngs and messages by hym sent, procured, moved and stirred Henry callyng hymself Erle of Richemound, and Jasper late Erle of Pembroke, beyng than beyond the See in Britayn, great Enemyes of owre said Soveraign Lorde, to make a great Navye, and bryng with theym an Armee and greate nowmber of people Straungiers from Britayn over the See, and to arrive in this Reame, to the destruction of the most Roiall persone of oure said Soveraign Lorde, and also to th'entent, not onely to destroie the most Roiall persone of oure said Soveraigne Lorde and his true Subgetts, but utterly to destroie and subverte this his Reame; by reason of the which procurement, mocions, writyngs, messages and sendyngs, the said henry callyng hymself Erle of Richemond, and Jasper callyng hymself Erle of Pembroke, and thair adherents, beyng Enemyes to oure said Soveraigne Lorde, comed falselye and traiterously, as false Traitours and Rebells, the said XVIIIIth day of October, the yere abovesaid [1483], out of the partye of Bretayn, with a greate Navie and Armye of Straungiers, within the co[a]stys and corps of this Reame, at Plymmouth in the Countie of Devon', and there falsly and traiterously to have arrived.

Some of this is inaccurate, but it is important to note that Henry had become a force and threat to Richard III. Moreover, the fear of "subverting" the realm is a reference to usurpation, something Richard obviously did not want to happen. The text is such that Henry, as well as Buckingham, could have been the ones viewed as the intended king. With the death of Buckingham, after which this was written, there could be little doubt of who would succeed Richard III in the event of a successful invasion.

The rolls mention other "diverse false and traiterouse Proclamacions" against Richard III, a hint at a full-scale propaganda campaign being waged by Henry and his supporters. Henry took full advantage of Richard's unpopularity and the by now well-known belief that he had murdered his nephews. In a letter Henry signed as king, written from Brittany, he stressed two points: 1) His gratification at his supporters' willingness "to advance me to the furtherance of my rightful claim, due and lineal inheritance" of the crown; 2) The knowledge that his future victory will overthrow "that homicide and unnatural tyrant, which now unjustly bears dominion over you."[26] The reference to "homicide" was clear to everyone opposing Richard III, or to those having doubts about him.

The parliamentary rolls also tell of Henry's mother and her part in the rebellion. As with Buckingham, she was accused of sending messages and tokens to Henry to come to England with an invasion force. She also took out loans for "great somes of Money" from London and elsewhere in England in support of the enterprise, and the impression is that she was quite busy helping both Henry and the duke of Buckingham prepare for their rebellions. Although Margaret was now watched more closely, her husband, Thomas Lord Stanley, escaped recrimination and was made constable of England one month after Buckingham began his fatal rebellion.[27] Richard was throwing a political bone to a potential enemy.

Whether her continued efforts to aid her son influenced Stanley's decision to hesitate at Bosworth Field rather than immediately support Richard in battle may never be known. It is true that Richard held Stanley's son, Lord Strange, as a hostage for sacrifice should the leery lord waiver in support. But given Stanley's past hesitations in battles and politics we might very well view him as the most consistent player in this late-medieval drama.[28]

Polydore Vergil adds further information about Henry's first try at the throne. Apparently, Margaret Beaufort was in touch with the queen, Elizabeth Woodville, still in sanctuary at Westminster Abbey, about the planned rebellion. The queen agreed to a marriage between her eldest daughter, Elizabeth of York, and Henry Tudor in return for supporting Richard III's overthrow. If this story is true—and it appears so—then it would be difficult to believe that the two princes were still alive and being abandoned by their mother in favor of a rival claimant who in effect would be hostile to her family. These were strong, politically-astute mothers of kings and would-be kings. They both had a common enemy: Richard III.

---

[26] *Letters of the Kings*, I, p. 161.
[27] *Calendar of Patent Rolls 1476-85*, p. 367 (18 Nov. 1483).
[28] See Chrimes, *Henry VII*; Ross, *Richard III*; Barry Coward, *The Stanleys Lords Stanley and Earls of Derby 1385-1672* (1983), *passim*.

The events of late-1483 were capped off by a propaganda ploy that brought the plotting of two ambitious mothers closer to fruition. In Rennes Cathedral on Christmas day, Henry's fellow Lancastrian exiles and disgruntled anti-Richard Yorkists witnessed his pledge to marry Elizabeth of York once he gained the throne. Not only did it pose the image of a future monarchy that united the white rose of York with the red rose of Lancaster, however weak Henry's bloodlines, it also forced Richard III's hand.

On 1 March 1484, Richard pulled off a coup for his cause by talking Elizabeth Woodville and her daughters into leaving sanctuary. This blocked off communication between the dowager queen and Richard's enemies, and it ensured that Henry's vow—clearly heard throughout England—could never be fulfilled so long as he had Elizabeth of York in custody. Unfortunately, this politically important move by Richard was to be followed with a series of disasters that ultimately led to his undoing, while feeding the propaganda flames of the Tudor supporters.

A month after Elizabeth Woodville left Westminster, Richard III's ten-year-old son and only heir, another Edward, died. Almost immediately rumors spread that Richard had seized his niece, Elizabeth of York, for the purpose of marrying her to beget an heir, and that he planned to do away with his wife, Anne. Not only did a rumor of another plot by Richard solidify his perception as a murderer, the marriage ploy to his niece was made even more awkward since he had declared his brother's children, including Elizabeth of York, bastards so he could acquire the throne.

It is most likely that this was Henry's supporters at work and we can gain a glimpse of what was taking place from a source none other than Richard III himself and a letter he sent to the mayors and councils of cities throughout the realm that very April. Richard told of "divers seditious and evil-disposed persons both in our City of London and elsewhere within our realm" who were "sowing seeds" of noise and slander against him and his supporters. This was accomplished by setting up bills, sending messages that included "false and abominable lies," and "bold and presumptuous open speech". Richard enjoined the city fathers in London, York and elsewhere to take down the seditious bills "without reading or showing the same to any other person." It would have been useful if someone had preserved one of those bills for us to read today.[29]

---

[29] *Letters of the Kings*, I, p. 158 for York; *Historical Manuscripts Commission*, 11th Report, App., Pt. III (1887), p. 106 for Southampton.

Richard also seemed to have worried about people questioning his title and right to the throne. He harped on it in the January 1484 parliament and in April reiterated his claim to a London livery company.[30] His personal loss at the death of his son, and the rumors about his alleged homicidal behavior, forced him to try and destroy the source of his woes: Henry Tudor. In June, Richard agreed to send Brittany 1,000 archers in return for Henry Tudor. But rather than working through the now frail Duke Francis, Richard plotted with Peter Landais, the Duke's treasurer and an ambitious man seeking his own power base.

Somehow Bishop Morton, in Flanders, heard of the plot and got the news to Henry in time for a clandestine escape to France only hours ahead of Landais' men. Although one historian suggests that Lord Stanley might have tipped off his stepson, it is hard to believe that Richard III, at this time, would have told the husband of Henry's mother of the plan. Given his personality, it is even harder to think of Stanley being involved in something as dangerous as intrigue.[31]

Richard's plot was not only desperate but foolish. To send troops to Brittany was to risk war with France. No wonder Charles VIII welcomed Henry Tudor and his followers with open arms. Moreover, the French government was helping Tudor's war of words and damaging rumors. When the Estates-General met in France from 15 January to 13 March 1484, the chancellor, de Rochefort, mentioned the murder of the princes by Richard III. Richard's blunder in trying to procure Henry was mirrored by his failure to remove Elizabeth of York as a potential queen by marrying her off to one of his loyal supporters. His actions for the rest of 1484 centered only on Henry Tudor's expected invasion, whenever or wherever it would take place.

A further setback for Richard came late in 1484 when John de Vere, earl of Oxford, escaped from a ten-year imprisonment at Hammes Castle near Calais and joined Henry, adding an important lord and military man to the enterprise. On 7 December, Richard issued a proclamation which, in effect, admitted to the reality of his situation. After slandering the rebels and suggesting that they were under the rule of Duke Francis—this a last ditch effort to sway potential rebels with anti-foreign sentiment—Richard said that their leader was Henry Tudor, who through ambition had taken "the name and title of royall astate of this Realme of England, where unto he hath no maner interest, right, title or colour, as every man wele

---

[30] Ross, *Richard III*, p. 186.
[31] Chrimes, *Henry VII*, pp. 29ff; Ross, *Richard III*, p. 199 and for Stanley.

knoweth."[32] The last phrase "as every man well knoweth" suggests that Richard may have been putting up his own bills telling of the spurious claims Henry was making. The proclamation does recite a charge of Henry being a bastard twice over, once through Owen Tudor—called a bastard himself—and secondly through Margaret Beaufort and an unlawful liaison between her great-grandparents, John of Gaunt and his mistress and future wife, Katherine Swynford. Henry IV had barred their offspring from the throne, an action that probably would not have held up in court.

This proclamation is interesting in what it says about Henry Tudor's behavior as a would-be king. It stated that Henry had already promised and handed out archbishopricks, bishopricks, dukedoms, earldoms, knighthoods and other titles and offices. This apparently had been practiced by Henry for some time and we here glimpse how baffling it must have been for Richard to try to counter this exiled "king of England" who was acting out the role of royalty to perfection: he was doing "kingly things". Worse, Richard was at the mercy of repeated rumors about what he did with his nephews. If the princes were alive, he didn't use the easiest way out by producing them for public view.

Richard tried to take charge of events by concluding a formal truce with Duke Francis in March, 1485, since he greatly feared the possibility of invading ships from that strategic duchy.[33] Yet no sooner was Richard trying to secure his position but another disaster hit: his wife, Anne, died on 16 March. Once again the rumors began to spill out over England, this time that Richard killed his wife and was yet again going to marry his niece, Elizabeth of York. The rumors may have been effective. Commines, commenting on Anne's death, noted laconically "some say he made her away."[34] It is easy to imagine that Henry encouraged this story.

By June 1485, Richard made ready for the expected invasion of Henry Tudor. On 23 June, he reissued his proclamation of 7 December and called his people to arms. The rest, we might say, is history. Henry landed near Milford Haven in Wales on 7 August, gathered forces in addition to his foreign contingent and English exiles, and fought against Richard's forces near Market Bosworth on 22 August. Lord Stanley held off support for Richard—and for his stepson, Henry—long enough to force Richard to gamble on a desperate charge against Tudor, only to fall and die in battle.

---

[32] Found in various forms in *Brit. Libr.*, Harleian MS. 433 and here taken from the *Paston Letters*, III, pp. 316-20.
[33] *Cal. Pat. Rolls 1476-85*, p. 545.
[34] *Commines*, I, p. 398.

Henry's long exile ended and, almost poetically, so did his pretense as king—a pretense lasting almost as long as the reign of his rival and victim, Richard III.

Henry Tudor, now Henry VII, continued his propaganda against Richard III throughout his long reign, adding a store of tales and lies that would make their way into Shakespeare's play. He also followed in his deceased father-in-law's footsteps—Edward IV—by speaking of being restored to his realm.[35] Although Edward had been a Yorkist and Henry VII represented the Lancastrians, the victor of Bosworth Field was careful to tread lightly on Edward's name since he was soon to marry his daughter, Elizabeth of York. In one document we see Henry VII referring to Edward as "our noble progenitor King Edward IV of foremost memory".[36] Predictably, Richard III did not fare well. He was usually referred to as "Richard late in deed and not in right King of England", and on occasion simply "our great enemy the late duke of Gloucester".[37] It was only after Henry was well-established on the throne that the pejoratives petered out. In his last parliament in 1504, a statute referred to his defeated rival only as "King Richarde the therd".[38]

Unfortunately for Henry, others with ambitions similar to his own were taking notes, and his reign was plagued with pretenders and Yorkists claiming to be king, including impersonators of the dead princes. More than once, he had to don armor and defend his throne, and his fate could easily have gone the way of Richard III. Such royal impostors took their toll on Henry who, though liberal with pardons, could also be harsh with rebels, including William Stanley, his step-uncle, who helped him win his crown. Henry had him executed in 1495 for conspiring with a rival who would be king.

The first Tudor king was well aware of these dangers. So was his second son, the future Henry VIII, who set about destroying members of the Yorkist dynasty so he could sleep better at night. As with most propaganda campaigns, when they work they are often emulated. Henry VII won his campaign of words with a victory in battle. The possibility of someone following his lead was to haunt him for the rest of his life.

---

[35] *Brit. Libr.*, Lansdowne MS. 511 fos. 20-v.
[36] T.N.A.: P.R.O, E 404/85, 30 Nov. 1504.
[37] T.N.A: P.R.O., PSO 2/1, 9 Feb. 1486; C 251/27 no. 13; C 82/280, 1 Dec. 1505; PSO 2/1, 18 Sept. 1485.
[38] 19 Hen VII c. 5 (1504) (*The Parliament Rolls of Medieval England 1275-1504*, Vol. XVI, Henry VII, 1489-1504, ed. Rosemary Horrox (London, 2005)), p. 332.

Chapter Two

A Country Under Contract: Early-Tudor England and the Growth of a Credit Culture[*]

Introduction

One of the critical questions concerning Henry VII's reign involves how he managed finances and obtained income. While that does not suggest a very striking subject compared to Henry Tudor defeating Richard III for the crown of England—"A horse! a horse! my kingdom for a horse!"—governments nonetheless run on cash. Unless things have changed after this writing, the United States government inflicts itself periodically with the possibility of not paying its debts, and it makes for a weakness in governance and in economic stability. In the realm of monarchy, poor kings rarely fared well. Not being able to live on their own meant seeking sources of income and often sharing power to obtain it. It seems as though Henry VII did very well. How did he do it?

By 1485, royal income came largely from royal lands and prerogative rights (money from wardships, marriages, fees and the like). Then there were grants from parliament, including customs on trade. From near bankruptcy under Henry VI to a rise in trade and population during the course of the 15th century, by the end of Henry VII's reign his total revenue was in excess of £100,000 annually. Yet after 1504, he did not need parliament for money and hardly asked for much in his last one. At the same time, there is a wealth of evidence that shows how Henry VII spent much of his day: going over financial accounts and often writing his name or sign manual (H R, for Henricus Rex) on every page. He scrutinized the books and scrolls of his treasurer of the chamber and his

---

[*] Reprinted with permission. The article was first published in *Essays in Economic and Business History*, Vol. XXIX (2011), pp. 75-86.

financial ministers. In a letter between mother (Margaret Beaufort) and son, we learned that Henry's eye sight was going bad. No wonder!

He also cultivated new sources of income that were not really new: prosecuting old and new contracts in the form of bonds and driving in money owed on them. What he did do unlike kings before him was pursue these obligations with a vengeance. This is discussed throughout the book, along with a tabulation of one potential source of revenue from such bonds in Chapter Eight.

Nevertheless, I always thought it would be helpful to place Henry VII and his financial activities into a context not only of England before his time but also in view of the Continent. Culling from research used in my other work plus some new exploration into English records, I had an opportunity to present a relatively short explanation of the development of England's credit economy and what I believed was taking place during Henry's reign. It was published in a journal reaching mainly non-English history and economic scholars and a wide range of interests, especially of the European kind.

Many of the historical explanations for the growth of modern English credit and finance often overlooked the late-medieval and early-modern periods. They favored instead a delayed fruition by focusing on economic growth in late-Tudor and Stuart England and the anticipation of the founding of the Bank of England in 1694. Moreover, European practices regularly dominated the discussion to show both borrowing and influence, especially from the Italian city-states.

However, as I hoped to demonstrate, England developed methods of credit and business transactions through the use of written obligations long before Continental financial instruments: they pervaded all aspects of English law, administration and finance. The central theme that has focused my investigations of the reign of Henry VII involved the intensification of using and prosecuting these written contracts to bring law and order to the realm and a steady flow of revenue to the crown.

This article provided an overview of how a bottom-up system developed and expanded through English common and statutory law, ultimately becoming the main form of statecraft for the first Tudor king. Henry VII's success in business, finance and the prosecution of the law stemmed from his recognition that, upon acquiring the throne of England, a country under contract *already existed among private parties, public courts and a developing centralized government.*

Beginning in the late-12th century, the European economy underwent rapid changes for reasons that are not completely understood. Both markets and production expanded, along with the parallel development of urban centers. Financial instruments facilitated this growth, including written contracts, provisions for banking and credit, and bills of exchange. These transactional devices may have been created in part to skirt the laws and anathema of usury prosecuted by the church.[1] Also fueling this expansion was an increase in species as silver was mined in Eastern Europe, contributing to the transformation of the lord-vassal relationship from one of service or in-kind responsibility to one of cash payment.[2]

Some have argued that it was the ruling elites who created demand for goods, markets and the methods to obtain luxuries and commodities by developing credit processes that worked for both buyers and sellers.[3] But few disagree with the observation that European credit and financial advances, with especial concentration in the Italian city-states, became models for later economic developments in other countries. Whether England was a beneficiary of these advances or was already pursuing a separate track for financial innovation is the subject of this paper.

Traditionally, when historians studied the economic and financial developments of late-medieval England that contributed to the rise of the modern state, emphasis was usually placed on the ends, not the means. For example, royal government finance has been analyzed from the perspective of transitional economies, such as the shift from the export of wool to the finishing and export of cloth; or from fiscal changes based on efficiencies in land revenue collection and the changing role of parliament in its struggle to establish both a governmental identity and greater involvement in taxation, spending and policy.[4] The duchy of Lancaster—which was the largest household and portfolio of land holdings in England

---

[1] S.H. Rigby, *English society in the later middle ages: Class, status and gender* (London, 1995), pp. 127-43; Diana Wood, *Medieval economic thought* (Cambridge, 2002), p. 5; John H. Munro, "The medieval origins of the 'financial revolution': usury, rentes, and negotiability," *The International History Review*, 25 (Sept. 2003), pp. 505-562.

[2] For example, Peter Spufford, *Money and its use in medieval Europe* (Cambridge, 1988).

[3] Edwin S. Hunt and James M. Murray, *A history of business in medieval Europe, 1200-1550* (Cambridge, 1999).

[4] E.g., W.C. Richardson, *Tudor chamber administration 1485-1547* (Louisiana State U., 1952); B.P. Wolffe, The *royal demesne in English history: the crown estate in the governance of the realm from the Conquest to 1509* (Ohio UP, 1971).

before 1399 when it became part of the royal demesne—has been frequently cited as a model for more effective government administration and finance.[5] However, until most recently the duchy had not been analyzed from the viewpoint of the means by which it would become a model in the first place.[6]

The same is true for finance and economic development at the local level of English society, stressing the developing role of regional and municipal elites and the parallel decline of the manorial system in favor of an increasingly non-feudal society with a shift in judicial power from the lord of the manor to the legal courts in London. Again, often lacking from these discussions are the means by which such changes were facilitated.

Written obligations

Those means in fact relate to how English men and women commonly conducted daily interactions involving purchases, borrowing, trade, land transactions, legal disputes and contractual agreements: through a document called a written obligation—which was sealed and often signed between parties—and its enrolled offspring, the recognizance. These *de facto* contracts, collectively described as bonds, had existed in England for centuries. By the reign of the first Tudor king, Henry VII (1485-1509), it is not difficult to describe the realm he administered as a country under contract.[7] The judiciary functioned at both the local and national level through such bonds. They had several uses: for appearance at court; to abide arbitration, especially in actions of debt but also for consummating land transactions; to keep the peace; and to promise allegiance to the crown. The use of these contractual debts facilitated revenue collection both locally and through royal departments in a country where species remained at a premium. They were utilized to purchase goods and services, to transact trade, to secure offices such as a sheriff or customs

---

[5] Robert Somerville, *History of the duchy of Lancaster*, 1 (London, 1953). For an analysis of the duchy and its relation to the crown politically as well as financially under the Lancastrians, see Helen Castor, *The king, the crown, and the duchy of Lancaster: public authority and private power, 1399-1461* (Oxford, 2000).

[6] Mark R. Horowitz, "Policy and prosecution in the reign of Henry VII," *Hist. Research*, Vol. LXXXII, no. 217 (Aug. 2009), pp. 412-58. [Chapter Three]

[7] For examples and discussions of a cross section of society engaged in the use of written obligations, see Horowitz, "Policy and prosecution," *passim*; Sean Cunningham, "Loyalty and the usurper: recognizances, the council and allegiance under Henry VII," *Hist. Research*, Vol. LXXXII, no. 217 (Aug. 2009), pp. 459-81.

official, to obtain wardships of minors or to acquire ecclesiastical appointments. Because collateral or third-party guarantors (sureties) were usually involved in a bond, which often included penalties for non-payment or late-payment, they were the precursors of modern debit and credit instruments. Moreover, all classes of society used such written instruments.[8]

So, for example, in the year 1478 the widow of a London grocer had in her possession among the debts owed her husband twenty-nine written obligations that she planned to sell. According to her husband's wishes, she first had to offer them to two tradesmen, and if they had no interest in purchasing them then she could make them available to a grocer and a fishmonger. However, they could acquire the obligations only if they purchased them "at an equal price with others, without fraud, they shall have the same."[9] It is important to think of these instruments in the way the public viewed and utilized them at the time: binding, negotiable, perpetually viable, enforceable, fungible and omnipresent.

What follows is a brief example of the language in a simple written obligation: "William is bound by obligation in £30 to pay Robert £20 by the feast of Easter next coming, or to forfeit his goods and lands." The bond would be dated, and in this example there is a built-in penalty of 50 per cent—William must pay £30 instead of the £20 he owes Robert only if he fails to fulfill his payment obligation by the feast of Easter. A condition may or may not be stated in the bond, such as the reason for the debt. In this instance, the condition relates to the penalty: pay £20 on time or forfeit £30 in cash or in goods and lands. There could also be co-signors, or sureties, for William. The obligation would then add a phrase such as "Henry and John each are bound in £10 for William to fulfill the conditions of the obligation." They as well could lose their pledged amounts, which clearly gave them an incentive to make sure William paid on time.[10]

---

[8] Horowitz, "Policy and prosecution," pp. 413ff; P. Nightingale, "The intervention of the crown and the effectiveness of the sheriff in the execution of judicial writs, c. 1355–1530," *Eng. Hist. Rev.*, Vol. cxxiii (2008), p. 5.

[9] *Calendar of Close Rolls 1476-85*, no. 449, discussed in Horowitz, "Policy and prosecution," p. 414. In London, written obligations were purchased and assigned to third parties from an early date. By the 15th century the courts recognized this application of bond sales and afforded purchasers similar rights to those of the original bondholders. (Caroline M. Barron, *London in the later middle ages. Government and people 1200-1500* (Oxford, 2004), pp. 61-2.)

[10] Ranulf de Glanvill (d. 1190), the 12th century justiciar to King Henry II, explained at length the process and validity of this aspect of a bond in a work attributed to

Robert, who was the creditor, would take physical possession of the written obligation, which each party put their seal to and possibly signed. In theory, he would return the document to William upon fulfillment of the agreement. For non-payment or late payment, Robert could go to court and sue William and his sureties, producing the obligation as proof of the debt.

Regarding penalties, those written into these bonds could also represent interest on a loan, thus escaping the prohibitions against usury although perhaps the fear of damnation was less worrisome than may be apparent.[11] For the present example, William borrowed £20 and owed his creditor £30—a 50 per cent interest charge if this was a simple loan. The historian Michael Postan noted long ago that such deceptions were quite common in medieval loans in England, and no doubt they became more prevalent after the use of moneylenders declined with the expulsion of the Jews in 1290.[12] Even Robert Grosseteste, who was consecrated bishop of Lincoln in 1235, admitted that usury was hidden in contractual debts.[13] Moreover, it has been observed that forward contracts on the sale of wool

---

him. (Glanvill, X, ed. G.D.G. Hall (London, 1965), I, 2-8, 12, pp. 118-26.) Modern historians using the printed summaries of bonds, such as those in the *Calendar of Close Rolls*, can fall into the trap of missing exactly how much each surety contracted for unless the original documents are viewed. For a discussion on this critical subject, see Mark R. Horowitz, "Henry Tudor's treasure," *Hist. Research*, Vol. LXXXII, no. 217 (Aug. 2009), pp. 578-9. [Chapter Eight]

[11] European merchants may have compartmentalized their consciences in formulating contracts with interest written into them, although a few sought forgiveness for their sin upon reaching their deathbeds. (Kathryn L. Reyerson, "Commerce and communications," in *The New Cambridge Medieval History V, c. 1198-c. 1300*, ed. by David Abulafia (Cambridge, 1999), pp. 64-5.) Elsewhere it has been argued that the "financial revolution" occurred in the 13th and 14th centuries as a response to harsh usury doctrines, but at least in the case of England contract law developed out of common law where interest or penalties were customarily part of the process. (Elaine S. Tan, "An empty shell? Rethinking the usury laws in medieval Europe," *The Journal of Legal History*, 23 (Dec. 2002), pp. 177-96; Munro, "Financial revolution," pp. 505-562.)

[12] M.M. Postan, "Credit in medieval trade," *Econ. Hist. Review* (1928), p. 2; "Private financial transactions in medieval England," *Vierteljahrschrift fur social- und Wirtschaftsgeschicte*, 23 (1930), pp. 26-75; Robin R. Mundill, "Christian and Jewish lending patterns and financial dealings," in *Credit and debt in medieval England c. 1180-c. 1350*, ed. by P.R. Schofield and N.J. Mayhew (Oxford, 2002), pp. 46ff.

[13] S. Menache, "Matthew Paris's attitudes toward Anglo-Jewry," *Journal of Medieval History*, 23 (1997), p. 154; James McEvoy, *Robert Grosseteste* (Oxford, 2000).

by English monasteries since the 14th century carried interest rates averaging 20 per cent.[14]

Legal difficulties with sealed contracts

One weak point in a written obligation was the means to identify its authenticity should an action at law ensue. Seals became the final proof of a written agreement in England and northern France, while on much of the Continent the notary validated a document. As one historian noted, "England ever remained emphatically a land of seals, the employment of which became essential to the authentication of all public and private documents."[15] When Ralph de Grendon acknowledged a debt of £200 to the bishop of Bath and Wells in a bond enrolled at chancery and due in 1291, he did not own a seal. To authenticate the bond, two people present during the process were required to use their seals, one of them being an agent of the bishop.[16] In an action at law, loss or defacement of a seal led to the suspension of an action on a written obligation. This stance remained firm throughout the late-medieval period, summed up by a case before king's bench in 1527, which concluded that if a seal fell off a written obligation it could render it valueless.[17] A stolen or lost seal—much like identity theft today—could also prove to be financially hazardous. Henry de Perpoint came to chancery at Lincoln in 1280 and said he had lost his seal, and therefore any instrument found stamped with it after the present date was to be void and of no effect.[18]

Another vulnerability pertaining to these contracts, which could prove devastating for the debtor, was how to ascertain that a debt or stipulation

---

[14] Adrian R. Bell, Chris Brooks and Paul R. Dryburgh, "Interest rates and efficiency in medieval wool forward contracts," *Journal of Banking and Finance*, 31 (Feb 2007), pp. 361-80. At one manor in Havering, Essex, obligations were recorded with penalties ranging between 150 and 200 per cent. (M.K. McIntosh, "Money lending on the periphery of London, 1300-1600." *Albion*, 20 (1998), pp. 557-71.)

[15] T.F. Tout, *Chapters in the administrative history of mediaeval England*, 6 vols. (Manchester, 1920-33), I, pp. 122-3; Horowitz, "Policy and prosecution." pp. 454-58.

[16] *Cal. Close Rolls 1288-96*, p. 118 (1289).

[17] O.W. Holmes, Jr., *The common law* (Boston, 1881), p. 261; Theodore F.T. Plucknett, *A concise history of the common law*, third ed. (1940), p. 348; A.W.B. Simpson, *A history of the common law of contract, the rise of the action of assumpsit* (Oxford, 1975), pp. 90, 267.

[18] *Cal. Close Rolls 1279-88*, p. 63.

in an obligation had been fulfilled. Despite their long history, there was no set procedure for cancellation of a bond. This may have been a major reason for increasing actions to recover debts, with the creditor denying payment received on the bond or the debtor failing to recover the actual written bond from the creditor with or without a written acquittance.[19] Technically, an obligation was discharged upon completion of the stated condition or performance of the agreement, either by the debtor or his assignees. There were several ways this could occur. They could be nullified at law by certain pleas, or as the 13th century English jurist Henry Bracton noted "as where an obligation has been extorted by fraud or duress; (or) by an exception of *res judicata*, as where one has been acquitted of an obligation by judgment."[20] A creditor could also discharge an obligation fictitiously by declaring that the conditions were fulfilled when in fact they were not. Alternatively, a written bond could be discharged by novation (*novationem*), or the transference of a contract from one person to a second. This cancelled the original obligation and created a new one, often with sureties and a new penalty. Finally, the simplest completion of an obligation was for the debtor to perform the condition.

However, once the condition of an obligation was met it was essential that the debtor either physically obtained the actual sealed obligation from the creditor—at which time it should have been destroyed—or a written acquittance stating the bond was now null and void forever. Whether through a debtor's carelessness or for some other reason, the problem involving custody of the written instrument became a legal nightmare. It is no wonder that a recognizance for 2,000 marks enrolled in Edward III's reign carefully stipulated that each of four installments would not be paid until an acquittance for each payment was forthcoming; the fourth and final payment was to release the actual written bond.[21] Failure to receive

---

[19] Numerous acquittances, or written discharges of an obligation, are extant, in direct contrast to the dearth of written obligations because they were most likely destroyed once they were obtained by the debtor. In the University of Chicago Bacon MSS. (3185-4053), some one hundred acquittances are preserved from the years 1320 to 1785.

[20] *Bracton on the laws and customs of England*, II, trans. by Samuel E. Thorne (Harvard U. P., 1968), p. 288.

[21] From the close rolls, 48 Ed III, quoted in *Select cases concerning the Law Merchant*, I, ed. by Charles Gross, Selden Society V. 23 (1908), p. lvi (15 July 1374).

such proof could result in a greedy creditor's prosecution of the instrument at law, even if the conditions of the bond had been met.

This view of the strength and force of a written contract prevailed throughout the late-medieval period, culminating in the case of *Donne vs. Cornwall* in 1485 at the start of Henry VII's reign.[22] In this case, the defendant paid money owed on a bond and then received the actual instrument, although he "foolishly failed to destroy it." The plaintiff wrongfully recovered the written obligation, brought an action on it, and the court decided that the defendant's plea regarding the circumstances was not good: the bond existed, so it was viable.

Recognizances: enrolled, pre-judged obligations

There also developed the practice of having these private debts between parties "recognized" and recorded before the crown or a local court or council as an extra guarantee for validity and future payment. In the early-13th century in King John's reign, William of Berningham came to the king's court and recognized a debt to the bishop of Ely for 10 shillings per year for certain lands. The debt was enrolled by a clerk on the *Curia Regis Rolls* for future reference and possible action at law. In another obligation, contracted at Edward III's court held in Northamptonshire in 1350, Richard Gluneul, chevalier, recognized a debt of £20 to Richard de Fryseby and John de Chorper, payable within the same year.[23]

These recognizances, like the written obligation, represented a consensual transaction between two parties. However, they were enrolled on a permanent record before an official tribunal; copies or "certificates" were made as further proofs. It was, in effect, a judgment; the debtor admitted openly that the debt was good and by his consent. This made the burden of proof easier for a creditor seeking an action for default or non-performance of an agreement. Although ostensibly a safeguard for validating a written obligation, the recognizance also shortened the process for an action on debt since the debtor's liability was already established. The royal chancery, where many of these debts were recorded, became a national archive that could play a relevant role in judicial proceedings on records of obligations held by that department. The chancellor and his

---

[22] Quoted in Simpson, pp. 99-100. (See *Yearbooks*, 1 Hen VII.P.F.14, pl. 2.)
[23] *Curia Regis Rolls*, Vol. II, 3-5 John, p. 211; Northamptonshire Record Office, Fitzwilliam MS. 2045.

officials also began to render judgments on debts and deeds recorded in
their presence.[24]

Contracts and the crown: Statutes Merchant and Staple

Obligations owed the crown (*ad usum regis*) functioned in much the
same way as private transactions, the most common being a debt for a
given sum. These debts were written, signed, sealed, and retained by the
exchequer, various royal departments or courts of law, or any number of
officials, returnable to the debtor upon completion of the conditions,
financial or otherwise. When Walter, bishop of Exeter, contracted a debt to
King Edward II for £80 10s 9d, payable by 24 May 1318, the exchequer
retained the obligation until payment was made to the treasurer and
chamberlains. In a loan of 500 marks to the abbot and convent of
Westminster Abbey in 1307, the debt was to be repaid at the exchequer in
London.[25] In each case, a written obligation to the crown took the form of
a customary private debt. In effect, age-old local practices for transacting
business and legal matters became imprinted at the royal governmental
level for finance and the administration of law. It was a striking example
of change taking place from the ground up.

The wool trade between England and the Continent contributed to the
steady rise in the use of written debts. Customs on wool, begun in 1275,
represented not only an additional source of income for the monarch but
also the start of governmental encouragement for the wool trade in the
form of statutes. These included laws that simplified the means by which
merchants could transact and recover debts. However, it is important to
remember that validation by recognizance predated the later statutes for
merchants, and written obligations were as well enrolled in the early
Letter-Books of the common council of the corporation of London and
other municipalities before their expanded usage by the crown.[26] The

---

[24] Simpson, p. 126; Postan, "Private financial instruments," pp. 35-6.
[25] T.N.A.: P.R.O., C 81/1661, exchequer warrants; Westminster Abbey Muniments
MS. 12191, 18 Aug. 1 Ed II. (The abbot was Walter de Wenlock.) The exchequer
was the repository for most records and official documents, e.g., an order to deliver
from Northampton all the chirographs, bonds, tallies and charters, etc. to the king's
exchequer, from the chest there. (*Cal. Close Rolls 1279-88*, p. 4.)
[26] E.M. Carus-Wilson and Olive Coleman, *England's export trade 1275-1547*
(Oxford, 1963), pp. 1-2; Hubert Hall, *Select cases concerning the law merchant*,
Selden Society (London, 1932), 46, III, pp. xiii-iv. The chamberlain of London
took recognizances before 1283. (n. 5.)

government now attempted to codify and regulate such enrollments by statute, and both the royal government and the merchants benefited from these long-standing traditions and procedures.

The Statute of Acton Burnell (1283) set out to correct abuses suffered by merchants involved in contracting debts.[27] A merchant who wished to "make sure of his debt" could now appear with his debtor before the mayor of London, York, Bristol and other towns designated by the king. The creditor, if not satisfied by the due date, could bring the actual obligation before the mayor for comparison with the enrollment. After validation, the mayor was empowered to seize the movable goods of the debtor, order an extent of his possessions and imprison him for insufficient collateral.[28]

Despite this attempt to standardize procedures for merchants locally, recognizances by Statute Merchant were also enrolled on the close rolls at the evolving royal "department" of chancery. On 26 May 1306, a memorandum was recorded stating that Sir William le Vavassar came into chancery and acknowledged before the chancellor that he was paid £10 6s 8d owed him in a "statute of Acton Burnell" by Elias de Whitely; le Vavassar now agreed that the written obligation he held for the debt "shall be hereafter of no value." The probability that le Vavassar was not a merchant widened the gap between the intended use of the Statute and what actually occurred. The use of the Statute Merchant by non-merchants led to the Ordinance of 1311, which temporarily suspended all debts by Statute unless between merchant and merchant.[29] Clearly, there was a

---

[27] *Statutes of the Realm*, 11 Ed I. The literature on this statute and the Statute Staple is important but often neglected. The volumes edited by Hubert Hall are tedious but mandatory reading for an in-depth discussion of these laws (II, III, Selden Society, Vols. 46, 49 (1929, 1932).) See also the articles by Postan; Plucknett, pp. 348-9; Simpson, pp. 126-30, 253-4, 487. Summaries of the statutes are found in Carl Stephenson and Frederick George Marcham, eds., *Sources of English constitutional history* (New York, 1937), pp. 173-4, 228-30. For a more recent discussion, see Christopher McNall, "The business of statutory debt registries, 1283-1307," in *Credit and debt in medieval England*, pp. 68-88.

[28] See, for example, the long but interesting suit on a Statute Merchant in Edward II's reign, summarized in English. (Brit. Libr., Add. MS. 4524 fos. 102-120.) One penny for every pound of the debt was to go to the royal clerk. These procedures differed slightly for a market fair, and the statute was amended two years later (13 Ed I, *Second Statute of Merchants*).

[29] *Cal. Close Rolls 1302-7*, p. 442. Examples of recognizances and procedures on Statute Merchant and Staple from the close rolls are found in Hall, III, pp. liiiff. Postan surveyed Letter-Books A and B of the corporation of London and found

growing need for written debt procedures and management among all classes of society, and the government sought expediencies to help. Self-interest was part of the motivation, as royal intervention and facilitation of debts helped increase duties and fees to the crown and its administrators.

In 1353, parliament passed the Statute of the Staple.[30] Because of the growth in trade during the first half of the 14th century and the need for revenue by Edward III to help sustain the Hundred Years War, this statute provided for certain staple towns to be established in England, circumventing both the commercial activities and potential profits at the urban centers outside England handling the staple trade. Fifteen towns were designated and the procedure for taking the enrollment of debts and adjudicating them was modified from the earlier Statute Merchant. Although instigated for the use of merchants, others once again took advantage of enrollments by Statute Staple, a circumstance that was finally ended in 1532.[31]

Both types of recognizances relied on the chancery to obtain writs against a debtor for non-payment. But when these writs and the status of the cases were returned to chancery, many pleas commenced there. This was hardly surprising, not only from the inducement of fees coming to the clerks at chancery, but also from the fact that litigation under statutes Merchant and Staple could be transferred to chancery by a writ of *certiorari* to obtain a remedy. Here was the beginning of the connection between written obligations being both filed and litigated at chancery, and at a time before chancery went "out of court" to become a separate institution.

The steady expansion in overseas trade during the 15th century insured the pervasiveness of enrolled recognizances and written obligations, especially for debt. In fact, sales credits based on these bonds formed the financial basis for English medieval trade.[32] Monarchs often borrowed

---

that 75 per cent of the 600 recognizances entered were between merchant and merchant. The Ordinance of 1311 was never strictly enforced and became more lax as enrollments increased and fees accumulated. (Postan, "Private Financial Instruments," p. 39.)

[30] *SR*, 27 Ed III, St. 2, c.9.

[31] *SR*, 23 Hen VIII, c. 17. See Simpson, p. 129. At one point, a statute amending the 1353 one extended the "statute staple" to "every person, be he merchant or other." (36 Ed III, c. 7.) The enrollments for bonds by Statute Merchant and Statute Staple lacked any reference to cancellation of debts, which as discussed earlier led to many actions at law.

[32] Postan, "Credit in medieval trade," p. 87.

money from the Staple against the future customs duties; these transactions were accomplished by written obligations acting as tallies or receipts, in effect making the written bond negotiable "currency" for payment.[33] But it is again important to stress that obligations and recognizances were in existence before the statutes Merchant and Staple, before the first customs duties in 1275 or the great increases in the wool and cloth trades. These laws reflected English custom and tradition—the acceptance of written and recorded bonds as a successful means to make transactions between parties viable and enforceable.

Henry VII and his "bond policy"

By Henry VII's reign, private transactions had evolved to where such bonds existed in perpetuity until fulfilled and cancelled, or forfeited and prosecuted; sons, daughters, executors and future heirs could owe upon the written obligations taken out decades earlier.[34] Such precedents were well-established. In the mid-13th century, John the son of Hugh died. An entry on the chancery rolls noted that if the executors of John failed to find sufficient surety for debts owed the king, the amounts due would be taken from their lands and movable goods.[35]

The formation of Henry VII's pervasive bond policy for ruling England was therefore no accident or stroke of genius, although as a method of statecraft it clearly was *sui generis*. It must be remembered that Henry spent the last fourteen years of his life in exile before defeating Richard III in battle and becoming king in 1485. He had little or no experience in running or financing a government, let alone even knowing how to be a king. Fortunately, his mother Lady Margaret Beaufort had both managerial experience and knowledge of key personnel who through

---

[33] W.I. Haward, "Financial transactions between the Lancastrian government and the merchants of the staple from 1449 to 1461," printed in *Studies in English trade in the fifteenth century*, Eileen Power and M.M. Postan, eds. (New York, 1966), pp. 303-6, 296ff.). Another discussion in this volume shedding light on 15th century trade is E.E. Power, "The wool trade in the fifteenth century," pp. 39-91.

[34] The liability of heirs and executors for debts on bonds of the deceased was upheld in a suit in 1253. (Paul Brand, "Aspects of the law of debt, 1189-1307," in *Credit and debt in medieval England,* p. 32.) For an example of one of many "old bonds" prosecuted in the reign of Henry VII, see Mark R. Horowitz, "Richard Empson, minister of Henry VII," *Bull. of the Inst. of Hist. Research*, 55 (1982), pp. 46-8. [Chapter Four]

[35] *Cal. Close Rolls 1254-6*, p. 114.

her influence would become Henry VII's chief ministers and administrators. Their financial and legal backgrounds centered on household finance or debt collection, and several had worked at the duchy of Lancaster where written obligations were utilized for finance and justice.

It was these men and their backgrounds and expertise that formed the basis for the first Tudor king's bond policy. Reynold Bray had been the steward and receiver-general in the household of Sir Henry Stafford, second husband of Lady Margaret. Account books for their finances included entries of obligations. At the beginning of Henry VII's reign, Bray was appointed chancellor of the duchy of Lancaster, where bonds continued to be taken both for judicial purposes and revenue collection. James Hobart, a deputy-steward at the duchy prior to Henry's accession, became the king's attorney-general and entered into many bonds with his fellow councilors on behalf of the king. Richard Empson had been the attorney-general of the duchy under Richard III and now worked closely with Bray; he would eventually succeed him as chancellor of the duchy. Edmund Dudley became both Henry VII's chief administrator of bonds and the president of the council. Both Empson and Dudley remain for posterity the infamous "bond prosecutors" who lost their heads because of their behavior in vigorously prosecuting obligations and recognizances. Many other working councilors of the new monarch had been employed in a Tudor household or were connected with Bray. They as well had experience in taking and collecting bonds.[36]

These ministers and officials schooled Henry VII in the execution and management of obligations and recognizances, not only for the many bonds taken from people to appear in court or keep the peace, but also in the collection of debts owed the crown from land revenues, trade, taxes and prerogative rights. Henry had both royal and local administrative records searched for old recognizances still due, and he kept boxes of obligations in his chamber, many of which were prosecuted.[37] The close rolls at chancery were both scrutinized and transformed into records of recognizances due the king. Contemporary men and women were upset and angry at this intensification of bond prosecution, but not to the point

---

[36] Horowitz, "Policy and prosecution," pp. 424ff, for an in-depth discussion of Henry VII's "working councilors" prosecuting his bond policy. [Chapter Three]

[37] Henry kept bonds and documents in his own "litell coffer", and a servant of one of his bond policy ministers delivered to the king's treasurer of the chamber nineteen obligations of good abearing (good behavior) in one box, two obligations in another box, and twenty-one obligations in a third box (Brit. Libr., Add. MS. 21480 fos. 167, 180v, 184).

of a "recognizance revolt". After all, the first Tudor king was simply following the laws and customs of the realm as they pertained to written obligations, although with an enthusiasm not seen before or since his time. Many bonds had lapsed unpaid, and through efficiencies and commitment Henry VII sought to obtain any and all revenues due the crown.

Not only did Henry become the first solvent English monarch in centuries in large part from this policy, he as well brought peace, stability, affluence and security to a land rife with unruliness and local power struggles during the period romantically known as the *Wars of the Roses* (c. 1455-85).[38] This was in part due to his vigilance in placing people in bonds for good behavior and allegiance to the king: hundreds of people were under such financial vulnerability should they be found in contempt of their obligations. Henry's ministers prosecuted these bonds vigorously, with the result of not only filling the royal coffers but also garnering respect for the law and making a commitment to a secure monarchy. His accomplishments, and indeed much of his infamy, were the result of this ubiquitous use of bonds; this ushered in a Tudor dynasty well-versed in the use of "credit" and contractual agreements to achieve and maintain prosperous rule. Henry and his ministers recognized the efficiency and effectiveness of bonds as a means to an end, and they took advantage of the fact that such contracts were in use for centuries as an acceptable, common way to transact business, law and finance.

Obligations in various forms were in use before the Conquest in 1066 and they became the mainstay for most aspects of everyday transactions in England.[39] Henry VII inherited a realm under obligation, figuratively and literally, and he took full advantage of the age-old, cultural adherence to English law and custom. It was the intensification of this use of bonds and their prosecution that brought him wealth and stability, but also accusations of greed and graft, mainly through the misuse of these legal instruments by two of his ministers, Richard Empson and Edmund Dudley.

Nevertheless, the reliance on written obligations would continue through the 16th and 17th centuries at both the local and national level. It is therefore important to understand that long before modern finance fully reached fruition in England, culminating in the late-17th century establishment of the Bank of England, there was a thriving credit

---

[38] For Henry VII's treasure and success with his bond policy see Horowitz, "Henry Tudor's treasure," pp. 560-79.

[39] Holmes, *The common law*, pp. 254ff.

society—one that was, to use a traditional phrase, in practice since "time out of mind". But it was based primarily on English custom and tradition, and not directly on Roman law or various Continental practices.

CHAPTER THREE

POLICY AND PROSECUTION IN THE REIGN OF HENRY VII[*]

Introduction

This article—the crux of how I view the reign of Henry VII in the realms of finance, administration and law and how it contributed to the development of the modern English state—almost lost its way from over-ambition. I like to describe it with a sentence that lends itself to a whimsical but telling visual:

"Suddenly, he ran out of the house, jumped on his horse and rode off in all directions."

The article originally encompassed the entire topic of how Henry VII used written contracts, or bonds, in a variety of financial and legal areas to bring law and order to the realm while enhancing his treasury. Not only did I want to show the origins of this royal policy, which I thought had been overlooked or misunderstood, but also how it played out with the cities and towns of England and with ordinary citizens, often harshly. I hoped to use a strange case about a man named Thomas Sunnyff as an example of the larger picture of what was taking place at the local level.

I sent a draft of what had become a very long article to John Guy at Cambridge, whom I have known for some time and for whom I have great respect as a historian, careful researcher and friend. John patiently read it and wrote me back, telling me what I clearly needed to hear and probably suspected once I "jumped on my horse". His conclusion: I actually had several articles, not one! He was right.

Therefore, I decided to write the Thomas Sunnyff segment first, which appears as Chapter Five. I then concentrated on the cities and towns and how the use of bonds was folded into a means by which Henry VII gained

---

[*] Reprinted with permission. The article was first published in *Historical Research*, special 500th Anniversary issue on the death of Henry VII, ed. Mark R. Horowitz, Vol. LXXXII, no. 217 (Aug. 2009), pp. 412-58.

a measure of control over municipalities. That is now Chapter Six. I also had the opportunity to discuss my thoughts about the cities with James Lee, who had done a lot of work on town elites. As it turned out, our views were quite complementary as to Henry's relations with urban centers. At the same time I was working on the town piece, I laid out how I wanted to attack my major thesis about Henry's policy and how it was implemented. Fortuitously, Henry VII's death provided me with a place to publish it.

After the Sunnyff article came out, I suggested to Historical Research *that they might consider doing a special issue on the 500th anniversary of the death Henry VII for the year 2009. The editors liked the idea, especially since they knew that the year would be flooded with commemorative publications for the 500th anniversary of the beginning of the reign of his better-known offspring, Henry VIII. As mentioned in the Preface, I was asked to be the Guest Editor, write the Introduction, contribute articles and pick the scholars on both sides of the Pond. The article that follows is the third destination of my horse ride.*

These are my beliefs on how Henry VII succeeded in establishing his dynasty and moving England into the modern era. I addressed certain issues that I felt were often taken for granted. For example, I wanted to discuss how the king's chamber became the national repository for cash owed the crown as well as an administrative "department" for prosecuting bonds. Historians often held up the duchy of Lancaster as the model for chamber finance. The duchy, originally a huge portfolio of lands held by the duke of Lancaster, came into the royal demesne when Henry of Lancaster became Henry IV in 1399.

But how exactly the financial aspects of the duchy worked was never detailed despite a seminal book by Sir Robert Somerville in 1953—a year after Walter Richardson published his work on Tudor chamber administration. In looking at this question, I discovered that the duchy used bonds to drive in revenue, much as the chamber did under Henry VII. And it was no surprise that many of the king's councilors who used these instruments for the king's policy were connected to the duchy, including all three chancellors there during Henry's reign: Reynold Bray, John Mordaunt and Richard Empson. This connection formed the royal policy.

Sir Robert also discovered two books of entries seemingly kept at the duchy during the reign that involved proceedings before several of Henry VII's working councilors, in effect providing valuable information about what they did in light of the lack of most of the proceedings of the council. Because the phrase "council learned in the law"—often spelled "counsel"—appeared at intervals, Sir Robert concluded this was a special council charged with prosecuting prerogative and other royal rights. It has been called the council learned *ever since. Respectfully, I had doubts.*

Lords and ladies kept their own "council/counsel learned", as did the city of London. Counsel did not always mean council, nor was it viewed that way in Henry VII's reign or beyond. It meant people. Even Hall's Chronicle *referred to Empson and Dudley as "bothe learned in the laws of the realme", without a mention of counsel. John Guy has talked about spelling and what council/counsel meant at the time, and to me it is tenuous to create a court or council out of a phrase. Moreover, quite often the "counsel learned" participants were referred to simply as "counsel". They did their work wherever they happened to be, and they were sometimes called "counsel for the time being". That hardly suggests an institution or court—there was no "exchequer for the time being".*

Indeed, Thomas Cromwell referred to the "counsel learned" at a time when it was supposed to have disappeared. To me it probably never was. It pertained to personnel, with individuals promoting the king's policy and rights. I would recommend those interested in these "new men" of Henry VII (mainly lawyers and non-churchmen, breaking from the past) to consult Steven Gunn's well-researched book on them.

Another area for exploration involved whether Henry VIII continued his father's bond policy and to what extent he reversed many of the debts owed his father. I discussed what was the accepted view that indeed people had their bonds cancelled in the new reign—a clear departure. Yet in viewing the actual documents involved rather than printed summaries, it could be determined that many were cancelled after they were paid! *The policy thus continued well into the new reign.*

I also wanted to show how Henry VII was directly involved in prosecuting his policy beside scrutinizing accounts. It became evident to me that the king was actually assigning work to his councilors. One account book I came across in the National Archives had a thick cover. In examining it carefully, I saw what looked like very faded writing on the back. Using an ultraviolet light the letters emerged—it was Henry VII's handwriting. As discussed below, Henry was instructing Edmund Dudley to use the book to drive in money owed on the bonds recorded in it.

Finally, the entire thesis rests on the fact that bonds were used in England for centuries before Henry VII's reign [Chapter Two]. His royal policy was thus created from the bottom up, not the top down. There was no learning curve for English men and women about what the king was doing. That it could be harsh or intrusive was another story.

Whether Henry VII was an innovator, renovator or simply lucky has
not been definitively ascertained in the years since S.B. Chrimes's
biography of the king, although a recent work has provided greater
clarity.[1] One unapologetic admirer of Edward IV proffered the opinion
that the first Tudor's reign "was not a type of kingship appropriate to late-
medieval England". This presumed, of course, that Yorkist successes and
failures were somehow appropriate in a world that was supposed to stand
still in a medieval pose.[2] Such an argument, or a disdain for Henry VII, did
not advance the unravelling of how and why this usurper succeeded in
bringing stability to the realm amid intermittent uprisings, unprecedented
solvency to the monarchy, and viability to a dynasty in less than twenty-
four years—about the same period of time in which all three Yorkists lost
their thrones at least once (and two of them also shared the label "usurper"
with the first Tudor).[3] It was fortunate for both Henry VII and the
development of the modern state that he did not share a belief in repeating
the "medieval" failures of the past, or in doing royal business as usual.

One significant image of the shape-shifting first Tudor, supported by
mounting evidence, is that of the hands-on ruler who, working directly
through trusted and competent ministers, officials and servants, actively
prosecuted the laws of the realm to secure not only a more orderly, law-
abiding society but also a potentially enormous source of royal revenue
previously untapped with any regularity by his predecessors.[4] Whether the

---

[1] S.B. Chrimes, *Henry VII* (Berkeley, Calif., 1972); S. Cunningham, *Henry VII*
(2007).
[2] C. Carpenter, "Henry VII and the English polity", in *The Reign of Henry VII*, ed.
B. Thompson (Stamford, 1995), pp. 11-30, at p. 22. Carpenter seemingly
undermined her understanding of what Henry VII actually accomplished by noting
that her views were "not based on any original research on the reign" (p. 11, n. 1).
[3] Carpenter, pp. 14, 19. She also castigated those who utilize government records
to determine what the government was doing. Such statements as wondering why
Henry VII used chamber finance "when there was a perfectly good exchequer" (p.
28) demonstrate the need to study and understand government records and
documents within the context of the political and economic realities of the time.
However, explorations into central archives nonetheless must be supplemented
with local evidence to show the interplay between the realm at large and the royal
government. The present study hopes to illustrate how longstanding customs and
practices throughout the shires and towns of England became a centrepiece of
royal statecraft.
[4] See, e.g., D. Grummitt, "Henry VII, chamber finance and the 'new monarchy'",
Hist. Research, Vol. LXXII (1999), pp. 229-43, at pp. 241-2; M.R. Horowitz,
"'Agree with the king': Henry VII, Edmund Dudley and the strange case of

"exaction" of money due on both law enforcement and financial debts called obligations and recognizances was harsh or par for the period will continue to be discussed and debated.[5] So, too, will the deeds and malversation of the only two proponents of these activities to lose their heads for their efforts: Sir Richard Empson, knight and Edmund Dudley, esquire.[6]

Nonetheless, this perspective is not new to the study of early Tudor history. G.R. Elton noted that "the king was trying to restore solvency and power to the crown, but he was also trying to bring peace, justice and order to the realm; rightly he regarded the first as the necessary condition for the second".[7] Both F.C. Dietz and W.C. Richardson spent time discussing what can collectively be called bonds as aspects of finance and chamber administration, an important examination of government that continues today.[8] But it was Henry's contemporary court observer Polydore Vergil who perhaps first recognized a behavioural pattern and mode of governance that was more steadfast than serendipitous: "the king claimed that he tolerated these exactions of set plan, in order thereby to maintain the population in obedience".[9]

This "plan"—or what we today would call a major policy—involved taking and driving in debts, fines and penalties arising from the various written obligations and the enrolled or filed recognizances taken by royal

---

Thomas Sunnyff", *Hist. Research*, Vol. LXXIX (2006), pp. 325-66, at pp. 325-6 [Chapter Five]; and various writings and papers by Grummitt, Steven Gunn, John Guy, Dominic Luckett, John Watts, Margaret Condon and Sean Cunningham, among others.

[5] It more or less began tangentially with the Elton-Cooper debate of a half-century ago (G.R. Elton, "Henry VII: rapacity and remorse", *Historical Jour.*, i (1958), pp. 21-39; J.P. Cooper, "Henry VII's last years reconsidered", *Historical Jour.*, ii (1959), pp. 103-29; G.R. Elton, "Henry VII: a restatement", *Historical Jour.*, iv (1961), pp. 1-28. Of interest is that, as Chrimes observed, of the seventy-five pages of discussion barely two were devoted to recognizances. (Chrimes, p. 310).

[6] Of note is that both men signed their surnames differently from the spellings given to them for centuries. Dudley signed his name "Dudeley"; Empson wrote "Emson". There are numerous samples of both in the various documents for Henry VII's reign housed at The National Archives.

[7] G.R. Elton, "A restatement", pp. 27-8.

[8] F.C. Dietz, *English Government Finance 1485-1558* (Urbana, Ill., 1920; New York, 1964); W.C. Richardson, *Tudor Chamber Administration 1485-1547* (Baton Rouge, La., 1952).

[9] *The Anglica Historia of Polydore Vergil*, ed. D. Hay (Camden 3rd ser., lxxiv, 1950), p. 131.

officials, courts and central and local departments from citizens high and low for a multiplicity of reasons. These included payments for customs duties and farms; licences to trade; entry into lands; promise of allegiance or keeping the peace; securing an office (and sometimes paying for its discharge at the end of tenure); ecclesiastical livings; wardships and marriage; renegotiation of an old debt; appearance in a court of law or before a judicial proceeding or conciliar court; payment for pardons—in fact, debts to the crown, real or potential, for just about anything one could incur involving money or behaviour.[10] One critical quarter for ministerial activity related to political and societal stability involved bonds concerning the law and its maintenance, among them those for appearance at court, good behaviour ("good abearing") and keeping the peace, bail and fines. This vital area did not simply target the enclave of the nobility, but all stations in life.[11]

---

[10] Although there are varying definitions of a recognizance and its relation to an obligation, this author views the former in its legal description as an obligation of record, which was entered into before a court or record or an authorized official or magistrate, with a condition to complete a specific act (appearance, keep the peace, pay a debt). It differed from an obligation because it was witnessed only by the record and not by a party's personal seal (see appendix). Medieval English society knew the difference, although sometimes circumstances could dictate. In an entry of debts in Henry VII's chamber account for 31 Oct. 1504, Anne Tropnell was recorded as owing the king £66 13s 4d "opon an oblig"—with the word "oblig" crossed out and "recoig" written next to it. The next time she was listed for the same amount, on 2 Apr. 1505, it was called a recognizance. It was enrolled at chancery as a recognizance on 28 March 1504, with payments due by instalments. This was for a wardship (T.N.A.: P.R.O, E 101/413/2/3 fos. 165, 213; *Calendar of Close Rolls 1500-9* no. 314; *Calendar of Patent Rolls, Henry VII, 1494-1509*, p. 432). The same correction occurred for George and Walter Herbert (T.N.A.: P.R.O., E 101/413/2/3 fo. 198). Recognizances usually required sureties, which was not often true for an obligation: "John Treguram and Pieter de Opuciis are bound in an obligation to pay [100] li. by Hallowtide next coming or else to find sufficient sureties by that day to be bound in a recognizance to pay the same [100] li." (quoted, with modernized spelling, in M.R. Horowitz, "An early-Tudor teller's book", *Eng. Hist. Rev.*, Vol. XCVI (1981), pp. 103-116, at p. 105 and n. 2, from Brit. Libr., Add. MS. 21481 fo. 290). [Chapter Nine] However, see the obligation discussed below recorded by William Mordaunt, acting as a surety.
[11] See Sean Cunningham, "Loyalty and the usurper: recognizances, the council and allegiance under Henry VII", *Hist. Research*, Vol. LXXXII, no. 217 (Aug. 2009), pp. 459-81. J.R. Lander's article on bonds related to the nobility ("Bonds, coercion and fear: Henry VII and the peerage", in *Florilegium Historiale: Essays Presented to Wallace K. Ferguson*, ed. J.G. Rowe and W.H. Stockdale (Toronto, 1971), pp.

Indeed, given the surfeit of bonds investigated and discovered, taken, filed, enrolled, renegotiated (compounded) and either prosecuted or arbitrated during the reign involving both private and public parties, it is not difficult to reach a stark conclusion: when it came to English men and women interacting between each other or with a local government, a royal court or an official requiring a promise, oath or debt, Henry VII ruled an England under obligation, legally and literally.[12] What has not been fully appreciated for the period is that most business was conducted through written debts, not through actual cash payment.

A reminder for modern historians of the ubiquity of bonds as a critical finance tool is an enrolment in chancery on 4 October 1478 involving Alice Gairstang, widow of a London grocer. The entry, in the form of an indenture between the widow and two mercers, noted that she possessed among the debts owed to her husband twenty-nine written obligations that she wished to sell. It stated that Alice was required to give the right of first refusal to the two mercers, or then to a grocer and a fishmonger, but only if they "buy those obligations at an equal price with others, without fraud, they shall have the same".[13] It is important to think of these instruments in the way they were viewed and utilized at the time: binding, negotiable, enforceable, fungible and omnipresent.[14]

The present discussion takes the view of Henry VII's use of bonds as a far-reaching "bond policy", one that evolved through the experience and activities of his trusted councillors and the recognition that the king could do the king's business in much the same way as his subjects conducted affairs in their own lives. Moreover, it involved English men and women of all walks of life, and not just the high born. In this way, it became a true

---

327-67) overshadowed what was actually taking place throughout the realm, although it has been touched upon since, e.g., M.M. Condon, "Ruling elites in the reign of Henry VII", in *Patronage Pedigree and Power in Later Medieval England*, ed. C. Ross (Gloucester, 1979), pp. 109-42, at pp. 119-20.

[12] It has become clear that, under Henry VII, fiscal policy affected all groups in society, and that it was based on precedent and tradition (e.g., P.K. O'Brien and P.A. Hunt, "The rise of a fiscal state in England, 1485-1815", *Hist. Research*, Vol. LXVI (1993), pp. 129-76).

[13] *Cal. Close Rolls 1476-85* no. 449.

[14] In London, written obligations were purchased and assigned to third parties early on, and by the 15th century the courts acknowledged this practice and provided purchasers with the same rights as the original bondholders (C.M. Barron, *London in the Later Middle Ages: Government and People 1200-1500* (Oxford, 2004), pp. 61-2).

national policy, one that folded in other political necessities pursued by the king.[15]

It was the long-established traditions and procedures for binding parties through a credit system of payment that allowed Henry's bond policy to take form and expand.[16] (see appendix) In fact, the policy could not have succeeded if it was in conflict with the accepted daily intercourse of society. This included a shift in the view of the centre. John Watts has aptly pointed out that while dynastic associations and affinities were still important by 1485, such loyalties were tempered by the "habits of obedience to the crown", and that Henry Tudor therefore had a blank slate. Gerald Harriss noted that society wanted a more effective government.[17] In this regard, the new king and his ministers could be viewed as perspicacious. However, it was both the specification and intensification of prosecuting all manner of obligations and recognizances that separated Henry VII from previous regimes. What needs to be explained is how this policy came about and developed during the course of the reign almost to subsume much of the business of the king and his close and trusted officials and ministers. Moreover, it would be helpful to assess his policy and its impact on the realm—one that did not simply vanish upon his death 500 years ago.

It should come as little surprise that many of the answers lie not only in the accepted traditions and customs of the kingdom but also in the very personal nature of Henry's reign. Relying on trusted friends or even allies of one's parents or family members to run a government is hardly a unique

---

[15] Margaret Condon wrote of the "conscious" and purposeful policies of Henry VII during his reign that separated him from the Yorkists and the past: the large-scale secularization of clergy appointments, who were now not so much theologians as administrators; the paucity of peer creation, in part a reflection of the strength of the king as opposed to Edward IV's rule; the shift in power at the local level to the gentry from the nobles, straining and minimizing the inherent gentry-lord relationship (Condon, "Ruling elites", *passim*). The bond policy of the royal government went far beyond these targeted actions to pervade and encompass the entire realm.

[16] "By the later Middle Ages the use of credit was ubiquitous". (J.L. Bolton, *The Medieval English Economy, 1150-1500* (1980), p. 303.

[17] J. Watts, review of S. Cunningham, *Henry VII* (review no. 624) <http://www.history.ac.uk/reviews/paper/watts2.html> [accessed 21 Nov. 2008]; and J. Watts, "'A New Ffundacion of is Crowne': monarchy in the age of Henry VII", in Thompson, pp. 31-53, at pp. 35-6; G.L. Harriss, "Political society and the growth of government in later medieval England", *Past & Present*, cxxxviii (1993), pp. 28-57, at pp. 32-7.

concept, whether one studies the Caesars or the recent two-term U.S. presidency at the start of the present century. What strikes a special chord during Henry VII's sovereignty is the relation between the shared expertise and talents of his ministers and the accepted procedures of law and finance already in practice throughout the realm since "time out of mind"—Henry's councillors were experienced in taking and prosecuting bonds, and they applied what they knew to help run the royal government. This allowed the policy to flourish and succeed with little public outcry during the reign. The king was not so much innovating as executing age-old procedures to great effect and, as contemporaries would argue, often with a vengeance and an intensity never seen before or since his time.[18]

The purpose here, therefore, is not to return to an Eltonian view of persistent, planned bureaucratic developments but rather quite the opposite.[19] Henry VII was a pragmatist schooled in what might be called "pure politics": the pursuit of self-interest, self-preservation and the means to obtain and maintain both through the use of power. He knew this required actions to achieve the objectives of a financially sound, law-enforcing monarchy that could lead to a viable dynasty—something that his immediate predecessors failed to achieve. What was purposeful involved a bond policy to bring those objectives to fruition, and it came about not through deliberate design but from an understanding of what worked and what did not—with a critical reliance on learned councillors familiar with and committed to this *modus operandi*, in sharp contrast to the administrations of Henry VI and Edward IV.

Furthermore, while designations such as "office", "court", "council-counsel" and "department" are helpful for present-day historians to discuss areas of administration, finance and justice, they are obfuscating because responsibilities and tasks devolved upon the king's councillors and faithful men, not the titles they assumed.[20] Even today in our self-described

---

[18] E.g., *Hall's Chronicle*, ed. Sir H. Ellis (1809). Such a view was echoed by Raphael Holinshed, *Chronicles of England, Scotland and Ireland* (6 vols., 1807-8), iii; *A Survey of London by John Stow*, ed. C.L. Kingsford (3 vols., Oxford, 1908-27), i; Francis Bacon, *The History of the Reign of King Henry VII*, ed. J. Rawson Lumby (Cambridge, 1885).

[19] G.R. Elton, *The Tudor Revolution in Government: Administrative Changes in the Reign of Henry VIII* (Cambridge, 1953).

[20] This is discussed in the duchy of Lancaster section below. John Guy proffered the terms "counsel" and "consall" as the consultative process and "council" or "consaill" as a deliberative institution, but noted that from the earliest times to Elizabeth I "the two usages were utterly confused" (J.A. Guy, "The rhetoric of

modern world the same types of players may be found running
governments while blurring bureaucratic responsibilities and organization
charts to achieve the political needs of the leader. Indeed, it could be
argued that Henry Tudor might have felt some familiarity with how
statecraft in many countries functions in the 21st century.

Monarchs, nobles, gentry, clergy, merchants and artisans alike kept
accounts of the various bonds they entered. They preserved original
documentation in boxes, "coffins" or "caskets" for future reference,
especially when it was necessary to begin or defend an action at law.[21]
Such actions were not uncommon and all classes were represented in the
king's courts: half of the defendants in king's bench from East Anglia
between 1422 and 1442, for example, were yeomen or husbandmen.
Moreover, credit and debt "was part of everyday life, not just for
merchants, but for peasants and the upper classes".[22] Although there is a
dearth of surviving private household accounts and journals from the late
15th century, it is clear that those people who kept such books recorded
everything from private transactions to daily diets.[23] Two such accounts

---

counsel in early modern England", in *Tudor Political Culture*, ed. D. Hoak
(Cambridge, 1995), pp. 292-310, at p. 292). The confusion may, in part, be our
own. E.g., historians might consider treading lightly on the notion of a "council
learned in the law" for Henry VII's reign, as opposed to "learned counsel"
(lawyers and learned men) doing the king's bidding in certain areas involving the
law and finance (R. Somerville, "Henry VII's 'council learned in the law'", *Eng.
Hist. Rev.*,Vol. LIV (1939), pp. 427-42). This is discussed below. In Henry's time,
the modern definition of office was often referred to as a "room", and "finding an
office" sometimes meant discovering an action at law.

[21] For an example of a "casket", see T.N.A.: P.R.O., C 244/156 no. 138, a casket
where letters, writings and muniments were kept. For "coffin", see the following
section on the duchy. There are printed examples as well: in 1464-5, a servant of
Sir John Howard paid 16d for a "lyttle coffere" and 1d was "paid fore a box" (*The
Household Books of John Howard, Duke of Norfolk, 1462-71, 1481-3*, intro. by A.
Crawford (Stroud, 1992), p. 487).

[22] P. Nightingale, "The intervention of the crown and the effectiveness of the
sheriff in the execution of judicial writs, c.1355-1530", *Eng. Hist. Rev.*, Vol.
CXXIII (2008), pp. 1-34, at p. 5. For king's bench, see P.C. Maddern, *Violence
and Social Order: East Anglia, 1422-42* (Oxford, 1992), p. 40.

[23] M.K. McIntosh, "Money lending on the periphery of London, 1300-1600",
Albion, xx (1988), pp. 557-71, at p. 560. McIntosh studied the manor of Havering,
Essex, and noted that the obligations for delivery of goods or cash often

are vivid illustrations of the care and scrutiny given to personal business affairs by the time Henry VII became king and exemplify the pervasiveness of written obligations.[24]

The first is that of William Mordaunt, brother of Sir John Mordaunt, the friend and councillor of Henry VII and chancellor of the duchy of Lancaster. William became an important servant of justice, receiving a commission of the assize in 1490 and one for gaol delivery a year later—commissions he held for the remainder of the reign. Besides his role as a county judge, Mordaunt also had connections in the City. He was a treasurer of the Middle Temple and the chief prothonotary in the court of common pleas. Numerous folios in the files at common pleas include his name as author of the records and he undoubtedly sued many cases there on behalf of the king, perhaps as a "learned counsel" to the king's councillors.[25] His fortune was owed in part to the influence generated by his brother, John, and by the two men with whom he served on county commissions: Sir John Fyneux (chief justice of the king's bench) and Sir Robert Reed (justice of the king's bench and chief justice of the common pleas).[26]

His account book, ostensibly kept for the Middle Temple, contains numerous entries of a personal nature that allow a glimpse of an early

accumulated, forming an internal system of "stored or owed credit". She found obligations with penalties running between 150 and 200 per cent (p. 563).

[24] See, e.g., D. Youngs, "Estate management, investment and the gentleman landlord in later medieval England", *Hist. Research*, Vol. LXXIII (2000), pp. 124-41, at p. 140. There are, of course, other accounts which demonstrate how obligations were used. George Monoux, draper and alderman of London, began a ledger in 1507, soon after his election, that included indentures he entered into involving the use of obligations to "bind" the parties to the agreement (Brit. Libr., Add. MS. 18783 fos. 3v-4, 6v-7; A.B. Beaven, *The Aldermen of the City of London* (2 vols, 1908-13), ii, found online at <http://genealogy.patp.us/aldermen_1400.shm> [accessed 21 Nov. 2008]).

[25] T.N.A.: P.R.O., CP 40/87 fos. 61, 115; Chrimes, p. 150. Mordaunt sued for the government in king's bench as well (*Cal. Close Rolls 1500-9* no. 298). Queen Elizabeth of York, referring to him as "attourney in the Commen place", gave him 20*s* for services rendered, as she did to his brother (40*s*) and other learned counsel of the king (privy purse expenses, Elizabeth of York, 8-15 Mar. 1503, excerpted online at <http://www.r3.org/bookcase/wardrobe/ward15.html> [accessed 21 Nov. 2008]).

[26] Reed and Mordaunt were justices on the same gaol delivery (T.N.A.: P.R.O., E 404/85, 1 May 1505).

Tudor civil servant making private transactions.[27] Items include money spent for his gowns or lent to his wife, Anne, and "ffeez due to be paid", some to the king. Payments were made for legal fees for various reasons, such as the 6s 8d paid to Humphrey Coningsby, serjeant-at-law and learned councillor of Henry VII, "for his councell in the corp[or]acon of the Gild of Thaxted".

What stands out in the account book are entries of Mordaunt's written obligations for the payment of sums for wardships, obtained by his brother John. A grant for the wardship of John Leventhorp was awarded to William Mordaunt and William Gascoign, his cousin, on 12 May 1506 by letters patent. The entries begin with the payment of £10 as partial settlement of £40 due to Wistan Brown, a gentleman-usher of the chamber who may have received moneys for the king and helped Mordaunt with the grant in return for a fee. The due dates of the remaining payments were then listed along with a final memorandum to have the written debt returned to Mordaunt when paid in full—the all-important dénouement in discharging a written obligation if a written acquittance was not obtained.[28] He ended this entry with another payment notation: "& then have I paid C [100] li. for lev[en]thorp ward to wystan broun & for hym— x [10] li.".

Mordaunt not only contracted debts for personal gain but as a surety for others: "I am bound in ij oblig[ations] eyther of x mrc [marks] as suerte for Thomas Sprot[t] to m[aster] wode wherof x marc must be paid at Seint Andrew day & at m[i]dsomr aftr x mrc". Sprott was a witness for a release and quitclaim of lands to John Mordaunt and Wistan Brown and an acquaintance of William Mordaunt. "Master Wode" was the chief justice of common pleas, Thomas Wood, and this might explain Mordaunt's willingness to enter into two debts as surety for a family friend who owed money to his mentor at court. William also lent money and it was not beyond him to make a profit: on 1 April 1504, he recorded a loan to his

---

[27] Northamptonshire Record Office, Stopford-Sackville MS. 3689. There is no pagination. The book, partially destroyed and difficult to read, is seventy folios in length and runs from 1499 to 1516, with headings indicating term times. It is indexed as an official account book of the Middle Temple, although there are many private dealings within the folios.

[28] For mentions of acquittances recorded in an account book, see *The Estate and Household Accounts of William Worsley, Dean of St. Paul's Cathedral 1479-97*, ed. H. Kleineke and S.R. Hovland (2004), pp. 51, 53, 66, 76, 83.

brother, John, for £50 upon which £53 6s 8d was due—a modest but useful 6.67 per cent return on his familial investment.[29]

Special influence for gain was not the case with Dame Alianore Townshend, second wife and widow of Sir Roger, a justice of common pleas. Her husband kept a "vault" of documents and deeds, in part for use in potential litigation. The majority of suits he initiated at common law on his own behalf involved debts on obligations, most likely to force arbitration and settlement. At times, he and his family recovered lands in lieu of money owed on bonds for the purchase of sheep and produce.[30] It was possibly because her husband was both old and a busy royal justice that Alianore had to learn the business of running various lands and manors, for which she kept an account book.[31] The book provides a common view of how households throughout England ran their estates and conducted everyday affairs, with written obligations an important vehicle to make things work.

In August 1492, Sir Roger made Alianore his executrix in a new will; he died on 9 November 1493.[32] Alianore entered into numerous business contracts involving the fruits of the cultivation of her lands.[33] One such

---

[29] It would be interesting to learn if this loan was related to the two obligations for £50 each owed to the king by the Mordaunt brothers and William Gascoign "hanging opon the said lord Grey". The amounts were recorded in the king's chamber book as paid on 19 Nov. 1502 and 4 Dec. 1503 respectively (Brit. Libr., Add. MS. 59899 fo. 130v). William also acted as a surety for John regarding a fine of 4 marks owed to the Middle Temple (*Middle Temple Records*, ed. C.H. Hopwood (4 vols, 1904-5), i, p. 6).

[30] C.E. Moreton, *The Townshends and their World: Gentry, Law and Land in Norfolk, c.1450-1551* (Oxford, 1992), pp. 104-6, 112, 120-2.

[31] Brit. Libr., Add. MS. 41305. All references are to this document.

[32] *Inquisitions Post Mortem*, Hen. VII, i, no. 1143. For that date, Alianore noted it as the day of Sir Roger's "dessessyng". There is an enlightening non sequitur about Sir Roger's demise: although Townshend's will reads like most late medieval endeavours, replete with bequests of alms to the poor and funds for masses for his soul, he added a personal, seemingly proto-Calvinist conviction regarding his salvation, "which is above all werkes unto whom it is appropured to have mrcy as by all holy scripture plainly it apperith, and that in everich our [hour] that the sinner soroweth his synnes the which cõmyth oonly of the grace, charite and infynite mercy of our savyour crist Jhu of the wych numbir of contrite synners I mekely and humbly besechith him that I may be oon and come of the numbir predestinate to be savid" (T.N.A.: P.R.O., Prerogative Court of Canterbury (Register: Vox 2), PROB 11/10).

[33] It should not be thought that a woman partaking in "business" affairs in Tudor

transaction was entered under the heading "10 Henry VII" (1494-5) and shows the operation of an executrix of a will recovering debts owed to the decedent by obligation:

> This bull made at Reynhm [Raynham manor] the thursday next after ower lady day the Assumpcon in the xth yere of kyng harry the vij[th] wittenesse that I Dam' Alianor Tonneshend hath rec[eived] of John hewer Willm Curson & John Swyft of oxbysborgth xx[li] at div[r]s tymes w[t] y[t] x marke that my husbond rec[eived] in his lyve at penteney in p[art] payme[n]t of an obligacon of 1 [50] marke in wich the seid John Willm & John stande bounden In to my husbond befor In wittenesse wher of to this biel I have sette my seal yeven the yere & day a bove wreten.

This was a copy of the original obligation, recorded by Dame Townshend's clerk or receiver-general for future reference. Other debts, however, demonstrated that Alianore Townshend personally supervised her husband's estates. One folio, headed "ffor wole sales", listed a debt on 3 March 1493, more than a half year before the death of her husband and evidence that she was already managing the manor: John Bradman, "cytcyn & salter of London", William Yorke "gentilman" and William Bradman "cytycyn & fyshemongr of london bynde hem by ther obligacon to pay to my lady dame Alianor Townesend xxj li. vj s viij d. At the fest of ye Natyvyte of sent John Baptysts [29 August]", 1495. These three men were listed in five other obligations, each for £21 6s 8d and each due at the same feast in years extending from 1496 to 1500. Other obligations retained by Alianore Townshend were delivered for collection, including several overdue by John Bradman. William Dene, one of her agents, often received Alianore's unpaid written debts and conveyed them to Nicholas Nynes, a "gentleman" of chancery and one of her representatives in London.[34] What legal action Nynes may have resorted to is not known from the account book. Nor can it be determined that the overdue debts were ever paid. The book was a record of contracts and miscellaneous

---

England was unusual. It was not, as per the example of Katherine Nerbourne who petitioned the king for a licence to buy 100 tuns of Gascon wine (T.N.A.: P.R.O., C 82/232, June 1502). Women ruling the roost predated Alianore (see the brief discussion on Alice de Bryene of Acton, Suffolk, who kept a daybook of household expenses and died in 1435 having run her estates as a widow for forty-nine years, in M.R. Horowitz, *The Monumental Brasses of England* (University of Illinois, Urbana, Il., 2002), pp. 30-1).

[34] Moreton, p. 107. Nynes later became a sheriff in London (T.N.A.: P.R.O., E 404/85, 2 May 1505).

agreements, not an account of issues and receipts.[35] For the most part they were private transactions involving the toil of her lands and her local or London buyers.[36]

The records kept by William Mordaunt and Alianore Townshend are indicative of the widespread practice of contracting debts for future payment in a well-developed credit society based in part on written obligations and not on immediate payment in cash or in kind. Sureties and agents were necessary to guarantee an agreement and to facilitate collection at the appointed, stipulated time, and it was quite common to renegotiate debts for future ones or when they were in default. Many indentures enrolled at chancery bound each party in a recognizance to perform the conditions of the agreement or to abide by the decisions of arbiters—a literal example of binding arbitration, with forfeiture of those bonds going to the crown.[37] This mimicked the private indentures entered into outside the scope of royal government.[38] Because less than ten per cent of lawsuits filed at common pleas reached a verdict in Henry VII's reign, such actions were often initiated to force arbitration—a usually peaceful solution to potentially violent disputes in many circumstances.[39]

---

[35] A few notations indicate that arrears were collected, putting the residue owed into new obligations for future payments (fo. 15v)—a common procedure that was emulated vigorously by Dudley, Empson and their fellow councillors.

[36] Two interesting notes show that Dame Alianore also dealt with the government. A list of documents kept in a box by the writer of her account book included "a quietans of the kyng of C merke" and an acquittance of "Sr Raynald Bray" (fo. 21v). Both acquittances may have related to obligations she fulfilled. She was listed in one of the king's chamber books on 10 Apr. 1495 as owing the crown £30 upon an obligation (T.N.A.: P.R.O., E 101/413/2/2 fo. 84v). Sir Roger was on several commissions with Bray and must have known him (W. Campbell, *Materials for a History of the Reign of Henry VII* (2 vols., Rolls ser., 1873-7), ii, 477-8; *Cal. Pat. Rolls 1485-94*, pp. 502-3).

[37] One entry in John Heron's list of recognizances kept in his chamber book noted that two men forfeited their recognizances for the breaking of an arbitration before the lord chancellor (Brit. Libr., Add. MS. 21480 fo. 169v.)

[38] E.g., the head of Llanthony priory in Gloucestershire entered an indenture with three people to let a farm. Two of them, a mercer and a weaver, entered bonds for £20 to perform the covenants in the lease (*A Calendar of the Registers of the Priory of Llanthony by Gloucester, 1457-66, 1501-25*, ed. J. Rhodes (Bristol and Glos. Archaeol. Soc., 2002), nos. 196-7, 23/26 June 1508).

[39] D.J. Guth, "Enforcing late-medieval law: patterns in litigation during Henry VII's reign", in *Legal Records and the Historian*, ed. J.H. Baker (1978), pp. 80-96, at p. 87. At king's bench, where 20 per cent of crown pleas reached a verdict, just

When the first Tudor became king, it was over a realm that was already viewing arbitration, and therefore compromise, as a viable alternative to the factional disputes of the mid-15th century, drawing people closer to the central courts and central authority to assist in the process.[40] This was occurring at a time when manorial courts were in decline and local litigants sued in alternative jurisdictions.[41] Henry's councillors were involved in numerous suits to pursue peaceful results to disputes while maintaining a central governmental presence in the localities.[42] It was the written obligation and its enrolled or recorded form as a recognizance that allowed a way for society to function and a means to enforce the oaths and promises between both private and public parties for finance and for legal solutions.

Upon Henry VII's accession in 1485, the largest "private" estate and household in England was the duchy of Lancaster, and it is important to review briefly the way in which it worked to obtain an understanding of how Henry VII's bond policy developed for the entire royal government. Since its incorporation into the royal demesne holdings in 1399, the duchy remained an important supplement for moneys employed by the 15th-century kings. It also adjudicated disputes through its own court of learned counsel and auditors, similar to the learned councillors of nobles and magnates (often referred to as their "council learned").[43] Indeed, the earl

---

1 per cent did so for private suits (E. Powell, "Arbitration and the law in England in the middle ages", *Trans. Royal Hist. Soc.*, 5th ser., xxxiii (1983), pp. 49-67, at p. 51, citing M. Blatcher, "The workings of the court of king's bench in the 15th century" (unpublished University of London Ph.D. thesis, 1936); C. Whittick, "The role of the criminal appeal in the 15th century", in *Law and Social Change in British History: Papers Presented to the Bristol Legal History Conference, 14-17 July 1981*, ed. J.A. Guy and H.G. Beale (1984), pp. 55-72, at p. 72).

[40] D. Tilsley, "Arbitration in gentry disputes: the case of Bucklow hundred in Cheshire, 1400-65", in *Courts, Counties and the Capital in the Later Middle Ages*, ed. D.E.S. Dunn (Stroud, 1996), pp. 53-70; M.T. Clanchy, "Law, government and society in medieval England", *History*, lix (1974), pp. 73-8; Moreton, p. 194.

[41] C. Briggs, "Seignorial control of villagers' litigation beyond the manor in later medieval England", *Hist. Research*, Vol. LXXXI (2008), pp. 399-422, at p. 421.

[42] S.J. Gunn, "Sir Thomas Lovell (*c*.1449-1524): a new man in a new monarchy?", in *The End of the Middle Ages? England in the 15th and 16th Centuries*, ed. J.L. Watts (Stroud, 1998), pp. 117-53, at p. 133.

[43] "Most, if not all, of the great magnates retained a group of legal specialists known collectively as 'the council learned', some of whom also held administrative posts on their employer's estates, and were therefore constantly on

of Oxford, one of Henry's staunchest supporters and councillors, wrote to the king's chief minister, Reynold Bray, about a matter before him that he was examining along with "thadvise of my councell learned".[44] The king's mother, Lady Margaret, also had a council learned, which assisted her in hearing cases at her manor at Collyweston.[45] The continuing procedure of administering the duchy lands as a household with the dual roles of revenue generation and adjudication of disputes promoted efficiency in accounting and collection, in contrast to the tedious process of tallies and paperwork at the exchequer at Westminster. The exchequer of the duchy received all the profits of lands and justice. What has not been fully appreciated is that the means by which this was carried out rested in part upon the written obligation.

This has been largely overlooked in favour of an explication of duchy organization and procedure for the first Tudor's reign. For the years before 1485, there has been little discussion about what facilitated the duchy's efficiency in the areas of finance and justice—the written obligation.[46] After Henry became king, the "council learned in the law" was dubbed by Somerville seventy years ago as a committee of royal councillors using the duchy chambers as a prerogative and conciliar court. This has overshadowed

---

hand to offer professional advice" (C. Rawcliffe, "The great lord as peacemaker: arbitration by English noblemen and their councils in the later middle ages", in Guy and Beale, pp. 34-54, at pp. 37-8). See additional discussion in her article "Baronial councils in the later middle ages", in *Patronage, Pedigree and Power*, ed. C. Ross (Gloucester, 1979), pp. 87-108, at pp. 90-4).

[44] Westminster Abbey Muniments, MS. 16075. See also a reference to the earl of Northumberland's "lernyd Councell" (Corporation of London Records Office, Repertories of the Court of Aldermen 2 (1505-13), fo. 24 (4 Mar. 1507)). Oxford noted that a privy seal now moved the case to the "Councill of the king", most likely the lawyers and learned councillors headed by Bray, and not the larger council of which the earl was a member. The "council learned" of Henry VII should be viewed this way, as they were at the time. So a memorandum of a recognizance dated 8 July 1502 involving payment of a farm for the king's use to Reynold Bray, Thomas Lovell and John Mordaunt—all referred to as part of the "council learned" by Somerville—simply called them the "kings moost noble counsail" (T.N.A.: P.R.O., C 244/150 no. 62.)

[45] M.K. Jones and M.G. Underwood, *The King's Mother: Lady Margaret Beaufort, Countess of Richmond and Derby* (Cambridge, 1992), p. 87.

[46] For a history of the duchy, see R. Somerville, *History of the Duchy of Lancaster*, i, *1265-1603* (1953). Somerville did not discuss obligations or the various ways they were utilized by the duchy and its councillors and officials, although he gave a slight hint of their existence (p. 201).

any discussion of the actual workings of the duchy council and court and has thus left a void as to which came first—duchy procedure or royal conciliar activity there—and why.[47] Indeed, it would perhaps be more useful to look at these activities in the duchy as being pursued by councillors who were "learned" in the areas they worked in on behalf of the king, rather than an institutional entity for that purpose—activities that paralleled the work of the "counsel learned" of other great households.

This was expressed at the time in a recognizance entered into by several men involving payments due to six councillors of the king on his behalf whom Somerville identified as members of the "council learned": Thomas Lovell, John Mordaunt, James Hobart, Richard Empson, John Hussey and Thomas Lucas. If any of the recognizors or their heirs died within four months new persons were required to guarantee payment "or ellys suche othyr as the kings lernyt Counsell *for the tyme being* shall accept to be bounden in like fo^{r}me and condicion"—a reference to people, not polity.[48]

The officers of the duchy were required to take out bonds for their good behaviour and true accounting while in office, similar to the bonds required of sheriffs, customers and other royal officials that were usually filed at the royal exchequer. Upon completion of office, they also needed to obtain either those written bonds—which was preferable—or a written discharge (acquittance). For example, on 20 January 1509, three men were bound by recognizances for £100 to Sir Richard Empson, chancellor of the duchy, for John Butler to farm the duchy holdings of Ogmore in Wales. Over a year later, at the beginning of Henry VIII's reign, Butler had the obligation returned to him by command of "m[aster] fitzjames" and "m[aster] bonhm", the new attorney-general and receiver-general of the duchy respectively.[49] Butler came in person to the duchy council chamber in Blackfriars, one of several meeting places. In the presence of Richard

---

[47] Somerville, "Henry VII's 'Council learned in the law'", pp. 427-42.

[48] T.N.A.: P.R.O., C 255/8/5 no. 63, 29 Mar. 1504 (author's italics). Additional bonds were required (nos. 64 and 79, the latter using the same phrase). The matter involved the wardship of two daughters, for which payments were made to the king's chamber (Brit. Libr., Add. MS. 21480 fo. 46). For the phrase "lerned Counsell for the tyme being", see also T.N.A.: P.R.O., C 244/157 no. 21. The phrase is not mentioned in the printed summary of its enrolment on the close rolls (*Cal. Close Rolls 1500-9*, no. 535).

[49] T.N.A.: P.R.O., DL 41/34/1 fo. 46. For John Fitzjames and John Bonham, see Somerville, *Duchy of Lancaster*, pp. 402-3, 407.

Lussher, the "auditor of the same contrey", it was certified that Butler had fulfilled his duty in office and he retrieved the obligation.

The main function of these and other duchy officials was the collection of revenues accruing from farms and leases and, not surprising given the duchy's household origins, it was accomplished in part through the use of obligations for future payment. This method continued throughout the 15[th] century. When Richard III appointed a new chancellor of the duchy in the summer of 1483, among the items delivered to the new official were "iij coffyns wherin bee obligacions yat c[r]tain [per]sonnes bee bounden unto ye said king Edward [IV] for paiement of thair fermes according to yendentures betwix thaim made".[50] This use of written obligations for payment at the duchy continued unabated through Henry VII's reign.

The duchy council and its receiver-general were responsible for the collection of revenues on these obligations, which often included a penalty for non-payment. The receiver-general was charged with following through on revenue collection and the acquittance of those bonds. Along with the duchy chancellor and attorney-general, he was a key officer for discharging accounts and providing information for potential adjudication for non-payment. He worked in conjunction with the clerk of the duchy council to keep records of these transactions, and one such book of obligations has numerous entries, many from the reign of Henry VII. One entire section from the reign involves the taking and receiving of obligations by William Heydon, clerk of the duchy council, and John Ward, one of the duchy receivers; Heydon was probably the author and/or keeper of the book. Although no reasons are given for the obligations, notations were made that money was paid to the receiver-general.[51] The receiver-general also retained the actual obligations. A typical example is the entry from 25 March 1507, written by Miles Gerrard, who held the office from 1505 to 1509. He referenced an obligation "of x li. of John Stanley Esquire" that he had received of William Heydon. Stanley was

---

[50] T.N.A.: P.R.O., DL 25/3631; Somerville, *Duchy of Lancaster*, p. 391, where he noted the delivery but not the contents. This was but a small part of the records being conveyed. The new chancellor also received fifteen keys "in a ledder bagge" which opened chests kept at St. Bartholomew's in London, "wherin remaigne the kings evidences belonging to ye duchie of Lanc".

[51] T.N.A.: P.R.O., DL 41/34/1 fos. 158-164v. There are a large number of obligations listed in this document from the reign of Edward IV to the time of Henry VIII. On the last page, among the doodles the name "heydon" is written nine times.

constable of Tutbury castle and bailiff of the new liberty in Staffordshire
in the duchy, as well as an esquire for the body. Gerrard signed the entry.[52]

Judicial proceedings were held in the various duchy chambers through
its council sessions and the work of its own attorney since the time Henry
IV was duke of Lancaster. The council was usually populated with royal
servants and officials as well as the king's appointed chancellor of the
duchy and attorney-general, and disagreements were settled effectively
and usually in short order.[53] They included both civil and criminal matters,
which were therefore prosecuted by duchy officials who were also royal
servants—a situation that continued during Henry VII's reign with those
learned counsel who worked there.[54] Many disputes involved the
collection of revenues based on written obligations—it was critical to
drive in "old bonds" related to revenue if the king was to obtain his
money, much of it committed to the royal household or for other
assignments. Proceedings also included the various bonds for appearance
and for the keeping of the peace, and they were issued in the same manner
as in other courts of law: Robert Blundell and his sureties appeared before
two of the barons of the duchy's exchequer to enter a recognizance of £40,
the condition being to keep the peace against another person and to appear
at the next term session of the exchequer.[55] By 1483, when Richard
Empson was attorney-general at the duchy, he could by statutory law
submit a bill "into eny of the Kyng's Courtes by wey of enformation,
shewying in the same to the Court, what and wherin the Kyng, or eny
other to his use, shuld be unlawfully hurted or wronged in any thing to
hym apperteynyng in the right of the same Duchie". The duchy and its
officers thus had wide-reaching authority to pursue every legal avenue to
obtain what was due to the king.[56] Bray, Empson and their fellow
councillors would use this power for all obligations and recognizances
owed to Henry, and not just those related to the duchy of Lancaster.

It was the dual use of bonds at the duchy for revenue and the
maintenance of law and order and adjudication of debts owed to the crown

---

[52] T.N.A.: P.R.O., DL 41/34/1 fo. 161v; *Cal. Pat. Rolls 1494-1509*, p. 373;
Somerville, *Duchy of Lancaster*, p. 373.
[53] Rawcliffe, "The great lord as peacemaker", pp. 38-9.
[54] *Pleadings and Depositions in the Duchy Court of Lancaster*, i: *Time of Henry
VII and Henry VIII*, ed. H. Fishwick (The Record Soc., xxxii, 1896), pp. vii-viii.
[55] T.N.A.: P.R.O., DL 41/11/26, 4 Sept. 1505.
[56] *The Charters of the Duchy of Lancaster*, ed. W. Hardy (1845), pp. 337-9; *Rotuli
Parliamentorum*, vi. 208.

that became the model for Henry VII's royal bond policy,[57] in large part because of the experience and expertise of those councillors at the duchy who did the work as opposed to members of the king's greater council who proffered advice. It is perhaps no coincidence that the earliest records of proceedings in the duchy date to 1485, when Henry's successive chancellors there also became key financial and judicial councillors for the royal government.[58] When petitions were addressed to Empson at the duchy, it was recognized that the activity of the councillors there was part and parcel of the work of Henry VII's government: "Unto the Ryght Honorabull and Worshypfull Knyght, Master Empson, Chauncelar of the Dowche Chamber and oone of the Kyngg's Councell".[59]

Household finance in England and its large-scale exemplar at the duchy of Lancaster became the basis for Henry VII's pervasive bond policy. It was centred on the king's chamber and his "working councillors", notwithstanding the documentary intimations of earlier chamber activity under the Yorkists.[60] Clearly, this did not come about through the machinations of a monarch with little or no administrative, managerial, legal or financial experience—one who spent half his pre-regnal life abroad in exile dependent on those foreign rulers, relatives and family supporters who somehow saw advantage in keeping him alive and sustaining him.[61] When

---

[57] J. Baker, *The Oxford History of the Laws of England*, vi: *1483-1558* (Oxford, 2003), p. 221.

[58] *Pleadings and Depositions in the Duchy Court*, p. v. Of course, such records from earlier times could be missing, but the pervasiveness of recording-keeping and record-retention throughout Henry VII's reign suggests otherwise.

[59] *Pleadings and Depositions in the Duchy Court*, p. 48.

[60] The paucity of direct evidence, including the lack of chamber books, has plagued a detailed study of Yorkist chamber administration, such as it was, since discussed early on by F.C. Dietz and later W.C. Richardson (Dietz, p. 67; Richardson, *Tudor Chamber Administration*, p. 109). The well-known letter of Richard III (26 Apr. 1484)—appointing Edmund Chaderton his treasurer and receiver of the chamber and ordering him to "render faithful account or reckoning to ourselves only and to no other" for all the "receipts paid or delivered by our officers or minister or by any other persons whatsoever to the said Edmund to our use"—is suggestive of early Tudor administration and procedure ("Topic 4. Restoring effective royal government, 1471-1509" <http://www.dur.ac.uk/r.h.britnell/SEMINAR%204.htm> [accessed 21 Nov. 2008]).

[61] Michael Jones, who has written on the first Tudor's experiences pre-Bosworth, suggested to this author that if Henry learned anything with regard to household

Henry became king in August 1485, he was assisted by his mother, Lady Margaret Beaufort, and his uncle, Jasper Tudor, duke of Bedford, in placing people in key governmental positions. And as has been demonstrated throughout history, it was such loyal and royal supporters who influenced and helped to establish a polity for running the realm based on their own areas of expertise.

What may have surprised both minister and monarch alike was how quickly the first Tudor grasped the potential of a bond policy and consciously decided that he wanted to expand it and manage it. Furthermore, he well understood that simply enforcing the laws of the realm—which involved not only generating positive cash flow but also actively pursuing peace and order and the sure payment on contractual obligations to maintain both—would have little adverse effect on a citizenry that had tired of instability and were long attuned to the age-old practices of written bonds.[62]

How did Henry's policy take form? When looking at the personnel upon whom the new king relied to help him rule England, it is hardly coincidental that most of those involved in Henry's bond policy cut their financial teeth in household finance, either through their tenure at the duchy of Lancaster or in private households; through prosecution of legal disputes as "learned men" in the law; or through connections with, or extreme loyalty to, the households of the king's family. The intent of this section is not simply to revisit the sometimes scattered biographies of

---

finance it was by observing, not by doing (see his article, which lists most known references to date about Henry in Brittany: "'For my lord of Richmond, a pourpoint . . . and a palfrey': brief remarks on the financial evidence for Henry Tudor's exile in Brittany, 1471-84", *The Ricardian*, xiii (2003), pp. 283-93). Perhaps Henry's closest brush with personal finance while in exile involved signing his name, "henry de Richemont", to a loan of 10,000 crowns of gold from Francis, duke of Brittany, dated 29 Oct. 1483, promising to repay it "on the word of a prince". [See Chapter One] Nonetheless, Francis required a co-signer, which role was undertaken by Henry's uncle, Jasper Tudor (Brit. Libr., Add. MS. 19398 fo. 33).

[62] Edward IV was initially viewed as the panacea for the instability of Henry VI's reign, a hope that went unfulfilled. One assessment of his tenure states that the people of England were not sorry to see him go in Sept. 1470 and "lacked enthusiasm for his return" in Mar. 1471 (C. Richmond and M.L. Kekewich, "The search for stability, 1461-83", in *The Politics of 15th-Century England: John Vale's Book*, ed. M.L. Kekewich and others (Stroud, 1995), pp. 43-72, at p. 50). The authors quote an observation made at the time from Warkworth's *Chronicle*: "The people looked after . . . prosperyte and peece, but it came not" (p. 46).

Henry VII's key trusted servants and ministers, but rather to pinpoint and highlight those attributes they held in common, which in turn influenced the course of the statecraft that Henry was to pursue.[63] It is perhaps fitting first to look at Henry's mother and the prime mover in helping her son to gain the throne of England: Lady Margaret Beaufort, countess of Richmond and Derby. Her three marriages, strong will and aptitude for political survival afforded her opportunities to learn household finance and to manage its accounting and personnel, while at the same time adjudicating disputes relevant to her lands.[64] Those account books and rolls that survive relating to her estates suggest a firm understanding of the credit and legal culture of her time, including the use of written obligations.[65] After her son became king, she ran her own court of equity and Henry often delegated cases to her at her principal residence of Collyweston in Northamptonshire.[66] She could be both ruthless and acquisitive in her business methods, and until her death in 1509 she acted as an arbiter in many disputes and relied on household officials to assist her in both fiscal and judicial matters.[67]

One of those officials was Reynold Bray, whose early career was as steward and receiver-general in the household of Sir Henry Stafford, son of the first duke of Buckingham. When Stafford became Margaret Beaufort's second husband sometime before 1464, Bray continued in his

---

[63] What follows is based on the *Oxford Dictionary of National Biography* (Oxford, Sept. 2004; online edn., Jan. 2008) <http://www.oup.com/oxforddnb/info> [accessed 21 Nov. 2008]; *History of Parliament, 1439-1509*, ed. J.C. Wedgwood (1936); and information gleaned from the various works of R. Somerville, W.C. Richardson, S.B. Chrimes, S. Gunn and D. Grummitt, unless otherwise noted.

[64] Margaret never recognized her contracted marriage to John de la Pole (dissolved in 1453).

[65] The accounts include several housed at St. John's College, Cambridge (D91.17, D102.10, D102.2, D102.6, D91.20, D91.21, D91.16, D91.19, D102.1, D91.14, D91.13, D92.11, and a book of inventories—D91.15—which include 19 obligations due at her death) and several at the Westminster Abbey Muniments repository when she was married to Lord Stafford (e.g., W.A.M., MS. 5472). The author wishes to thank Malcolm Underwood, archivist, St John's College, Cambridge and Richard Mortimer, keeper of the muniments at Westminster Abbey Library, respectively, for their kind correspondence and insight regarding these documents.

[66] M. K. Jones, "Lady Margaret Beaufort, the royal council and an early Fenland drainage scheme", *Lincolnshire Hist. and Archaeol.*, xxi (1986), pp. 11-18, at p. 11.

[67] Rawcliffe, "The great lord as peacemaker", pp. 39, 53.

position of managing their estates and legal matters while developing a personal relationship with the countess and her family. Part of the experience he gained as receiver-general involved searching documents to assist Margaret in her various legal disputes—an activity he was to raise to a deliberate national effort. He became part of the Tudor conspiracy to put Henry on the throne, and Bray joined him in exile and fought with him at Bosworth Field. His loyalty, experience and trustworthiness cannot be overstated, nor his influence on the king as the foremost policymaker, office recruiter and chief minister. Three weeks after Bosworth, Bray became chancellor of the duchy of Lancaster. He thus moved from a long tenure as a major household officer of a noble family to being the chief executive of the largest household in England. He was soon after appointed treasurer of England, for only a short time, but maintained his working relationship at the exchequer in taking bonds from office-holders and in the oversight of customs, land revenues and the auditing of accounts. Additional appointments in the Welsh marches, northern England and the duchy of Chester ensured that those jurisdictions would be brought into Henry VII's financial and judicial policy.[68]

Other men with experience at the duchy, in household finance or with financial instruments and contract law, joined Bray as part of a group of working councillors involved with pursuing the king's "plan" for securing law and order and financial solvency. They also exhibited an overt dynastic loyalty or benefited from well-placed connections with the royal family. The same day Bray became chancellor of the duchy of Lancaster, Richard Empson, a member of the Middle Temple, was named its attorney-general, a position he had held under Edward IV but quickly lost under Richard III. He attended most of the duchy council meetings under the Yorkists and gained experience on royal commissions and from his

---

[68] M. Condon, "From caitiff and villain to *pater patriae*: Reynold Bray and the profits of office", in *Profit, Piety and the Professions in Later Medieval England*, ed. M.A. Hicks (Gloucester, 1990), pp. 137-68, at pp. 138-9; M.R. Horowitz, "Richard Empson, minister of Henry VII", *Bull. Inst. Hist. Research*, lv (1982), pp. 35-49, at p. 39. [Chapter Four] It should not be lost that Margaret Beaufort's third husband, Thomas Lord Stanley, was a well-seasoned administrator of both personal and royal household finance, having served as receiver-general in Lancashire for the duchy of Lancaster in the reign of Edward IV (C. Ross, *Edward IV* (Berkeley, Calif., 1974), p. 382).

charge "to ov^{r}see the kings said evidences".[69] He and Bray held several joint stewardships and Empson was one of the inner circle of councillors named an executor to Bray's will; his son, John, married the niece of Bray's wife. The last duchy meeting recorded in Richard's reign was attended by several learned counsel, including Richard Empson and a deputy steward, James Hobart of Lincoln's Inn from Norfolk. Hobart became Henry VII's attorney-general in 1486, perhaps through the influence of Empson and Thomas Lovell (discussed below), the latter also of Lincoln's Inn and Norfolk.[70] John Cutte was a receiver of forfeited lands during Richard III's reign. Under Henry VII he became receiver-general in the duchy of Lancaster and under-treasurer of the exchequer, thus blurring "departmental" responsibilities—as did all working councillors—when it came to pursuing royal policy. He worked closely with Bray and Empson in channelling money from the duchy and the royal exchequer to the king's chamber, as well as conveying recognizances due for payment.[71]

John Mordaunt, of the Middle Temple like Empson, was a member of Bray's own estate council and succeeded him as chancellor of the duchy; Empson would follow Mordaunt in that position. He fought for Henry at Bosworth, became a king's serjeant-at-law and was an attorney to Prince Arthur and chief justice of Chester—an institution that used obligations

---

[69] J.H. Baker, "The legal education of Richard Empson", *Hist. Research*, Vol. LVII (1984), pp. 98-9; T.N.A.: P.R.O., DL 5/2 fo. 2; Horowitz, "Richard Empson", *passim*.
[70] T.N.A.: P.R.O., DL 5/2 fo. 15; *Records of the Honourable Society of Lincoln's Inn, The Black Books*, i: *1422-1586* (1897), pp. 100, 109, 119. The black books kept by the Inn included bonds. Hobart's patent for office was enrolled 3 Nov. 1486. (*Cal. Pat. Rolls 1485-94*, p. 138).
[71] B.P. Wolffe, *The Royal Demesne in English History: the Crown Estate in the Governance of the Realm From the Conquest to 1509* (1971), p. 296 (app. D); *Cal. Pat. Rolls 1494-1509*, p. 424; A.F. Pollard, *Reign of Henry VII from Contemporary Sources* (3 vols., 1913), i. 153. An example of payments to the chamber: in May 1503, John Cutte, the receiver-general of the duchy of Lancaster, delivered to the chamber £5,062 6s 2d for one year's revenue in the duchy (T.N.A.: P.R.O., E 101/413/2/3 fo. 99). There are many mentions of Cutte delivering money to the chamber or to individuals, e.g. the £2,303 14s 5d "received of Sr R Bray by the hands of John Cutte" for money lent to the king's cofferer (T.N.A.: P.R.O., E 101/413/2/2 fo. 84v). Cutte was also an executor of Bray's will, and in his own will (1521) he asked for prayers for the souls of Henry VII and Reynold Bray (T.N.A.: P.R.O., P.C.C. (Register: Maynwaring), PROB 11/20). [See Chapter Nine.]

and recognizances for finance and the course of justice.[72] He was also a commander at Stoke (1487). Thomas Lovell, who fought at Bosworth, helped to put down the Northern Rising (1489) and battled at Stoke and Blackheath (1497). He became Henry's chancellor of the exchequer, receiver of land revenues, treasurer of the chamber and later treasurer of the household—offices putting him in direct contact with Bray, Empson, Cutte and other royal councillors charged with royal finance and the maintenance of law and order.[73] It was Lovell and Bray who helped to divert money destined for the exchequer to the king's chamber from the very outset of the reign.[74] Lovell was a bencher at Lincoln's Inn and as treasurer kept and audited accounts; he also knew Hobart there.[75]

John Heron, who was Lovell's assistant before succeeding him as treasurer of the chamber, became the "traffic controller" in the bond

---

[72] Both the councillors of the duchy of Lancaster and the members of the prince's council met at St. Bartholomew's for their deliberations—the same place various evidences for the duchy of Lancaster were housed (discussed earlier). By the 15th century, recognizances for the peace dominated enrolments at the Chester exchequer court (T. Thornton, "Local equity jurisdictions in the territories of the English crown: the palatinate of Chester, 1450-1540", in Dunn, pp. 27-52, at p. 40).

[73] Brit. Libr., Cotton MS., Titus B.XII fo. 53v, pub. in M.J. Bennett, "Henry VII and the northern rising of 1489", *Eng. Hist. Rev.*, Vol. CV (1990), pp. 34-59, at p. 36. Lovell entered private business deals with his fellow councillors, from whom he also found opportunities, e.g. he succeeded Empson as high steward of Peterborough monastery. A signet for his appointment as chancellor of the exchequer for life was dated 9 Oct. 1485 (T.N.A.: P.R.O., PSO 2/1).

[74] Chamber finance began almost immediately. Five days after Bosworth, Sir John Guildford delivered payments for customs to the chamber and required a written discharge at the exchequer (T.N.A.: P.R.O., PSO 2/1, 30 [*sic*] Feb. 1486). John Currin used evidence of payments to diplomats from the chamber to suggest that the shift from the exchequer began in Nov. 1486 ("'Pro expensis ambassatorum': diplomacy and financial administration in the reign of Henry VII", *Eng. Hist. Rev.*, Vol. CVIII (1993), pp. 589-609, at p. 597).

[75] *Lincoln's Inn, The Black Books*, p. 148. Lovell also gave money towards completing a new building. In 1489, he and Hobart were joint stewards in the duchy of Lancaster in East Anglia charged with increasing duchy rents, an exercise Empson also pursued. A book of Empson's "improvements" for the north parts for 1505-8 has annotations and changes in rent value that are in his hand (T.N.A.: P.R.O., DL 41/29/10). For the farm of Highrilley (or Horleyhead), rented at £6 13s 4d annually, it was now increased to £8 (a rise of about 21 per cent), which nonetheless was noted as "to[o] dere" and the renters could only pay an additional 10s or "[th]ey will lose it" (fo. 14).

policy, keeping records of bonds and negotiating them, meeting with the various councillors and the officials at the exchequer and chancery, and spending time with Henry VII in scrutinizing books, rolls and records. He would become more than just a treasurer keeping the books, but the actual recipient of funds on bonds—a development perhaps recognized in a shift of language when he started to be referred to as "our Receyvo^r for oure said Chambre".[76] Edmund Dudley, grandson of John, Baron Dudley but remaining an esquire his entire life, studied at Gray's Inn and stayed on the periphery of the inner circle of councillors until later in the reign. He served in the English army in France (1492) and advised Henry VII on the treaty of Etaples, which provided the crown with a large annual stipend. In 1506, he was named president of the council. He was involved with James Hobart at various chancery common law pleadings.[77] There is evidence that he worked with Bray in pursuing written obligations for the king before his formal royal service in September 1504.[78]

Thomas Lucas became Henry's solicitor-general and worked closely with Empson, Dudley, Lovell and Hobart. He began his career as secretary in the household of Jasper Tudor. John Hussey, a former surveyor of the lordships in Lincolnshire held by the duke of Clarence, helped to quell Francis Lovell's rebellion (1486) and fought at both Stoke and Blackheath. He obtained stewardships with Bray in the duchy of Lancaster and was a steward of two of Margaret Beaufort's manors. He was appointed comptroller of the household and became master of wards in 1503, a post he held until 1513 when Lovell, his kinsman by marriage, succeeded him; his patron was Reynold Bray. True to the way Henry VII governed, the king delayed Hussey's patent for failing to take out a bond for office.[79] He was present at the peace negotiations in France where he may have met Edmund Dudley, if not sooner. Hussey's eldest son married the niece of Thomas Lovell.

---

[76] T.N.A.: P.R.O., E 404/84, 12 Nov. 1503, 20 Nov. 1503. [See Chapter Nine.]

[77] See T.N.A.: P.R.O., C 43/1 nos. 30(b), 32, where Dudley signed the documents, as did Hobart and his successor as attorney-general, John Ernley.

[78] T.N.A.: P.R.O., E 101/413/2/3 fo. 19 (July 1503), Bray and Dudley together pursuing an obligation of statute merchant for certain lands of Sir John Turbervile in Sussex—Dudley's home county—valued at £313 6s 8d. See also D.M. Brodie, "Edmund Dudley, minister of Henry VII", *Trans. Royal Hist. Soc.*, 4th ser., xv (1932), pp. 133-61.

[79] Jones, "Lady Margaret Beaufort", p. 14; Horowitz, "Richard Empson", p. 44 and n. 82.

Three other councillors spent much of their time engaged in pursuing the king's financial and judicial rights through the bond policy. Henry Wyatt, who may have begun his Tudor support with Buckingham's rebellion in 1483, became clerk and then master of the king's jewels early in Henry's reign, and often worked with Dudley to collect on obligations.[80] He fought at Stoke and Blackheath and at one time was ransomed from Scottish imprisonment. He took and delivered obligations to the king, and was one of those responsible for collecting the benevolence money owed to the crown.[81] John Ernley, who succeeded Hobart as the king's attorney-general in 1507, was admitted to Gray's Inn around the time Edmund Dudley was there; he later acted as one of Dudley's feofees. Edward Belknap, who fought at Stoke and gained early experience in revenue collection as receiver for the Warwick and Spencer lands, was named surveyor of the king's prerogative late in the reign.[82] Of the working councillors it was these men, following the lead of Reynold Bray and the king, who formed the core group facilitating royal policy.

Others assisting in the effort had similar backgrounds or accomplishments. William Smith, who became bishop of Lincoln, headed up the king's council in the marches. He started his career in the service of Margaret Beaufort, before becoming surveyor and receiver-general for the Warwick, Salisbury, Spencer, Berkeley and Morley lands in 1499. He remained close to Bray[83] and was named one of the executors to his will. Humphrey Coningsby, a king's serjeant-at-law who worked closely with his fellow

---

[80] E.g., the £200 delivered to the king's chamber by the hands of Edmund Dudley and "Harry Wiott" in partial payment of £600 owed by the earl of Devonshire (T.N.A.: P.R.O., E 101/413/2/3 fo. 227, 20 May 1505).

[81] Brit. Libr., Add. MS. 21480 fos. 175v, 177.

[82] T.N.A.: P.R.O., E 101/413/2/2 fo. 44. He took bonds as part of his pursuit of moneys owed to the king, and he often worked with Empson, Dudley and Heron in administering them (T.N.A.: P.R.O., E 101/517/15 fos. 3-v, 5-v; E 101/517/14 fos. 3, 5.) His patent for office dated 1 July 1508 is missing, but an enrolment on 19 Aug. explains his authority and the procedures he was to follow (*Cal. Pat. Rolls 1494-1509*, p. 591). W.C. Richardson noted that the enrolment allowed Belknap to appoint deputies ("Surveyor of the king's prerogative", *Eng. Hist. Rev.*, Vol. LVI (1941), pp. 52-75, at pp. 63-6). In fact, a petition signed by Henry VII not only listed 31 proposed deputies representing all the counties but also authorized Empson, Hussey, Southwell and Dudley to "take sureties of [all] of the seid deputies by obligacons" for £40 each unless they were joined with "any other Counties"; then the bonds were to be for £20 (T.N.A.: P.R.O., PSO 2/3, n.d. but after 1 Aug. 1508).

[83] *Cal. Pat. Rolls 1494-1509*, p. 168.

councillors sitting at the various duchy chambers, began his practice as an attorney at common pleas; he later acted as a feofee for Bray. His clients included Queen Elizabeth and Peterborough abbey; Empson served as steward of the liberty of Peterborough around the same time. William Cope, Henry's cofferer, was a servant of Margaret Beaufort and lifelong associate of Bray and one of his executors. He was a feodary of the duchy in Wiltshire and Hampshire, as well as steward for various lordships. He also received revenues from the Isle of Wight and paid them to the chamber.[84]

Robert Southwell started his career as an auditor in the exchequer. He was a member of Lincoln's Inn and most likely gained the attention of Thomas Lovell and James Hobart there. He began assisting Bray in auditing the accounts of revenue officials, bypassing his old department and delivering money to the king's chamber.[85] He became the chief butler of England and kept books of audit for royal lands, wards and butlerage. After Bray's death, Southwell headed up an audit function with the bishop of Carlisle, Roger Leybourn.[86] He was also a receiver for several holdings of Cecily, duchess of York and delivered money directly to the king's chamber.[87] Christopher Bainbridge, master of the rolls at chancery, took bonds and recorded them while acting alongside the working councillors; he was admitted to Lincoln's Inn when Lovell and Hobart where there. Finally, it would be remiss to exclude John Morton, the quintessential

---

[84] *Cal. Pat. Rolls 1494-1509*, pp. 168-9; T.N.A.: P.R.O., E 101/413/2/2 fo. 58v.

[85] T.N.A.: P.R.O., E 101/413/2/2 fo. 45. Regarding Southwell, see Margaret McGlynn, "'Of good name and fame in the countrey': standards of conduct for Henry VII's chamber officials", *Hist. Research*, Vol. LXXXII, no. 217 (Aug. 2009), pp. 547-59.

[86] See M.R. Horowitz, "Cash and kings: Henry VII's land revenue management", paper read at the *Sixteenth Century Studies Conference*, 1983, p. 4 and n. 8; J.A. Guy, "A conciliar court of audit at work in the last months of the reign of Henry VII", *Bull. Inst. Hist. Research*, xliv (1976), pp. 289-95. Leybourn succeeded William Sever as bishop of Carlisle. Sever received a commission as surveyor of the king's prerogative on 12 Apr. 1499 and collected grants from parliament in the north on behalf of the crown (T.N.A.: P.R.O., E 404/83). Condon correctly posited that Sever's appointment was made in the spring of 1499 ("Ruling elites", p. 117 and n. 40). He was translated from Carlisle to Durham in 1502 (Hatfield House, Cecil Papers, 207/1 fos. 9-10). The author wishes to express his gratitude to the 7th marquess of Salisbury for permission to peruse the account books of William Sever, and to Mr. Robin Harcourt Williams, librarian and archivist to the marquess, for providing copies for review.

[87] E.g., T.N.A.: P.R.O., E 101/413/2/3 fo. 59, 16 Apr. 1503.

Tudor supporter, apologist and future chancellor and cardinal, who had experience in taking and administering bonds directly for the government since Edward IV's reign.[88]

The purpose of the above recitation regarding these royal officials and their experience and connections relates to what now should be quite evident: that the councillors responsible for administering Henry VII's bond policy from the start of the reign shared much in common, including the ability to facilitate that policy. They were likely to attract Henry's confidence and those of lifelong supporters such as his mother, Bray, Mordaunt and Lovell for the same reason. Most had household and financial experience, often through the graces of Margaret Beaufort, who clearly helped her son to form his government, or through their work at the duchy of Lancaster or exchequer. Most of them fought in one or more battles to win or uphold Henry's claim to the throne—Henry noticeably liked his ministers to fasten their swords alongside their ambitions, much as he was to do personally, beginning with Bosworth Field. Most had legal backgrounds, sometimes at the same inns of court, or arranged private business deals and familial marriages with each other, or worked in the same areas of government, often overlapping. The majority had experience in the administration of debts, revenue and obligations. Most served as M.P.s (Lovell, Empson, Mordaunt and Dudley were also speakers of the commons), which helped in the exercise of control by the central government over the gentry. They were on numerous commissions of the peace and special commissions throughout the reign, making their presence known in all corners of the realm on behalf of the king.

These men were an interconnected, fiscally astute and politically seasoned group loyal to the leader—commonalities found long before and after the reign, although perhaps not always with experience so closely tied to the development and needs of royal policy.[89] None were noblemen or ecclesiastics except the bishops of Lincoln and Carlisle, whose fiscal responsibilities lay away from Henry's court and whose activities were

---

[88] Morton was master of the chancery rolls under Edward IV from 1472 to 1478, the first civil lawyer in that office (C.S.L. Davies, "Bishop John Morton, the Holy See and the accession of Henry VII", *Eng. Hist. Rev.*, Vol. CII (1987), pp. 2-30, at pp. 3-4). He had first-hand knowledge of bonds (see, e.g., *Cal. Close Rolls 1468-76*, nos. 1088-9, 1210, 1452).

[89] See S.J. Gunn, "The structures of politics in early Tudor England", *Trans. Royal Hist. Soc.*, 6th ser., v (1995), pp. 59-90. Gunn discusses the importance of the "interrelationships of the political actors".

mainly administrative.[90] They were picked for their loyalty to Henry and his family, their connections with each other and their experience in law, administration and finance, much of it stemming from household finance and expertise gleaned at the duchy of Lancaster or in the law courts.[91] Not growing up in the household of an English monarch, Henry VII could afford to have an open mind as to how to rule England efficiently and effectively while exhibiting a willingness to follow and then to support and lead those who could help him attain financial and dynastic stability.

From the beginning of Henry VII's reign, obligations and recognizances for all aspects of governance continued to be used as in the past at the various common law and conciliar courts and financial departments.[92] Bray and Empson ran the council meetings and sessions of the duchy of Lancaster, which became one of the focal points for royal conciliar governance for both finance and law *ex cathedra*. They also worked with other councillors across courts, departments and jurisdictions to ensure that moneys due to the crown were accounted for, and that all bonds for the maintenance of justice—especially for keeping the peace and appearing at a court or commission—were either enforced or collected upon for default. Many of their cohorts sat on the assizes and at the sessions of the peace, where they could also keep track of the various writs of justice requiring bonds for appearance, good behaviour, payment and demands for written records. Bray, Hobart, Cutte and Empson were familiar with the roles of the J.P.s from their tenure at the duchy of Lancaster: it was the duchy chancellor who appointed judges and J.P.s and regulated the sessions of the peace.[93]

---

[90] Richard Fox, a university-trained councillor under Henry VII referred to as "of excellent wit and learned", was bishop of Winchester and lord privy seal. He entered into bonds on behalf of the king. (Chrimes, pp. 34-5). Fox was a protégé of Margaret Beaufort.

[91] Bureaucrats worked together and conducted private business with each other throughout the 15th century, and they gained experience in the various departments of state. Henry IV introduced several duchy of Lancaster servants into his new government. They were schooled in the principles of administration: "Secretarial, financial and with a strong injection of law" (R.A. Griffiths, "Public and private bureaucracies in England and Wales in the 15th century", *Trans. Royal Hist. Soc.*, 5th ser., xxx (1980), pp. 109-30, at pp. 119-21, 123).

[92] Richardson, *Tudor Chamber Administration*, p. 141.

[93] R. Somerville, "Lancashire justices of the peace in the 15th and 16th centuries", *Trans. Hist. Soc. of Lancs. and Cheshire*, cii (1951), pp. 183-8.

Hobart, Cutte and Empson also had been involved in the many commissions sent out during the last years of the Yorkists to enquire how best to "improve" the king's revenue from the duchy estates—a concept used time and again in the first Tudor's reign for all his financial, judicial and prerogative rights. Edward IV had difficulty collecting payments due from duchy farmers and tenants, and more than any previous monarch he attempted to make this aspect of revenue generation more effective. Letters in the form of privy seals were sent to those held to be in arrears, and the duchy council put offenders in prison for non-performance: practices Bray and then Empson and his colleagues expanded during Henry VII's reign. Richard III recognized the potential of duchy efficiency and profit, and drew up a plan based on the duchy's 1399 charter for receivers to collect revenue from all forfeited lands and make their accounts directly to auditors appointed by the king, bypassing the exchequer.[94] He called for these receivers to be of a different ilk than the traditional "lordes, knightes, and esquires" who often kept revenue that was due to the monarch: Richard wanted people who would be "lerned men in the law".[95] The last Plantagenet did not implement his plan. Henry VII, Reynold Bray and a small group of working councillors did, and their activities centred on the use of bonds.[96] They in effect fulfilled the last Yorkist's desire to rely on royal officials who were "lerned men in the law."

As has been seen, the duchy used bonds for various sources of income due to the king. These obligations even facilitated the collection of fifteenths, as when the exchequer was ordered by privy seal to discharge

---

[94] Somerville, *Duchy of Lancaster*, pp. 248-51, 257; Dietz, pp. 65-7, discussing Richard III's plan, styled "A Remembraunce made, aswele for hasty levy of the kynges revenues", pr. in *Letters and Papers Illustrative of the Reigns of Richard III and Henry VII*, ed. J. Gairdner (2 vols., Rolls ser., 1861-3), i. 81-5. Even as late as 1508, Lovell, Hobart, Lucas and others continued on duchy commissions (Somerville, *Duchy of Lancaster*, p. 267).

[95] *Letters and Papers Richard III and Henry VII*, i. 84.

[96] Richard III probably did not see any advantage to pursuing a bond policy, although there are glimpses that he was familiar with their use in government. (see M.R. Horowitz, "Henry Tudor's treasure", *Hist. Research*, Vol. LXXXII, no. 217 (Aug. 2009), pp. 560-79). [Chapter Eight] The keeper of a privy seal book for his reign noted that "iij obligacions of marchaunts of London" were kept in "my maister[s] casket"—a notation similar to John Heron's reference to boxes of such bonds stored in Henry VII's chamber. There were also entries of obligations, including an order to the exchequer to discharge a former sheriff's bond for office "by reason of a recoignaunce" (Brit. Libr., Harleian MS. 433 fos. 1v, 42v).

Andrew Buk and his fellow collectors from Cambridgeshire for their payments directly to the king's chamber. They had, in fact, been bound to Bray, Lovell and other councillors for £115 19s 8d "to content theim at certain daies conteyned in their sev^rall obligacons" for the second fifteenth granted two years earlier—again, the never-ending quest to drive in overdue payments.[97] This procedure was used outside the duchy as well.[98] Emulating both duchy procedures and household finance, the working councillors—including the treasurer of the king's chamber (first Lovell and then John Heron)—utilized bonds and began keeping stacks of obligations for payment, or memoranda of them. They also created long lists of obligations and enrolled or filed recognizances that were noted as outstanding, paid or wanting in partial payment.

The bond policy, which encompassed all obligations and recognizances involving finance and justice, began to bifurcate—placing people in new bonds and seeking out and examining old ones that were potentially in default for non-performance of conditions. The reason for this was first and foremost the inherent delay in obtaining moneys owed to the crown in the area that could anachronistically be called "accounts receivable"—a situation shared by all households and creditors. The king also wanted to ensure that those under bond to keep the peace or to appear at a court were in fact living up to the conditions imposed upon them, especially when it

---

[97] T.N.A.: P.R.O., E 404/83, 4 Feb. 1499. The money was received in the chamber. It continued to be collected throughout the reign and forwarded to the chamber. A privy seal dated 9 Dec. 1506 noted that collectors in Lancs. alone owed the king £1,650 13s 4d for "sundry" fifteenths and tenths from previous grants. Miles Gerrard had now given John Heron £825 6s 8d and required a discharge at the exchequer as money paid directly to the chamber (T.N.A.: P.R.O., E 404/86).

[98] In an account book for 1501-2 of William Sever, bishop of Carlisle (and later Durham) involving the collection of moneys on behalf of the king in the northern parts, a notation of payment was made for £256 13s 1d as part of the fifteenth and aid due from the West Riding of Yorkshire. An entry was added "Besides and above lxxj^{li} iij^s xj^d [£71 3s 11d] that the forsaid collecto^rs be bounded by obligacon to content and pay unto the kings grace as above" (Cecil Papers 212/9 fo. 10). Henry VII wrote his sign manual in the book four pages later. In another version of the account, the bishop received £66 9s 4d from several collectors for the second fifteenth in the West Riding as partial payment for the total due. Three of the men were now bound "to Maister Bray and me the forsaid Bishope in sev^rall obligacions to the kings behouf and use" to pay £53 3s 6d on a specified date (Cecil Papers 207/1 fos. 7-8). Sever was no doubt beholden to Bray for his advancement. In a letter to Bray regarding his yearly accounts he referred to himself as "yor own Man W duresme" (W.A.M., MS. 16028).

came to the issue of peace bonds as an attempt to thwart potential civil unrest.

This was not difficult to implement since the processes and practices were already in place and functioning, both at the royal administrative level and at the local levels of finance, justice and government, especially for real debts owed to the crown for its ordinary and extraordinary income. Nor was it problematic to deduce that many of those previously under obligation might be in forfeit. All that was required to make the policy responsive was to ascertain if such conditions were either met or the amounts or penalties for non-performance had been prosecuted for payment to the crown and then collected.[99] However, a caveat mentioned earlier bears repeating: those seeking set administrative procedures and the institutionalization of the policy need to be cognizant of the fluidity of government, past as well as present. Moreover, people living at the time were perhaps more aware of the confusion inherent in any policy put into execution than are today's historians.

Robert, abbot of St. Mary's in York, expressed this view in a confidential communication to Reynold Bray. He reminded Bray that the abbot and another party entered an obligation to "send up before candlemesse next coming" three obligations with conditions under the convent seal, following the directions "of a papir signed w^t the hand of maister mordaunt". The abbot now sent both Mordaunt's letter and the obligations to Bray to be delivered to the king. He then pleaded with Henry VII's chief councillor that after making the delivery to the king Bray would have them cancelled and returned to the bishop of Durham, who administered such bonds in the north. Robert ended his letter asking of Bray to "know yor mynd to whome at my daies of payment I shall send up my paiements and of whome I shall receive my bounds for the discharge of me and this hens".[100]

---

[99] The intimidating penalty written into a bond for non-performance was not a Tudor invention. The money penalty clause (*sub pena*) was used in writs dating back to at least 1363, if not earlier (W.M. Ormrod, "The origins of the *sub pena* writ", *Hist. Research*, Vol. LXI (1988), pp. 11-20, at p. 11).

[100] W.A.M., MS. 16050, n. d., but between Dec. 1502 and Aug. 1503. Robert Wanhope's election to the abbacy was enrolled 5 Dec. 1502; he received his temporalities by patent 3 Feb. 1503 (*Cal. Pat. Rolls 1494-1509*, pp. 302-3). Bray died 5 Aug. 1503. Procedures were quite fluid. In the bishop of Durham's account books previously mentioned, he noted that in borrowing money from Henry VII for his temporalities, he was required to have the abbot and convent of the Blessed Lady next to York enter into obligations for the debt "wyth paynelty". These bonds

The first step for policy implementation involved identifying what non-performing obligations and recognizances were scattered throughout the central and itinerant courts, treasuries and repositories. It was next required that they be recorded or stored at fixed locations with easy access, such as the chancery, the duchy chambers, the king's chamber or with certain ministers. It was then essential that such bonds were prosecuted for payment or renegotiation where applicable, and for discharge when it was determined that conditions were fulfilled. These were procedures well known to private household accounting and to the machinery of the duchy of Lancaster. Privy seals became the instrument of choice for summoning parties before the councillors, whether at the duchy, star chamber or individually, or for ordering written discharge (acquittance) for a bond.[101] The signet office was also used, especially for directives to government departments regarding bonds. Henry appreciated the work of the various clerks there. In 1497, he signed a signet letter noting that because the clerks of the signet had been diligent in the king's "manifold causes and businesses", as well as securing paper, parchment and wax at their costs, he rewarded them with £10 each.[102] The king and his working councillors kept them very busy.

The point at which the bond policy moved from initial implementation to fully-fledged operation is not self-evident. As seems to be the case throughout Henry VII's reign, documentation is a fickle servant of discovery. Chancery enrolments provide little indication of initial policy execution, although they offer strong evidence as to when the intensification of the bond policy occurred.[103] The various rolls, memoranda, books, writs and lists stored at The National Archives are helping historians come to the realization that they do not necessarily conform to century-old classifications and, therefore, administrative or political solutions for Henry's statecraft.[104] What has become clear is that this was a resolute

---

were to be delivered to Humphrey Coningsby, one of the king's working councillors, by Easter 1502 for subsequent delivery to Henry VII "w[th]owt any fayll or ffawt" (Cecil Papers 207/1 fos. 9-10).

[101] E.g., the two privy seals for appearance before Edmund Dudley, printed in Horowitz, "'Agree with the king'", pp. 365-6. See also Horowitz, "Richard Empson", p. 46; J.A. Guy, *The Cardinal's Court: the Impact of Thomas Wolsey in Star Chamber* (Hassocks, 1977), p. 83.

[102] T.N.A.: P.R.O., E 404/82, 9 Oct. 1497.

[103] Horowitz, "Henry Tudor's treasure".

[104] The various lists, books and rolls of obligations and the chancery writ series at The National Archives (especially C 244) suggest a large increase in bond-taking

effort on the part of the king and his working councillors—who together constituted his government.[105] And while the first surviving books of receipts in the chamber, kept by Lovell and then Heron, begin recording obligations four years after the start of the reign, there is evidence that this policy commenced from the outset, with some changes from the past.[106] Beginning in October 1485, pardons for outlawry were enrolled on the patent rolls for non-appearance before the "justices of the Bench". They involved not only non-appearance during the first few months of the reign but also from the reigns of Edward IV and Richard III. Most of these were for pleas of debts between private parties, but recognizances would have been taken to guarantee appearance. Because paying for pardons was a *sine qua non* under Henry, it is likely that payment was required to vacate those bonds for appearance.[107] Similar pardons for non-appearance, including those from offences under the Yorkists, continued to be enrolled throughout the reign. Many of those bonds for appearance were pursued for prosecution and collection by Edmund Dudley twenty years later.

At the same time, those people who were potentially harmful to the stability of the new dynasty were forced to take out peace bonds, either because of their actions before or soon after Bosworth or because of their affinities—a procedure common before Henry VII's reign and until recently the central theme of the first Tudor's predilection for bond-taking among the upper echelons of society.[108] Indeed, one might perhaps wonder if Henry ever heard stories about his grandfather, Owen Tudor, and one in particular pertaining to his release from Windsor castle after taking out a

---

during Henry VII's reign, as do the various chancery rolls and, of course, the numerous obligations recorded in the chamber books. But one must always be wary of the fact that conclusions are being drawn from surviving documentation and even from the way in which they are classified. Nonetheless, that documentation and some of the conclusions suggested from it are congruent with the commentaries during the reign about the increased usage of bonds over time (see Cunningham, "Loyalty and the usurper").

[105] John Watts observed that Henry VII and his close advisers were in fact the government running England (Watts, "'A Newe Ffundacion of is Crowne'", p. 50).
[106] T.N.A.: P.R.O., E 101/413/2/2, entitled "the kinges Boke of his Receiptes. heron."; S. Cunningham, "'To keep all Englishmen obedient through fear': Henry VII, the council and rule by recognizance, 1485-1509", paper read at All Souls' College, Oxford (Nov. 2002) regarding T.N.A.: P.R.O., C 54/375-6, a recognizance roll; and his article "Loyalty and the usurper".
[107] *Cal. Pat. Rolls 1485-94*, pp. 1-4.
[108] Lander, pp. 267-300; Condon, "Ruling elites", pp. 119-20; Cunningham, "Loyalty and the usurper".

recognizance for £2,000—the concept of bonds apparently ran in the family.[109] Such control could and probably did help to quell potential revolts under the first Tudor by making them literally costly, and by hindering any local aristocratic intentions against the monarch not only through their obligations but also those of their affinities and would-be followers.[110]

This meant that Henry VII had to enforce the conditions of these bonds or they would be of no effect on the populace. He seems to have had great confidence in his position as king soon after Bosworth, and it is clear that he had no qualms about such enforcement throughout his reign, against both the principals and their sureties.[111] Less than two months after Bosworth, memoranda of recognizances were filed at chancery for sureties to guarantee that their recognizors kept the peace and their allegiance to Henry VII. However, they involved parties from all walks of life and not simply nobles. They included a grocer, a cordwainer, a fuller, several yeomen, gentlemen, knights and a lord.[112]

That confidence also meant that Henry could be magnanimous if the occasion warranted, something often lost on the chroniclers of his reign. On 26 July 1498, Thomas Wotton, vicar of Chiswick, was bound in 50 marks as a surety for William Lound (Lund), a rector and chaplain, whom Wotton thought "would have bien [the king's] true and faithful liegeman". Lund apparently "offended your grace" and Wotton requested a pardon from paying the forfeiture because of his poverty by having the king sign a bill to that effect and give it either to the chancellor or the keeper of the rolls. Henry VII signed the bill and a note at the bottom stated that it was received by the master of the rolls on 1 May 1501 by the hand of James Hobart, the king's attorney, no doubt to grant the pardon since Lund also received one two days earlier.[113]

---

[109] R.A. Griffiths, "Tudor, Owen (*c.* 1400-61)", *O.D.N.B.* (<http://www.oxforddnb.com/view/article/27797> [accessed 21 Jan. 2009]).

[110] Cunningham, "Loyalty and the usurper".

[111] A. Cameron, "Complaint and reform in Henry VII's reign: the origins of the statute of 3 Henry VII, c. 2?", *Bull. Inst. Hist. Research*, li (1978), pp. 83-9, at pp. 83-6.

[112] T.N.A.: P.R.O., C 255/8/4 nos. 167-9, dates ranging from 14 to 18 July 1486. Thirteen other memoranda of recognizances were dated between 17 Oct. 1485 and 18 Aug. 1486 (nos. 152-4, 156-66; C 255/8/5 nos. 59-61).

[113] T.N.A.: P.R.O., C 82/218; *Cal. Pat. Rolls 1494-1509*, p. 237. Wotton said his benefice was valued at 13 marks annually, plus the houses were in "ruyn & decaye and [he] hath no frends to helpe hym"; he also had a "poor modre". One can only

On 8 July 1489, John Radcliff, Lord Fitzwalter was under recognizance with three sureties "by him made in our Chauncerie". There is no record of it being enrolled on the close rolls summarized in the *Calendars* but it was filed in chancery as a memorandum "more plainely may appere of recorde".[114] However, a year after Fitzwalter was attainted (1495), the sureties were in forfeit of 1,000 marks each for this bond. One of them, John Wyndham, did not suffer the stigma of Fitzwalter's attainder because the king ordered a tally to be cut at the exchequer for the amount and given to the surety "by way of reward". A second, Robert Drury, was also released by a signet letter with the king's sign manual.[115] The third surety, Sir Robert Brandon, actually forfeited his 1,000 marks, and apparently there were eight sureties in other recognizances for the perfidious lord who were in forfeit, each for £1,000.[116]

Bonds were being taken and recorded early in the reign and it can be surmised that the working councillors were busy locating existing obligations and recognizances while taking new ones. Henry VII would

---

wonder if the king smiled sardonically as he affixed his sign manual to the bill after reading it. Since Lund's pardon was enrolled, it is most likely that he paid for it, a "fee" demanded frequently by Dudley later on.

[114] T.N.A.: P.R.O., C 255/8/5 no. 100. It nonetheless has an enrolment mark on it, and Sean Cunningham has informed the author that it is found on T.N.A.: P.R.O., C 54/376, m. 10, dated 28 July 1489, noting the three sureties to be discussed.

[115] T.N.A.: P.R.O., E 404/82, 26 Nov. 1496; C 255/8/5 no. 100; Chrimes, p. 139. Fitzwalter was referred to as "oure rebell the late lord ffitzwater" (T.N.A.: P.R.O., C 82/245). He was the only noble involved in Sir William Stanley's treason, and it has been suggested that unlike Edward IV, who had a propensity to side with the stronger of two parties in a dispute, Henry VII did the opposite—in this case siding against Fitzwalter in a star chamber suit which may have pushed the lord into rebellion (T.B. Pugh, "Henry VII and the English nobility", in *The Tudor Nobility*, ed. G.W. Bernard (Manchester, 1992), pp. 49-110, at pp. 53-4). Fitzwalter was executed and his son placed in a £5,000 bond, which according to Lander was the cost for obtaining a reversal of his father's attainder (Lander, p. 334). See David Grummitt's article, where he notes that Fitzwalter's relation with Henry VII was in "terminal decline". ("Household, politics and political morality in tghe reign of Henry VII", *Hist. Research*, Vol. LXXXII, no. 217 (Aug. 2009), pp. 393-411.

[116] T.N.A.: P.R.O., E 101/414/16 fo. 127v. In a chamber book of payments for 1495-7, a list of memoranda included a note that eight sureties forfeited their £1,000 recognizances but also stated that Wyndham, Drury and Brandon forfeited their 1,000 marks each for Fitzwalter's treason (E 101/416/6 fo. 122). The fact that the names of Wyndham and Drury were crossed out, but not Brandon's, suggests that this list was the original and required updating and recopying into E 101/414/16.

become deeply involved in such searches. In 1498, he ordered an inventory of all the rolls and records "made in the courte of Chauncery of King Edwarde the iiij^{te}" during his first decade of rule—records going back thirty-seven years.[117] The chancery files were constantly scrutinized throughout the reign since a large number of bonds or memoranda concerning recognizances were stored there. For example, on 29 November 1500, two sureties came to chancery and recognized debts of £20 for Thomas Blake's appearance in star chamber, plus his promise not to harm certain people named. Almost eight years later, Robert Rydon, clerk of the council, received a writ from the king summarizing the bond, which was in "filacus cancellar". It enjoined Rydon to certify whether or not Blake appeared at the appointed time. Rydon replied that on 31 January 1501, Blake in fact had appeared at chancery, confessed to whatever allegations were before him, and was dismissed along with his sureties. The recognizance on file, however, was discovered uncancelled, which is why the king wanted to know its status.[118]

Henry started placing people high and low into bonds for traditional royal business. In various parishes in the hundred of Hoo in Kent, eighteen yeomen and two gentlemen entered into bonds to the king for £600 to observe conditions in indentures taken a year after the reign began.[119] Henry also received payment on forfeitures on bonds directly into the chamber or into the exchequer throughout the reign, and again not just from those of high estate. When the king discovered that three yeomen from Suffolk forfeited their recognizances of 100s each that were taken before the justices of the peace for the appearance of one of them at the appointed day, a total of £15 was "paide unto us in oure Chambre". They

---

[117] The inventory, ordered on 7 Oct. 1498 (and not 1499 as printed), is found in *The Egerton Papers* (Camden Soc., 1st ser., xii, 1840), pp. 1-3. It included all the records on file at chancery.

[118] T.N.A.: P.R.O., C 244/147 no. 105(a)(b)(c). Henry VII was just as diligent with the exchequer. On 18 Nov. 1505 he informed the barons there that because "we have certayne knowleige by you" of various sums of money received at the exchequer the previous year, he wanted it assigned for specified purposes. This privy seal, signed by Henry, went into great detail, listing sums collected from parliamentary grants, sheriff's accounts and other payments going back not only to "the second yere of o^r raigne" but also to the twelfth year of the reign of "o^r noble p[ro]genitor king Edward the iiijth [1472-3]", more than thirty years earlier (T.N.A.: P.R.O., E 404/85).

[119] *A Descriptive Catalogue of Ancient Deeds*, ed. H.C. Maxwell Lyte (1900), iii, A.9509.

now required a discharge at the exchequer. The same was true of two yeomen and three husbandmen of Kent, forfeiting 100 marks "paide unto us in oure Chambre", although the king "for div^{r}se consideracons" remitted part of the amount. Often these forfeitures would be collected at the exchequer for assignment to royal officials or servants. A "franklyn" and a gentleman from Devon were bound by recognizance for John Splotte, also a gentleman, to keep the peace against all the king's liege people and specifically against a certain clerk, plus to appear at the next sessions of the peace in Exeter. A year later Splotte "made assaulte upon oon John Stabbot", thereby triggering the condition involving all the king's liege people even though it was not against the named clerk. Indeed, any breaking of the peace against a private person was also a breach of the king's peace, and therefore involved potential forfeiture of money to the crown. All three men now surrendered amounts totalling £40, which went as royal rewards.[120]

Henry personally ordered special commissions not only to seek out the records of obligations and recognizances but also to take new ones and drive in old ones. Moreover, these commissions were charged with finding any and all revenue due to the crown.[121] Towards the end of the reign, Henry entrusted his working councillors to draw up commissions that he authorized, such as the all-encompassing one described in a bill he signed that was based on articles authored by Richard Empson and John Hussey. It recorded the names of the commissioners followed by a list of "enquerry" for a large number of potential offences, including all wards, marriages, lands without licence, special liveries, wastes, sales of woods, treasure trove, inquisitions by escheators, lands in-chief within the duchy of Lancaster or elsewhere, misprisions, extortion, all "usserers", escapes, and "all forffayters off reconnyssance be fore the Justyces off pace

---

[120] T.N.A.: P.R.O., E 404/83, 12 Jan. 1501; E 404/84, 13 Nov. 1502; E 404/84, 11 Feb. 1502. See the note in John Heron's account book that a vicar in Devonshire forfeited 40 marks by recognizance "for breking of peax opon the p[ar]isshe clerke" (Brit. Libr., Add. MS. 21480 fo. 180).

[121] Developed in the 14th century, the commissions of the peace were created to enforce statutes of the peace, receive indictments and conduct jury trials. Henry VII transformed the commission, making it an agency of the government for administration and fiscal policy, with one or more councillors sitting in every county (see D. Loades, *Power in Tudor England* (Basingstoke, 1997), pp. 72-3; Harriss, "Political society", pp. 46-9).

sheryffs or othervyse in sessions". Empson, Lucas and Hussey signed the articles.[122]

These special commissions were an adjunct to the responsibilities of councillors and commissioners of the peace and the judges of the assize; the aforementioned bonds taken before J.P.s were clearly discovered by those hearing cases. For example, on 12 February 1502 it was recorded that two London gentleman were in forfeit of their peace bond against all liege people and a named person that was taken during the assizes in 1491—an eleven-year-old bond.[123] The aftermath of rebellions provided a special opportunity for such commissions and the taking of bonds. Henry VII realized that by replacing retribution with reprieve, he could tap into a source of income and inculcate respect for the law and civil obedience at the same time: the king understood early on that most rebels were worth more alive than dead.[124] Recognizances were taken by three royal officials

---

[122] T.N.A.: P.R.O., C 82/294, 8 Dec. 1506. A summary of the commission recorded on the patent rolls does not mention the councillors or their involvement (*Cal. Pat. Rolls 1494-1509*, pp. 507-8). For other commissions drawn up specifically by Empson or Dudley, see M.R. Horowitz, "'Contrary to the liberties of this city': Henry VII, English towns and the economics of law and order", *Hist. Research*, Vol. LXXXV, no. 227 (Feb. 2012), pp. 32-56. [Chapter Six] One example was the signet to the chancellor for two commissions to be drawn up by the squire for the body and Edmund Dudley, "concernyng oure right and Interesse as by oᵣ said Counsaillo'" will show you (T.N.A.: P.R.O., C 82/313, 20 May 1508).

[123] T.N.A.: P.R.O., E 404/84. As will be discussed, bonds could be decades old (see the example of a bond prosecuted almost twenty years later in Horowitz, "Richard Empson", pp. 47-8).

[124] E.g., after the northern rebellion in 1489, Henry VII had small groups of rebels executed. Yet while in York, "the king pardon some day iii C [300] knelyng on their knees and some day ii C [200] some day mor and some day lasse so that season his grace pardont upon a xv C [1500]" (Brit. Libr., Cotton MS., Titus B.XII fo. 55v; Bennett, p. 58). Those who were reprieved paid for this act of mercy. In an earlier disturbance in Oxfordshire, John Sant abbot of Abingdon was indicted for treason, summoned before the king's council and bound in 2,000 marks to pay two instalments of £800 each (21 May 1486). He rebelled yet again and on 27 Sept. 1490 he entered an obligation for 2,000 marks to pay £1,000 in instalments, for which he made several payments to the king's chamber. He lost his lands by act of parliament of 13 Jan. 1489, but had his abbacy restored in 1492. His pardon, enrolled on 2 Feb. 1493, apparently cost £31 11s, paid in the hanaper—this before the service of Edmund Dudley (D. Luckett, "The Thames Valley conspiracies against Henry VII", *Hist. Research*, Vol. LXVIII (1995), 164-72, at pp. 166-8; *Cal. Pat. Rolls 1485-94*, pp. 403, 316, 421; *Cal. Close Rolls 1485-1500*, nos. 99, 540,

in Somerset, Dorset and Wiltshire "for the fynes of theim that offended w^t the Lord Audeley the smyth & othr the hole sum where of was [£4,629 8s 8d]". Additional recognizances for the same insurrection totalled £9,319 17s 6d. Notations in the chamber accounts indicated that payments were received. When other offenders beyond the commission entered into bonds, they were known to the king because he "hath a boke".[125]

The king also used bonds as a preventative measure once a rebellion was in the offing. On 5 October 1501, he signed a warrant directing a commission to deal with the recent rebels supporting Edmund de la Pole, earl of Suffolk, who was still at large.[126] Writs of *dedimus potestatem* were sent to the J.P.s in Oxfordshire, "for theym to take sureties by recognisance of the p[er]sonnes . . . resorting to o^r said countie for their true liegance unto us after the fo^{r}me and condicon as is expressed in o^r said other l[ette]res". Two days earlier, Henry VII had sent the chancellor "the names of suche p[er]sonnes as were s^{r}vnts of o^r Rebel". Any man on the list failing to appear and enter into a bond was to be committed to ward "tyl they fynd suertie".[127]

Henry went from accepting and then managing the bond policy to taking the lead, and he began to tell councillors on how to write obligations and seek them out. In signing warrants to Humphrey Coningsby concerning parcels of land, he instructed the learned councillor and serjeant-at-law, who worked with Empson at the duchy of Lancaster, that "he must deliv[e]r t[e]rme mich[aelmas] anno xxj^o [1505] p[ro]x[imo] ij obligacons as foloweth". He then specified the names, the language and the amounts for the two obligations. The king also set policy by example, including what became the *modus operandi* of bond review: determining the status of a bond, learning the particulars of those involved, and negotiating for a final disposition. The recognizance taken on 28 December 1492 by several sureties, including Nicholas Nyens and

---

672). Bacon noted sardonically that "the less blood he drew, the more he took of treasure" (p. 213).

[125] Brit. Libr., Add. MS. 59899 fos. 116v, 200v. This was for the Cornish rebellion. Its leaders were Lord Audley, Michael Joseph and Thomas Flamank, who were executed. The rebellion ended at Blackheath on 17 June 1497.

[126] Suffolk was finally captured and, beginning on 24 Apr. 1506, spent the rest of his life in the Tower (Chrimes, pp. 290, 344). He was executed in 1513.

[127] T.N.A.: P.R.O., C 82/223, 5 Oct. 1501; C 82/332, 3 Oct., with no year given, but clearly 1501. This last document should be reclassified and stored in C 82/223. For another source related to these bonds, see Cunningham, "Loyalty and the usurper".

William Campion of London, for 1,000 marks "ev^{r}ych of theym" for Henry Hudson's allegiance, lay filed at chancery for a decade. Then on 26 February 1502, Henry VII signed a bill "at our Maner of Richemonde" ordering the cancellation of the recognizance "only touchyng the bondes of the seid Nicholas [and] William and for noon of the other p[er]sones named in the seid recognisaunce but that the seid recognisauce touchying the seid [other] p[er]sones to be and stond at all tymes in strength and virtue".[128]

Forfeitures to the crown on various bonds, including old ones "on the books", continued at a steady pace, involving people from every level of society. Because ordinary and extraordinary revenue and the profits of justice—and the difficulty in collecting it—were a main concern of the government, forfeitures by sheriffs for their misdeeds in office or their failure to collect revenue as spelled out in their recognizances were both a source of income and a check on incompetent or dishonest appointees.[129] As the "conspicuous instrument of the royal will",[130] the sheriff was a key component for the king's bond policy for law and order and financial stability.[131] Much of the effectiveness of the sheriff, or lack thereof, depended in part on the strength or weakness of the monarch: Henry V confronted the deficiencies in law and order through a strong effort to centralize law enforcement, with the sheriff as a keystone. In a recent study of the enforcement of statute staple recognizances by sheriffs from c.1355 to 1530, Henry VII seems to have had the greatest success in aligning

---

[128] Brit. Libr., Add. MS. 59899 fo. 189v; T.N.A.: P.R.O., C 255/8/4 no. 74(a)(b)(c). Hudson soon entered a £1,000 bond for allegiance.

[129] This included the care Henry VII took in appointing sheriffs, with many examples seen in the chancery warrants, e.g. a slip of vellum stating simply that Peter Bevyll was to be sheriff in Cornwall, signed by Henry VII (T.N.A.: P.R.O., C 82/230, 30 Apr. 1502, listed in the *Calendar of Fine Rolls 1485-1509*, no. 740). The same was true for escheators, e.g. John Blyke's appointment for Oxfordshire and Berkshire, signed by Thomas Surrey, treasurer of the exchequer, and sent to chancery with a note (in the same ink as the signature) stating "My lord the kings pleasure is that this man for grete [con]sideracons be admyttid eschetour and the othir last maid to be discharged". It was enrolled on the fine rolls on 30 Dec. 1504 (T.N.A.: P.R.O., C 82/267, Dec. 1504 (*Cal. Fine Rolls 1485-1509*, no. 811)).

[130] R. Gorski, *The 14th-Century Sheriff: English Local Administration in the Late Middle Ages* (Woodbridge, 2003), p. 3. Gorski discusses the sheriff in terms of wealth, status and locality but makes no mention of how he was literally "bound" to the centre by recognizance for his performance in office.

[131] Cunningham, *Henry VII*, p. 170.

sheriffs with the central will.[132] That success was linked to bonds for office.

But, as outlined above, it had been a major task to ascertain at the exchequer who was under bond, where the bonds were kept and what steps had been taken to ensure performance or payment on default. On 27 February 1500, Henry spelled out his bond policy regarding sheriffs to his chancellor, Cardinal Morton, reiterating that "it is ordeyned and provided that nomaner personne elected and chosen Shirif of any countie . . . shal have out our l[ett]res patents touching his shirifwik unto the tyme he shal have founde g[oo]d and suffisaunt suertie in our Eschequier to yelde ther a iust accompt for thesame".[133] Reynold Bray, with his positions at the duchy, the exchequer and as chief minister of the king, was afforded the flexibility needed to make sure that bonds continued to be taken of new sheriffs, and there is ample evidence to show that efforts were made to hold them accountable and to collect on forfeited bonds.[134]

Diligence was the key, whether for ensuring that bonds were taken or that appointments were made that benefited the king, without any political agendas on the part of the sheriffs. Bray and his successors seem to have had a great deal of success through their collective scrutiny. A signet from the king to the prior of Tynemouth and a clerk enjoined them to take a recognizance by writ of *dedimus potestatem* of Sir Humfrey Lisle and his sureties to be sheriff of Northumberland because he "hath dilayed hiderto to fynde sureties as in suche caas is accustomed" in order to get his letters patent for office. The recognizance was to be drawn up by "our trusty counsaillor" the bishop of Carlisle. The signet letter was returned to chancery with an attached memorandum of a recognizance taken of Lisle and four sureties for his office.[135] When it was bruited that Thomas

---

[132] Nightingale, pp. 18-19, 25ff. It was concluded that Henry departed from the Yorkists in his diligence to control sheriffs through legislation and central direction by the chancellor: "Thus Henry VII was able to enforce statute staple recognisances to a degree never before achieved. . . . No longer, it seems, did it depend on the individual personality of the king, or on his ability to terrorise his subjects. Instead, its effectiveness had been institutionalized" (p. 25). Nightingale notes that sheriffs could be held accountable by entering bonds for office, which Henry had no qualms about prosecuting.

[133] T.N.A.: P.R.O., C 82/201.

[134] E.g., the E 404 warrants for the reign at T.N.A. and the copy of Dudley's account book (Brit. Libr., Lansdowne MS. 127).

[135] T.N.A.: P.R.O., C 82/330, n.d., but most likely the first quarter of 1506. Lisle was originally committed to the county on 1 Dec. 1505, but his appointment was

Hasilrig, named sheriff of Warwickshire and Leicestershire, was "suposd that he had been reteyned with soom lords ther", his appointment was cancelled. However, Hasilrig appeared before the king and "shewed that he is nat reteyned nor bilonging to any p[er]sonne but merely unto us, and would endevor hym with al effect to s[e]rve us truly in the said rowme". The king signed a signet to this effect, addressed to Reynold Bray and the bishop of Salisbury.[136] The political ramifications were stunning. The county sheriff, once all-powerful in his dual roles in local justice and in revenue collection, was becoming more closely linked and beholden to the monarch, not the magnate.[137]

The king's plans were carried out with alacrity by other working councillors. In one telling privy seal given to Edmund Dudley and John Cutte late in the reign, Henry VII noted that since 1485, both sheriffs and escheators had forfeited—and continued to forfeit—"div^{r}s theyr recognisaunces" that they and their sureties entered into before the barons of the exchequer to the late John Dynham, lord treasurer, and "Sr Reynold Bray knight to our behouf". These included bonds for both the execution of their responsibilities in office and for any accounts due on revenue collections.[138] Cutte succeeded Bray in this role, and the king now gave

---

vacated for failing to enter a recognizance for office. He finally obtained it on 9 Apr. 1506 (*Cal. Fine Rolls 1485-1509*, nos. 843, 845).

[136] T.N.A.: P.R.O., C 82/332, n.d. Hasilrig was appointed on 15 Nov. 1500 (*Cal. Fine Rolls 1485-1509*, no. 708).

[137] Local lords historically had some influence in the choice for both sheriff and justice of the peace (G.L. Harriss, "The dimensions of politics", in *The McFarlane Legacy: Studies in Late Medieval Politics and Society*, ed. R.H. Britnell and A.J. Pollard (Stroud, 1995), pp. 1-20, at p. 6; Gorski, pp. 16-19).

[138] Under-sheriffs could be culpable as well, and sheriffs paid to name them. Sir John Warburton paid Dudley £40 cash for the right (Brit. Libr., Lansdowne MS. 127 fo. 5). They would then enter into bonds or contracts with their under-sheriffs, such as Sir John Howard's retention of an under-sheriff by obligation (*Household Books of John Howard*, p. 472). An indenture drawn up on 6 Dec. 1501 noted that the sheriff of Wiltshire deputed Christopher Nicholas "to be his undershreve" (*Ancient Deeds*, vi, C.5196). Indentures could include bonds for performance. The one made on 15 Nov. 1499 between Thomas Cotton, sheriff of Cambridgeshire and Huntingdonshire, and Walter Lorkyn, to be his under-sheriff, stated that Lorkyn had to perform all his duties faithfully and account for all profits to Cotton, as well as enter a bond to this effect "in the sume of xx li." (Huntingdon Record Office, Conington Estate Papers, 3/15/1). The folded strip that held the now missing seal was made from a writ that cannot be read except for the date (13 Mar. 1499) and the name "mordaunt" at the bottom. One might surmise it was a directive from

him full power to "assesse compounde & agre for us & in oure name w^t all & ev^{r}y the seid recogniso^{r}s & their mayn[per]no^{r}s for their fynall ends & discharges of ev^{r}y the seid recognisaunces". Cutte was also empowered to assign the moneys collected for fees and wages for the king's servants or for other purposes, and to provide acquittances to those paying their debts; Dudley was to work with him.[139] Although a learned councillor who was later referred to as one who "had no lernyng in the lawe other then a litill exp[er]iens", Cutte nonetheless became a key figure in the bond policy that extended into Henry VIII's reign.[140]

The exchequer was ordered by the king to forward tallies to those making payment without "other charge to be sett uppon theym or eny of theym for the same", including pardons they would receive for discharging their bonds. Henry also stated that the warrant would act as a discharge for Cutte and Dudley for these responsibilities by both the current and future monarchs. This is a glimpse of one role in the area of bonds that Bray pursued from the outset, in this case for those bringing revenue to the exchequer. It was passed on to his executor, John Cutte, and to his successor as the king's personal finance minister for bonds, Edmund Dudley. It must have become obvious to Henry VII that this component of bond policy needed attention. A privy seal to the exchequer the previous year noted that "where abouts ten yeres past" the sheriff of Lincoln kept a felon in jail "according to thordre of o^r laws". The felon escaped and the sheriff now forfeited his recognizance in the sum of 100s from his goods and lands, to be given as reward to one of the king's servants.[141] Although one historian considered this prosecution of bonds for erring sheriffs to be ruthless, it was in fact putting into effect the will of a monarch bent on making royal officials accountable and culpable—and at a level not seen before his time.[142]

John Mordaunt to the sheriff, but the brittle strip would have to be removed and unfolded for content identification, which the author hesitated to undertake.

[139] T.N.A.: P.R.O., E 404/85, 16 Apr. 1506.

[140] Brit. Libr., Cotton MS., Titus B.IV fo. 112, n.d., letter from Thomas Denys to Cardinal Wolsey asking for the office of under-treasurer of the exchequer previously held by Cutte.

[141] T.N.A.: P.R.O., E 404/85, 30 Nov. 1504.

[142] Nightingale, p. 33. She nonetheless concluded that "Henry VII achieved some real improvement in the administration of local justice in ways that people wanted, that is by making the sheriffs better servants of the people as well as of the crown" (p. 34).

When Edmund Dudley succeeded Bray as the chief royal official for taking and collecting bonds, he continued this policy of reviewing shrieval recognizances for possible forfeitures.[143] He even notched it up by often requiring sheriffs, under-sheriffs and escheators to pay for the discharge of their bonds for office at the end of their tenure, although as just noted in Henry's directive such officials were not in theory subject to other fines once they executed their responsibilities.[144] While an *argumentum ex silentio* is never proof of any position, it might be assumed that those sheriffs and under-sheriffs involved with collecting revenue from various land and judicial sources who were not in Dudley's book or the chamber books and lists of bonds were in fact doing a good job in bringing cash and bonds to the chamber. This could especially be true given the close scrutiny of exchequer records by the king's councillors.

There was also a steady closing of the gap between chancery administration of old and new bonds and direct royal involvement by the king, his chamber and his working councillors. Searches through the records were assisting in this endeavour. A series of recognizances enrolled at chancery in November 1496 involving a large number of laymen for the loyalty and "good aberyng" of Thomas Warde, a merchant of the staple, and his appearance before the king was brought to light in May 1501. Henry signed a bill cancelling the recognizances of two of the sureties (a salter and a "pasteler") and it was sent to William Warham, keeper of the chancery records and rolls and the future chancellor and archbishop of Canterbury. Both bonds were marked cancelled on the close rolls. Then a separate petition to the king to release another surety at least four years later noted that Thomas Warde had now "dyed in the towre". That surety, a "pewterer", was "att [the] poynt of owtlawry" because of the "force of the said recognisaunce". He successfully pleaded poverty "and

---

[143] Other councillors also pursued forfeitures on the recognizances of sheriffs who did not perform their duties. E.g., Sir Walter Griffith, sheriff of York, forfeited £100 to Humphrey Coningsby on behalf of the king for the escape of a prisoner. The money went to the chamber and a tally for payment was cut at the exchequer, where Griffith's bond most likely resided (Brit. Libr., Add. MS. 21480 fo. 186v).

[144] From Dudley's account book: Henry Tey paid £100 (40 marks in cash, the rest by obligation) to John Heron for a pardon for his offences as sheriff; Sir William Say paid £100 (100 marks by obligation) for the discharge of his "shrefwike"; John Parys paid £10 in ready money and £10 by obligation to discharge his office of three years; John Maynwaring paid £40 (£20 in cash, £20 by bond) for a discharge (Brit. Libr., Lansdowne MS. 127 fos. 4, 5, 13v, 19). It is possible that these sums were renegotiated forfeitures on bonds.

havyng wyf and chyldren lyke to be perisshed for defaute" if he had to pay on the bond, and the king signed the petition as sufficient warrant for the recognizance to be cancelled at chancery.[145] Prosecutions on bonds were taking place because they were being scrutinized in the rolls and files.

Henry VII personally directed the intensification of bond administration, consolidation and prosecution, with the chancery as a central point for a process that moved to the working councillors and the king and his chamber. At the end of 1499, he informed all chancery officials that recognizances in cases of treason and misprision by "subjects or strangers" were to be enrolled, perhaps a reaction to the uncertain intentions of the earl of Suffolk and the final act in the Perkin Warbeck revolt.[146] The king noted that these bonds had not hitherto been enrolled and he now ordered those working at chancery to enrol them within eight days of receipt. Failure to do so meant a fine of 20s to the officers, with two-thirds going to the king and one-third to the chancellor: an incentive for the chancellor to keep tabs on his clerks. In true policy fashion, Henry ordered that those forfeitures also had to be enrolled—most likely as recognizances!—under a further penalty of 10s within a month after the infraction was incurred. Failure to do so meant the loss of office. The king made sure his chancery clerks had the means to do his will, stating that, "to avoid any excuse", all chancery officers would have access to every recognizance on file for enrolment within the eight-day period. To make the point stick—as if it were somehow missed—each clerk was to be bound to Henry VII in 20s for "each day after the eight that he fails to enrol the same, with a further fine of 10s for failure to subscribe his name to the same".

Although some have argued that this command had little immediate effect with regard to bonds for treason and misprision, there clearly was an increase in administrative activity, but not necessarily on the close rolls.[147]

---

[145] T.N.A.: P.R.O., C 82/218, 6 May 1501; C 82/329, n.d. but after 27 Nov. 1505; *Cal. Close Rolls 1485-1500*, no. 957; *Cal. Close Rolls 1500-9*, no. 447. Warde required a pardon with many others in 1505 for possible trade violations (*Cal. Pat. Rolls 1494-1509*, p. 449).

[146] *Cal. Close Rolls 1485-1500*, no. 1199, enrolled 8 Dec. 1499. Warbeck was executed on 16 Nov.; the earl of Warwick on 29 Nov. Edmund de la Pole, earl of Suffolk, had fled to Calais the previous May.

[147] McFarlane noted a rise in bond enrolment on the close rolls after 1500, and Lander felt that while recognizances for the nobility did not rise until 1502, he agreed with McFarlane that perhaps all bonds were now recorded "as a precaution" by the chancery clerks (McFarlane, review of *Calendar of Close Rolls 1500-9*,

In the surviving *corpus cum causa* writs, which included memoranda of recognizances taken at chancery, such bonds were filed throughout the reign but with increased frequency.[148] During the period 1498-9, old recognizances found among these eighty documents were now beginning to be prosecuted with some regularity.[149] For the period 1499-1502, the number of writs filed came to 315 documents, and from 1502 to the end of the reign a total of 815 were filed, with a large number as memoranda of recognizances.[150] The 1499 enrolment directive may have been the result of the continuing escalation of the bond policy, but a large jump in enrolment occurred later on because of particular circumstances and the decisions made by the king.

Those circumstances, with their potential for instability for the crown, emerged over time while the working councillors followed the king's determination and Bray's conciliar leadership in increasing their activities regarding bond policy. They included Henry VII's intermittent illnesses after 1499, which became more serious by 1507; the death of Cardinal Morton in September 1500; and the loss of Henry's heir and his wife within a ten-month period (2 April 1502 and 11 February 1503 respectively). But perhaps the biggest prospective blow to his statecraft was the death of Sir Reynold Bray on 5 August 1503. Henry had relied heavily on this architect of both his governance and his magnificent chapel. Fortunately, the king possessed councillors who for the most part had been executing his financial and judicial activities through his bond policy for eighteen years with Bray.

Ever cautious, Henry did not immediately elevate anyone to replace Bray and even took his time before giving John Mordaunt the chancellorship of the duchy of Lancaster in 1504. Whether the king saw this trusted official and councillor to his mother as Bray's eventual replacement may have become moot because of two occurrences that year: the recognition of Edmund Dudley as a capable and loyal councillor who was made speaker of the commons in January; and the death of Mordaunt

---

Eng. Hist. Rev., Vol. LXXXI (1966), pp. 153-4; Lander, p. 335). See Horowitz, "Henry Tudor's treasure" regarding enrolments at chancery.

[148] T.N.A.: P.R.O., C 244 series.

[149] T.N.A.: P.R.O., C 244/146.

[150] T.N.A.: P.R.O., C 244/147-50 (1499-1502); C 244/151-9 (1502-9). A few of the twenty-one documents in the last batch of writs (C 244/159) were dated from 1510 to 1511.

on 11 September.[151] Interestingly, Dudley dated the first time he "entered the service of o[r] said sov[r]aigne lord" to the same day Mordaunt died, which does beg the question of whether he received his position by default.[152] Within a month of Mordaunt's death and Dudley's elevation, Richard Empson was named keeper of the duchy seal, and its chancellor a year later. Empson would thus preside over the working councillors to pursue the bond policy that included prosecuting the king's financial and judicial rights using the various duchy chambers, as Bray had done. Henry VII therefore had made up his mind to continue the same polity and policy established in 1485, except that Bray's dual roles were now assumed by two men who would forever be linked with the first Tudor's mode of governance and its amplification: Empson and Dudley.

Dudley and the king began working closely together. Numerous bills were signed by both of them for a variety of actions.[153] When William Halls was approved to be the clerk of the peace in Devon, a bill for his letters patent was signed by Dudley and Henry VII; unsurprisingly, Halls had to pay 40 marks cash to Dudley for the office. Dudley most likely had his book of bonds with him when he signed the bill, and perhaps he and the king decided on the amount together.[154] They also perused the same book of recognizances, and Henry VII signed every page of Dudley's own book.

---

[151] Horowitz, "Richard Empson", pp. 40-1. Henry VII's last parliament began 26 Jan.

[152] Brit. Libr., Lansdowne MS. 127 fo. 1. A petition signed by Henry VII and Dudley addressed to the treasurer, barons and chamberlain of the exchequer, rehearsed the terms of an annuity of 100 marks for Dudley since Sept. 1504, for "our trusty and right welbeloved Consaillor" (T.N.A.: P.R.O., C 82/278, 29 Oct. 1505). Steven Gunn suggested that Bray may have been Dudley's patron ("Edmund Dudley and the church", *Jour. Eccles. Hist.*, li (2000), pp. 509-26, at p. 523).

[153] It should be noted that Henry signed numerous writs and letters with other working councillors as well, usually pointed to their particular activities. This is evident in the various privy seal and signet warrants found in the C 82 and E 404 series of documents at The National Archives.

[154] T.N.A.: P.R.O., C 82/293, 2 Nov. 1506; Brit. Libr., Lansdowne MS. 127 fo. 31, dated the same day. Payments for offices varied in amounts, e.g. clerkship of Hull (£106 13s 4d); auditorship in Cornwall (£40) and in the exchequer (40 marks); clerkship of the peace in Lincolnshire (50 marks) and in Leicestershire (20 marks) (Brit. Libr., Lansdowne MS. 127 fos. 31-33v). Empson probably possessed a similar book, for which an entry was reconstructed along the lines of Dudley's activities (Horowitz, "Richard Empson", p. 42).

The king relied on Dudley to pursue all avenues of potential revenue and possible forfeitures on bonds for those failing to adhere to the law or to administer their offices competently. As noted above, Henry also gave Dudley, and Empson, great latitude in drawing up commissions for that purpose.

Dudley may well have been the prime mover in discovering not only these shortfalls related to bonds but also inefficiencies and oversights elsewhere in government. For example, the king sent a signet letter to the chancellor after learning that those administering the royal forests were "suche symple p[er]sonnes [who] as in tyme passed have been promoted therunto and nowe occupie those rowmes". Because of these incompetent officials "the game w[t]in o[r] forrests be gretely diminisshed and destroyed". Henry now told the chancellor that "fromhensfurth take thadvise of o[r] right trusty counseillour Edmonde dudley, Justice of oure said forests" in making out any writs or warrants by his command to remove any officials and replace them "as he shall thynk moost expedient". Dudley was undoubtedly the source to whom Henry referred when he spoke of "learning" about the problem. As if to ensure that his chancellor and archbishop of Canterbury would indeed bow to the will of an esquire, the king concluded "ffaile ye not to confo[r]me you thus to doo as we trust you and as ye tender our pleas[ure]".[155] Henry VII invested more power and authority in Dudley. In a letter to the chancellor, the king commanded "for y[e] bishop of Winchest[r]" to make out under the great seal writs of "Ne exeas Regnum (not to leave the realm)" "after [such] maner fo[r]me and effecte as our trusty Counsaillo[r] Edmund Dudley shall shewe unto you".[156] It is not difficult to see how animosity towards Dudley could have built up over time as other royal officials had to bend to the will of an over-mighty esquire solely because of the king's unwavering support.

Part of the increase in bond policy activity can be attributed to this decision by Henry VII that Dudley should pursue obligations and recognizances as Bray had done, only with greater assistance from the king. One example of this shift after 1504 can be seen in recognizances involving Sir Henry, Lord Clifford. Three years earlier, the king received payment on one of ten recognizances for £100 entered into by Clifford for yearly receipts for the farms and issues of certain manors in York.[157] The

---

[155] T.N.A.: P.R.O., C 82/320, 8 Oct. 1508.
[156] T.N.A.: P.R.O., C 82/286, 21 June 1506.
[157] *Cal. Close Rolls 1500-9*, no. 114. A notation in the summary states that all bonds were cancelled by successive warrants down to 18 July 1518, but fails to mention that cancellation occurred because payments were made.

money was originally to be paid to four of the working councillors for the king's use: Mordaunt, Hobart, Empson and Lucas. Henry later signed a warrant to cancel that one bond at chancery because the money was paid to the king "fforseyng alwayes that al the othr recognisancs remayne in ful strength and effect as it apperteigneth".[158]

Nevertheless, after Dudley's activities on behalf of the crown were well under way, a new set of bonds for Lord Clifford marked a different procedure. The king sent a list of recognizances to chancery via Thomas Routhale, the king's secretary but also one of the masters in chancery—yet another blur of "offices" that helped in the implementation of policy.[159] The list included four bonds entered on 22 April 1506 by Lord Clifford and his sureties for the total payment of 1,300 marks. These recognizances were taken by Routhale and subsequently signed by Henry VII. A signet letter by the king was also sent with the recognizance list to the master of the rolls at chancery, Christopher Baynbridge, who had recently succeeded William Barons at that position; Dudley had been Barons's patron.[160] The king ordered the bonds to be "spedely and suerly entred and enrolled amongs other Rolls and Records in our Chauncery".

However, Henry VII further commanded that the master of the rolls was then "w^t all diligence [to] sende unto our right trusty counsaillor Edmund Dudley the true copyes of the said recognisaunces subscribed with your hand".[161] In fact, the recognizances were enrolled, Dudley received the bonds, and Clifford compounded these and other recognizances with Dudley for a pardon for numerous offences.[162] There was no involvement with the other councillors; Dudley was doing the king's bidding on his own when he was not working with his colleagues, much as Bray had done. He had become an important conduit between the

---

[158] T.N.A.: P.R.O., C 82/246, 26 July 1503.

[159] Routhale, like so many other working councillors, took recognizances and obligations on behalf of the king before Dudley's entry into royal service. See, e.g., John Hussey's bond of 1,000 marks to keep his two brothers, William and Robert, on their good behaviour and on time to appear "byfore the kings seid secretary" to take out bonds for £500 each for their allegiance (T.N.A.: P.R.O., C 255/8/5 no. 95, 9 Jan. 1502).

[160] Gunn, "Edmund Dudley and the church", p. 523. Barons, a graduate of Oxford and Bologna, became bishop of London.

[161] T.N.A.: P.R.O., C 82/284, 27 Apr. 1506.

[162] *Cal. Close Rolls 1500-9*, no. 622; Brit. Libr., Lansdowne MS. 127 fo. 22v; *Cal. Pat. Rolls 1494-1509*, p. 466. The pardon did not exclude payment of the 1,300 marks or the payment of £700 on other recognizances owed by Clifford.

king and his chancery when it came to bonds. This did not preclude other councillors from continuing the execution of the bond policy with chancery involvement, whether Dudley worked with them or on his own. Joanne Pickering's recognizance for 500 marks taken in chancery on 10 July 1503 required her to find sureties for a bond of 400 marks "such as our Counsell lerned shuld accept". The bond, which was "in our Chauncᵉy remaynyng of recorde", was ordered cancelled in November 1504.[163]

Dudley also became involved with determining possible forfeitures on judicial bonds, many of which had been in abeyance at the various law courts since the beginning of the reign. This was to be accomplished either through his own searches or through lists of obligations and recognizances compiled by others and given to him to prosecute, and he had help from the king. Indeed, on the inside cover of a book listing the recognizances forfeited at king's bench from the beginning of the reign, Henry VII wrote a note in his own hand: "A declaracon of all the recognicions forfait in the kyngs bench from Anno pᵐo of oᵣ Reign [1485] unto mich[aelmas] Anno 20° [1504] [and?] yᵗ E Dudley hath [further] charge to make out proces for all thoes yᵗ be unpaied".[164] The twenty-folio book, written in Latin and organized by court terms, noted that the recognizances were kept at the exchequer. Several months later (1 February 1505), Dudley received another book of obligations by order of the king, based on records from the start of the reign "towching dyvᵣse o[the]r matyers". The twenty-seven folios listed everything from bonds for appearance at common pleas or the king's "counsaill", keeping the peace and good behaviour to obligations for hunting hawks in the king's forest, keeping allegiance, prohibiting Calais merchants to sail in certain waters or the making of bricks. It was delivered to Dudley and his servant, John Mitchell, by John Heron to prosecute the bonds on behalf of the king.[165] Heron signed almost every

---

[163] T.N.A.: P.R.O., C 82/252. The recognizance was for semi-annual payments, most likely for a wardship, and it was not enrolled.

[164] T.N.A.: P.R.O., E 101/516/17. An ultraviolet light was required to bring out the notation and the handwriting was compared to four pages of script written by Henry VII during the timeframe 1502-4 (E 101/413/2/3 fos. 1-4). Despite Henry's reference to recognizances through the autumn of 1504, when Dudley entered his service, the book apparently ends in the summer of 1503, suggesting that it had been prepared for (or by) Bray just before his death and was now assigned to Dudley.

[165] T.N.A.: P.R.O., E 101/517/11, cover and fos. 3, 7v. The book is mentioned in Condon, "Ruling elites", p. 133 and n. 10; it is discussed in Horowitz, "Henry Tudor's treasure".

page, mimicking the monarch he served. Most revealing is that, of the large number of obligations for "good abearing", a majority involved non-nobles.

Besides seeking out old bonds for prosecution, Dudley and the king kept a close eye on potentially new ones that related to both finance and law and order. One example is the signet signed by Henry VII to the chancellor, asking for a commission under the great seal involving the bishop of Exeter, Robert Willoughby, Lord Broke and John More "according to a bill of certain Articles signed w^t o^r hand". Although Henry signed it, at the bottom of the three articles is found "p[er] me Ed[mund] Dudeley p[ro] Rege", the obvious author and perhaps the discoverer of the matters. The first article involved a Devonshire man "which is lunacy and hath be oute of his mynde by [the] space of xxv yeres". He was seised of lands worth 200 marks per annum, without permission from any king, past or present. The second article involved "a grevous and heynous murdr" in Devon by a man and a woman. The man was hanged, but the woman escaped with the help of John Lilbert, one of the justices of the peace, although he knew "that she was p[ar]tie to the said murdr". The third involved a man who robbed his mother of gold and silver and was later captured. However, the justice of the peace decided "to lett hym goo by maynp[ernours]", which the article states "shuld not have byn doon by the law & good discrecion".[166]

No doubt Henry VII and Edmund Dudley saw financial possibilities, including the taking of new bonds. Although obligations or recognizances relating to the last two articles may not have been very lucrative, the surviving lists and files of such bonds for the reign show numerous very small amounts. The king was focused on upholding the law and making sure that the justices were accountable and the populace was aware of their monarch's commitment to law enforcement. Henry VII was unequivocally the force behind this policy of prosecuting bonds, both to activate the somnolent process of law and to collect money from those who disrespected it or ignored it, or who might potentially break it.

---

[166] T.N.A.: P.R.O., C 82/294, 28 Dec. 1506. It was enrolled at chancery on 16 Jan. 1507, but the printed summary only lists the three commissioners and the reason for the commission, being "to enquire of lands and idiots, murders, homicides, escapes of felons in the county of Devon" (*Cal. Pat. Rolls 1494-1509*, p. 507). There is then a notation that the commission was vacated by writ of *supersedeas*, although it appears to have been reinstated with additional commissioners the following March (*Cal. Pat. Rolls 1494-1509*, p. 546).

Although Dudley acted as his personal bond minister, with Empson in a similar position overseeing the working councillors for day-to-day activities, the king directed the overall policy. He accomplished this through his councillors, who like Dudley worked from books and lists of obligations due to the crown, usually in specific areas of prerogative rights or judicial fines owed to the king.[167] Henry also ruled through his directives that encompassed the realm, mainly through letters he signed personally—a signature that was sought after as the ultimate royal stamp of approval.[168] Sheriffs and justices were well aware of their king's commitment to maintaining the laws and to acquiring what was deemed his just due as monarch. They could expect to hear from him frequently: a not uncommon communication was the signet letter he signed at Richmond ordering a commission in Derbyshire and Nottinghamshire to inquire about wards, lands *in capite*, livery, marriages, loans, murderers, idiots, unlawful acquittals and "all forfaictures of recognisaunce takyn bifore the Justicis of peax Shiriffs or othrewise in sessions".[169]

While historians have sometimes been sceptical about a shift in policy or priority under Henry, especially when it came to increasing the prosecution of old bonds, what actually occurred was an intensification of, and procedural change in, a bond policy that commenced at the outset of the reign. Elton denied any effort to collect on old bonds when he wrote his articles, concluding that "the alleged evidence for a marked deterioration in the last years rests either on statements of interested parties or can be paralleled from the earlier years". He did concede that "it does look as though the last years of Henry VII witnessed a more

---

[167] One can only wonder how many files of obligations and recognizances must have existed. There is a reference to another repository for bonds in one of the surviving council books at the duchy of Lancaster: "Thobligacon of Willm Ap Rys & divrs other r[e]mayneth in the kings box of obligacons in the Ambry" (T.N.A.: P.R.O., DL 5/2 fo. 104). An ambry was a small cupboard or closet for storage. There were boxes of obligations in the king's chamber, and Dudley had them all over his house (Horowitz, "Richard Empson", pp. 47 n. 103, 42).

[168] People at the time understood the weighty authority of these various missives and the king's propensity for signing documents. A typical example was when the abbot of Woburn petitioned the king for a patent a half year after Perkin Warbeck's execution. He requested Henry's signature, "and that this bill signed w^t your moost victorious hand may be sufficient warrant to your Chaunceller of Englond" for a patent under the great seal "w^tout sueng prive signet prive seale or other warrant" (T.N.A.: P.R.O., C 82/205, 12 June 1500).

[169] T.N.A.: P.R.O., C 82/330, 30 Nov., n.d., but after 27 Aug. 1492, when the king changed his sign manual.

particular attention to the collection of debts and fines owed the king".[170] But his use of fifteen extant *scire facias* writs to show that all but one of the "old" debts put for recovery were taken by 1499 missed most of the surviving evidence, or the fact that searches, and collections, on old bonds began from the start of the reign. Overlooked as well were the bonds on file and Dudley's lists and books of bonds taken since 1485 and handed to him by the king for prosecution and collection.

Then there are the close rolls that survive from the reign, the summaries of which, as noted above, seem to suggest a huge increase in bond enrolment (and therefore bond activity) after 1500 or 1502.[171] The plethora of recognizances appearing on the dorse of these rolls later in the reign has led to an optical illusion that needs to be recognized. Henry VII's chancery did begin to enrol recognizances on the close rolls with greater frequency when compared to surviving rolls from the Yorkist period. But what appears to be a boutade of new obligations and recognizances towards the end of the reign was in fact a purposeful, concerted and expanded effort to discover, list, scrutinize and act upon any and all records involving bonds old or new *ad usum regis*, whether for actual debts or future behaviour. There was a jump in enrolments on the close rolls from 1500 to 1501, from nineteen recognizances due to the king or his councillors on his behalf to sixty-nine, and as discussed above, it may have been related to a 1499 proclamation involving bonds for treason. In 1502 the number was sixty-eight but it then dropped to thirty-six in 1503. It was in 1504 that the number of bonds enrolled spiked to 122, with many enrolled later in the year; and from 1506 to 1508 the number never dipped below 213 per year. This coincided with Edmund Dudley's employment and the appointment of Richard Empson as successor to John Mordaunt at the duchy of Lancaster. But it involved an administrative enhancement for the bond policy: using the close rolls as a source of documentation for potential or real money due to the crown on recognizances. The jump in enrolments was an archival move for record consolidation of an ongoing bond policy that resulted in the steady growth of the taking and prosecuting of recognizances and obligations after 1485, not 1502 or 1504.

It is difficult to ascertain the magnitude of bonds being taken, prosecuted and cancelled upon payment as the reign progressed. Almost a

---

[170] Elton, "A restatement", pp. 28, 12.
[171] *Cal. Close Rolls 1485-1500* and *Cal. Close Rolls 1500-9*; see Horowitz, "Henry Tudor's treasure", for an analysis of enrolled bonds summarized in these *Calendars*.

half century ago, R.E. Latham noted in the 1500-9 volume of the *Calendar of Close Rolls*: "It is clear from the original recognizances surviving in unsorted Chancery Files that the great majority were not enrolled".[172] One complication lies in the probability that bonds were enrolled but that the actual rolls have not been identified or are missing. For example, the C 255/8 series (4, 5, 7-12) at The National Archives have the M^o enrolment mark on them yet are missing from those close rolls that have been identified for the reign and printed in the two-volume *Calendars*. File four has 169 memoranda of recognizances, mostly for good behaviour, that cover the first ten years of the reign: "old" bonds. File five contains 105 memoranda, with about a third from the last nine years of the reign and the majority from earlier years. Sean Cunningham has discovered a "missing" chancery roll that in fact contains the enrolment of the majority of these bonds.[173] It is the circular argument that we do not know what we do not know.

Another challenge involves the lists and books of bonds kept by councillors that cannot be accounted for either in the chancery and exchequer records or in the chamber account books. Dudley's books of old bonds, two of which have been mentioned, may represent a combination of bonds filed at various royal repositories, as well as within the king's chamber. This loose tracking of bonds is what led to more and more of them being entered on the close rolls as part of the effort to consolidate their administration and prosecution. Moreover, they were not simply those taken by the inner circle of councillors who predominated in the entries, such as Lovell, Empson, Mordaunt, Dudley, Hobart and Lucas. When, in January 1507, Hugh Kedinghale petitioned for the farm of Lewesham for twenty-one years, he paid £10 for the privilege. A bill to this effect was signed by Henry VII, Robert Southwell and Roger, bishop of Carlisle. But it also noted that six sureties "standeth bounden" to Southwell, Carlisle and John Heron since 1505 for 200 marks to pay a lesser sum in three instalments. This was gleaned from locating the recognizance on the close rolls, most likely through the efforts of Heron.[174] How many "bonds in boxes" Southwell and Carlisle kept may never be known.

---

[172] *Cal. Close Rolls 1500-9*, pp. viii-ix.
[173] Cunningham, "Loyalty and the usurper".
[174] T.N.A.: P.R.O., C 82/295, 29 Jan. 1507; *Cal. Close Rolls 1500-9*, no. 523. As if to make the memory of the bond perfectly clear, after the words "standeth bounden" Henry VII wrote in the words "b[y] reco[g]nysance".

In a list of recognizances from Henry VII's reign created by the command of his heir, Henry VIII, it was noted that the entries came "out of divrse boks signed w[th] thand of o[r] derrest fadre".[175] The first Tudor's signature or sign manual "H R" ("Henricus Rex") could also be found on warrants, pardons, lists, nominations for office and a variety of other documents, suggesting that he spent an inordinate amount of time involving himself in all aspects of finance and law.[176] Indeed, Henry put his name to every act of parliament after 1497—the date of the earliest known original act. He signed each membrane, a practice emulated by all three of his grandchildren once they became the monarch.[177] The king was scrutinizing and signing documents even after being observed as very ill in the spring of 1507.[178] He was well enough that September to cross out the words "for term of life" and sign his name to a petition for letters patent requested by Richard Empson for certain manors.[179] Henry continued to sign bills and letters, often with Dudley or Empson, well into 1508 and 1509.[180] True to his micro-management style, he was working at least a week before his death when he signed a general pardon in a shaky hand at both the top and bottom of the document.[181]

Henry VIII tried to emulate his father as the ultimate royal administrator, but the seventeen-year-old's world view was closer to that of Henry V than Henry VII. He initially began signing John Heron's accounts, but he also purchased a collar of "Esses" (SS) reminiscent of

---

[175] T.N.A.: P.R.O., SP 1/1 fo. 104; *L&P*, I.i. no. 309.

[176] Steven Gunn felt that occurrences of Henry's signature on accounts diminished after 1504 along with his eyesight, which clearly was a factor ("The courtiers of Henry VII", *Eng. Hist. Rev.*, Vol. CVIII (1993), pp. 23-49, at p. 24). But the number of accounts that the king scrutinized had also multiplied, perhaps limiting the use of his sign manual. The king's ministers also began signing documents on his behalf, with or without his being present.

[177] J.I. Miklovich, "The significance of the royal sign manual in early Tudor legislative procedure", *Bull. Inst. Hist. Research*, lii (1979), pp. 23-36, at p. 24.

[178] *Calendar of State Papers, Spanish*, suppl. to vols. i and ii, no. 14 (p. 90).

[179] T.N.A.: P.R.O., C 82/304.

[180] E.g., T.N.A.: P.R.O., C 82/310, 314, 319, 324.

[181] T.N.A.: P.R.O., C 82/326 (delivered 16 Apr. 1509). For a discrepancy on the date of Henry's demise, see S.J. Gunn, "The accession of Henry VII", *Hist. Research*, Vol. LXIV (1991), pp. 278-88. Chrimes thought that neither Henry VII nor his son could have had much personal input to the pardon issued two days after the first Tudor's death, but this document suggests a king involved in his administration to the end (Chrimes, p. 315).

Lancastrian lore with a focus on the reclamation of a lost France.[182] With the advice of his grandmother and certain of his father's councillors, he also issued a pardon two days after his father's death that encompassed recognizances and other offences, although the exception of "detts and accompts" clearly signalled that the bond policy was not going to vanish along with Henry VII.[183]

And it certainly did not. John Heron continued to list both recognizances and obligations owed to the crown, beginning eight days after the death of Henry VII.[184] Henry VIII signed almost every page of the recognizances, and many were annotated as paid or vacated. For the rest of the reign, bonds continued to be taken, filed, prosecuted and collected upon as before. Thomas Wolsey's rise to power included his personal involvement in seeking out money owed on debts to Henry VII, beginning in August 1514.[185] In a collection of books and records for the exchequer, compiled late in Henry VIII's reign (1541-2), it was noted that anyone taking an obligation to his own use in the name of the king would suffer imprisonment—an attempt to avoid the abuses that occurred in the previous reign under the direction of Empson and Dudley, which may still have been a problem. It also noted that obligations owed to Henry VIII that went unpaid were nonetheless viable and due "to the heirs or executors of the kinge". Regarding bonds taken at the various financial courts for payment by sheriffs and officers of the crown (for example, exchequer, duchy of Lancaster, court of wards), it stated:

> And where sundrie p[er]sons stand bounden to the kinge in div[r]s great sumes of money by recognizaunce, or other bonds in the said sev[r]all Courts for debts due the kinge for purchase of lands and goods, p[er]formance of condycons and sundrie other Causes, And albeit the same p[er]sons have well and trulie satisfied the same debts, or p[er]formed the Condicions of

---

[182] See Brit. Libr., Add. MS. 21481, *passim*, and fo. 31 (2 June 1510) for the purchase of a collar of SS, a badge worn by the supporters of Lancaster since the days of John of Gaunt. A secular cult of Henry V, hero of Agincourt, came about early in Henry VIII's reign (C.S.L. Davies, "Henry VIII and Henry V: the wars in France", in *The End of the Middle Ages? England in the 15th and 16th Centuries*, ed. J.L. Watts (Stroud, 1998), pp. 235-62, at p. 237).

[183] Horowitz, "'Agree with the king'", p. 356.

[184] See Brit. Libr., Add. MS. 21481 fos. 289-305v for recognizances, fos. 318-352v for obligations.

[185] S.J. Gunn, "The Act of Resumption of 1515", in *Early Tudor England: Proceedings of the 1987 Harlaxton Symposium*, ed. D. Williams (Woodbridge, 1989), pp. 87-106, at pp. 93-4.

the same Recognizaunces, or other bonds, yet the same Recognizaunces or other bonds cannot be made void wth out the kinges speciall warrantt wch shoud be greate unquietnes, to the kinge and verie Chardgable to his subiects, to suie from tyme to tyme for the same.

Because people in the past had lost their official acquittances, "whereby greate daunger maie growe to them", it was ordered that as the written discharge was given to the debtor the recognizance should be cancelled and made void at the same time.[186] This showed that more than thirty years after Henry VII's death, bonds were still a cornerstone of finance and justice and the dominant credit instrument for debt, trade and acquisition.

The exchequer, as it was wont to do during a new reign, reverted to storing obligations and the ready money paid upon them. This forced Henry VIII, through the recommendations of his father's experienced councillors, to rein in both the bonds and the cash. And once again, it was John Cutte who was asked to fill the role of royal liaison between the exchequer and the chamber. It took not only privy seals but acts of parliament to ensure that obligations and recognizances were delivered to the king's chamber, with the tellers of the receipt at the exchequer assisting in this endeavour. But while there remained instances where money and bonds still stayed at the exchequer, it was evident that the new king agreed to maintain the role of his chamber as the national treasury, at least as far as bonds were concerned.[187] Given his proclivities for war, this fitted well with his need for large amounts of cash expeditiously.

Finally, it should be pointed out that for ordinary English men and women, entering into obligations continued unabated as a way of life. Between 1550 and 1580, disputes on non-performing obligations rose to hundreds of thousands of suits per annum.[188] However, most were no doubt filed to force arbitration and settlement, a practice well established since long before the first Tudor became king. Recognizances continued to be used throughout the 16th and 17th centuries to "bind over" people to keep the peace and behave themselves. By 1600, recognizances for the peace were acknowledged as a means to coerce antagonists into avoiding

---

[186] Brit. Libr, Cotton MS., Titus B.IV fos. 57, 58v-59.

[187] Horowitz, "An early-Tudor teller's book", *passim*.

[188] C. Muldrew, *The Economy of Obligation: the Culture of Credit and Social Relations in Early Modern England* (Basingstoke, 1998), p. 3. Muldrew is much too late in suggesting that the "culture of credit" began in the mid-16th century or that written debts could be exchanged for other debts and started to be recorded in account books in the 16th and 17th centuries (pp. 3, 100, 109).

brutal acts at a time when there was a growing sense of abhorrence of violence—arguably a concern throughout Henry VII's reign and one reason he intensified their administration and prosecution.[189] A study of recognizances for peace and appearance extant for the borough of Colchester during Elizabeth I's reign noted that "the recognizance not only aided in the prevention and control of crime but also provided a ready to hand means to supervise and to regulate the lives of persons considered undesirable or dangerous to the community"—conclusions at which Elizabeth's grandfather and his councillors arrived almost a century earlier, but overlooked in this review.[190] There could also be a malicious use of bonds, as in the days of Empson and Dudley, but bonds and sureties had a continuous role in private and public transactions and matters of law. As one author has noted, "the simple recognizance, that laconic, much neglected and undramatic instrument of law enforcement, was arguably crucial to the keeping of the public peace at every social level".[191]

What about the recognizances and obligations from the old reign that were viewed as illegal, harsh or even spurious by the new reign? J.R. Lander concluded that numerous bonds were cancelled and vacated at the beginning of Henry VIII's reign without payment upon them, a deduction based on the summary entries in *Letters and Papers* in the reign of Henry VIII where the word "cancelled" was printed: forty-five recognizances the

---

[189] S. Hindle, *The State and Social Change in Early Modern England, c.1550-1640* (Basingstoke, 2000), pp. 97ff, 105.

[190] J.B. Samaha, "The recognizance in Elizabethan law enforcement", *Amer. Jour. Legal Hist.*, xxv (1981), pp. 189-204, at p. 189. Samaha concluded the peace bond's main purpose was the prevention of violence and serious threats to public order, and it was effective since most people in recorded recognizances honoured their conditions (pp. 194, 197). Unfortunately, he disregarded the fact that these bonds had been in use for centuries, especially at the local level for appearance at court, law enforcement and keeping the peace. His assertion that "the criminal trial must yield its exalted place [to recognizances] as the centerpiece of the administration of justice" misses the pervasive usage of bonds for this purpose in Henry VII's reign, who is never mentioned. (p. 204). E.g., such statements as the recognizance being called upon "to do the job" of maintaining order in Elizabethan alehouses by binding the keepers to have a licence ignored Henry VII's "national" licensing of alehouses in 1495, which gave J.P.s the authority to take sureties for good behaviour from those who kept such houses (<http://www.camulos.com/inns/3licence. htm> [accessed 21 Nov. 2008]).

[191] Hindle, *The State and Social Change*, p. 111-15. To Hindle, recognizances were an overt demonstration of the participatory nature of state formation in England.

first year, 135 more over the next five years.[192] Indeed, many bonds were cancelled without payment, and Lander noted that fifty-one of them were said to have been extortionate, although one might argue that any debtor to the crown hearing of a general pardon on bonds might plead this story.[193]

These cancellations suggested a change in policy from the previous reign, or at the very least a recognition that the policy was unjust and in need of remedy. But an examination of the actual chancery warrants for vacating recognizances shows that a large number were cancelled *upon payment*, and not simply cancelled as printed in the summaries. In fact, only weeks after Henry VII's death, bonds were prosecuted for payment with new ones taken by many of the same ministers and officials who worked closely with Empson and Dudley.[194]

This is gleaned by comparing some of the printed summaries of bonds listed simply as cancelled in *Letters and Papers* with the actual warrants upon which they were based. For example, Elizabeth Strykland and her sureties were bound in a recognizance of £100 taken in the old reign to pay 100 marks to Thomas Lovell, Richard Empson, John Hussey, Edmund Dudley and Thomas Lucas on behalf of the king on 3 May 1509, twelve days after the death of Henry VII; she in fact paid so that she could have her bond cancelled. A recognizance taken on 30 November 1506 of Sir

---

[192] Lander, p. 352 and n. 170. He did note that many bonds from the old regime were paid or compounded, and that the practice continued into the reign of Henry VIII. Brodie and Elton previously came to this conclusion (Horowitz, "'Agree with the king'", n. 134).

[193] Hall noted that in the first year of the new reign, "executours made restitucion of great sommes of money, to many persons taken against good conscie[n]ce to the sayde kynges vse, by the forenamed Empson and Dudley" (*Hall's Chronicle*, p. 514). Dudley admitted that many people were dealt with harshly, if not illegally (C.J. Harrison, "The petition of Edmund Dudley", *Eng. Hist. Rev.*, Vol. XXXVII (1972), 82-9).

[194] Lander made the same judgement regarding notations of "vacated" or "cancelled" recognizances printed in the summaries of the *Calendar of Close Rolls*. E.g., two recognizances were entered into by four men for £100 each to pay £80 at Martinmas in 1505 and in 1506 to Hobart, Empson, Hussey, Dudley and Lucas for the king's use. In the *Calendar*, they are annotated as "cancelled by warrant" with no mention of payment, drawing the conclusion that no money was ever paid (*Cal. Close Rolls 1500-9*, no. 418(ii)). Yet the two warrants for cancellation for the two recognizances state that £80 was paid on 3 Nov. 1505 and again on 7 Nov. 1506 to the treasurer of the king's chamber (T.N.A.: P.R.O., C 82/279; C 82/293). The *Calendar* entry also lists the bonds under 3 Dec. 1504, with no mention of the dates of discharge in the successive two years.

Richard Woderove and his sureties for £100 to pay 100 marks to certain working councillors was cancelled after being "paid & p[er]formed". Sir Robert Drury and others were bound in a recognizance on 20 November 1504 for £250 for Drury to pay two instalments of £100 each, one on 15 February 1508 (which he did) and later on 24 June 1509. He made that payment and his bond was then cancelled. Robert Brudenell, a "learned councillor" of Henry VII, and his sureties owed 50 marks in a bond to Lovell and others to the use of Henry VII taken in July 1506; he paid it on 24 June 1509 to have it cancelled. Thomas Cokayne and three sureties were bound to Thomas Lovell and others for £100 on 14 July 1506 to pay 100 marks the same day Brudenell's bond was due; the bond was cancelled 26 October 1509, but after the money was received by the treasurer of the king's chamber. Sir Thomas Curwen and two others were bound by recognizance on 13 July 1507 in 100 marks to pay £50 at a certain date; Curwen paid the amount to John Heron and his bond was cancelled on 14 November 1509. The same was true of Edward Jerningham, bound to Henry VII and paid in full in the new reign to have his recognizance voided. The recognizance of Thomas Troyes and two others, taken on 20 February 1505, were paid in full and then cancelled on 9 November 1509.[195] In a review of surviving chancery warrants two years after Henry VIII's reign began, recognizances were still being cancelled upon payment. This cannot be determined solely from reading the summaries in *Letters and Papers*.

Meetings were in fact held by Henry VIII's councillors about the myriad bonds owed his father to see how many of them should be respited and how many should be either collected or compounded.[196] The reviewers were for the most part his father's men: Thomas Lovell, Richard Fox, John Heron, Thomas Lucas, James Hobart and Thomas earl of Surrey among them. Heron delivered the bonds to the various parties involved, although it was clear that not all money was returned—there were also books "of the recepts of their first paiements signed w^t the kings hand", referring to Henry VII.[197] By 1530—more than twenty years later—there were at least four files of old obligations kept in the chamber, mainly from Henry VII's

---

[195] T.N.A.: P.R.O., C 82/338 (*L&P*, I.i. no. 132(34)); C 82/336 (*L&P*, I.i. no. 54(3)); C 82/337 (*L&P*, I.i. no. 94(99)); C 82/338 (*L&P*, I.i. no. 132(18), which only states the £40 penalty, not the 50 marks actually due—this omission occurs in other *L&P* entries); C 82/341 (*L&P*, I.i. nos. 218(59), 381(108)); C 82/342 (*L&P*, I.i. no. 257(63), (84), (34)).

[196] *L&P*, I.i. no. 1493.

[197] T.N.A.: P.R.O., SP 1/2.

reign; the last file was annotated as "desperate".[198] The thirteen folios read like Edmund Dudley's account book, with annotations against each name and sums of money due on bonds from both reigns. There were listed Tom White and a surety in an obligation for £10 to "save harmeles" another party; Sir William Parker in an obligation of £26 13s 4d, made to Empson; £500 worth of obligations entered into by collectors of an aid and a subsidy to make a true payment; and a recent obligation of 400 marks to be paid "when the kings lerned counsail shulde determyn the title & possession of certein lands".[199]

A separate section listed bonds to Sir Robert Southwell for the payment of farms and the "good abering appara[n]ce and suche like condicion not appering bifor the treasourer of the chamb[e]r whether they war observed or not and the most p[ar]ts of them void & expired". These were similar to those taken at the duchy of Lancaster and later in Henry VII's chamber and represented the bond policy in full force during his reign. They were also comparable to those listed in books given to Dudley for collection, and the suggestion here is that while these were very old, some of them had been paid or most likely compounded for lesser amounts.

But what is striking are the number of bonds noted as "put to be sued", or those marked "sol" ("paid"). Clearly, after more than two decades, the bonds taken in Henry VII's reign were viewed as in full force and actionable—Tudor history was repeating itself, with ministers of the king prosecuting "old bonds". They probably included bonds taken by Empson and Dudley that were questionable but nonetheless now prosecuted and not simply cancelled. As if to distance the first Tudor from his ministers, one bond for £10 entered into by Richard Warrings was annotated "a bil[l] on pap[er] to Edmonde Dudley no me[n]cion of the king. It is put to be sued".[200]

There was also reference to another book of obligations, given to that great Tudor organizer, Thomas Cromwell. Next to several listed for the duke of Buckingham was written "Thise be mencioned in an other boke geven to m[aster] cromwel". In his remembrances when he was Henry VIII's principal secretary, Cromwell wrote "Recognisances forfeited for non observance of the peax or for apparance bifore iustices", and he

---

[198] T.N.A.: P.R.O., SP 1/59, inventory of old obligations *temp* Henry VII kept by Sir Brian Tuke, treasurer of the chamber (found in *L&P*, IV.iii. no. 6798). The original document is used for this discussion.
[199] T.N.A.: P.R.O., SP 1/59 fos. 16, 17, 20.
[200] T.N.A.: P.R.O., SP 1/59 fo. 20.

involved himself with their collection. He also made a note about taking sureties from men in the Tower, not unlike the behaviour seen in Henry VII's reign. Cromwell similarly reminded himself to "speke w^t the kynges lerned Counsaill for the fynisshing of the boke of the Staple"—the same procedure of consulting with the king's working councillors, who were men learned in the laws and processes administering obligations and recognizances and charged with prosecuting them for collection or fulfilment.[201] These were words and actions familiar from the first Tudor's reign.

Henry VII's bond policy literally "bound" a large number of English men and women of high and low birth to the centre through the administration of law, the enforcement of peace and the collection of revenue and debts due on financial arrangements, offices and responsibilities. While all of these measures existed before his time, they were never utilized by an English monarch with such intensity, or determination. The influence of his working councillors, who were brought together largely through their connections with the king's mother and uncle and their own colleagues, cannot be overemphasized.[202] Nor can the experience they offered the king from working in households, whether of a lord or lady or the largest household in the land—the duchy of Lancaster. Where G.R. Elton saw a developing bureaucracy, culminating in the work of Thomas Cromwell and the birth of the modern state under Henry VIII, David Starkey rejected this view and replaced Elton's state bureaucracy with a departmental state run by the privy chamber. Ironically, both admitted that proximity to the king was the decisive factor in how the government worked, yet resisted the notion of the ruler's friends as all-important for state development in favour of the creation of institutions.[203]

---

[201] Brit. Libr., Cotton MS., Titus B.I fos. 157v, 427, 436. Richard Riche also took recognizances, including those for behaving in a desirable way toward the king and realm (T.N.A.: P.R.O., E 315/352).

[202] Nevertheless, Henry VII did not simply clean house, an action most competent rulers avoided; he kept many of the "bureaucrats" in place to maintain continuity. Moreover, at least thirty-five of his councillors also served as councillors to Edward IV (S.J. Gunn, *Early-Tudor Government, 1485-1558* (New York, 1995), p. 23).

[203] See D. Starkey, "Court history in perspective", in *The English Court: from the Wars of the Roses to the Civil War*, ed. D. Starkey and others (1987), pp. 1-24, for the arguments pro and con concerning Elton's Tudor revolution. For a good summary of the political historiography of Tudor England, see S. Alford, "Politics

Henry VII knew better, and he was fortunate to have men qualified and well versed in the use of legal instruments who could serve his purposes regardless of what "offices" or "departments" they occupied. He was pragmatic more than bureaucratic, and his willingness to work with his councillors to stabilize his reign and ensure a viable dynasty bore fruit. He was also astute enough to realize that as king it did little good to wait for cash to come in; credit worked well in the form of obligations and recognizances, and negotiations through compounding and drawing out payments even better. Relying on well-established procedures at the exchequer for payments on bonds did not result in timely cash flow; administering those debts through his trusted councillors and in person offered a quicker response time, especially when collectors such as sheriffs could be made accountable. The same was true with the profits of justice from old, inactive recognizances.

The first Tudor also realized that while the monarchy was the historic centre of the realm it did not always appear that way to "foreign" interests in the shires, especially when local or seigniorial courts overshadowed the central courts, or judicial commissions were headed by local magnates. Henry's numerous commissions of the peace and special commissions were peopled with trusted officials, many from the gentry, who may or may not have had power bases in a locality but who nonetheless represented the king first. Such close scrutiny of the shires from Westminster also meant a careful search into records for any prerogative rights of the king in abeyance, or any forfeitures on peace or appearance bonds uncollected or lacking in prosecution. People could complain about an old bond suddenly surfacing, but they did not question its legitimacy or viability after centuries of acceptance.[204]

This recognition of legal instruments, and therefore a "national" force of law behind them, helped to move England to become a more law-accepting if not law-abiding nation.[205] It was an important step towards a nation state and a sense of linkage to the centre, and it is often lost in the discussions about state development. When the law as a precursor to the

---

and political history in the Tudor century", *Historical Jour.*, xlii (1999), pp. 535-48.
[204] E.g., the exchequer warrant dated 18 Mar. 1504 concerning William Chapplayne of Norfolk, bound by recognizance on 14 Oct. 1491 in £40 in chancery to keep the king's peace. When he broke the peace thirteen years later, the king learned of the bond "as we bee p[er]fitely enfo[r]med"—undoubtedly from a search. Chapplayne now forfeited the £40 (T.N.A.: P.R.O., E 404/84).
[205] Horowitz, "'Contrary to the liberties of this city'".

state is addressed, it usually turns to the growth of parliament.[206] This view led Christopher Brooks to suggest why legal studies have made little impact on the general and political history of England during the three centuries following 1500: there has been no "analytical perspective capable of doing justice to the complex and multi-faced role of law in society".[207]

The present discussion is an attempt to offer one aspect of this perspective, and to suggest answers to key questions. If it was the law that bound the commonweal together over time, what was the actual mechanism that allowed this to happen? If this was a bottom-up process, what was taking place in the villages, towns and shires, how did it work, why was it working and how did it influence the procedures of law, order and justice at the top? The development of equity courts or statutory law alone cannot explain adherence to, and belief in, a national law, especially the latter when so many statutes were for particular groups or individuals, and not a few of them had little means of being enforced. Henry VII and his working councillors found that mechanism to suit their own purposes, and it was in fact one that had been operating for centuries: the written obligation. It allowed him to become the most solvent king since the Conqueror; and it permitted him to bequeath a realm with a developing national law, and respect for it, that would prevail over local influences. Nonetheless, it was a process—something the first Tudor king could appreciate when he stepped into his chamber for the very first time.

---

[206] E.g., A. Harding, *Medieval Law and the Foundations of the State* (Oxford, 2002). Harding does note that local justice was the main political dialogue between the monarch and the realm, and that law was the "state of the realm" (pp. 185, 263).

[207] C.W. Brooks, *Lawyers, Litigation and English Society Since 1450* (1998), p. 179.

Appendix

An England under obligation

To understand how Henry VII's bond policy could even materialize beyond the experiences of his working councillors, it is essential to recognize that all of these bonds, and the procedures to create and prosecute them, were well-established instruments of administration, finance, law and politics long before 1485. Furthermore, written, sealed obligations ("writings obligatory") between private parties or with the royal government were in use before the Conquest. The "surety" or pledge became both an acceptable guarantee for performance of an agreement and a customary legal component of the written obligation. The origins of such guarantors dated back to private feuds between families when hostages were required to assure peace and co-operation.[208] In early Norman England, sureties were offered to guarantee the payment of a debt by the debtor, who would seek out such persons to trust him to fulfil his obligation. This included keeping the peace and allegiance to the king, both political requirements for the maintenance of law and order.[209] One of the earliest contracts enforced by law was the bailment of a prisoner and the finding of "mainpernors" to ensure his appearance for trial, this an extension of the practice of taking hostages.[210] But although the procedure was traditionally viewed as "putting up a body" for another, liability only extended as far as a fine for non-performance, or confiscation of lands and chattels, and not the actual punishment due to the defendant.

---

[208] O.W. Holmes, Jr., *The Common Law* (Boston, Mass., 1881), p. 248. Numerous examples exist in the 12th-century histories of Henry of Huntingdon (*c.*1080-1160) and Orderic Vitalis (1075-*c.*1143), where the early-Norman kings used hostages to guarantee an agreement (Henry of Huntingdon, *Historia Anglorum*, trans. Thomas Forester (1853; repr. 1968); Orderic Vitalis, *The Ecclesiastical History of England and Normandy*, trans. M. Chibnall (Oxford, 1969-80). The practice dated back to Roman law when a body was bound in ropes and chains and turned over to the creditor (R. Zimmerman, *The Law of Obligations: Roman Foundations of the Civilian Tradition* (Capetown, 1990), p. 5).
[209] At the local level, breaking an oath was seen as a threat to law and order and an assault on both traditions and the law (J. Lee, "'Ye shall disturbe noe mans right': oath-taking and oath-breaking in late medieval and early modern Bristol", *Urban Hist.*, xxxiv (2007), pp. 27-38, at p. 36).
[210] Orderic Vitalis, pp. 249-50; T.F.T. Plucknett, *A Concise History of the Common Law* (3rd edn., 1940), p. 341.

If change occurs from the bottom up or from the localities to the central authority—and Penny Tucker's discussion regarding the influence of the London constitution on that of royal government is suggestive of this observation[211]—there is perhaps no better example of the effect of local customs and procedures on the centre than the written bonds between private parties, which formed the basis of a credit society to allow judicial and economic processes to flourish.[212] This was recognized by the 13th-century legalist Henry Bracton. His comprehensive work, *De Legibus et Consuetudinibus Anglie*, set down in writing the laws and opinions of his time, codifying precedents for future generations and future lawmakers.[213] In a revealing discussion on why written obligations were originally devised, Bracton simplified the theory behind the custom: "Stipulations and obligations were devised to enable everyone to acquire that which is to his interest". The crux of the agreement binding people together was the written instrument, "as where one states in writing that he owes; . . . It is not that the letters themselves or the written characters bind (nor) the meaningful language they express, but both the language and the written letters unite to effect the obligation".[214] Bracton's discourse on the various types of covenants and actions at law for non-performance were perceptions of his time, often confused by the lack of precedent in Roman law that he obdurately sought in vain, or by a misunderstanding of English custom.[215] But his mission was the message: bonds were a way of life, and he sought to fit them into a central body of law governing the realm.

One weak point in a written obligation was the means to identify it as the defendant's should a judicial action ensue. This problem was met by the use of seals.[216] Seals became the final proof of a written agreement in

---

[211] P. Tucker, "Reaction to Henry VII's style of kingship and its contribution to the emergence of constitutional monarchy in England", *Hist. Research*, Vol. LXXXII, no. 217 (Aug. 2009), pp. 511-25.

[212] Horowitz, "'Contrary to the liberties of this city'".

[213] Trans. by Samuel E. Thorne (Cambridge, Mass., 1968), vol. ii. See also F.W. Maitland, *Select Passages from the Works of Bracton and Azo* (Selden Soc., viii, 1895).

[214] Bracton, ii. 287. For stipulations, see A. Watson, *The Laws of Obligations in the Later Roman Republic* (Oxford, 1965), ch. 1.

[215] Maitland, who was openly hostile to the "Romanist", attacked his confusion, concluding with the terse statement "we can hardly attribute to Bracton a full knowledge of what he is about" (Maitland, p. 147).

[216] Holmes, p. 261. For creating a seal and the hazards for its survival, see D. Marcombe, "The confraternity seals of Burton Lazars Hospital and a newly

England and northern France, while on most of the continent the notary provided the mechanism for validating a document.[217] As Tout observed, "England ever remained emphatically a land of seals, the employment of which became essential to the authentication of all public and private documents".[218] In an action at law, loss or defacement of a seal led to the vacation of an action on a written obligation.[219] This stance remained firm throughout the late medieval period, summed up by a case before king's bench in 1527, which concluded that if a seal fell off a written obligation it could render it valueless and not actionable.[220]

Conversely, it was critical for the debtor or bound party to have an obligation cancelled or discharged upon fulfilment. This process sometimes got sticky, and often reprehensible, in at least two major areas of contract law with a long tradition and acceptance by English society. The first was when the condition of a debt was fulfilled by the debtor but the actual written debt itself was never cancelled by the creditor or debt-recording agency or official, for example, a local court, the chancery, the exchequer or one of the ministers of the king. Problems could also arise if an original obligation was converted into a new one, without the first one

---

discovered matrix from Robertsbridge, Sussex", *Trans. Leicestershire Archaeol. and Hist. Soc.*, lxxvi (2002), pp. 47-58, at pp. 53-4.

[217] T.F. Tout, *Chapters in the Administrative History of Mediaeval England* (6 vols., Manchester, 1920-33), i. 122. Notaries were nonetheless used in England. On 26 Apr. 1481, a London grocer gifted a draper his goods, chattels and debts for a consideration (a piece of silver) "and in token thereof he has affixed his seal and that of William Campe notary for greater corroboration of the premises" (*Cal. Close Rolls 1476-85*, no. 791). Such enrolments included a second person to validate a document if a party's seal was not well known.

[218] Tout, i. 123.

[219] Plucknett, p. 348. This prevented spurious contracts: "the courts were prudently suspicious of any signs of monkey business" (A.W.B. Simpson, *A History of the Common Law of Contract: the Rise of the Action of Assumpsit* (Oxford, 1975), p. 90).

[220] Cited in Simpson, p. 267. The courts wrestled with the "lost seal" during Henry VII's reign. In a case before common pleas in 1488, two debtors sealed an obligation but one seal either fell off or was removed. The plaintiff argued that the debtor whose seal remained on the obligation owed him money; the defendant pleaded that it was "not his deed" because of the missing seal of the other debtor. Chief Justice Bryan said that the defendant could plead that it was "not his deed", but it was argued that since one debtor's seal remained, the debt was good. Bryan reiterated that the missing seal meant the obligation was no longer the one the debtor originally sealed (*Yearbook*, Hil. 3 Hen. 7, plea 20 fo. 5a).

being cancelled.[221] Many debts were cancelled orally, but by 1485 the law had evolved to the point where a contract stood viable forever unless it was cancelled by some form of written acquittance; destroyed after the condition was met; or renegotiated into a new bond that had language annulling the previous one.[222] When four men entered a bond on 10 March 1496 for Sir Charles Somerset as part of his indenture for an office in Cardiff, it was superseded by a new bond with different sureties (guarantors for the bond) seven years later. However, the old bond was never cancelled, which meant that it was still viable. Henry VII ordered the keeper of the rolls at chancery to enrol "the newe recognisaunce" and to have "the old recognisance to be uttrely annulled made voide and cancelled furthwt".[223]

Although Edmund Dudley has been cast as the belligerent bond-master for the reign, he in fact spent a great deal of time not just taking, renegotiating and collecting on bonds, but also discharging them with written acquittances. One example is the seven-line "Recepi" dated 26 September 1506 stating that Sir John Arundell of Lanherne paid £80 for the king's use, £40 in gold and £40 by obligation. It was written in a hand similar to an entry in one of the king's chamber books, and it was signed "Ed[mun]di Dudeley".[224] The fact that it was preserved among the

---

[221] The legal concept of *novatio* involved an old obligation converted into a new one—the former became inoperative *ipso iure* and was not enforceable (Zimmerman, p. 758). However, that was not always the case and care was given to cancel the original bond.

[222] *Donne vs. Cornwall* (1485), quoted in Simpson, pp. 99-100. The defendant paid money owed on a bond and then received the actual instrument, although he "foolishly failed to destroy it". The defendant claimed that the plaintiff wrongfully recovered the written obligation and brought an action on it, but the court decided that the defendant's plea regarding the circumstances was not good: the bond existed, so it was viable, or in modern parlance "a contract is a contract". It was a person's own fault if he or she failed to obtain cancellation of a bond and it was sued upon (Baker, *Oxford History of the Laws of England*, vi. pp. 41-2).

[223] T.N.A.: P.R.O., C 82/250, 11 Sept. 1503; *Cal. Close Rolls 1500-9*, no. 211.

[224] Truro, Cornwall Record Office, MS. AR3/384. Arundell was a knight of the body and entered into numerous recognizances and obligations as party to land transactions and moneys owed to the crown (T.N.A.: P.R.O., C 82/364 (*L&P*, I.i. no. 784(30)); *Cal. Close Rolls 1485-1500*, nos. 83, 399, 945; *Cal. Close Rolls 1500-9*, nos. 209, 959; *Cal. Pat. Rolls 1485-94*, p. 332; *Cal. Pat. Rolls 1494-1509*, pp. 107, 552, 567). Dudley made an entry in his account book related to this payment (Brit. Libr., Lansdowne. MS. 127 fo. 32v, 11 Nov. 1506) The *O.D.N.B.* states that by 1508, Arundell was a receiver in Cornwall; he paid Dudley 450

Arundell papers in Cornwall attests to the great concern for keeping such acquittances safe to prove that a bond had been cancelled.

The second area of contention involved conditions for future actions or behaviour, such as keeping the peace or appearing at a court of law or before a king's councillor at a certain time and place, or a place to be determined. Not only did Henry and his councillors often force people to take out written bonds for a future behaviour or action, they also ordered that the files and rolls of such recognizances kept at the various royal, itinerant and local courts be actively searched, seeking to prosecute overdue or unfulfilled conditions in those bonds for collection, sometimes many years after they were contracted.[225] The courts grappled with the distinction between "good behaviour" and "keeping the peace", but did not stand in the way of the king's prosecution of such bonds.[226] In more sinister circumstances, a bond for future behaviour could be interpreted as an actual debt for payment due to the crown. Technically this was illegal but nonetheless might be prosecuted by over-animated ministers, with or without the king's knowledge.[227]

---

marks (350 in cash) for the privilege on 1 Nov. 1507 (P.Y. Stanton, "Arundell family (per. 1435-1590)", *O.D.N.B.* (<http://www.oxforddnb.com/view/article/41331> [accessed 21 Jan. 2009]); Brit. Libr., Lansdowne MS. 127 fo. 50). This Sir John should not be confused with Sir John Arundell of Trerice from another branch of this ubiquitous Cornish family (see C.R.O., MS. AR/24/16, where both Johns acted as arbiters in a matter).

[225] See, e.g., Lander, pp. 328-67; C. Rawcliffe, "Henry VII and Edward, duke of Buckingham: the repression of an 'over-mighty subject'", *Bull. Inst. Hist. Research*, liii (1980), pp. 114-18.

[226] A year into Henry VII's reign, all of the justices, the chancellor, the treasurer and various lords of the king's council gathered at Whitefriars to discuss the case of two knights, each bound to the king in £3,000 for their "good behaviour" (*de bene gerendo*). The knights—Sir Richard Crofts, treasurer of the king's household, and Sir Richard Corbet—were accused of displaying swords, daggers and other weapons openly in Westminster hall, raising the question of whether they forfeited their bonds. The justices were undecided (the reason for the meeting), although they expressed the view that surety of the peace could not be breached without fighting but that it could be forfeited by an assembly of people or the actual weapons, even without breaching the peace. They also argued that if the bound parties behaved themselves, it was not a breach of the peace (*Yearbook*, Mich. 2 Hen. 7, plea 7 fos. 2v-3). Corbet was later in breach of a recognizance of the peace (T.N.A.: P.R.O., E 404/82, 3 Dec. 1496).

[227] That is apparently what happened to Thomas Sunnyff, haberdasher of London, as detailed in Horowitz, "'Agree with the king'", pp. 325-66. [Chapter Five]

Henry VII and his working councillors crafted a national policy for royal finance and justice based on centuries of private transactions between parties and the various remedies at law afforded to them. That it worked and worked well attested to the acceptance by English men and women of procedures that they had been using in their daily lives—indeed, six London parishes today still retain receipts for "hocking", an apparently old rural Easter ritual where men and women bound each other "in order to extract playful fines".[228] Less-than-playful excesses and dubious or illicit exactions occurred during Henry VII's reign, and people were harmed by the misuse of both the bond policy and the power to enforce it. But no recognizance revolt resulted, in part because the national policy was congruent with local experience, although greatly intensified by the first Tudor king.

---

[228] "Ecclesiastically-sponsored theatre in London, 1422-1642", *Guildhall Library Manuscripts Section Newsletter*, x (Winter 2007/8). The author wishes to thank Penny Tucker for this reference.

CHAPTER FOUR

RICHARD EMPSON, MINISTER OF HENRY VII[*]

Introduction

As noted in Chapter Nine, I spent 1977 in England researching my PhD thesis on Henry VII. Besides listing documents to view at the major archives, I planned to visit other repositories in London such as the Guildhall, Westminster Abbey and the National Register of Archives, as well as a few county record offices. At the time, the National Register was off Chancery Lane near the Public Record Office. I had no idea what to expect there other than volumes listing documents in various holdings throughout England. One catalogue on Northamptonshire mentioned a "Peter Empson", and I was curious.

I believe I was like most students reading about Henry VII's reign regarding Richard Empson and Edmund Dudley, the first ministerial casualties for serving a Tudor monarch. They were almost a catch phrase—"Empson and Dudley"—and I was intrigued about what they did and why they lost their heads while others doing the same thing kept theirs intact. I also wanted to know about their rise to power, especially since neither was a churchman—the usual medieval path to royal employment. Nonetheless, very little scholarship had been devoted to either man.

I began with Dudley. In 1932, D.M. Brodie published an article entitled "Edmund Dudley, minister of Henry VII." Then in 1948 she put out an edition of Dudley's Tree of Commonwealth, *written while prisoner in the Tower. It was advice for a king on good rule, presumably written to appease the new king, Henry VIII, and perhaps save Dudley's head. That did not happen. In 1972, C.J. Harrison published a copy of a "petition" of Dudley's that he had discovered. It related to people Dudley claimed were treated unfairly with written bonds for various debts. I read these*

[*] Reprinted with permission. The article was first published in the *Bulletin of the Institute of Historical Research* (now *Historical Research*), Vol. LV, no. 131 (May 1982), pp. 35-49.

publications while a graduate student and then turned to do the same for Empson. As I soon learned, there was not much to read about him beyond a short essay in the Dictionary of National Biography, *which basically pulled from old secondary sources. Empson was missing in action.*

That is why I was curious about the references to Peter Empson, presumably Richard's father. I spent a day at the Register, writing down all references to Peter from lists of deeds kept at the Northamptonshire Record Office. The dates were the right time frame and I planned a day trip to Northampton to view the deeds plus other documents related to the reign. (The two privy seals I found there are discussed in Chapter Five.)

It was, in fact, Richard Empson's father, and the deeds help dispel the first of several myths about this minister. To belittle Empson by denigrating his origins, Peter Empson had always been referred to as a sievemaker (basketmaker), making him landless and therefore unimportant and common. That was hardly the case after looking at the deeds. I now began keeping a side ledger of notes on Richard Empson as I reviewed various documents throughout 1977. I wanted to see what else I could learn about him and how a "new man" could rise to power through connections and achievements. In delving further into his work as a councilor, an image started forming of someone politically-connected, well-trained and prepared to help prosecute Henry VII's bond policy.

I started looking into other sources long after his death to see how the "legend" of Empson and Dudley grew. It led me to references in the House of Commons records in James I's reign. I showed these to a friend and 17th century historian, Conrad Russell, while attending a seminar he co-chaired at the Institute of Historical Research. (He later taught at Yale and colleges in London and became 5th Earl Russell, taking his seat in the House of Lords—who knew?) We chatted about how Empson and Dudley were alive and well in the minds of members of parliament (M.P.s) more than a century after their deaths. (In a later essay, I would use other references to them that I located, found in Chapter Seven.)

I also drew a map of London from one in the archives at the British Library representing the time Empson and Dudley lived there; then I took a long walk! From all the references I found about their houses and sharing a courtyard to do their evil deeds, that walk and map suggested that they did not live near each other at all—but it was a nice story.

Finally, when I returned to Chicago and began collating my notes before starting my thesis, I also wrote an article on Empson, picking a title that would pay homage to Brodie and her important article on Dudley. I called it "Richard Empson, minister of Henry VII." Happily, much work has been done on both ministers since the article on Empson appeared.

On 17 August 1510, the first two important ministers to suffer destruction during the reign of the Tudors were executed on Tower Hill in London. One of the officials, Edmund Dudley, has left the historian of the period a vivid portrait of his activities and beliefs through the survival of various documents written by him.[1] Of the other victim, Sir Richard Empson, little is known. Unlike his fellow minister, he left no treatise on administering the state or any account of his personal or official conduct.[2] Furthermore, despite the survival of letters, deeds and records pertaining to Empson's public and private life, this confidant to Henry VII has been unceremoniously lumped together with Dudley. The two ministers have remained for posterity the coeval villains of Henry VII's reign, thus spiriting from Richard Empson a separate identity to show his origins, what he achieved and where his own purported infamy might lie.[3]

The materials relating to Empson are such that a preliminary study can be made to discover both his career and the opportunities pursued by a late-15th century gentleman to become an important minister of state. Because the vilification of Empson has preceded vivification, it is also desirable to untangle a few of the *causes célèbres* attributed to him, many of which have acquired an aura of validity after five centuries of repetition. The purpose here is not to cleanse a soiled reputation but to uncover any facts that may elucidate those activities which precipitated the fall of a minister engaged in executing the whims and commands of his monarch.[4] Moreover, it must be remembered that Henry VII's statecraft

---

[1] For references to his treatise, "The Tree of Commonwealth", see D.M. Brodie, "Edmund Dudley: minister of Henry VII", *Trans. Royal Hist. Soc.*, 4th ser., xv (1932), p. 134 n. 1. A copy of Dudley's account book and fragments are found in Brit. Libr., Lansdowne MSS. 127, 160, and Harleian MS. 1877. His "petition" is printed by C.J. Harrison, "The petition of Edmund Dudley", *Eng. His. Rev.*, Vol. LXXXVII (1972), pp. 82-99. I would like to thank Professor Conrad Russell for his helpful suggestions upon reading a draft of this article, and my wife Barbi for typing and proof-reading the final draft.

[2] Francis Bacon claimed to have seen an account book of Empson's, the only reference to such a book (F. Bacon. *History of the Reign of Henry VII*, ed. J.R. Lumby (Cambridge, 1885), pp. 192-3). From Bacon's references, however, it appears that he mistook Dudley's book (Brit. Libr., Lansdowne MS. 127) for Empson's.

[3] There has never been an article on Empson, and a recent biographer of Henry VII noted "little modern work has been done on Empson" (S.B. Chrimes, *Henry VII* (U. of California, 1972), p. 317 n. 2).

[4] S.E. Thorne believed that the two ministers had been rehabilitated (*Prerogativa Regis* (1949), p. xi). Recent research, however, leaves their traditional reputations

centred on his personal chamber, bypassing many of the exchequer procedures for administration and finance. He also sought to prosecute the prerogative rights of the crown to their greatest financial advantage. Such policies required dependable, competent ministers experienced in these areas of governance. That Empson, and Dudley, were exponents of this programme speaks of the institutions and procedures of the time and not any ministerial machinations.

Empson himself might have been surprised to learn that history has left him the son of a sievemaker (i.e., basketmaker), yet precious little has altered this view. None of the 16th century chronicles or histories mentions his origins.[5] John Stow, writing nearly a century after the executions, was the first writer to give Empson a past, stating that he "suddenly rose from poverty (as being the Sonne of a Sieve-maker, in Tocester [Northants]) into inestimable authority and riches".[6] Once the eloquent history of Henry VII's reign by Francis Bacon appeared in 1622, the occupation of Empson's father became settled in the tradition of Stow until the mid-19th century and George Baker's work on Northamptonshire.[7] Baker discovered that Empson's father, Peter, was probably a man of local consequence, but the temptation to fall back on Francis Bacon was too great, and he also concluded that "Empson was of mean original, being the son of a sieve-maker at Towcester". Modern writers, when they do seek a beginning to Empson's life, continue along the lines established by Baker.[8]

---

well intact (e.g. F.C. Dietz, *English Public Finance*, 2nd ed., 2 vols. (1964), Ch. iv; W.C. Richardson, *Tudor Chamber Administration*, 1485-1547 (Baton Rouge, 1952), pp. 141-58; Chrimes, *Henry VII*, pp. 133-4, 211-14, 310-17).

[5] *The Anglica Historia of Polydore Vergil*, 1485-1537, ed. D. Hay, Camden 3rd ser., lxxiv, 1950), p. ix; *Hall's Chronicle*, ed. Sir H. Ellis (1809), p. 499; R. Holinshed, *Chronicles of England, Scotland and Ireland*, 6 vols. (1807-8), iii, pp. 531, 536-7.

[6] J. Stow, *The Annals of England* (1600), p. 813.

[7] Bacon, p. 190; J. Weever, *Ancient Funerall Monuments* (1631), p. 417; T. Fuller, *The History of the Worthies of England*, ed. P.A. Nuttall (3 vols., 1840), ii, p. 510; Edward, Lord Herbert of Cherbury, *The Life and Reigne of King Henry the Eighth* (1672), p. 6; *State Trials*, comp. T.B. and T.J. Howell (34 vols., 1816-28), i, p. 283; G. Baker, *The History and Antiquities of the County of Northampton*, 2 vols., 1822-41) ii, p. 139.

[8] *D.N.B.*, s.v. Empson; J.C. Wedgwood, *History of Parliament: Biographies, 1439-1509* (1936), p. 300; *Luffield Priory Charters*, ed. G.R. Elvey, Northants. Record Soc., xxii, xxvi, 1968-75), ii, p. xxxiv. The error of referring to Empson as "Sir Thomas Empson", who was actually Richard's heir, was initiated by Hall and "Arnold's *Chronicle*" and perpetuated by the *State Trials* (*Hall's Chronicle*, p.

Peter Empson of Towcester married Elizabeth Josephs, a coheiress to estates situated near those of her husband.[9] There is no documentary evidence that he practiced a profession. He was already a man of some means in 1444 when he was named a juror for the assizes,[10] and he spent the next twenty-five years in the property and legal affairs of his town and adjoining villages. He witnessed several deeds of enfeoffment for lands in Towcester, often with men of importance such as the bishops of Lincoln and Ely. He obtained a cottage in Towcester with lands in neighbouring villages, including Easton Neston where his son would one day live. Peter Empson continued to witness grants and transact property conveyances with important local families until his death in 1473. The year of his death marked the first participation of his son Richard in local property transactions.[11]

From the study of his family acquisitions in Northamptonshire, little can be gleaned regarding the early life of Richard Empson. Where he obtained an education is unknown, but by 1473 it can be maintained that he was a lawyer in his early twenties in active pursuit of local properties to supplement his inherited estates.[12] Richard Empson was but one ambitious

---

512; *The Customs of London, otherwise called Arnold's Chronicle*, ed. J. Douce (1811), p. xliii; *State Trials*, i, p. 283; *A Selection of Cases from the State Trials*, ed. J.W. Willis Bund (2 vols., Cambridge, 1879-82), i, pp. 71-3). For Thomas Empson, see M.R. Horowitz, "An early-Tudor teller's book", *Eng. Hist. Rev.*, Vol. XCVI (1981), pp. 103-16. [Chapter Nine]

[9] *Luffield Priory Charters*, ii, p. xxxiv.

[10] *Calendar of Patent Rolls 1485-94*, p. 374. The following deeds were used to trace the activities of Peter Empson: Northamptonshire Record Office, Fermor-Heskith MSS., Muniments of Title Deeds, F/18/2, F/15/8, F/16/9, D/1/3, E/24/6, F/14/8, F/17/12, F/15/10, F/25/9, E/25/6, D/19/16, E/27/1a, F/19/3, F/1/11, D/6/13, F/2/5, F/19/8, 11; Towcester Charity Records, Deeds, TC 16.

[11] N.R.O., Fermor-Heskith MSS., MTD, F/2/5, D/6/11, D/1/6. The *D.N.B.* states that Richard entered such transactions in 1476, which is three years too late.

[12] There is no evidence to show that Empson attended a university, although this does not preclude the possibility that he in fact studied at one (see E. Russell, "The influx of commoners into the university of Oxford before 1581: an optical illusion?", *Eng. Hist. Rev.*, Vol. XCII (1977), pp. 723, 737-8). C.H. Cooper wrote that Empson studied and practiced common law but could not confirm where he was educated (C.H. and T. Cooper and others, *Athenae Cantabrigienses* (3 vols., Cambridge, 1858-1913), i, p. 14). Empson was connected with Sponne's charity in Towcester, also referred to as "Towcester College", but it cannot be assumed that he obtained any formal training there. For Sponne's charity, see *Victoria History of*

county man trying to build both his holdings near Towcester and local alliances which could prove useful for a future career in government. Sir William Catesby, father of the future councillor of Richard III, and his brother John, a serjeant-at-law, were local landholders in the service of the king.[13] In 1475, Richard Fowler, chancellor of the duchy of Lancaster, obtained property in Easton Neston, including a tenement held with the lord privy seal (John Russell), Richard Empson and others—perhaps Empson's initial encounter with royal officials.[14] Sir Thomas Billing (chief justice of king's bench) acquired properties in the county with the Catesbys and other men known to Empson.[15] The careers of these men were rising under Edward IV and no doubt Richard Empson hoped to follow their example.

Empson's early career was typical of his contemporaries and their own accomplishments, without any suggestion of future success. Almost without exception, every person Richard Empson associated with in county affairs under Yorkist rule was a member of parliament, a sheriff of Northamptonshire, an officer in the duchy of Lancaster, a member of the various royal commissions for the county or any combination of these responsibilities.[16] The influence many of these men had on the careers of Empson and other men cannot be overstated. When Empson first entered royal service in 1475 as a justice of the peace for the county, he sat with others who had served on previous commissions and who were his associates in local land settlements.[17] In 1478, Empson attained his first major appointment: the office of attorney-general for the duchy of

---

Northamptonshire, ii, pp. 181-2; *Northants. Notes and Queries*, i (1886), p. 74, iii (1890), p. 29; N.R.O., Fermor-Heskith MSS., MTD, D/19/16; see below, and n. 21.

[13] *Cal. Pat. Rolls 1467-77*, p. 158; *Calendar of Close Rolls 1476-85*, no. 611.

[14] N.R.O., Fermor-Heskith MSS., MTD, E/26/9, E/1/4. Russell became rector of Towcester on 6 Aug. 1471 and may have know the Empsons (*D.N.B.*, s.v. John Russell).

[15] *Cal. Pat. Rolls 1467-77*, p. 531.

[16] E.g., Robert Broun (auditor for Queen Elizabeth, 1465; commissioner of array, 1484; auditor for south parts in duchy, 1485); Richard Burton (J.P. for Northants., 1483; escheator for Northants. and Rutland, 1483); John Eltonhead (M.P. for Old Sarum, 1467-8; escheator for Northants. and Rutland, 1471; J.P. for Northants., 1467-77) (R. Somerville, *History of the Duchy of Lancaster*, 1265-1603 (2 vols., 1953-70), i, p. 441; *Cal. Pat. Rolls 1467-77*, pp. 623-4; *Cal. Pat. Rolls 1476-85*, pp. 567-8; Wedgwood, p. 299; *Calendar of Fine Rolls 1471-85*, nos. 45, 801).

[17] *Cal. Pat. Rolls 1467-77*, p. 624.

Lancaster.[18] He undoubtedly owed this office to the influence of Thomas Billing, John Catesby, Richard Fowler and other important officials of the duchy known to him through business associations.

For the remainder of Edward IV's reign, Empson retained his office as attorney-general and continued on various royal commissions.[19] He attended every meeting of the duchy council save one, and on 10 February 1481, Empson probably presided over the session through the absence of the chancellor.[20] He also pursued interests in county affairs where he still spent much of his time. In 1481, Empson and a local associate were elected collectors for the support of Sponne's charity in Towcester.[21] In the 1470s he became involved in the concerns of Luffield priory, from which he later received an annuity.[22]

Only glimpses of Empson's work at the duchy may be discovered. In May 1480, Empson petitioned the king's council for letters of privy seal to summon two instigators of a riot in Yorkshire. He reported that an officer of the duchy had distrained the cattle of a Yorkshire man for failing to pay his rent "according to the law". Eighty men gathered and released the beasts, and Empson was now concerned because it meant "the king's great hurt and let of payment of his duties".[23] In 1482, he traveled to Fotheringhay castle to make search of the feodary rolls of the duchy and separate them from those of the duchy of York.[24] The experience gained at the duchy would prove to be invaluable for his later success under Henry VII.

The tenacious attorney for the duchy suddenly saw his budding career stunted by the last Yorkist monarch while the fortunes of many of his associates blossomed, including three men who became trusted councillors to Richard III: William Catesby, Richard Ratcliffe and Francis, Viscount

---

[18] Somerville, *Duchy*, i, p. 406. He received the reversion of the office 1 July 1477, but did not obtain it until the end of 1478.

[19] *Cal. Pat. Rolls 1476-85*, pp. 144, 214.

[20] T.N.A.: P.R.O., DL 5/1 fos. 53, 47.

[21] *Northants. Notes and Queries*, iv (1892), p. 253; *V.C.H. Northants.*, ii, pp. 181-2.

[22] *Luffield Priory Charters*, ii, p. xxxiv, no. 766c.

[23] T.N.A.: P.R.O., SC 8/338/1211.

[24] Somerville, *Duchy*, i, p. 243. See also T.N.A.: P.R.O., DL 5/1 fo. 85v. Empson was not a feodary as has been misinterpreted from this journey (J. Hurstfield, *The Queen's Wards* (2nd ed., 1973), p. 234).

Lovell.[25] Under the protectorate of Richard, duke of Gloucester, Thomas Keble was appointed attorney-general of the duchy of Lancaster. The day after Gloucester declared Edward V a bastard, Richard Empson was referred to as the "late" attorney-general of the duchy, and Keble held the office under Richard III.[26] Why Empson fell from royal favour is uncertain in view of his close ties with supporters of Richard III. One obvious reason might be a connection with the execution of William Lord Hastings, but more evidence is needed to establish such a link.[27] It is also possible that Empson appeared less than enthusiastic about Richard III's usurpation. This may have pushed him into the group of royal officials who were purged after Richard III's accession, including several in the duchy.[28] Whatever the reasons, Empson did not obtain any office under the new king although he was still retained of counsel in the duchy of Lancaster.[29]

What he thought of Henry Tudor's possible invasion will probably never be known. He at least was deemed loyal enough by Richard III for inclusion with the Catesbys on a commission in Northamptonshire to ascertain the supporters of Buckingham's futile rebellion.[30] The day after Richard III's proclamation against "Harry, earl of Richmond and all the other king's rebels", Empson and his county associates received a commission to array the county.[31] Empson could hardly have been enthusiastic about the outcome at Bosworth Field on 22 August 1485. He owed his career to men who were unable to retrieve his once-bright future

---

[25] These councillors were the infamous "Cat, the Rat, and Lovell our dog" (*D.N.B.*, s.v. Ratcliffe). For their connections with Empson and his associates, see N.R.O., Fermor-Heskith MSS., MTD, E/27/3, E/28/5; *Cal. Pat. Rolls 1476-85*, p. 505; *Cal. Close Rolls 1476-85*, nos. 1397, 945.

[26] Somerville, *Duchy*, i, 406.

[27] Only circumstantial evidence points to a possible relationship between Hasting's death and Empson's fall. Hastings became chief steward of the duchy of Lancaster in 1470; he was previously the steward for Higham Ferrers (Northants.), a post Empson held under Henry VII. Thus there were two official opportunities for the men to know each other (Somerville, *Duchy*, i, p. 422; T.N.A.: P.R.O., DL 12/1 no. 57). Both Empson and Hastings knew the Catesbys well. Hastings was the patron of Sir William Catesby, and the two men with John Catesby and others obtained land grants in 1479 just 12 miles from Towcester (Baker, i, p. 242; *Cal. Close Rolls 1476-85*, no. 611). Whether or not these events can place Empson, Hastings, and the Catesbys in the same "group" demands further investigation.

[28] Brit. Libr., Harleian MS. 433 fos. 23r-v.

[29] T.N.A.: P.R.O., DL 5/2 fo. 2.

[30] *Cal. Pat. Rolls 1476-85*, p. 393.

[31] Brit. Libr., Harleian MS. 433 fo. 273v; *Cal. Pat. Rolls 1476-85*, p. 492.

under Edward IV. Other men of influence known to him had lost their lives or lands under Richard III, including Earl Rivers, whom Empson represented as his attorney.[32] Richard III was a known quantity to Richard Empson; should Henry Tudor win the day and the throne, Empson's greatest challenge would be to disavow the Yorkist ties he had cultivated for over a decade.

Three days after Bosworth Field and the triumph of Henry VII, William Catesby was beheaded for high treason; three months later, numerous attainders were passed against Richard III's supporters.[33] Richard Empson, however, not only survived the upheaval of revolution, he quickly allied with the usurper and his adherents, notably Reynold Bray, one of the king's most trusted ministers.[34] Three weeks after Bosworth Field, Empson was once again appointed attorney-general for the duchy of Lancaster, the same day Bray was named chancellor of the duchy.[35] Empson's unexplained ostracism by Richard III afforded him a fresh start with different faces and a new king.

Empson's acquisition of lands and manors during the reign of Henry VII continued to reflect the concerns of an ambitious careerist establishing new alliances and large estates. He augmented his holdings in Easton Neston and neighbouring villages, and after 1490 he began acquiring interests in several counties, often with Bray and other councilors of the king well-acquainted with Empson through royal commissions and offices.[36] Although Empson and others obtained numerous properties in and around Middlesex, his residence in London is not known until late in the reign.[37] In 1507, after he was chancellor of the duchy of Lancaster,

---

[32] Wedgwood, p. 300.

[33] *Rotuli Parliamentorum*, vi, pp. 275-8.

[34] A survey of Bray's career is found in Richardson, *Chamber*, pp. 451-8.

[35] *Materials for a History of the Reign of Henry VII*, ed. W. Campbell (2 vols., 1873-7), i, p. 549: Somerville, *Duchy*, i, p. 392.

[36] His known property transactions are too numerous to list in full. A few references follow: N.R.O., Fermor-Heskith MSS., MTD, U/35/3, E/31/3, D/28/1, D/2/26, D/24/2, 3; Brit. Libr., Sloane MS. 747 fos. 38r-v; T.N.A.: P.R.O., E 326/5446, E313/10/10; *Cal. Pat. Rolls 1494-1509*, p. 54; *Cal. Close Rolls 1485-1500*, no. 928; *Calendar of Inquisitions Post Mortem, Henry VII*, i, nos. 655, 749, 753, 922.

[37] *A Calendar to the Feet of Fines for London and Middlesex*, ed. W.J. Hardy and W. Page (2 vols., 1892-3), ii, 1, 4, 5, 6, 7, 9; *Warwickshire Feet of Fines*, ed. E. Stokes, F.C. Wellstood, L. Drucker and others, Dugdale Soc., xi, xv, xviii, 1932-43), iii, no. 2748; *Cal. Pat. Rolls 1485-94*, p. 338; *Cal. Pat. Rolls 1494-1509*, pp. 54, 214; *Cal. Close Rolls 1485-1500*, nos. 567, 905, 1117; T.N.A.: P.R.O., E

Empson secured a lease of lands and tenements near Bridewell along the Thames. Afterwards, he leased a mansion with orchards in St. Bride's parish called "Le Parsonage".[38] Stow alone referred to a second house owned by Empson adjacent to Edmund Dudley's in St. Swithin's Lane "wherein they met and consulted of matters at their pleasures".[39] Dudley did own a house in the parish of St. Swithin but around the corner from Stow's intriguing scenario.[40] Empson's known residence stood near council chambers of the duchy at Bridewell and Blackfriars where he occupied much of his time. Stow's story of a house over a mile from Empson's work and in close proximity to Dudley's abode fits the legend better than the evidence.[41]

Empson's responsibilities under Henry VII expanded from the opening of the reign. In 1486 alone, he became steward for life of two lordships in Northamptonshire, received a joint grant for a farm of swans in the duchy lands in Lincoln, sat on a commission "de walliis et fossatis" near his home county, participated on commissions determining lands held *in capite*, and was appointed a J.P. for his county.[42] His efficiency in executing these and other offices, for which there is ample evidence, encouraged further responsibilities as the reign progressed.[43]

Empson also continued to dominate county affairs. He represented Northamptonshire in parliament from 1489 to 1504; in 1491 he was

---

326/5192; *Catalogue of Ancient Deeds*, vi, no. C.5745; iii, no. A.5507 (Westminster Abbey Muniments, MS. 16015).

[38] W.A.M., MSS. 13601-2.

[39] *A Survey of London by John Stow: Reprinted from the Text of 1603*, ed. C.L. Kingsford (3 vols., Oxford, 1908-27), i. p. 224.

[40] Guildhall Library, Corporation of London Record Office, Journals of the Court of Common Council, xi fo. 20v; T.N.A.: P.R.O., E 154/2/17.

[41] Confusion between the residences of Dudley and Empson continued after Stow. In the lord treasurer's notes of a speech by James I, it was stated that Dudley was a Northamptonshire man "and there lived"; Empson was said to have lived in London (*Commons Debates* 1621, ed. W. Notestein, F.H. Relf and H. Simpson (7 vols., New Haven, 1935), v, 71). See below.

[42] *Cal. Pat. Rolls 1485-94*, pp. 64, 103, 133, 495; *Material for Henry VII*, i, pp. 380, 460.

[43] Empson was a proficient receiver of farms and offices granted to him, e.g., payments to the king's chamber for Catesby's lands (*Rot. Parl.*, vi, pp. 490-2; T.N.A.: P.R.O., E 101/414/6 fos. 101v, 115; E 101/414/16 fo. 81v; Brit. Libr., Add. MS. 21480 fo. 32v; T.N.A.: P.R.O., E 404/82, 25 Mar. 1498; E 404/83, 14 Mar. 1499, 30 Mar. 1500, 20 Mar. 1501; E 404/84, 10 Mar. 1502, 19 Mar. 1503).

chosen Speaker.[44] In 1486, he was once again involved with Sponne's charity in Towcester. Four years later he became recorder of Northampton, a position he also obtained for Coventry.[45] He was named to every commission of the peace in Northamptonshire and in neighbouring counties during the reign. He continued to act in the affairs of Luffield priory and in 1496, when the king ordered an inventory for that institution, it was delivered to Empson's care.[46] He also found time to practise law and to represent people in his locality.[47]

His work as attorney-general for the duchy was often blurred with a parallel body of councillors deliberating in the duchy chamber, the "council learned in the law". This group of royal officers of state, mostly lawyers and headed by Reynold Bray, held proceedings from at least 1495 to adjudicate suits involving the laws of the realm and the rights of the king. It became one of several platforms of justice on which Henry VII's councillors presided and rendered decisions.[48] Although Empson had acquired administrative experience as a duchy official before Henry VII's reign, his activities under Bray brought him closer to the role of an important councillor to the king through this dual aspect of the duchy. In 1497, Bray informed Henry VII of an escape from ward at Peterborough and promised that the guilty gaoler would be fined 100 marks. The debt was to be sealed in a written obligation, "and Richard Empson to see the

---

[44] Wedgwood, p. 300; *Rot. Parl.*, vi. p. 440; Brit. Libr., Harleian MS. 2252 fo. 28v.
[45] *Northants. Notes and Queries*, iv (1892), p. 253; *Records of the Borough of Northampton*, ed. C.A. Markham and J.C. Cox (2 vols., Northampton, 1898), i, p. 312, ii, p. 103; *Records of the Guild of the Holy Trinity . . . Coventry*, ed. M.D. Harris and G. Templeman (Dugdale Soc., xiii, xix (1935-44), ii, p. 170; T.N.A.: P.R.O., C 244/154 no. 5(b); C 244/158 no. 50(b).
[46] *Cal. Pat. Rolls 1485-94*, pp. 482, 495, 497, 503; *Cal. Pat. Rolls 1494-1509*, pp. 631, 652, 663; *Luffield Priory Charters*, ii, nos. 766c, A9, A10 (W.A.M., MS. 3007). Endorsements of writs by Empson returnable to chancery are found in T.N.A.: P.R.O., C 244/149 no. 11(a); C 244/154 no. 19(a); C 244/157 no. 8(a)(b).
[47] *Cal. Inq. Post Mortem, Henry VII*, i, no. 372; T.N.A.: P.R.O., E 40/8418.
[48] T.N.A.: P.R.O., E 101/414/6 fo. 125; R. Somerville, "Henry VII's 'Council learned in the law'", *Eng. Hist. Rev.,* Vol. LIV (1939), pp. 427-42. Sir Robert believed the committee was called into existence about 1500 when the records begin. This view has been accepted elsewhere (*Select Cases in the Council of Henry VII*, ed. C.G. Bayne (Selden Soc., lxxv, 1958), p. xxv; Chrimes, *Henry VII*, p. 150). In the repertories of the aldermen's court in London, an entry for early 1497 alludes to a document to be drawn up and delivered to "the kings learned council" (C.L.R.O., Repertories of the Court of Aldermen, i, fo. 13v).

sureties [for the obligation] taken for the same".[49] In a variance between two parties in 1502, "Master Empson" and other lawyers were ordered to view the area of contention "to examine the matter".[50]

At the death of Bray in August 1503, Empson was an accomplished councillor of the king and a leading minister in the duchy of Lancaster. He was already sitting in the courts of requests and star chamber, and in February 1504 he became a knight of the Bath when the future Henry VIII was created prince of Wales.[51] When Henry VII finally appointed a new chancellor of the duchy almost a year after Bray's death, it went to his trusted friend Sir John Mordaunt. But Mordaunt's sudden death in September 1504 thrust Empson into the forefront as the leading councillor in the duchy and the logical successor to his close associate and mentor Reynold Bray.[52]

The king, ever cautious in his appointments, once again left the chancellorship of the duchy in abeyance, but within a month of Mordaunt's death Empson was styled "keeper of the duchy seal". On 3 October 1505 he was officially granted the chancellorship for life.[53] For the remainder of the reign, his activities at the duchy as chancellor and presiding officer of the king's councillors sitting there were aligned with the polity and procedures established by Bray.[54]

A major responsibility pursued by Empson and his colleagues during the last years of Henry VII's reign involved the taking and prosecuting of written obligations, or bonds—legal instruments utilized by the law courts and the various departments of state. These "writings obligatory" placed a

---

[49] T.N.A.: P.R.O., E 101/414/16 fo. 131. See also T.N.A.: P.R.O., DL 5/2 fo. 7v.

[50] T.N.A.: P.R.O., DL 5/2 fo. 24v (also fo. 52).

[51] *Angelica Historia*, p. 6; *Select Cases in the Court of Requests*, 1497-1569, ed. I.S. Leadam (Selden Soc., xii, 1898), p. cii; Brit. Libr., Hargrave MS. 249 fo. 54, Lansdowne MS. 160 fo. 309, Add. MS. 11595 fo. 74; *Rot. Parl.*, vi, 532. Empson and 1,320 other men were eligible for knighthood (Brit. Libr., Harleian MS. 813 fos. 62-77).

[52] Somerville, *Duchy*, i, p. 392. Empson was named an executor of Bray's will (N.H. Nicolas, *Testamenta Vetusta* (2 vols, 1826), i, 447). Mordaunt continued to sit in the duchy chamber until the time of his death in 1504 (T.N.A.: P.R.O., DL 5/4 fo. 16v). His death is customarily placed between the dating of his will, 5 Sep., and its probate, 6 Dec. (*D.N.B.*; Somerville, *Duchy*, i. p. 392), although an inquisition for his properties gives his death as 11 Sept. (*Cal. Inq. Post Mortem*, Henry VII, iii, no. 875).

[53] T.N.A.: P.R.O., DL 12/3 nos. 55, 62; DL 5/2 fos. 74, 78, 89r-v; Somerville, *Duchy*, i, p. 392.

[54] T.N.A.: P.R.O., DL 1/2 fo. 65; DL 5/2 fos. 97, 109, 123; DL 5/4 fos. 116, 157v.

person in a legally constituted debt, be it for money, allegiance, the payment of farms and customs duties or the promise of good behaviour ("good abearing"). Bonds for the collection of debts on farms in the duchy possessed a long history, and books were kept recording such transactions and their discharge upon payment to the receiver-general of the duchy.[55] This procedure for payment was emulated by the king's chamber where bonds with various stipulations were stored and recorded.

Obligations for royal finance increased in usage during the reign and the close rolls at chancery became a record for many of the bonds taken by the king's councillors *ad usum regis*. Such enrolments of obligations were called "recognizances", a term signifying a bond enrolled or filed at a judicial tribunal. Beginning in 1502, Empson's name appeared in over fifty entries of recognizances on the close rolls, most of which were for the payment of moneys due to the crown.[56] Payment was forthcoming on most bonds payable to Empson and other councillors. In 1504, William Boughton and three sureties were bound by two recognizances to Empson, Dudley and three other councillors. The condition stipulated payment of £80 on 11 November 1505 and £80 on the same day in 1506. The payments were duly received in the king's chamber on 3 November and 7 November of those years.[57] Many such bonds filed as memoranda were also duplicated on the close rolls for easy reference. Robert Spencer and three sureties were bound by recognizance in chancery for the payment of £40 to Empson, Mordaunt and others. A memorandum of the bond was filed at chancery; it was later enrolled on the close rolls where it was cancelled a year later following payment to the king's chamber.[58] Similar bonds were filed without duplication on the close rolls, many taken by the king's councillors.[59]

Empson's personal involvement in taking written bonds for various conditions cannot be as readily discovered as that of his historical cohort, Edmund Dudley. While hundreds of bonds recorded by Dudley survive,

---

[55] E.g., T.N.A.: P.R.O., DL 41/34/1 for the reigns of Edward IV-Henry VIII.
[56] This figure is determined from entries in *Cal. Close Rolls 1500-1509*. For bonds of allegiance taken of the nobility and enrolled on the close rolls, see J.R. Lander, "Bonds, coercion, and fear: Henry VII and the peerage" in his *Crown and Nobility, 1450-1509* (1976), pp. 267-300.
[57] *Cal. Close Rolls 1500-09*, no. 418 (ii); T.N.A.: P.R.O., C 82/279, 3 Nov. 1505; C 82/293, 7 Nov. 1506.
[58] T.N.A.: P.R.O., C 244/154 no. 20; *Cal. Close Rolls 1500-09*, no. 321; T.N.A.: P.R.O., C 82/280, 4 Dec. 1505.
[59] *Cal. Close Rolls 1500-09*, pp. viii-ix.

Empson has left little trace of such activity.[60] A formula for reconstructing Empson's "missing" account book based on Dudley's administrative techniques may be possible, if indeed Empson did keep such an account as claimed by Bacon.[61] A petition by Sir Thomas Knight for a pardon was signed by Henry VII and Edmund Dudley in November 1505. On the 16th of that month, Knight paid Dudley £200 "for his pardon": £100 in ready money and £100 by obligation.[62] Many other examples exist where Dudley signed a petition addressed to the king and received payment for the privilege.[63]

By working backwards from petitions signed by Empson and the king, Empson's involvement with written bonds can be determined. In 1506, writs of attachment were awarded against Thomas Wodeshawe by the "council learned".[64] Wodeshawe, a collector of the customs in the port of Southampton, was listed in the chamber accounts as owing the king £100. By the end of 1505 only £15 had been paid, the likely cause of his arrest.[65] In February 1507, Wodeshawe petitioned the king for a pardon. It was signed by Henry VII and Richard Empson, although enrolment in chancery did not occur until two years later.[66] No record has been found of a payment for Wodeshawe's pardon, but in view of prevailing policy in Henry VII's reign there is little doubt that such payment was required, and in this instance any bond for payment would have been taken by Empson.[67]

Another form of personal authority exhibited by Dudley and attributed to Empson involved the holding of private "courts" within their homes, although the romantic notion of clandestine meetings between them cannot

---

[60] See above, n. 1.

[61] See above, n. 2.

[62] T.N.A.: P.R.O., C 82/279, Nov. 1505; Brit. Libr., Lansdowne MS. 127 fo. 13.

[63] See the pardon of Sir John Risley, T.N.A.: P.R.O., C 82/296, Feb. 1507; *Cal. Pat. Rolls 1494-1509*, p. 535; Brit. Libr., Lansdowne MS. 127 fo. 38v.

[64] T.N.A.: P.R.O., DL 5/4 fo. 88v.

[65] T.N.A.: P.R.O., DL 5/4 fo. 63; T.N.A.: P.R.O., E 404/84, 28 Nov. 1502; E 101/517/2, m. 3; E 101/516/30 m. 2. The writs were addressed to the sheriffs of the county and town of Southampton.

[66] T.N.A.: P.R.O., C 82/296, Feb. 1507; *Cal. Pat. Rolls 1494-1509*, p. 621.

[67] One recognizance enrolled in chancery and later paid and cancelled was discharged by a warrant signed by Henry VII and Empson, suggesting that Empson was involved with the original debt (*Cal. Close Rolls 1500-09*, no. 674; T.N.A.: P.R.O., C 82/295, 30 Jan. 1507). An inventory written in Henry VIII's reign of old obligations from the previous reign listed Thomas Wodeshawe as owing £100 (T.N.A.: P.R.O., SP 1/59 fo. 16).

be reconciled with their known residences.[68] If Dudley did use his house for the king's business, he surely was equipped for it. After his attainder, an inventory of his goods listed boxes of obligations and "evidences" found in almost every room except the bedroom.[69] The 16th century writers mentioned hearings before Empson at his house in St. Bride's parish.[70] It is possible that what was meant concerned the council chambers at Blackfriars and Bridewell near his house, but there are also documented references to "the council chamber at St. Bride's in Fleet Street" and appearance before Empson "in the parish of St. Bride's in London".[71] These allusions to a chamber in St. Bride's have been proffered as evidence that Empson may have used his house since it is assumed that no duchy chamber existed outside those at Westminster, Blackfriars and Bridewell.[72] Yet the "council learned" also met at Greenwich, Richmond or wherever a few of the relevant councillors happened to be, and the references suggest that there was a chamber in Fleet Street where councillors deliberated. The duke of Buckingham's case was heard before "the justices assembled at the Church of St. Bride's" (off Fleet Street), and it is most certain that large ecclesiastical buildings, including those at Blackfriars and Westminster, were best suited for judicial proceedings.[73] Whether or not Empson held private court or opened his house to the "council learned" cannot now be discerned.

Dudley and Empson did work together as professed by the chronicles, but usually with other councillors of the king. Rarely does a document contain only their names.[74] Dudley's work on the "council learned" meeting at the duchy appears to have been minimal.[75] When a customs official of Yarmouth was ordered to appear before Dudley and Empson,

---

[68] See above, and nn. 40-1.

[69] T.N.A.: P.R.O., E 154/2/17.

[70] Holinshed, iii, p. 553.

[71] T.N.A.: P.R.O., DL 5/2 fo. 101; DL 5/4 fos. 152v, 153 (Bridewell); DL 41/34/2 fo. 146 (Blackfriars); DL 41/34/2 fo. 160, DL 5/4 fo. 127 (St. Bride's).

[72] Somerville, "Council Learned", pp. 430, 442 n. 2.

[73] Quoted in A.W.B. Simpson, *A History of the Common Law of Contract* (Oxford 1975), p. 340.

[74] E.g., T.N.A.: P.R.O., C 82/320, Oct. 1508; *Cal. Close Rolls 1500-09*, no. 837.

[75] T.N.A.: P.R.O., DL 5/2 fo. 101v. Somerville believed Dudley to be an integral member of the "council learned" ("Council Learned", pp. 430-1), but this is true only for his role as a "learned councilor" performing the same duties. Most of his work was accomplished away from the duchy court.

his hearing was before Empson alone.[76] The widow of Sir Roger Ormeston was ordered to appear before Dudley and other councillors in London. She in fact came before Empson in the duchy chamber at Westminster and was told to remain "unto the coming of Master Dudley".[77] Empson was the central figure for the proceedings of the "council learned"; Dudley spent much of his time with the king and other councillors away from the duchy chambers and infrequently used Empson's facilities for the king's business.

Where the two councillors become more visible together is during the last two years of Henry VII's reign when the king was sick much of the time. In March 1507, Henry VII was in a grave state of health. He ordered the writing of his will—which included Dudley and Empson as two of the executors—and commanded "Master Wolsey" to receive money for the saying of 7,209 masses for the king's soul. Empson was forwarded a royal letter, perhaps for his appearance at court, and Dudley and other councillors were given funds to redeem certain persons from prison: the gesture of a dying king.[78] Henry VII recovered by July, but relapse occurred in March 1508, when myriad masses were again ordered.[79] During the last months of his life, Henry VII was completely incapacitated, to the point where Empson, not the king, ordered the payment of money to a royal servant.[80] Dudley in the meantime, was receiving royal matters for the king, who died on 21 April 1509.[81]

The relationship of Empson, and of Dudley, with Henry VII was not dissimilar from that of councillors such as Edward Belknap, Thomas Lovell, John Hussey and Robert Southwell with the king. Where Empson had his own conciliar court at the duchy and Dudley his private accounts and ad hoc perambulations from department to king's chamber, Southwell held his own court of audit for the king, taking bonds for various conditions, and Hussey as master of wards often worked with Dudley to ferret out old debts or take new ones.[82] Edward Belknap's responsibilities

---

[76] T.N.A.: P.R.O., DL 5/2 fo. 101.
[77] T.N.A.: P.R.O., DL 5/4 fo. 101v.
[78] Brit. Libr., Lansdowne MS. 1 fo. 115; T.N.A.: P.R.O., E 36/214 fos. 70, 73r-v; *Hall's Chronicle*, p. 502.
[79] T.N.A.: P.R.O., E 36/214 fos. 87v, 122v. In Aug. 1508, the king was reported to be *in extremis (Calendar of State Papers, Venetian*, 1202-1509, no. 906).
[80] T.N.A.: P.R.O., E 36/214 fo. 161.
[81] T.N.A.: P.R.O., E 36/214 fo. 163.
[82] A book of proceedings before Southwell's court is found in T.N.A.: P.R.O., E 315/263. Hussey was appointed "master of our wards" on 13 Aug. 1503, although

as surveyor of outlawries, marriages and other royal prerogatives complemented the work of his colleagues.[83] All were busy at their occupations while the king slowly drifted to his death.

Henry VII's relations with Richard Empson seemed to embody a posture of guarded trust. After Empson's appointment as attorney-general for the duchy, there was little immediate response by the king to his capabilities or potential. The first major assignment occurred in September 1497, when Empson received 1000 marks from the king to be delivered for the relief of Exeter against Perkin Warbeck's rebellion.[84] Few other personal missions are found until Henry VII's extreme illness in 1508 when the king began to rely on Empson and other councillors to govern the realm. In that year, Henry VII signed several warrants to the chancellor of England for commissions under the great seal listing articles that Sir Richard Empson "shall devise and send upon you".[85] On a more personal level, there is evidence that Henry VII stayed with Empson at Easton Neston on at least one occasion.[86]

Rewards were few and inconsequential. In 1495, Empson was given £13 6s 8d as a reward, perhaps for legal services rendered, and such tokens proceeded in trickles.[87] Empson's petitions for office were met with royal scrutiny and supervision. When in 1507 Empson sought the stewardship of manors in Northamptonshire for life, Henry VII crossed out the words "for

---

his patent was delayed until he acknowledged a bond for office (T.N.A.: P.R.O., C 82/332, 13 Aug. 1503; *Cal. Pat. Rolls 1494-1509*, p. 334; T.N.A.: P.R.O., C 255/8/5 no. 83). He is erroneously referred to as Sir John Hursey in Chrimes, *Henry VII*, p. 129.

[83] W.C. Richardson, "The surveyor of the king's prerogative", *Eng. Hist. Rev.*, Vol. LVI (1941), pp. 52-75.

[84] T.N.A.: P.R.O., E 101/414/6 fo. 87. Warbeck listed Empson as one of many bad influences on the king (Brit. Libr., Harleian MS. 283 fo. 123v; *The Reign of Henry VII from Contemporary Sources*, ed. A.F. Pollard (3 vols., 1913-14), i, 153).

[85] T.N.A.: P.R.O., C 82/315, 17 July 1508; C 82/316, 21 Aug. 1508 (*Cal. Pat. Rolls 1494-1509*, p. 627).

[86] A grant to a household servant of the king was signed by Henry VII at the manor of "Easton" on 20 Aug. 1507. The next day, the warrant for the grant was delivered to Empson within his manor (T.N.A.: P.R.O., DL 12/1/2 no. 52).

[87] Brit. Libr., Add. MS. 7099 fo. 52; T.N.A.: P.R.O., E 101/414/6 fo. 13; E 101/414/16 fos. 17v, 48v; E 101/415/3 fos. 13v, 37v. He once received a reward from Elizabeth of York (T.N.A.: P.R.O., E 36/210 fo. 46v).

life" and inserted "during pleasure". The king proceeded similarly with Empson's petition for another stewardship in that county.[88]

Trained in the administration of the duchy of Lancaster, eager to follow the prosecution of the law as the attorney-general and a member of the various conciliar courts, Empson's triumph as a leading Tudor minister was also the culmination of twenty years of expedient royal policy for ruling England. Statecraft had been based upon enforcement of the laws and statutes of the realm, and its proponents were the king and his councillors. Such personal governance of the realm could end only with the death of the king, and any repudiation could be aimed only at the ministers of that king.

Two days after the death of his father, according to Edward Hall, young Henry VIII ordered the arrest of Sir Richard Empson and Edmund Dudley for constructive treason. Soon after, both men were arraigned separately and condemned to death.[89] The two ministers languished in the Tower of London until 17 August 1510 when they were beheaded on Tower Hill. The actual indictments upon which Dudley and Empson were tried and convicted speak of independent armed conspiracies by the two ministers to overthrow the king and seize the government, a prodigious project for a senior minister, for Empson was almost sixty. The chroniclers, Stow and Bacon do not mention these charges and Lord Herbert brushed them off as "how improbable soever".[90] Henry VIII, however, was faced with a dilemma of denouncing the financial policies of his father to satisfy an aggrieved populace without tarnishing the image of the ruler who was often the prime mover behind such policies. Dudley and

---

[88] T.N.A.: P.R.O., C 82/305, Sep. 1507 (*Cal. Pat. Rolls 1494-1509*, p. 554); T.N.A.: P.R.O., DL 12/1/1 no. 57. The distinction between these tenures was perhaps more marked under Henry VII than in later times. Dr. Aylmer, in an example from Charles I's reign involving tenures, saw little difference between "pleasure" and "life" except where individual personalities were concerned (G.E. Aylmer, *The King's Servants: the Civil Service of Charles I, 1625-42* (1961), p. 117). He noted, however, that for the "middle rank" of servants it was more difficult for the king to get rid of officers holding life tenures. Henry VII had little difficulty with either tenure, but it was important for him to use the distinction to remind an official whence the source of his good fortune sprang.

[89] *Hall's Chronicle*, p. 505.

[90] T.N.A.: P.R.O., KB 8/4 (Baga de Secretis); KB 9/453/144, 467; Edward, Lord Herbert, p. 10. The House of Lords in 1621 recognized that two sets of indictments were filed, one for an attempt to seize the king, the other for various exactions and "crimes" against the people and, presumably, in violation of the law. (*Common Debates* 1621, iv, 205.)

Empson, the two most visible ministers of the old reign, provided the scapegoats for the protection of the late king's soul.

According to the chroniclers and writers in the century after the demise of Dudley and Empson, their crimes were many and manifold but not treasonous. Hall accused them of prosecuting cases of "outlaries, olde recognisances of the peace and good abering, escapes, ryottes and innumerable statutes penal".[91] Other writers expanded on this theme, listing individual cases and examples.[92] The parliaments of James I made frequent mention of Empson, with or without Dudley, largely through the orations of Sir Edward Coke and the prosecution of Mompesson's case.[93] That the names Dudley and Empson became convenient clichés for heavy exactions and legal chicanery is exemplified in a passage by Jonathan Swift: "What if there be an old dormant Statute or two against [a man]? Are they not now obsolete to a Degree, that *Empson* and *Dudley* themselves, if they were now alive, would find it impossible to put them in Execution?"[94]

Although recent scholarship has begun to piece together the activities of Henry VII's ministers, little attempt has been made to learn Empson's personal role in those sordid affairs attributed to both Dudley and Empson.[95] Moreover, the survival of Dudley's account book and the jeremiad he penned in the Tower allow an analysis of that minister's participation in the offences popularly ascribed to him. Empson's involvement in the indictments filed at king's bench or the celebrated stories about him remain unstudied, and a few examples will address the veracity of these allegations.

---

[91] *Hall's Chronicle*, p. 502.

[92] Holinshed, iii, 531, 536; Stow, *Annales*, p. 812.

[93] For Coke's references, see *Commons Debates* 1621, ii, 125, 145, 161, 197, 231; iv, 92, 110, 136, 158; v, 43, 258, 260, 270, 281, 301, 523; vi, 14, 44, 266, 283, 301. Coke associated Mompesson with Empson through the anagram "Mo-empson" (v, 258). The earl of Salisbury, in a speech before the committees of both houses to obtain revenues for James I, veiled a threat by stating "I do not say the King shall send you an Empson and a Dudley, but this I say, the King must not want" (*Proceedings in Parliament* 1610, ed. E.R. Foster (2 vols., New Haven, Conn., 1966), ii, 301).

[94] J. Swift, "An argument against abolishing Christianity" (1708) in *The Prose Writings of Jonathan Swift,* ed. H. Davis (16 vols., Oxford, 1939-68), ii, p. 30.

[95] Above, n. 4. See also G.R. Elton, "Henry VII: rapacity and remorse", *Historical Jour.,* i (1958), pp. 21-39; J.P. Cooper, "Henry VII's last years reconsidered", *Historical Jour.,* ii (1959), pp. 103-29; G.R. Elton, "Henry VII: a restatement", *Historical Jour.,* iv (1961), pp. 1-29.

One indictment concerned Empson's use of the privy seal towards the end of the reign to force alleged lawbreakers to "settle" any accusations with a fine.[96] Although many of the king's councillors ordered privy seals for their various activities at the time, evidence exists which shows Empson's rather capricious use of the seal for what appears to be extortion.[97] In his petition to the chancellor of England after Empson's fall, Robert Best of Norwich stated that one Gregory Caus was summoned by privy seal "upon information made against him before Sir Richard Empson". Caus was accused of shipping goods from Southampton without paying any duties on them, for which he now paid a fine "of certain money betwixt him and the said Sir Richard agreed". Robert Best alleged that now Gregory Caus became an informer for Empson and endeavoured to bring fines upon "diverse innocent people", including the present petitioner who was terrified of "the rigour and unreasonable punishment of the said Sir Richard [Empson] before whom he feared to have little justice". Caus forced Best to enter an obligation of £40 to abide by the award of two aldermen of Norwich for all matters between Caus and Best. The aldermen awarded Caus £10, which Best promptly paid. Caus, however, now brought an action of debt against Best on the £40 bond for performance, and the petitioner asked the chancellor to remove the case to chancery.[98]

Since petitions to the chancellor rarely failed to obfuscate the real issues in a suit, it is tempting to see this case as simply a matter of debt turned into one of extortion, thus taking advantage of Empson's reputation and Henry VIII's decree to right all wrongs committed in his father's reign.[99] But in this instance, the complaint contained elements of truth, both in the use of privy seals and informers. In 1507, Gregory Caus was in fact summoned before the "council learned" along with Richard Aylmer, one of the aldermen who arbitrated Robert Best's fine. The two men appeared together and were later dismissed after "be[ing] through [with the court] and their obligation [for appearance] rest[ing] with [Richard Empson is] delivered".[100] Whatever the men did to "be through" with Empson and his "learned council", it is not beyond the realm of possibility that they agreed to inform against lawbreakers, real or otherwise. The fact

---

[96] Brit. Libr., Add. MS. 41613 fos. 186-7.
[97] For privy seals sent by other councillors, see T.N.A.: P.R.O., E 36/214 fos. 75, 133, 141, 160.
[98] T.N.A.: P.R.O., C 1/289 no. 58.
[99] Stow, *Annals*, p. 815.
[100] T.N.A.: P.R.O., DL 5/2 fos. 108v, 109v.

that Caus encouraged his victim Robert Best to abide by the award of Aylmer and his fellow alderman smacks of collusion. When one considers that while Caus and Aylmer appeared before Empson, a man was awarded by the king for presenting "certain matters" before the king's council regarding three men lying in the Tower, it is quite proper to assume that men were frequently bought for their talents as informers.[101] Privy seals facilitated their work.

The charge of prosecuting old recognizances is a correct one, although there was nothing illegal or novel about it. Recognizances by "statute merchant" and "statute staple", ostensibly for debts between merchants but used by all classes of people, were sued upon for actions of debt years after their contracting.[102] Close scrutiny of recognizances filed at the various royal repositories became a common procedure during Henry VII's reign, and the treasurer of the chamber retained bonds for future collection.[103]

One example illustrates the rigour with which Empson, Dudley and Henry VII prosecuted an "old recognizance".[104] On 10 August 1487, Christopher Moresby and Lancelot Thirkeld acknowledged recognizances for £200 each to guarantee the appearance of Thomas Ratcliffe in chancery. Ratcliffe also acknowledged a bond of 500 marks for his appearance. In the interim, Ratcliffe was ordered to attend the king during his progress through northern England unless given licence to depart.

---

[101] T.N.A.: P.R.O., E 36/214 fo. 90. The families of Aylmer and Caus knew each other well and were important officials in Norwich. Robert Aylmer, the father of Richard, was mayor there in 1481 and 1492. The elder Aylmer's friend, Thomas Caus, was mayor in 1495 and 1503; his son was Gregory. Both Richard and Gregory, who may have grown up together, fared well: Richard became mayor in 1511 and Gregory was sheriff in 1516 (*The Mayors of Norwich*, 1403-1835, comp. B. Cozens-Hardy and E.A. Kent (Norwich, 1938), pp. 33, 36, 40-1).

[102] Examples of actions on these debts years after contraction are found in *Select Cases Concerning the Law Merchant*, ed. H. Hall (Selden Soc., xxiii, xlvi, xlix (1908-32), iii, p. lxix.

[103] In Oct. 1499, five years before Dudley's active service, two memoranda were noted by the treasurer of the chamber: "Memorandum of nineteen obligations of good abearing in one box"; "Memorandum of twenty-one obligations in another box" (Brit. Libr., Add. MS. 21480 fo. 167).

[104] This reconstructed from the following sources: T.N.A.: P.R.O., C 255/8/5 no. 58; C 245/45 no. 16(a)(b); C 82/294, Dec. 1506; C 82/301, July 1507; DL 1/2 fo. 84; DL 5/4 fos. 93v, 94v; *Cal. Inq. Post Mortem Henry VII*, ii, no. 292; *Cal. Close Rolls 1500-09*, nos. 613, 812; *Cal. Fine Rolls 1485-1509*, nos. 515, 529; Brit. Libr., Lansdowne MS. 127 fo. 36.

Henry VII finally granted Ratcliffe such licence, and he returned to his home in Cumberland where he resided until his death eight years later. In 1499, Moresby, one of Ratcliffe's former sureties, as well died, bequeathing his lands and chattels to his wife and daughter. The other surety, Lancelot Thirkeld, became a farmer of the subsidy and alnage on cloth in London. During all this time, a memorandum for the recognizances taken in 1487 remained in chancery uncancelled, and a record was never made of Ratcliffe's licence to depart, probably because it was given orally by Henry VII.

Almost twenty years after the bond was taken, the participants and their heirs were suddenly vexed with problems. Sometime in early 1506, Thirkeld was sued for the £200 owed on the 1487 bond. His lands and goods were seized by the crown. In March, he and two sureties entered four recognizances totalling the £200, although Thirkeld actually had to pay the lesser sum of £146 to the treasurer of the chamber in four instalments. The unfortunate surety petitioned the king repeatedly for a pardon, and in September he and John Ratcliffe, undoubtedly the heir of Thomas, appeared before the "council learned". Thirkeld did not fare well before the councillors. A writ of *scire facias* was issued on 4 December 1506 ordering his appearance in chancery the next term. He appeared and pleaded that, indeed, Thomas Ratcliffe had received a licence, but Thirkeld was nonetheless committed to the Fleet in 1507 by the king's council. Thirkeld petitioned the king once more, this time to be released from prison by promising to pay the debt when financially feasible. In June 1508, after his release, Thirkeld entered a bond for 500 marks for his allegiance to the king and his appearance before chancery; a further condition enjoined him to remain within twenty-one miles of London.

John Ratcliffe was dismissed from the conciliar court after the king's solicitor, also a member of the "council learned", informed the court that Ratcliffe had settled with the king. This referred to a fine of 200 marks for the discharge of Thomas Ratcliffe's old bond of 500 marks. It was paid by John Ratcliffe to Edmund Dudley in January 1507: 50 marks in cash and £100 by recognizance. At the same time, Henry VII signed a letter stating that the original recognizance was null and void for Ratcliffe only.

The other surety, Moresby, was dead, but his widow, daughter and son-in-law Humphrey Coningsby, a "learned councilor", were required to sue out a pardon in 1507 for the twenty-year-old bond. The fact that both Henry VII and Richard Empson signed the pardon strongly suggests that Moresby's executors either paid cash for the pardon or were placed in a recognizance by Empson for future payment of money as were John Ratcliffe and Thirkeld.[105] This was clearly legal extortion put to unmitigated use by Dudley, Empson and Henry VII. Empson ordered many people to the Fleet who came before him in the "council learned":[106] in the present case, he shared with Dudley the prosecution of this old bond.

Stow related a story about Empson which went deeper into intrigue than even the writer imagined. He asserted that there were many "opprobrious rhymes" written against Dudley and Empson during Henry VII's reign. One poem Stow discovered against Richard Empson was written by William Cornysshe of the king's chapel.[107] Although the poem is apparently lost, Cornysshe wrote another work while a prisoner in the Fleet in July 1504, and it survives.[108] This second poem has been viewed as a symbolic protest against Empson because the minister imprisoned the poet for writing the first one![109] Beyond Stow's mention of the first poem and the verbal lambaste by Cornysshe in his second effort, no other source alludes to Empson and his vituperative treatment of the righteous poet.

Ironically, a recognizance forced upon Sir Richard Empson for his own good behaviour provides evidence supporting this reason for Cornysshe's imprisonment. On 14 July 1504, the same month Cornysshe wrote his poem from the Fleet, Empson was bound by a recognizance for 100 marks payable to the king. The condition ordered Empson to

> do, keep and observe the king's peace against [William] Cornysshe of the king's chapel so that the same Cornysshe take no bodily hurt by the same Sir Richard neither by no one other by the consent, assent, procuring, abetting or stirring of the same Sir Richard.[110]

---

[105] In 1510, all three executors received pardons, perhaps for this debt (*Letters and Papers, Foreign and Domestic of the Reign of Henry VIII* (Kraus Reprint 1964-5), I. i. no. 438, pp. 221, 247). It is interesting to note that Empson "improved" the rent of a John Ratcliffe for certain properties in the duchy of Lancaster some time between 1505 and 1508 (T.N.A.: P.R.O., DL 41/29/10 fo. 14).

[106] T.N.A.: P.R.O., DL 5/2 fo. 94v; DL 5/4 fos. 111, 147, 153.

[107] Stow, *Annals*, p. 816.

[108] Brit. Libr., Royal MS. 18D.ii fos. 163-4, printed in J. Skelton, *Pithy, Pleasant and Profitable Works* (Menston, 1970, facsimile of 1568 ed.), no. 31. All quotations from the poem are from this edition.

[109] W. Chappell, "Some account of an unpublished collection of songs and ballads by Henry VIII and his contemporaries", *Archaeologia*, xli (1867-8), pt. ii, p. 380; *D.N.B.*, s.v. Cornysshe.

[110] T.N.A.: P.R.O., C 244/153 no. 136.

The effect of the bond was to last until at least 29 September 1505, enough time for Cornysshe to recover from his imprisonment and seek refuge in the king's chapel.[111]

Cornysshe, however, could not know of this bond during his stay in the Fleet, and his poem reflects the anger and fear of a man who had been wronged by an acrimonious minister for trying to tell the truth. He berated informers who "disgorgith theyr venome", one of whom probably informed Empson of Cornysshe's original poem. He reaffirmed his determination to tell the world of Empson's crimes in a pun on his present predicament:

> Yet trouth was drowned he not sanke
> But still dyd fleete above the water.

Cornysshe ended his poem on a pessimistic note regarding his own future, believing that although "God knowyth al, so doth not kyng Harry". Fortunately for the poet, the king was indeed aware of a minister's vindictiveness against a servant of the crown.

It would be most desirable to know the personal beliefs of Richard Empson or catch a glimpse of his personality, the lack of which leaves this important Tudor minister at the mercy of document and legend. But while Dudley spent his time of imprisonment offering opinions on the government and the prince, Empson was busy sorting out his estates.[112] As a man of his time, he had inclinations towards the devout. In 1506, he and his wife Jane were listed as members of the guild of St. Anne of Knowle in Warwickshire.[113] He also had a private chaplain, William Marshall, and he granted annuities and lands to parishioners in Easton Neston.[114]

A discussion of church affairs in what was perhaps the last correspondence before his death allows a ray of humour to permeate the otherwise stern, calculating image of Henry VII's minister. Upon being informed that his cattle had broken loose over the lands of a church in Northamptonshire, Empson replied from the Tower that it was the fault of the keepers, who were "beastly" for allowing the animals to roam freely. He promised that if his cattle were still at large he would order doors and locks, "for it is no profit to my cattle to be there [in the churchyard], there be better places I

---

[111] Cornysshe continued his career under Henry VIII (*D.N.B.*).

[112] T.N.A.: P.R.O., SP 1/1 fos. 157-161v; W.A.M., MS. 13603.

[113] *V.C.H. Warwick.*, ii, 122.

[114] N.R.O., Fermor-Heskith MS., MTD, E/29/11; W.A.M., MS. 25366.

know [for] them and more profitable".[115] It was perhaps the driving force in his life to make the laws of England profitable for his monarch. When Henry VII was dead and the cry for justice rang forth, all the loyalty and sedulity of a Tudor minister were of little profit to Richard Empson.

---

[115] T.N.A.: P.R.O., SP 1/1 fo. 161v.

CHAPTER FIVE

"AGREE WITH THE KING":
HENRY VII, EDMUND DUDLEY AND THE
STRANGE CASE OF THOMAS SUNNYFF*

Introduction

It was one thing to read about the harm inflicted on every day citizens of England during the reign of Henry VII when it came to legal chicanery, perjury, forged bonds and the intense prosecution of debts old and new. It was quite another to find proof. Most of what was known about the dark side of Henry's bond policy—discussed in greater detail in Chapter Seven—came from the London chronicles. Their authors collectively hated the policy and those who executed it, with the two most visible exponents of such activities being Richard Empson and Edmund Dudley. More evidence could be found in the court proceedings of London. However, these sources suggested to some historians that any graft or illicit behavior taking place was probably localized to the City.

In delving into the exchequer and chancery records for the reign, it became apparent to me that the bond policy was pervasive and enveloped all of England and Wales. The duchy council books furthered this view that people far from London could be caught in a web of prosecution. But again, the problem was to find an instant where, from start to finish, the process of all these allegations could be discerned and even followed.

I had run into Thomas Sunnyff first in D.M. Brodie's article on Edmund Dudley, mentioned earlier. He appeared again in passing three decades later in articles by J.P. Cooper and G.R. Elton on Henry VII's alleged rapacity and possible remorse over his actions. I vowed to take a peek at what was a long recitation of what happened to Thomas Sunnyff in his own words preserved in the Westminster Abbey Muniments archive.

* Reprinted with permission. The article was first published in *Historical Research*, Vol. LXXIX, no. 205 (Aug. 2006), pp. 325-66.

I was rewarded with a long, incredible tale of deceit, imprisonment, even murder involving an English citizen, Empson and Dudley, some of their minions and most probably the king. That this scroll even existed pointed to the proclamation issued by Henry VIII soon after the death of his father. It told all English men and women who were harmed in the old king's reign to file bills in court and plead their cases for redress "by reason of any light and untrue information or wrong surmises of Customers Comptrollers or [searchers] or any persons calling themselves promoters," as quoted in a journal of the common council of London. That is what Thomas Sunnyff did and why the document was written. It began my own intermittent thirty-year search to find out what happened, if it were true and how it related to the broader scope of Henry VII's policy—a policy that became corrupted. [See Chapter Seven]

Research I was doing on the reign periodically ran into relevant information for parts of Sunnyff's story. For example, the duchy council books had numerous mentions of privy seals sent to people with the vague command that they were required to appear before councilors for charges to be laid against them, with a large fine for non-compliance. It is probable that one or more one were sent to Thomas Sunnyff, possibly by Empson. C.G. Bayne, in his volume of cases heard in Henry VII's council, lamented that no privy seals existed today for us to see. Quite by chance, I discovered two of them in the Northampton Record Office while looking at deeds involving Richard Empson's father. These privy seals are actually a little unsettling to read and I obtained permission to print both of them. They appear as an appendix in this chapter.

A final note. When I taught a class on the Tudor kings at the University of Illinois (Chicago), I used a PowerPoint presentation to take students through the strange case of Thomas Sunnyff. The first year I did it, they were fascinated by mention of the murder of a child, and who might have done it. Although tangential to what we could learn from Sunnyff's misadventures about corruption, I decided to focus more on the murder in subsequent classes. After all, I had twelve suspects, running the gamut from a member of the lower class to the king of England! Moreover, I believed I knew who did it, and I would ask students to write down their choice after telling Sunnyff's story. Then I would go through the various documents, clues and revelations to solve the mystery. It led me to doing the presentation at various venues, from the University of Chicago and the University of Lincoln to a public library, and I entitled it "A Murder in Tudor England". If murder gets people's attention to learn about history, so be it.

It has become clear to historians of the period that Henry VII and his government pursued a policy of taking and prosecuting written bonds called obligations and recognizances with increasing vigour and alacrity during the course of his reign.[1] These involved not only real debts owed to the king (customs duties, rents and farms, payments for office and pardons, wardship, livery), but also debts for future behaviour, such as allegiance, appearance before a court of law or councillor, or good "abearing" (behaviour). As a result of the staggering amounts of potential income involved, the contemporary view of Henry as a greedy monarch largely arose from his pursuit of these bonds.[2] However, it might be argued that, given the needs endemic to the job of kingship, he was nothing more than perspicacious. Historically, governments, whether English or otherwise, have been well aware that effective rule required positive cash flow. Henry VII was no different from those whom he followed and those who succeeded him, except that he became one of the few solvent English kings since 1066.[3]

Rulers were also aware of the need to maintain and encourage order if they were to ensure effective and longstanding rule, a rare achievement for any length of time in the 15th century. While it may never be proven fully that Henry VII's motive for pursuing a policy of prosecuting bonds for most daily intercourse was to induce respect for the law and to establish order in the realm, he nonetheless succeeded in leaving England with two of the essential requirements for monarchical stability that Henry VI and the Yorkists failed to achieve: full coffers and a viable, unopposed heir to

---

[1] E.g., the various monographs and articles by J.R. Lander, S.B. Chrimes, J.A. Guy, Steven Gunn, Sean Cunningham, Dominic Luckett and David Grummitt.

[2] In a larger work in progress, the author has calculated the potential revenue from recognizances enrolled at chancery, which were only a small fraction of the total bonds in existence. Near the end of the reign, the amounts due on those enrolled bonds per year greatly exceeded the total annual income of the monarchy. (See M.R. Horowitz, "Henry Tudor's Treasure", Vol. LXXXII, no. 217 (Aug. 2009), pp. 560-79. [Chapter Eight]

[3] Henry recognized that traditional royal revenues were not adequate (A.J. Gross, "K.B. McFarlane and the determinists: the fallibilities of the English kings, *c*.1399-*c*.1520", in *The McFarlane Legacy: Studies in Late Medieval Politics and Society*, ed. R.H. Britnell and A.J Pollard (Stroud and New York, 1995), pp. 49-75, at p. 58). However, as Steven Gunn has commented to the author, sufficient revenue did not necessarily equate to successful kingship, e.g. in the cases of Edward II and Richard II, who were both deposed through their own rapacity and that of their favourites.

the throne.[4] Those accomplishments alone were hardly commonplace at the time. Henry VII ruled for twenty-four years as sole monarch of England; the previous twenty-four years saw five kings on and off the throne.

There was a darker side to Henry's royal policy of administering written bonds, one pointed out by many of the chroniclers of the time: the illegal or extra-legal binding or prosecuting of English men and women, high and low, for a multiplicity of reasons, or for no reason at all. That the populace accepted this policy—there were no "recognizance revolts" during the reign—attests to how far England had moved towards a law-abiding, or at least law-respecting, society. But there was an outcry against the sometimes nefarious use of bonds after Henry VII's death in 1509, and two of the most visible exponents of these activities, Sir Richard Empson and Edmund Dudley, esquire, were arrested, charged, on dubious grounds, with constructive treason and executed a year later. Clearly something was going on to require such harsh measures.

It is within this environment of prosecuting the laws of the land and securing the finances of the crown through written bonds that a strange case survives, recounting events taking place near the end of the reign and coming to light soon after Henry VII was dead and Empson and Dudley were in prison awaiting trial and execution. It involves a cross-section of society, from a common prostitute to the king himself. It also describes a series of events that, at the very least, must have been conceivable, since the injured party sought redress at law all the way to king's bench and would not have concocted a story that was beyond belief, and therefore relief. The fact that the plaintiff did receive relief from Henry VIII early in the young king's reign further suggests the veracity of the charges, if not the actual circumstances described in the complaint. The case is a vivid example of many such alleged situations where people were ill-treated by officials of the king. It also provides a means to review some of the vituperation flung by the various chronicles of the period at the last years of the reign, either for confirmation or dismissal. Finally, it is one of the rare occasions of an allegation against Empson or Dudley where both of these ministers of Henry VII were directly involved.[5]

---

[4] See, e.g., the article on bonds and instigating order in the north by S. Cunningham, "Henry VII and rebellion in north-eastern England, 1485-92: bonds of allegiance and the establishment of Tudor authority", *Northern Hist.*, xxxii (1996), pp. 42-74.
[5] This is not to say that the two councillors were never found working together, although surviving records point to few occasions. When the learned councillors

The matter is found among the documents preserved at Westminster abbey in the form of a first-person complaint by Thomas Sunnyff, merchant haberdasher of Ludgate in London.[6] It has been given little scholarly scrutiny beyond mention of its powerful indictment against Henry VII's councillors and the policies of the king himself. The complaint was first discussed briefly in a 1932 article on Edmund Dudley by D.M. Brodie as an illustration of the harsh measures taken by the king's ministers to enrich the crown, and as an example of the remorse felt by Dudley over those actions.[7] Almost three decades later, J.P. Cooper devoted two pages of an article to the case, briefly summarizing it as an example of the cruel treatment of citizens meted out by Henry's ministers.[8] G.R. Elton, attempting to show that the reign was reasonably devoid of rapacious behaviour on the part of the king and his councillors, conceded to Cooper that Sunnyff's case was "the only one known in which a man seems to have suffered quite innocently".[9] None of these historians sought to understand what was taking place, or why or how it might be a reflection of a royal policy in full force at the time.

In order to analyze the case with the objective of learning not only its authenticity but also what it says about the first Tudor's administration of law, justice and finance, it is important to put myth aside and seek corroborating evidence, both for this case and for the political climate that

---

met, especially at Westminster, individuals could be summoned by privy seal "to apere before Sr Richard Emson knight and Edmond Dudley squire to answere to such things as shalbe declared ayenst them" (T.N.A.: P.R.O., DL 5/2 fo. 101; and see also fo. 101v).

[6] Westminster Abbey Muniments, MS. 12249. The author is most grateful to the dean and chapter of Westminster for permission to use excerpts from this document and to transcribe the "confession" of Edmund Dudley that accompanies it. For the purpose of telling the story in the complaint, the writer of the document will be referred to as Thomas Sunnyff. This document is in poor condition with many tears, hanging parts along one side of the length of the scroll, deteriorated portions and rat damage. Dr. Richard Mortimer, keeper of the muniments, has informed the author that the manuscript is entering a restoration process.

[7] D.M. Brodie, "Edmund Dudley, minister of Henry VII", *Trans. Royal Hist. Soc.*, 4th ser., xv (1932), pp. 133-61, at pp. 153-4.

[8] J.P. Cooper, "Henry VII's last years reconsidered", *Historical Jour.*, ii (1959), pp. 103-29. The article was in response to G.R. Elton's discussion of a king who was neither rapacious nor remorseful when setting fiscal policy (G.R. Elton, "Henry VII: rapacity and remorse", *Historical Jour.*, i (1958), pp. 21-39).

[9] G.R. Elton, "Henry VII: a restatement", *Historical Jour.*, iv (1961), pp. 1-9, at p. 15.

might produce such a series of events. Richard Empson used his position as chancellor of the duchy of Lancaster to ferret out old debts for a variety of reasons, or to order people to take out new ones—a practice that he began in the reign of Edward IV and continued during and after the chancellorship of Reynold Bray.[10] Edmund Dudley worked mainly outside the sphere of councillors meeting with Empson at the various duchy chambers for this purpose. He was given long lists or books of obligations and recognizances due the king from a variety of sources, including those taken at chancery, common pleas or king's bench—records delivered to him by order of Henry VII.[11] The work of these and other councillors of the king and their minions often led to behaviour that was, in the eyes of contemporaries, coercive if not outright illegal, bringing to heel all stations of society through the use of written instruments and customary legal proceedings.[12]

For a clearer understanding of what was taking place in the complaint of Thomas Sunnyff, the intention here is first to summarize the allegations as they were written, then to analyze them and place them in the broader context of the reign. The case summary may appear closer to a recitation by Hitchcock than Holinshed because the facts and explanations are not immediately, if at all, apparent. Nevertheless, it allows the complaint to be expressed as it would have been received by those who read it at the beginning of Henry VIII's reign. Although no dates are given in the complaint, key ones ascertained from external sources will be used to provide a chronological framework. The summary of the complaint, and Dudley's separate alleged confession regarding Thomas Sunnyff that accompanied it, will be followed by an analysis in light of other records to determine both what occurred and what it might mean to an understanding of the activities of Henry VII and his councillors, and those carrying out royal policy. Regarding the date of the complaint, internal evidence suggests that it was written between 24 April 1509, when Henry VIII's

---

[10] M.R. Horowitz, "Richard Empson, minister of Henry VII", *Bull. Inst. Hist. Res.*, lv (1982), pp. 35-49 [Chapter Four]; R. Somerville, "Henry VII's 'Council learned in the law'", *Eng. Hist. Rev.*, Vol. LIV (1939), pp. 427-42.

[11] Horowitz, "Richard Empson", pp. 42-4; Brit. Libr., Lansdowne MS. 127, Dudley's account book (17th-century copy), fo. 55: "Itm deliv^{r}ed againe to the kingis highness the great book of Recogniz^{a}unce wch I had oons of his deliv^{r}aunce".

[12] E.g., *The Anglica Historia of Polydore Vergil, A.D. 1485-1537*, ed. D. Hay, Camden 3rd ser., lxxiv (1950), pp. 127ff.; *Grafton's Chronicle: or, History of England*, (2 vols., 1809, ii, pp. 230-1; *Hall's Chronicle*, ed. Sir H. Ellis (1809), p. 499).

pardon was announced publicly, and 17 August 1510, when Empson and Dudley were executed on Tower Hill. Bills filed at king's bench related to the case move the date to mid-1509.[13]

On the dorse of this rolled piece of parchment is written "The complaint of Thom[a]s Sunnyff ayenst Camby, and m dadley's Confession under it" (it will hereafter be referred to as the complaint). Inside the roll is a smaller document with the confession of Edmund Dudley. The complaint, which begins "ffyrst I ye sayd Thom^a s Sunnyff", was directed against John Camby, who was known to have been a henchman of Edmund Dudley. As Sunnyff's story unfolds in mid-April 1507, a mysterious woman named Alice Damston had been held prisoner—exactly where is not initially known—for seventeen weeks by John Camby.[14] Damston was incarcerated, according to the complaint, until she agreed to slander Thomas Sunnyff and his wife. At first, the author does not divulge the subject of the alleged slander, but it can be inferred that a legal proceeding or "inquest" into allegations against Sunnyff and his wife had been held: Sunnyff stated simply "we were [ac]quytte[d]". Alice Damston, he wrote, was being forced to say evil things about the haberdasher and his wife, but to no legal avail.

Sunnyff then noted that a servant of John Camby began to slander the couple publicly at Westminster Hall. Camby, meanwhile, "[l]abored to ye king['s] Counsell to cause my wyeff to be brentt [burned] & I to be hangyd". This is the first mention of royal governmental involvement. Sunnyff and a neighbour, Stephen Peacock, heard of these slanders and visited Camby in person, insisting that he hold his servant's tongue, as well as his own. Camby apparently refused. That same day, Camby came to Ludgate, close to where Sunnyff lived. He met with Stephen Peacock, who insisted that Thomas Sunnyff was "an honest man". Camby was unmoved but revealed the motivating force behind this unusual behaviour: he would leave Sunnyff alone if the haberdasher paid him £500 to have "don[e] w^t me [then]".

---

[13] See below.

[14] The chronology makes for torturous reconstruction. The focal point for working forwards and backwards is Sunnyff's mention of James Hobart as the king's attorney-general. Hobart was out of office by 8 July 1507 and John Ernley replaced him four days later (*Calendar of Patent Rolls 1494-1509*, p. 544). Alice Damston is presently referred to as "mysterious" because she could not be located anywhere in the state or Corporation of London records of the period, yet she is a central figure in the whole affair.

Events now moved rapidly. Sunnyff was summoned to appear before Sir Richard Empson, referred to as "[then] being of ye kings Counsell".[15] After meeting with Sunnyff, Empson told the hapless haberdasher that he "muste goo to warde [prison] for a c^{r}ten [matter] y^t was layd to my wyeffs charge as [Empson] was enformed". It is possible that it was John Camby, or his slanderous servant at Westminster Hall, who informed Empson. However, it is more likely that Edmund Dudley spoke to his fellow councillor of the matter after being briefed by Camby. All that is known for certain at this point is that Sunnyff's problem—and the debt of £500— had something to do with a "certain matter" involving his wife. Moreover, it had now moved up the ladder from perhaps the local assize to the chancellor of the duchy of Lancaster and a trusted minister of Henry VII.

Thomas Sunnyff was committed to the Fleet prison for six weeks, or roughly until the end of May 1507, writing that "in ye meane tyme ye sayd m[aster] Empson examyned ye matt^r & enqueryd [there]of & he could fyend no cause against me".[16] It was becoming clear to John Camby at this juncture that Empson was not going to move against Sunnyff. Nonetheless, the intrepid Camby now visited the warden of the Fleet to retrieve Sunnyff and bring him "afore m[aster] Dudley to Grenwych". Sunnyff, accompanied by his servant, was quickly conveyed to Greenwich by boat, where they found Dudley "in hys Chamber"—suggesting that Dudley either had use of a residence there or more likely that he used one of several locations where the king's councillors held meetings and judicial proceedings.[17] Dudley asked Sunnyff if Camby was present, and when the minister learned that he was not, he ordered Sunnyff to wait outside the chamber door until Camby's arrival.

Soon, Camby appeared and quickly asked Sunnyff if he had spoken to Dudley. Sunnyff revealed that he had not and Camby tried to coerce him into paying the £500 fine. Sunnyff remained resolute in his refusal—a remarkable posture given the perilous situation in which he found himself, but perhaps emboldened by Empson's dismissal of the case. Camby

---

[15] "m[aster] Dudley" is crossed out and replaced by Empson.

[16] The Fleet prison was often used by the chancellor of the duchy of Lancaster, titular head of the learned councillors meeting in the duchy chambers (e.g., T.N.A.: P.R.O., DL 1/2 fo. 84, where an old recognizance that "was nev^r spoken of" became activated and the party was "comyted to prison in the flete"). This is discussed in Horowitz, "Richard Empson", pp. 47-8.

[17] The learned councillors, or lawyers of the king, met at a variety of places, including Westminster, Bridewell, Greenwich, Richmond and Blackfriars (Horowitz, "Richard Empson", pp. 42-3 and n. 71.)

walked off to Edmund Dudley's chambers, and when both Dudley and Camby reappeared in the hall, the former confronted Sunnyff and "sayd to me y^{ese} wordes, 'Sunnyff—agree w^t ye king or ells you must goo to ye tower'".

The obstinate merchant, although realizing his danger, nevertheless refused to pay, saying "it was not ye king['s] will y^t I shuld yeld me gylty of ye thyng that I was never guilty of". Dudley now commanded Camby to take Sunnyff to the Tower of London. Camby, Sunnyff, the warden of the Fleet (who had remained nearby after depositing the party at Greenwich) and Sunnyff's servant located the boat on the Thames, but Camby ordered everyone out of the vessel except Sunnyff. When the warden retorted that he required a discharge for his prisoner, Camby replied "my worde shalbe suffycient discharge".[18] Camby and Sunnyff travelled towards the Tower—presumably Camby rowed—and soon they drifted past it. Sunnyff observed this and Camby said that the gates were shut, probably a reference to Traitor's Gate on the Thames.[19] When Sunnyff protested that the gates were clearly open, Camby insisted on taking him back to his home that night, so that they could return to the Tower in the morning. Once at Camby's house, Sunnyff was locked in a chamber, where he said he was kept not overnight but for four weeks, or until about 26 June.[20]

Meanwhile, a new "quest" was being held at the Grocers' Hall against Thomas Sunnyff's wife.[21] The text of Sunnyff's complaint is unclear at

---

[18] This "oral discharge" was a common occurrence in the reign, and caused much grief for defendants claiming that they had been orally discharged of a debt, or office, but had no written proof to support it. The same was true of "oral appointments" to office. An exchequer list of "wayers, serchers & gawgers of wools" from *c*.1501 noted at the bottom "yt ys thowght that ther ys div^{r}se other wayers serchers and Gawgers in div^{r}s portts of England which Occupy by the kyngs comaundement wherof we have no Record of the kyngs lres patentes in the Escheker" (W.A.M., MS. 12248).

[19] Henry III is credited with constructing the Thames-side gate, called Water Gate, which later became known as the infamous "Traitor's Gate".

[20] This date is crucial to the chronology, although it is not mentioned in the complaint. It is determined from bills submitted to king's bench as the date on which Thomas Sunnyff was incarcerated (T.N.A.: P.R.O., KB 9/453 no. 461; W.A.M., MS. 9260).

[21] It is unclear what Sunnyff meant when speaking of inquests. They seem to refer to actual court proceedings, whether at the assizes for gaol delivery or before the court of the mayor and aldermen of London or one of the sheriffs. It may have also been before a wardmote, which held inquests for, among other things, complaints involving prostitution (I.W. Archer, *The Pursuit of Stability: Social Relations in*

this point, but apparently several people involved in the judicial proceedings tried to approach Dudley to warn him that Alice Damston— who first accused Sunnyff and his wife of some "slander" and was now mentioned as residing in ward in the Counter—might stand as a witness for the defence.[22] Camby was unavailable, and it seems that Dudley never received the message because Damston was freed from her incarceration and testified that she had indeed slandered Sunnyff's wife.[23] As Sunnyff reported it, she "showyd how y^t her mast[er] nor her mastres nev^r knew of ye byrth nor of ye deth of ye chyeld but she sayd [that] it was dede born". Others now testified and confirmed her story.

Elizabethan London (Cambridge, 1991), pp. 78, 249). There is no mention of indictment, which would have required twelve or more citizens to swear under oath that there was sufficient cause to bring a party to a court of law. In 1496, a statute was passed whereby the indictment process, including the jury, could be circumvented by the justices of the peace, using their new ability to present felonies based solely on information (11 Hen. VII, c. 3). Richard Overton, in his *An arrow against all tyrants* (12 Oct. 1646), paraphrased Sir Edward Coke in stating that "by colour of which act, shaking this fundamental law, it is not credible (says he) what horrible oppressions and exactions—to the undoing of infinite numbers of people—were committed by Sir Richard Empson, Knight, and Edmund Dudley, being Justices of the Peace through England" (*The Levellers in the English Revolution*, ed. G.E. Aylmer (Ithaca, NY, 1975), pp. 68-70). This was before Dudley's active service but at a time when Reynold Bray and Richard Empson were already focusing on bonds and holding conciliar court proceedings at the duchy of Lancaster. Neither Empson nor Dudley was a J.P. "through England", but they represented numerous shires at different times, sometimes on overlapping commissions. As J.H. Baker noted, the statute "barely outlived Empson and Dudley", and it was repealed in 1 Hen VIII, c. 6. (J.H. Baker, "Criminal courts and procedure at common law, 1550-1800", in *Crime in England, 1550-1800*, ed. J.S. Cockburn (Princeton, N.J., 1977), pp. 18-19). A defendant could plead not guilty and "put himself on the country" ("po. se.", or "ponit se super patriam"), i.e., bring himself to trial to clear himself (Baker, p. 35.). This is one ploy that Sunnyff apparently tried to use in his struggles with John Camby.

[22] In the 15th century, the two "Counters" were in Cheapside and in the Poultry, and became alternatives to the old custom of having offenders stay in the house of the sheriff. They were used for minor offenders and usually people stayed the night, although longer stays were not uncommon. For operations and costs to prisoners, see a transcribed excerpt from the Corporation of London records in the time of Henry VI (*Munimenta Gildhallae Londoniensis*: i, *Liber Albus*, ed. H.T. Riley, Rolls ser., xii (1859), pp. 522-4).

[23] Sunnyff remarked early in his complaint that Damston lied, "as it apperyth by her owen Confession".

It is at this point that the cause for slander was divulged by Sunnyff: the death of a child at birth. Moreover, according to Sunnyff, the child in question was not only stillborn but also perhaps the child of Alice Damston, not his wife. Given the context of this revelation, it is most probable that the "master and mistress" of Damston were none other than Mr. and Mrs. Sunnyff. Where the demand for £500 fitted in is still unknown at this stage; nor is it obvious what motivated Camby's persistence and Dudley's ongoing interest.

Camby returned to the City, where he learned of Alice Damston's confession and, according to Sunnyff, "knew nott what to doo". In a fit of rage, Camby called those holding—and freeing—Alice Damston "false harlotts for cause [they] sufferd ye quest to speke w^t her, & he [Camby] being not at home".[24] He was not, however, prepared to give up, and next went to visit Alice Damston, convincing her to testify once again that Sunnyff's wife "kylde ye chyeld". She was also instructed to blame a certain official—"[m]aster ffenrother"—for coercing her into lying at the recent court proceedings by saying that the Sunnyffs were innocent.[25]

This Damston did, but those at the proceedings were not convinced, noting that "she varyed so ofte in her sayengs sayd unto m[aster] Dudley y^t y^{ei} could take no evydence by her words bycause Camby caused her to be so dyv^rs in her [tale]". This suggests that Dudley was either at the proceedings or involved in the entire matter against the Sunnyffs upon information given to him by Alice Damston, directly or through Camby. Moreover, there is the possibility that even Dudley was wavering in his belief that there was a credible action against Sunnyff. The examiners now went to the scene of the alleged crime where the "[chy]eld was caste ov'",

---

[24] "False harlot" was a common derogatory phrase at the time. (See, e.g., Corporation of London Records Office, Repertories of the Court of Aldermen 2 (1505-13), fo. 99v, "a false harlet & Userer"; *Norwich Consistory Court Depositions, 1499-1512 and 1518-30*, ed. E.D. Stone and rev. B. Cozens-Hardy, Norfolk Record Soc., x (1938), no. 271, "Thow art a fals harlot", no. 337, "false briber & a false harlot".)

[25] This was in all likelihood Robert Fenrother, goldsmith, one of the masters of the mint beginning in Dec. 1505. His petition to be a master, dated 20 Nov. 1505, was signed by Henry VII and Edmund Dudley after he agreed to enter into an obligation with Dudley to pay ready money and future cash instalments for the office (T.N.A.: P.R.O., C 82/280, 20 Nov. 1505, C 82/284, 14 Apr. 1506; Brit. Libr., Lansdowne MS. 127 fo. 13v (Dec. 1505); *Cal. Pat. Rolls 1494-1509*, p. 453 (20 Nov. 1505)). His role in the Sunnyff affair is unknown, but he did not suffer because of it. Fenrother retained his office in Henry VIII's reign (*L&P*, I.i. no. 185).

an allusion to the possible cause of death or to the disposition of the body after discovery—out a building or off a pier or bridge, but more likely into the Thames rather than into a burial plot. They also heard evidence from other people, presumably in the parish of St. Martin where the Sunnyffs resided. Once again, Sunnyff's wife was acquitted.

Camby now tried to prosecute Thomas Sunnyff on a charge of accessory to a crime—although no crime was found—and he continued to hold the merchant in custody. If true, this denial of customary bail was clearly illegal under the circumstances. Sunnyff told Camby to bring him to the assizes at Newgate because he believed he could be acquitted there just as he and his wife had been acquitted in the recent proceedings.[26] Two officials from those previous venues, Master Bodiham and Master Covell, now visited Camby and asked for Sunnyff's liberty since his wife had been acquitted "& nev[r] no faute coulde be founde in [Thomas Sunnyff]". Camby, more obsessed than ever according to the complaint, said that Sunnyff's freedom would cost him £500. The two officials told Sunnyff of their conversation with Camby, and he again refused to pay. The haberdasher now confronted Camby directly, demanding to know the reason for the £500 fine. Camby admitted that Henry VII desired it, saying that the king once pursued Sir Ralph Hastings until he obtained the manor of Wanstead, which he coveted. Camby did not fail to note that Sir Ralph had died, implying that Sunnyff could follow the same route.[27] The

---

[26] Between ten and twelve gaol deliveries were held at Newgate annually before the judges of the central courts, sitting with the mayor, recorder and senior aldermen. These were for the more serious crimes such as murder (Archer, *Pursuit of Stability*, p. 218).

[27] On 24 Oct. 1493, Hastings entered a recognizance for £1,000 to Henry VII to appear before the king and council in a year and to keep his allegiance—a lifelong Yorkist, he came close to being linked, through his chaplain and household steward, with Perkin Warbeck's conspiracy in 1489 (*Calendar of Close Rolls 1485-1500*, no. 737; *House of Commons, 1439-1509*, ed. J.C. Wedgwood (2 vols., 1936-8), i. p. 434 and n. 6). Earlier in the year he was one of seventeen sureties for the allegiance of John Hayes, and he was singled out from that bond to appear before the king at two future dates (*Cal. Close Rolls 1485-1500,* no. 686). Hastings had purchased a manor years before on the recommendation of Richard Page and Roger Appulton, the former a henchman of Edmund Dudley and business associate of Empson and Reynold Bray, who was named in a bill by Thomas Sunnyff (discussed below); the latter a surety with Page in an early bond (*Cal. Pat. Rolls 1485-94*, pp. 338, 163; *Cal. Close Rolls 1485-1500*, no. 338). The reference in the complaint to Hastings, who died in 1495, remains ambiguous, but he probably had early dealings with those involved in pursuing the prerogatives and finances of the

suggestion was clear: Henry VII knew of Thomas Sunnyff and wanted his money.

Sunnyff replied that "y^f ye kings good grace [knew ye tr]outh of my matt^r he wold not take a penny of me for m^{li} [£1,000]". Camby was adamant and purchased a writ to remove Sunnyff to king's bench, although it is not certain from which judicial jurisdiction he was being transferred.[28] Sunnyff gathered neighbours and business associates together to act as sureties in a recognizance for bail—apparently he was now incarcerated at one of the two Counters under the supervision of the sheriffs of London, where Alice Damston also resided. At the same time, Camby again tried to make Sunnyff pay him £500 for a full discharge of all offences—Sunnyff continued to refuse payment. Camby and Sunnyff appeared at king's bench with James Hobart, the king's attorney-general and fellow councillor of Empson and Dudley, who in Sunnyff's words "com^{a}unded y^t I shuld not be taken to baylle". The recognizance for bail was disallowed. A lawyer who happened to be present approached the bench and said it was against the law to refuse bail, but the judges answered that they "could not [contradict] ye kings Comaundm[ent] in so moche y^t Camby had brougth w^t hym ye kings atto^{r}naye". Sunnyff was committed to king's bench prison at Southwark for a month, from approximately 26 June to 24 July, although, as will be discussed, he probably remained in prison well into November.

---

king. Henry VII did obtain Wanstead, after he sent Thomas Lucas and James Hobart, his solicitor and attorney-general respectively, to the property on 16 July 1498 "for valuying of the same manor" (Brit. Libr., Royal MS. 14 B.xxiv, paper roll). It was at this manor that the king allegedly fell sick in or around 1499 although, as Steven Gunn has suggested to the author, the date may have been much later (*Letters and Papers Illustrative of the Reigns of Richard III and Henry VII*, ed. J. Gairdner, (2 vols., 1861-3), i, 233, 239). Indeed, when the plague befell London in 1499-1500, Henry VII and his court departed for Calais (M. Vale, "The 1490s: continuities and contrasts", in *Fins de Siècle, How Centuries End 1400-2000*, ed. A. Briggs and D. Snowman (New Haven, Conn.,1996), pp. 39-64, at p. 42).

[28] Presumably a writ of *certiorari* was issued to instigate a change of venue by having the records forwarded. Sunnyff may have been scheduled to appear at the Newgate assizes. A less likely possibility is that "king's bench" meant removing Sunnyff from the Counter to another prison. In the will of Richard Shore (d. 1510), a London alderman discussed below, money is bequeathed for the care of prisoners in several prisons, including "Newgate", "Ludgate", "the fflete", "the marshalsey", "the kyngs benche" and "in ev^{r}y of the two Counters in London" (T.N.A.: P.R.O., *Prerogative Court of Canterbury* (Register: Bennett), PROB 11/16).

With Sunnyff tucked away, Camby decided to collect the £500 without his co-operation, or indeed his presence. According to the complaint, Camby seized the haberdasher's lands and goods to levy a £500 fine.[29] As related by Sunnyff,

> [then] for drede of dyeng in p[r]sone in y[e] kings benche, & for losyng of all my goodds, I was fayn to agre to paye y[e] sayd sume of v.C li. [£500] besyed y[e] greatte costs & charge[s] y[t] I was at duryng y[e] tyme of my troubl & enp[r]sonme[n]t, wyth y[e] lose of my goodds & Custom[r]s; Consy[d]eering also y[e] greatt payn, vexa[tion], troubill & enp[r]sonme[n]t, [and] p[r]ncipally y[e] defama[tion] of my good name & fame, y[e] whych [Camby] can nev[r] restore to me [or] satisfye, yf [that] he had gyven a m li. [£1,000].[30]

Sunnyff was defeated and forced to "agree with the king". He noted that Camby "[did] as moche as in hym was to m[u]rder me and my wyeff for he has shortenyd o[r] lyves both and specially my wyeffs". In order to be released from prison, he now had to agree to pay the £500 "in money and bounds ev[r]y penny to y[e] kings grace for fe[a]r [tha]t I shuld have dyed in p[r]son by y[e] meanes of Camby".

According to Sunnyff, however, his ordeal did not end there. A year after his difficulties, in November 1508, a messenger from Camby told

---

[29] This was perhaps accomplished through the writ of *levari facias* or *fieri facias*, addressed to the sheriff. *Levari facias* ordered the seizure of a guilty party's goods and income from lands until the debt was satisfied; *fieri facias* enjoined the sheriff to seize and sell a defendant's property to satisfy a money judgement. The formula for the *fieri facias* writ included the phrase "quod fieri facias de bonis et catallis, &c." ("that you cause to be made of the goods and chattels &c.") (M. Pontani, "Pre-bankruptcy crimes and entrepreneurial behavior. Some insights from American and Italian Bankruptcy laws", *German Working papers in Law and Economics*, (2004), paper 14, pp. 1-29 at n. 3, referencing Black's *Law Dictionary*, ed. B.A. Gardner (7th edition, St. Paul, Minn., 1999). Camby was not averse to purchasing writs for his cause. The seizure is formulaically rehearsed in the king's bench returns (n. 20 above).

[30] Author's punctuation. One is struck by the language, which arguably is the precursor to the phraseology used for the modern day plea of "pain and suffering" and the pursuit of damages in excess of actual loss. Sunnyff no doubt was separated from his wife for long periods of time if these various incarcerations, and durations, took place. In a near-contemporary description of the duties of a gaoler in Kent, one responsibility was to "kepe ev[r]y freman so comytted by comaundement in the fre mannys towre and that he let not his wyf to come to hym and ly w[t] hym at her and his pleasure" (Brit. Libr., Stowe MS. 850 fo. 9).

him to come and "speke w^t m[aster] Dudley in all haste".[31] Sunnyff protested, saying that he had recently "come from m[aster] Dudley but evyn nowe from hys place"—perhaps to make a payment on his obligation.[32] Nevertheless, he was told to meet Dudley, not at his residence but at "ye boarshede at ffysshstreat ende", which was not far from

---

[31] The date is based on the discussion to follow. It is doubtful that Camby, often a stickler for legal formality, would have simply told Sunnyff he was being "summoned" without some legal document to that effect. It is therefore quite possible that Camby secured a privy seal through Dudley to accomplish the same thing, as he probably did to bring Sunnyff to Greenwich by boat. Dudley, Empson and other councillors regularly utilized privy seals near the end of the reign to conduct business and to facilitate judicial proceedings: Empson may have used one to summon Sunnyff before him at the duchy of Lancaster (Horowitz, "Richard Empson", p. 46 and n. 97). The privy seals did not always specify the place of meeting, only the councillor before whom the recipient was to appear, wherever he happened to be situated, or simply the "king and council". Such privy seals carried a penalty for non-appearance, and knowledge of them has come largely from references in other sources—C.G. Bayne said that no privy seal for appearance before the king's councillors was extant for Henry VII's reign (*Select Cases in the Council of Henry VII*, ed. C.G. Bayne, Selden Soc., lxxv, 1958), p. lxxxvii). However, the author has come upon two issued under the auspices of Edmund Dudley. They are reprinted with their original spelling at the end of this article and suggest how Dudley was able to force people such as Thomas Sunnyff to come before him or his colleagues and henchmen in the name of Henry VII. (see appendix)

[32] The story of Empson and Dudley meeting in a garden adjoining their residences to craft evil doings against English men and women is truly legend. It is found, among other places, in Stow (John Stow, *A Survey of London*, ed. C.L. Kingsford, (3 vols., Oxford, 1908-27), i, p. 224). The debunking of the legend is found in Horowitz, "Richard Empson", p. 39. Dudley, however, clearly conducted business at his home, and he built up an archive of written obligations owed to the crown and various "evidences" that occupied much of his time. An inventory of articles in his 20-room house, taken before his execution, listed numerous records found throughout his dwelling, including: "a litell Coffer w^t writyngs, a couffer w^t evydence sealed"; "A coffer with byllys & boxis w^t evidence"; the closet within the great chamber "Wherin ys conteyned div^{r}s evidence & other writyngs aswell belongyng to the seid Edmu^{n}de Dudeley as to dyv^{r}s other p[er]sons"; "dyv^{r}s obligacons conc^{r}nyng the kyng"; and "A boke of the statuts written" (T.N.A.: P.R.O., E 154/2/17). A summary of this inventory, printed in *L&P*, only lists the various rooms and areas of the house and the fact that there was plate, jewels and goods—not official documents (*L&P*, I.i no. 146). The inventory is reprinted in C.L. Kingsford, "On some London houses of the early Tudor period", *Archaeologia*, lxxi (1921), pp. 17-54, at pp. 39-42.

Dudley's house.[33] When Sunnyff arrived at the appointed place, he was greeted not by Edmund Dudley but by Camby and the lieutenant of the Tower, who led Sunnyff "by ye arm w^t on[e] of hys s^{r}v[a]nts as Camby hade Com^{a}undyd" to the Tower of London. Unfortunately, the document is torn and faded near the end, although it can be discerned that Sunnyff referred to a bill he possessed involving "m[aster] Shore m[aster] Knesworth and . . . m[aster] Grove"—who were the mayor and two sheriffs of London in 1505-6.[34] It was presumably from the Tower that Sunnyff wrote this complaint to "Master Bodyham of Watling Street", one of the judges at the early court proceedings who had heard the case against the haberdasher and his wife.[35]

Although the complaint ends here, there is a small scroll tucked inside it that has also been preserved at Westminster abbey. This is the

---

[33] This is determined from the location of the Boar's Head Tavern, made famous in Shakespeare's *Henry IV* as the watering hole of Falstaff and Prince Hal (*Henry IV Part I*, II.iv, III.iii; *Henry IV Part II*, II.iv; also possibly *Henry V*, II.iii). It was on the site later relegated to the statue of King William IV on Fish Street Hill just north of London Bridge. Fish Street, on the east side, ran from Friday Street to Bow Lane, along what is now Great Trinity Lane. It is in proximity to what was Candlewick Street (now Cannon Street), where Dudley's residence was situated. This tavern should not be confused with the Boar's Head across the Thames in Southwark. That tavern, referred to in a Paston letter of 1459 and demolished in 1830, was in fact owned by Sir John Falstaff. He bequeathed it to Magdalen College, Oxford (L. Wagner, *London Inns and Taverns* (1924), p. 80; H.C. Shelly, *Inns and Taverns of Old London* (1909), pp. 21-2; R. Bird, *The Turbulent London of Richard II* (1949), map following p. 156; F. Lambert, "Some recent excavations in London", *Archaeologia*, lxxi (1921), p. 56 and map).

[34] *The Great Chronicle of London*, ed. A.H. Thomas and I.D. Thornley (1938), p. 329.

[35] Roger Bodyham (Bodiham, Bodenham, Bodmin), gentleman of Great Dewechurch and of Watling Street, had a long career in law enforcement and justice for Henry VII. He delivered gaols in Herefordshire during the entire reign, was on commissions of the peace and at one time acted as sheriff of Hereford. He was included in a general pardon of 6 July 1510 (*Cal. Pat. Rolls 1485-94*, pp. 39, 133, 213, 242, 282, 318, 348, 415, 476, 488; *Cal. Pat. Rolls 1494-1509*, pp. 27, 53, 86, 146, 288, 294, 305, 327, 642; *Cal. Close Rolls 1485-1500*, no. 431; *Calendar of Fine Rolls 1485-1509*, no. 176; *L&P*, I.i. no. 38 (m. 17)). Curiously, Thomas Sunnyff received a judgment regarding a forged obligation "[by] the v^{r}d[ic]t of xij men at a nisi p^r[i]us at Herford a fore ye justic[es] of assice [*sic*]" (T.N.A.: P.R.O., STAC 2/25/9, l. 72 (of 105 lines)). The haberdasher may have come before Bodiham at those assizes and obviously trusted him as the recipient of the complaint.

"confession" of Edmund Dudley written on the dorse of the complaint. It is printed in full here.[36]

Sunnyff I crye youe and yor wyeff m^{r}cy and yf ev^r I have ougth at my liberte yf the kings executo^{r}s woll nott restore youe for trouth I woll for ther ys no matt^r y^t I have more remorce yn

Edmonde Dudley

Allso Sunnyff yor reco^{m}pence ougth to come of the kings executo^{r}s for the kinge hadde yor money ev^{r}y grotte and I no penny therof howe be it by Cause I was the executo^r of ye wronge rather than ye shall take reco^{m}pence yf I hade ougth as I have nougth I wolde reco^{m}pence youe my selfe and therfore I shall lowly besech the kinge and hys most honorable Counsell y^t ye maye be reco^{m}pencyd rather than sayll of suche poore goodds as wer myn for verely ye hade greate wronge

By me Ed^{m}do Dudley

If this is genuine, it was written from the Tower of London where, ironically, Dudley was awaiting his fate after Henry VII's death and from where, perhaps, Thomas Sunnyff was hoping to be released.

Upon careful examination of the complaint and the alleged confession, it becomes apparent that Dudley did not, in fact, pen the words attributed to him. It is not in his hand nor is it his signature, since there are examples of both from his will and from numerous documents that he signed.[37] Moreover, if the handwriting of the confession is compared with the complaint, it is evident that the same hand wrote both of them. If Sunnyff did write his own complaint, for it is not written in any official clerical hand, he also recorded a confession for Dudley. This, of course, would be most convenient considering that Dudley was in the Tower. Conversely, both documents could have been copied by one person from originals, perhaps even by Sunnyff. While this cannot be confirmed, the hand is consistent with early-16th century script, when Sunnyff or someone else could have written them. The only certainties, therefore, are that the writer

---

[36] The writer of the confession put an upper case "C" instead of a "B" for the word "By" in the second signature for Dudley. The author would like to thank Dr. Mortimer, keeper of the muniments at Westminster abbey, for sending him a copy of the confession to confirm spelling. Brodie printed the second part of the confession with minor spelling errors and mistaken words (Brodie, "Edmund Dudley", p. 154.)

[37] T.N.A.: P.R.O., SP 1/2 fos. 1-8; C 82 series, Henry VII's reign, *passim*.

was not Dudley, that he wrote both the complaint and the confession, and that the hand is contemporary. How it ended up in the collection of documents housed in the Westminster Abbey Muniments Room and Library is not known.[38] The confession will be revisited in light of similar correspondence known to be authored by Edmund Dudley.

To determine the truth, or otherwise, of the complaint it is necessary to look to external evidence, as well as to analyze more closely both the complaint itself and those persons detailed in the account. A suit was in fact filed by, or on behalf of, Thomas Sunnyff in the form of a bill in king's bench as part of the returns of *oyer et terminer* during the period July-October 1509, within six months of the death of Henry VII.[39] It claimed that men broke into and entered the home of Thomas and Alyce Sunnyff on Tower Rowe in the parish of St. Martin.[40] The couple were subsequently imprisoned, on 26 June 1507, until Sunnyff agreed to pay £500 to Edmund Dudley. The defendants named in the bill included Dudley, Camby, Richard Page (a clerk to Edmund Dudley) and there were others not named.

It is doubtful that whatever documentation might have accompanied this bill resembled Sunnyff's homeric complaint, since any return filed at king's bench would have been in Latin and much shorter in length. More likely, if there had been a longer recitation of the facts it would have mirrored another document stored at Westminster abbey, and also involving this case, with the words "a bill after the form of the law"

---

[38] Documents in the Westminster Abbey Muniments archives include numerous leases, quitclaims and copies of court proceedings from the time of Henry VII, many of them involving the king's ministers, including Richard Empson, Edmund Dudley and Reynold Bray. There is a collection of correspondence to Bray referred to as the Bray Papers (W.A.M., MSS. 16015-16080). One extant document was written by Empson after his incarceration in the Tower of London (W.A.M., MS. 13603, briefly summarized in Horowitz, "Richard Empson", p. 49). The abbey was used as a royal repository for records. One month after the death of Henry VII, payment was made to three officers of the exchequer of receipt for spending five days cleaning out three treasuries that contained the late king's records, including one kept at Westminster abbey (*L&P*, I.i. no. 46, 21 May 1509).

[39] T.N.A.: P.R.O., KB 9/453 no. 461.

[40] Although she is called Alyce (Alice) in various records, her husband referred to her as Agnes in his will (C.L.R.O., Journals of the Court of Common Council 10 (1492-1505), fo. 362v, for Alice; London, Guildhall Record Office, Testamentary Records in the Commissary Court of London, vol. II, 1489-1570, Register 10, fos. 27-28v, for Agnes).

written on the dorse.[41] This bill details, in Latin, a similar charge against Dudley, Page and Camby to the one found in the records of king's bench, and formally states that two pledges of proof (the fictitious John Doe and Richard Roe) attest to the veracity of the complaint. It also avers that on 26 June, in London in the parish of St. Martin in "Tower Rowe", the intrusion took place. The reason for the intervention was the recovery by Edmund Dudley from Sunnyff of a debt, with a penalty totalling £600 for the use of the king, against his goods and chattels and with the threat of imprisonment, unless Sunnyff committed to pay Dudley £500: £200 payable immediately and the rest presumably in written obligations with a schedule for future payments. He was also ordered to keep the peace or suffer damages to the value of £1,000, perhaps a clue to the £1,000 alluded to by Sunnyff in his complaint. At the very least, these two bills provide corroborating evidence aside from Sunnyff's complaint that an alleged violation of him and his wife occurred, involving imprisonment, the possible seizure of property and the demand of £500. The bills also name the alleged perpetrators as Edmund Dudley, John Camby and Richard Page—Richard Empson was not identified in either of them.

The various participants in this intriguing and unfortunate story provide further clues in helping to unravel and then reconstruct what may have actually taken place from 1507 onwards, starting with Thomas Sunnyff himself, by his own admission a wealthy merchant and landowner.[42] Surprisingly, this London haberdasher has left a faint trail of some of his activities, beginning in 1493. In that year, the sheriffs of London were ordered to arrest Sunnyff and have him brought before chancery at a specified date on a complaint of debt for £20 that he had failed to repay. The suit was brought by one William Huette, a servant of John Morton, chancellor and archbishop of Canterbury. The sheriff returned that Sunnyff was arrested and put in prison, and a week later two London haberdashers agreed to act as sureties in obligations for Sunnyff to appear at chancery.[43] As is evident in his complaint against Dudley and Camby, Sunnyff seems to have had a group of professional friends willing to bail him out when the need arose.

---

[41] W.A.M., MS. 9260. It is probable this bill was deposited at the abbey along with Sunnyff's complaint and Dudley's confession.

[42] In his will, dated 27 Mar. 1523, he mentioned his lands, buildings and rents, including properties in Essex and lands and tenements held of the bishop of London in Middlesex. Sunnyff also held both copyhold and freehold lands in Yorkshire (G.R.O., Test. Rec., vol. II, Register 10, fos. 27-28v).

[43] T.N.A.: P.R.O., C 244/142 no. 13(a)(b).

Sunnyff apparently made good on the debt and he does not appear in surviving official records again until 1498, this time as one of nine sureties bound in £500 each to the king for the allegiance of a priest—a large but not uncommon amount of money for a pledge of this nature for a non-noble.[44] This was the first mention of a debt incurred by Sunnyff for future performance—the good behaviour of another party. It is also the first time that the same amount found in his complaint can be located in an official record. It therefore remains to be seen if this obligation as surety for the good behaviour of a first party may have been converted into an actual debt due the crown nine years later, a practice that plagued many in England during Henry VII's reign.[45]

By 1500, Sunnyff was in trouble again, owing money to a widow in London. The sheriffs arrested him and kept him in ward, and once again he found sureties—two of them fellow haberdashers—to take out bonds for his release and appearance in chancery.[46] If the under-sheriffs of London were involved in the arrest, confinement and return of writ, it is suggestive of a link between this matter and the future involvement of Edmund Dudley and John Camby in the tribulations of Thomas Sunnyff in 1507. Dudley, a resident and important citizen of London, was named one of the under-sheriffs in November 1496. He left the office at the end of 1502, but stayed in touch with City officials throughout the reign.[47] If

---

[44] *Cal. Close Rolls 1485-1500*, no. 1051. Sunnyff is called a "mercer" (see discussion that follows). In a similar bond taken in 1492 for a vicar's good behaviour, each surety pledged 1,000 marks (T.N.A.: P.R.O., C 255/8/4 no. 74).

[45] See, e.g., the detailed account by Thomas Lord Dacre to the king's councillors early in Henry VIII's reign involving "diverse bonds and recognizances wrongfully made" during the previous reign. One alleged travesty of justice included his entering into a recognizance for 3,000 marks, taken by the bishop of Durham, "being one of the masters of the chamber", for Lord Dacre to keep the peace. According to Dacre, "Sr Richarde Empson and Edmond Dudeley anon after chaunged the same recognisaunce and made it a dett paiable at the feast of Saint [Michael] the Archangell [29 Sept.]", informing the luckless lord that "the saide late king had soo com[m]anded [hym] to doo". The bishop had since admitted that this was done "againste all right and goode conscience" (T.N.A.: P.R.O., SP 1/1 fo. 72).

[46] T.N.A.: P.R.O., C 244/147 no. 171(a)(b). The clerk made an error in the attached memorandum by referring to Sunnyff as John, most likely because it followed a surety named John. He was correctly identified as Thomas in the original *corpus cum causa* writ.

[47] C.L.R.O., JOR 10, fos. 81v, 230v; C.L.R.O., REP 1 (1495-1504), fo. 119; Edmund Dudley, *The Tree of Commonwealth, a Treatise*, ed. D.M. Brodie

Dudley actively administered the office during this period, he might have had his first encounters with the well-to-do haberdasher;[48] he may even have imprisoned Sunnyff in one of the Counters. Camby was an officer in one of the sheriff's houses in London, where defendants may have been detained before being moved to one of the two Counters.[49] He may also have become familiar with Sunnyff at this time.

There may even have been a personal motive. The Haberdashers' Company obtained the right from Henry VII to be incorporated as the Merchant Haberdashers, along with a new grant of arms, on 13 December 1502. This allowed them to enter into overseas trade, not just domestic manufacturing, to the dismay of the court of aldermen and especially the Mercers' Company, who worked closely with the Merchant Adventurers. Camby, a grocer, may have had business dealings with both the mercers and the haberdashers. Sunnyff was once referred to as a mercer, either by mistake or in reference to an earlier profession, and it is possible that economic rivalry played a part in the Camby-Sunnyff affair, although exactly how or why may never be known.[50]

(Cambridge, 1948), p. 2. In 1506, Dudley submitted a bill to the common council of London requesting that a current of water be diverted to his dwelling in Candlewick Street (C.L.R.O., JOR 11 (1506-18), fo. 20v). It was granted without the need for an inspection, which was usually required (e.g., C.L.R.O., JOR 10, fos. 365v-366v). Dudley was also paid an annual fee from the City chamber for life: £1 6s 8d, which was later increased to £3 6s 8d (C.L.R.O., REP 2, fo. 35).

[48] In his treatise written from the tower, Dudley noted his awareness of the various groups of people with money or influence, including "substanciall marchauntes" (*Tree of Commonwealth*, p. 46).

[49] *Great Chronicle*, p. 349.

[50] I.W. Archer, *The History of the Haberdashers' Company* (Chichester, 1991), pp. 17-18. In 1510, as a result of pressure exerted by the London aldermen, Henry VIII revoked the title of Merchant Haberdashers, although the company remained prestigious throughout the Tudor period. It is interesting that one of the inquests mentioned by Sunnyff was held at the Grocers' Hall. Members of different companies did interact, and co-operate. Richard Grafton, a member of the Grocers' Company, and Edward Whitchurch, of the Haberdashers' Company, became printers and partners, bringing out the 1537 Matthew Bible ("Printing in England from William Caxton to Christopher Barker: an exhibition", Nov. 1976-Apr. 1977, University of Glasgow). Some professions overlapped: William Maldon was referred to as a haberdasher and grocer during Henry VIII's reign (*Actes and Monuments of Matters Most Speciall and Memorable, Foxe's Book of Martyrs Variorum Edition Online* (v. 1.0) <http://www.hrionline.ac.uk/foxe/apparatus/person_glossaryM.html> [30 Dec. 2004]).

The next mention of Sunnyff is found in July 1506, before the common council of London.[51] An entry in the records of the court of aldermen noted that Sunnyff and two others entered into recognizances of £500 each to the chamberlain of the common council for future performance rather than an actual debt. The condition stated that the men were to abide by the orders of Thomas Knesworth, then the mayor of London, and the aldermen regarding any quarrels, transgressions, debts or arbitration with others—in effect to keep the peace and obey the law while the bond was active.[52] It was this Knesworth who was mentioned near the end of Sunnyff's complaint, along with his two sheriffs, Shore and Grove. Sunnyff's two co-debtors in the bond, Richard Covell and Stephen Peacock, later played a part in his complaint. Covell, a tailor and merchant, was revealed as being at the court proceedings that exonerated Sunnyff, and as the man who confronted John Camby about freeing the haberdasher.[53] Peacock, also a haberdasher, met with Camby and told him to stop slandering Sunnyff, whom he referred to as an "honest man".

Given the involvement of these men in the bond and in the tribulations of Thomas Sunnyff, the £500 repeatedly sought by Camby must be related to this obligation. Both Covell and Peacock were party to a bond of £500 with Sunnyff in 1506 and knew well that it was not a true debt but one for future behaviour. As friends, neighbours and business associates, it would therefore be reasonable that they would come to Sunnyff's defence several months later when he was accused of violating the condition of that bond,

---

[51] C.L.R.O., REP 2, fo. 13.

[52] This was a common bond utilized by city officials at their legal proceedings. In 1489, several people were "bounde by way and forme of Recognisaunce" to the mayor of Southampton in "good and lawfull money of Inglond" to abide arbitration. In 1495, a butcher of Southampton was bound "in an obligacion" to the mayor and his successors "w^t a condicion that he kepe the kings peice" (*The Book of Remembrance of Southampton, iii: 1483-1563*, ed. H.W. Girden, Southampton Record Soc. (Southampton, 1930), pp. 73-4).

[53] In 1505, he was one of many merchants receiving a pardon for shipping wools (*Cal. Pat. Rolls 1494-1509*, p. 448). A Richard Cavell was charged with trespassing on certain lands, for which his lawyer responded that the plaintiff "had more than he ought to have"—a novel defence (T.N.A.: P.R.O., C 244/156 no. 279(a)(b)). If this is Richard Covell, he was a landowner as well as a tradesmen, like Thomas Sunnyff (see also T.N.A.: P.R.O., C 241/275 no. 83). A Richard Cavell (Cannell) stood from Stamford in 1497 and 1504 as an M.P. and was described as a merchant of the staple. His will was proved on 11 Nov. 1508, and while he may have been a relation, he does not appear to be the friend of Thomas Sunnyff (Wedgwood, i, p. 166).

namely breaking the peace. They would also want to protect their "investment" as sureties, since both were liable for £500 in the event that Sunnyff defaulted on the bond.[54] John Camby and Edmund Dudley were focusing on this obligation, converting it into a real debt by taking advantage of the legal difficulties of Sunnyff's wife, Alyce, to leverage payment on the bond against her exoneration for an alleged crime. It also explains why Camby wanted to make Sunnyff an accessory, since it would activate the condition of the bond, namely keeping the peace.

Whether Sunnyff did anything in violation of this bond other than the allegation of being linked to the murder of a child is difficult to ascertain. Two months after entering into it, he and his wife required five sureties in a bond for £1,000 taken by the chamberlain of the City in the Guildhall regarding a variance with a single woman named Margaret Westbroke.[55] This suit, however, was a private one without royal implications such as breaking the king's peace. Moreover, the recognizance was vacated in November 1506, in effect nullifying the condition and rendering the bond harmless and of no effect. It therefore appears that Sunnyff's problem stemmed from the uncancelled £500 bond taken before the common council and the troubles associated with his wife's alleged involvement in a murder.

The various external documents and records that shed light on the complaint are often confusing chronologically, but they expand upon what occurred beyond the trip up and down the Thames and the summary imprisonments and alleged extortion of money. J.P. Cooper believed that the date 26 June 1507 referred to Sunnyff's last set of problems and imprisonment, when Richard Page was first mentioned as a henchman of Dudley and Camby.[56] This is not plausible given the existing evidence

---

[54] Forfeitures by sureties were real, and worrisome. On 8 May 1510, Hamnet Harrington wrote to Sir Robert Plumpton that "the shereff of the shire of Lancaster sent a bailife to my house with a wrytt, and hath seysed into the kings hand al my lands & goods vnto such tyme yat ye merchant of London be content of a c li. [£100] which Sir John Luth knight and I were surty to for you". That bond for debt was dated 1 Jan. 1500. Harrington found out that Plumpton received an extension for payment and wrote "I pray you to se a way yat I may be discharged, as shortly as ye can, so yat I may occupy my lands & goods" (*The Plumpton Letters and Papers*, ed. J. Kirby (Camden 5th ser., viii, Cambridge, 1996), p. 189 (208)). "Shortly" it was not to be: the obligation was voided on 9 May 1516 (n. 2).

[55] C.L.R.O., JOR 10, fo. 362v (26 Sept. 1506).

[56] Cooper, p. 121 and n. 113. Cooper ignored, or was unaware of, the bonds recorded by both Dudley and the chancery subsequent to this date, and Sunnyff's

from the waning years of the reign and the beginning of Henry VIII's kingship. Near the end of the haberdasher's stay in Southwark prison, on 21 July 1507, Dudley recorded a debt in his account book of £500 for the pardon of Thomas Sunnyff "for the murdering of the child", confirming the allegation mentioned in the complaint. It was to be paid by giving Dudley £100 in cash and £400 as a written obligation due the crown.[57] If the king's bench bill is accurate, both Sunnyffs were imprisoned twenty weeks ("viginti septimanarum") after the entry into their house on 26 June, dating their incarceration to the first part of November. They therefore remained in prison long after Dudley took the bond for a pardon.

Sunnyff failed to mention this new bond taken by Dudley for a pardon and the discharge of the old obligation, and he apparently refused to abide by it, which most likely kept him in prison. Despite Dudley's recording the debt, it is possible that Sunnyff only reluctantly signed and sealed an obligation for £400, although he appears to have paid the £100 in cash as partial payment for the £500 owed the king. (As mentioned earlier, Sunnyff admitted in his complaint that he paid the £500 "in money and bounds ev[r]y penny to y[e] kings grace".) Through the summer and autumn of 1507, Sunnyff seems to have persisted in refusing to pay the remaining £400 for his and his wife's freedom. If, in fact, the Sunnyffs continued to be exonerated of the crime, as alleged in the complaint, the haberdasher was correct in insisting that he owed the crown nothing, since there was no violation of his old obligation noted in the records of the City of London in 1506.

When Sunnyff's sureties arrived at king's bench in Westminster to post bail, James Hobart, the king's attorney-general, denied it, probably acting on behalf of Dudley or the king.[58] Some of those same sureties appeared in

---

statement that, after being released from prison upon payment to Dudley of cash and bonds, he was approached by Camby "a yere after yt I cam owte of p[r]son", and that he was then "led by y[e] arme" back to the Tower.

[57] Brit. Libr., Lansdowne MS. 127 fo. 46. These amounts differ from the ones recorded in the bill stored at Westminster abbey. The bill, written when Dudley was in the Tower, may have increased the amount paid with the hope of recovering additional cash.

[58] *Cal. Close Rolls 1500-09*, no. 813; Brit. Libr., Lansdowne MS. 127 fo. 48. James Hobart lost his office in 1507 and paid Dudley 700 marks in cash for a pardon in Nov. 1508 (fo. 49v). In an abbreviated list of debts based on Dudley's account book, and purportedly written by Sir Julius Caesar, the pardon is dated similarly but for 800 marks (Brit. Libr., Lansdowne MS. 160 fo. 321, repr. in *Archaeologia*, xxv (1834), pp. 390-3). It has been suggested that his demise came

chancery on 27 October 1507 and were bound in recognizances for Sunnyff's payment of 600 marks to the crown—or £400—in twelve instalments twice a year until 1513. They were entered on the chancery rolls.[59] This may well have been at the time when Sunnyff decided that he and his wife would be in mortal peril if they remained in prison, and these recognizances probably acted as bail bonds and as a means to guarantee Sunnyff's outstanding obligation to Dudley.[60] The recalcitrant Sunnyff had refused to pay more money since the 21 July obligation to Dudley beyond the initial cash offering of £100. Three months had passed, and it would not be out of character for Dudley to demand guarantors for Sunnyff's obligation in return for his freedom—a new bond to pay the old one.

Just five days after Sunnyff's sureties entered into the recognizances on his behalf for the remainder owed on the July bond, Dudley recorded a

---

through the efforts of unforgiving ecclesiasts in England (S.J. Gunn, "Edmund Dudley and the Church", *Jour. Eccles. Hist.*, li (2000), pp. 509-26, at p. 515). Hobart apparently was not well-liked by churchmen because of his actions against them. In a brief petition dated to 1504, Richard Nykke, the future bishop of Norwich, complained to William Warham, the chancellor, that actions of *praemunire* had been troubling clergymen throughout the realm regarding tithes. He noted that one of his priests had received from chancery a writ of *certiorari* (in preparation for transferring a case, presumably to the chancellor) "the wich the enemy of God and his churche Sr James Hubart wold not admytte. My lord, if ye helpe this prest in his mat^r and speke sharply to m. Hubart, I thynke the preists of this dioces shall lyve more at ease than they doo" (T.N.A: P.R.O., SC 1/44/83, 16 June *c.*1504; Gunn, "Edmund Dudley", pp. 516, 524). In Dudley's petition to right the wrongs against numerous people, the abbots of Gloucester and Chichester were listed as "hardlie dealt wth all for pramunires" (C.J. Harrison, "The petition of Edmund Dudley", *Eng. Hist. Rev.*, Vol. LXXXVII (1972), pp. 82-99, at p. 89 (no. 55)).

[59] *Cal. Close Rolls 1500-09*, no. 813. Sunnyff listed his original sureties for bail in his complaint as Master Peacock, Master Catesby, the goodman Godman, John Teasby, the goodman Burdon, John Atwell, Master Baker, Reynold Washe, "with other". One name cannot be read clearly. Those listed in the 12 recognizances for £40 each filed at chancery on 27 Oct. 1507 were Thomas Sunnyff, haberdasher of the parish of St. Martin, London; William Hudson, girdeler; John Teseby, tiler; Otwell Ingyll, William Baker and Reynold Wase (Walsh?), all haberdashers; and John Ball, brickmaker. The condition involved payments twice a year for six years of 50 marks each at specified days down to 1513, for a total of 600 marks (£400).

[60] In an analysis of peace bonds in Cheshire for the period 20 Hen. VI-3 Ric. III, it was posited that a bond with mainpernors was in effect a form of bail (D.J. Clayton, "Peace bonds and the maintenance of law and order in late medieval England: the example of Cheshire", *Bull. Inst. Hist. Res.*, lviii (1985), pp. 133-48 at p. 147).

new bond in his account book for Sunnyff and a surety for 400 marks. Sunnyff now owed the crown £400 (600 marks) for the July bond and 400 marks for this new bond, the latter presumably for a final pardon for all offences.[61] With this new bond in hand, Dudley took his time. He allowed the Sunnyffs to remain in prison for an additional three weeks before taking action to free the haberdasher and to exonerate him of both the 1506 obligation and the allegations against his wife in return for the two obligations now worth 1,000 marks to the king. On 24 November, a privy seal to the chancellor ordered a pardon for Thomas and Alyce Sunnyff for all possible crimes and misdemeanours, murders, corrupt bargains, recognizances, appearance before judges and surety, singling out Thomas for several offences that included bonds for keeping the peace, good behaviour and appearance before the king or his justices.[62]

That Sunnyff continued to be in physical danger after he left prison at the end of 1507, as he himself stated, is possible, although no surviving evidence supporting this claim has been located. On 13 February 1508, several months after agreeing to take out the recognizance in chancery with sureties for future payments, Dudley recorded a payment by Sunnyff of 50 marks as one of the semi-annual instalments due the king for 1,000 marks, a reference to the compounded bond.[63] In late 1508, Sunnyff asserted that he was again taken to the Tower of London without cause. Since Dudley did not record any further payments from Sunnyff after February, it is possible that the haberdasher continued to be obstinate about payment on the bond and spent the last five months of the reign in the Tower. If true, this is further evidence of vindictiveness from an over-mighty minister of Henry VII, for Sunnyff already had a pardon for all conceivable past offences, real or otherwise.

Those involved in the pursuit of Thomas Sunnyff also formed a fiscal and judicial cabal of sorts under the first Tudor, for which several would pay

---

[61] Brit. Libr., Lansdowne MS. 127 fo. 48, 1 Nov. 1507. In the margin is written a note that the bond was not kept because it was recorded earlier. It is doubtful that this refers to the 21 July bond but rather another obligation that compounded the two bonds.

[62] T.N.A.: P.R.O., C 82/307, 24 Nov. 1507.

[63] Brit. Libr., Lansdowne MS. 127 fo. 55v. For the theory of replacing old debts with new ones ("novatio"), see R. Zimmerman, *The Law of Obligations: Roman Foundations of the Civilian Tradition* (Cape Town, 1990), p. 758.

with their lives or their livelihoods after the accession of Henry VIII.[64] The author of the *Great Chronicle* had intimate knowledge of these men, their activities and their final dispositions; he also had access to records of the common council and aldermen's courts.[65] He wrote that in the autumn of 1506, soon after Sunnyff entered into his ill-fated bond with Peacock and Covell,

> this yere sprang much sorwe thorw the land, ffor by meane of a ffewe ungracious personys which namyd theym sylf the kyngis promoters many unleffull & fforgotyn statutis & actis made hunderyth of yeris passid / were now quykenyd & sharply callid upon to the grete Inquyetnesse of many of the kyngis Subgectis as well the Rych as the othyr that hadd any competent substaunce.

He also observed "Yit now & Specially syne Empson & dudley were sett In auctoryte, many moo In numbyr were callid beffore theym ffor many surmysid causis, [of] the which noon escapid wythowth payyng of ffynys lytyll or moch". Sunnyff's situation was clearly based on such a "surmise". The author of the *Great Chronicle* listed some of the old statutes that were now being prosecuted and added to the list "old Reconysauncis & boundis ffor pease or othir suyrtees that any man stood bounde to the kyng In his chauncery or sterr chambyr, Or other of the kyngys courtys". That jurisdiction was expanded to bonds entered into by principals and sureties before London courts. If any of these matters were brought to trial, "Then hadd they theyr ffalse Juryes soo ffyxid unto theym

---

[64] Vergil referred to them as "hangers on" and "aiders and abettors". Hall said that these men brought the names of possible offenders to Empson and Dudley (*Anglica Historia*, p. 151; *Hall's Chronicle*, p. 499). In the pardon issued soon after Henry VII's death was announced, wronged parties seeking redress included those prosecuted "by reason of any light and untrue info[r]macion or wrong surmyses of Custumers Comptrollers or [searchers] or any *p*sones calling theym self promoters" (C.L.R.O., JOR 11, fos. 68ff.).

[65] The author is thought to have been Robert Fabyan, an alderman of London (*Great Chronicle*, pp. xlvii-lxxvi). Stow, who owned and annotated it, believed that Fabyan wrote it (pp. xv-xvii). The latter part of the chronicle ends in the autumn of 1512; Fabyan died on 28 Feb. 1513. Ironically, "Robert Fabyan" was one of two sheriffs who arrested and imprisoned Thomas Sunnyff in 1493 (T.N.A.: P.R.O., C 244/142 no. 13(a)). In Apr. 1503, Fabyan was ordered by the court of aldermen to fulfill his agreement to be alderman"upon payne of enprisonemet". On 20 July, he was excused from office "p[r]textu inopie" (C.L.R.O., REP 1, fos. 135, 139).

that they were well assurid that they wold not passe agayn theyr meyndis, ffor alle was doon In the kyngis name & yit the moost proffyt cam to theyr coffyrs".[66] Apparently, Thomas Sunnyff escaped a false verdict regarding his wife and her alleged murder of a child. The unlucky tradesman and landowner was nonetheless targeted by at least three of these "ungracious personys": John Camby, Richard Page and Edmund Dudley.

Camby may have begun the whole affair in early 1507, bringing it to the attention of Dudley. He was in a position to hear many things. A grocer by profession, he held a job in a sheriff's house and almost lost his office because of his "wayward lyffe".[67] In an interesting observation for the case of Thomas Sunnyff, the *Great Chronicle* noted that people complained about Camby in connection with his "brybory fforcyble Injuryes ffacyng & pollyng and pety Bawdry or covert, by Reason of a stewe yt he kepyd by the watyr side" ("facing" referred to brow-beating and "polling" meant extortion and plundering;[68] "bawdry" was the practice of procuring women for prostitution; and "covert" could have referred either to a hiding place or to something concealed, which makes more sense in the context of "a stewe yt he kepyd by the watyr side", that is, a brothel).[69] In a petition written by Dudley from the Tower, he implies that

---

[66] *Great Chronicle*, p. 334.

[67] *Great Chronicle*, p. 349. He is referred to as John Canby. The author of the *Chronicle* spent a great deal of time discussing the life and demeanour of Camby, and one gets the sense that he knew him personally or had some gripe against him, or both.

[68] Empson and Dudley were accused of "brybory & pollyng" in the City (Gunn, "Edmund Dudley", p. 523). In a defamation case in 1523, one churchmen accused another of saying "Thou art a fals polling prest and a shaver, for thou hast used polling, but I wolnott be polled and shaved on the" (*Norwich Consistory Court Depositions*, no. 294). A "shaver" was one who fleeced, pillaged or plundered.

[69] It is not clear whether laws were rigorously enforced at this time against the keeping of stews and those who worked there, although neither John Camby nor Alice Damston seems to have suffered legally from their professions (see, e.g., M. Ingram, "Regulating sex in pre-Reformation London", in *Authority and Consent in Tudor England: Essays Presented to C.S L. Davies*, ed. G.W. Bernard and S.J. Gunn (Aldershot, 2002), pp. 79-95 at p. 81). An ordinance of 1382 passed by City officials prescribed certain punishments for a "common bawde", or prostitute (*Calendar of Letter-Books . . . of the City of London*, ed. R.R. Sharpe (11 vols., 1899-1912), *Letter-Book H*, p. 189). In 1489, a woman was convicted of being a bawd and, following the 1382 ordinance, was pilloried in Cornhill with a "rayhode" on her head, a white rod in her hand and the cause of her humiliation pronounced, before being conveyed to Newgate (*Letter-Book L*, p. 265). In Edward

Alice Damston was a prostitute.[70] This revelation suggests a clear connection between Damston, Camby's proclivities and side business, and the "facing" that she continued to receive from a promoter and perhaps her procurer—John Camby.

Camby accumulated money through his illicit and illegal activities and later fell in with Edmund Dudley, perhaps when the latter was an under-sheriff.[71] He did whatever the king's minister commanded, and it is not difficult to imagine that he was well-suited for the job of promoter. Camby received the office of weigher of wools, "an office of worshyp and of grete proffytt", on 29 November 1505, after securing a petition signed by Dudley and Henry VII, and after paying for the office in cash and obligations.[72] He also became a keeper of the Counter in the Poultry, which the *Great Chronicle* noted was "contrary [to] the myendis of the

---

IV's reign, the City fathers approved an ordinance "that Keepers of Stews should not harbour men or women at night, under penalty prescribed, and that they should find surety for their good conduct" (*Letter-Book L*, p. 136, 24 Nov. 1475). Defendants often denied such behaviour and ecclesiastical courts dismissed the charges (R.H. Helmholz, "Harboring sexual offenders: ecclesiastical courts and controlling misbehaviour", *Jour. British Studies*, xxxvii (1998), pp. 258-68 at pp. 260-1; and see S. McSheffrey, "Jurors, respectable masculinity, and Christian morality: a comment on Marjorie McIntosh's *Controlling Misbehavior*", *Jour. British Studies*, xxxvii (1998), pp. 269-78). Prostitution was tolerated nonetheless. In Southampton, prostitutes were required to have special identification: a "wenche of the stewys" was fined 8*d* in 1511 "for coming into the towne w^t owt hyr token" (*The Assize of Bread Book, 1477-1517*, ed. R.C. Anderson, Southampton Record Soc., xxiii, Southampton, 1923), p. 53). Prostitution was licensed on manors held by the bishop of Winchester in the Southwark stews. In 1506, there was an attempt to close them, but their final demise did not occur until 1546 (Ingram, pp. 81, 92; Archer, *Pursuit of Stability*, pp. 249-50; J.B. Post, "A 15th-century customary of the Southwark stews", *Jour. Soc. Archivists*, v (1977), pp. 418-28).

[70] See below; Harrison, "Petition", p. 90, no. 76.

[71] Camby acquired sufficient income to afford a household and to spend lavishly. Sunnyff said that when he was imprisoned in Camby's house for four weeks, he was held in a chamber where "I coulde noy speke w^t man nor cheyld but w^t y^em of hys house". The *Great Chronicle* noted that when Camby was arrested "many ffyne Gowne clothis & doblet clothis of sylk" were found in his chamber "which they lay cowchyd or pylid In" (p. 349).

[72] T.N.A.: P.R.O., C 82/279, 29 Nov. 1505; *Cal. Close Rolls 1500-09*, nos. 739, 676; *Great Chronicle*, p. 349. On 17 Nov. 1505, Camby paid Dudley £100 for the weigher's office, £50 in ready money, £50 by obligation. His patent was recorded 12 days later (Brit. Libr., Lansdowne MS. 127 fo. 13; *Cal. Pat. Rolls 1494-1509*, p. 470).

mayer the Shyrevys & alle auctoryte of the Cyte". Dudley and the king were apparently meddling with the perceived rights of the City in order to help Camby, as they did at one time with the appointment of a sheriff. In neither case did it sit well with the London elders.[73] Dudley's work with other legal councillors of the king at the duchy of Lancaster may have also brought Camby into the sphere of Empson and his associates and servants.[74]

Given the circumstances surrounding the relationship between Camby and Dudley, it is probable that Camby concocted the murder story against the Sunnyffs and told Dudley about it. The key witness—a prostitute named Alice Damston who may have worked for Camby at one time— was coerced by him into initially testifying to the murder. In fact, Sunnyff stated in his complaint that Camby had her "in hys kepyng as p^{r}soner . . . by ye space of xvij weks"—probably at the Counter where he was keeper—until she agreed to slander the couple.[75] She was not, therefore, a willing party to the falsehood. However, there are other possibilities. Damston might have been the inadvertent source of the rumour: if it were her child, she may have induced an abortion or it might have been stillborn, and the word got out once the body was discovered. Having a child would not have been helpful to her livelihood, even if she had now

---

[73] *Great Chronicle*, p. 349; and see pp. 332-3 on the promotion for sheriff of William Fitzwilliam by Dudley and the king. Henry meddled far and wide, including getting his man—Richard Empson—appointed as recorder of Coventry, but he failed to obtain a similar appointment for his candidate in York (L. James, "Urban recorders and the crown in late medieval England", in *The Fifteenth Century*, iii: *Authority and Subversion*, ed. L. Clark (Woodbridge, 2003), pp. 163-77 at pp. 171-3).

[74] Late in the reign, Dudley obtained manors and lands that were recovered by Camby and Miles Gerrard (*Cal. Close Rolls 1500-09*, no. 965). Gerrard was receiver-general at the duchy of Lancaster and paid money directly to the king's chamber, or to Dudley, in cash and bonds (T.N.A.: P.R.O., DL 12/3 no. 4; E 404/86, 9 Dec. 1506; DL 41/34/1 fo. 161b, 25 Mar. 1507). He was a squire for the body at Henry VII's funeral (*L&P.*, I.i. no. 201 (p. 16)). For Camby and Empson together, see T.N.A.: P.R.O., KB 9/453 no. 456. For council learned, see Somerville, pp. 427-42. Dudley had his own group of supporters and associates beyond the promoters. These included his brother-in-law, Andrew Windsor; Windsor's stepfather, Sir Robert Litton; and Dudley's cousin, Richard Dudley (S. Gunn, "The structures of politics in early Tudor England", *Trans. Royal Hist. Soc.*, 6th ser., v (1995), pp. 59-90 at p. 81).

[75] Later in the complaint, Sunnyff says that when Damston was scheduled to appear at the Grocers' Hall, men "cam to ye Counter to have ye sayd alyce".

given it up to work in the household of the Sunnyffs. The inference that the body may have been dumped somewhere before discovery supports the notion of an unwanted or stillborn child in need of secret disposal: Camby's "stew" by the waterside would have been a logical location for this grisly act. And if the brothel were less than "covert"—brothels are often a worst-kept secret, as this one was for the author of the *Great Chronicle*—when the body was discovered after being "cast over" it first became linked to Damston.[76] Less likely is the possibility that the child was Alyce Sunnyff's, with the stillborn birth becoming fodder for rumours about a murdered child. A married couple with a legitimate child—they already had a son named George—would have given their stillborn baby a Christian burial.[77] Moreover, Damston admitted that Alyce Sunnyff knew nothing about the dead child.

The end result was a story about a dead child connected to the home of Thomas Sunnyff and his wife. For whatever reason a rumour had made the rounds that Sunnyff's wife had murdered a baby. It probably began with, and was given credence by, the testimony of a prostitute who was forced to lie about what really occurred through the coercive measures taken against her by John Camby. The allegation was subsequently proven groundless in a court of law. This rather lurid bruit reached Dudley's ears through Camby, and the king's minister may or may not have known of its veracity. A search was made in the City records, and one of the "old Reconysauncis" found for possible prosecution that could encompass the alleged murder was the £500 bond of Thomas Sunnyff, a man almost certainly known to both Camby and Dudley.

During the course of Sunnyff's ordeal, it is possible that Camby, and Dudley, tried to rig or "ffyx" a jury to find in their favour against the Sunnyffs, although the haberdasher and his wife seem to have had great success in prevailing against the allegations. One chronicle noted that Empson and Dudley used "false perjured persons . . . which were by their commaundements empanyeled on every [in]quest, that the king was sure to wynne whosoever lost".[78] Perjury was undoubtedly a pervasive practice,

---

[76] In the 1570s, a handful of stews stood in close proximity to the Thames, on the north side where Camby's establishment had operated (Archer, *Pursuit of Stability*, p. 212). Archer noted that many people were brought before Church courts for prostitution who "were guilty of nothing more than the taking in of a pregnant single woman to be delivered". This is one possibility for what may have happened with the Sunnyffs and Alice Damston.

[77] G.R.O., Test. Rec., vol. II, Register 10, fo. 28v.

[78] *Grafton's Chronicle*, p. 231.

and not simply because the London chroniclers wrote about it. Soon after Henry VII's death, the London court of aldermen pursued such perjurers as, for example, on 8 June 1509: "At this co^{r}t it is decreed and adiuggyd that Henry Stockton ffishmonger and Robert Jakes sherman wich aswell by their own confession as other wyse been duly convycte of detestable p[er]iury shalbe disfraunchised from the lib^{r}tie of this Citie forever".[79]

Camby had business dealings with Richard Page who, as a named co-defendant in the formal bill filed by Sunnyff at king's bench, must have had a role in the affair that is not discussed explicitly in the complaint.[80] Page was referred to as a gentleman from Horton, Kent. From early in the reign, he seems to have travelled in the Reynold Bray-Richard Empson circle of officials with connections to the duchy of Lancaster, where Henry VII's councillors often "held court" for the king's prerogative and fiscal rights.[81] In 1490, Page and Bray, with other royal officers, obtained a licence to alienate lands and manors to several of the king's ministers, one being Richard Empson.[82] Page acquired several holdings during the reign—all through government connections—and was later employed by Dudley. In a star chamber proceeding where, among other things, he was accused of pulling a knife on an individual, Page was referred to as a clerk to Edmund Dudley.[83] The author of the *Great Chronicle*, corroborating independent evidence, mentioned Page and Camby as two of the "servantis of Dudley".[84] It is therefore likely that he worked in tandem with Camby during the whole Sunnyff affair.

At the core of Sunnyff's problem was the £500 bond for performance, one that he thought was inactive and irrelevant since he continued to keep the king's peace and to abide by any rulings of the common council of London. Sunnyff said as much in his complaint, telling Dudley that he

---

[79] C.L.R.O., REP 2, fo. 68v.

[80] *Cal. Close Rolls 1500-09*, no. 739 (18 July 1507), where Camby and Page were sureties for a recognizance. Page may have been mistakenly identified as the "servant" of Camby mentioned by Sunnyff in his complaint.

[81] Page was most likely related to his namesake, who died in 1493; that Richard Page was a lawyer from Horton and Shoreham in Kent, a "foreign" J.P. under Richard III who served as an M.P. for Plymouth under both Lancastrian and Yorkist rule, and a royal office-holder who was named king's solicitor in Jan. 1470. He was a friend of Bray, whom he named in his will (J.R. Lander, *English Justices of the Peace, 1461-1509* (Gloucester, 1989), p. 136; Wedgwood, p. 656).

[82] *Cal. Pat. Rolls 1485-94*, p. 338.

[83] *Cal. Close Rolls 1500-09*, no. 774; T.N.A.: P.R.O., STAC 2/25/8.

[84] *Great Chronicle*, p. 365.

"nev^r trespased to pay ony fine". It may have been Dudley who ordered a search into the records to see if the government had anything on Thomas Sunnyff, perhaps before his wife's acquittal, in the form of an obligation or recognizance that could be prosecuted. Dudley had cultivated many friendships in London before working for the king, and these helped him to obtain the office of under-sheriff. His appointment as speaker in the House of Commons at the start of 1504 probably also served him well in this regard. But after Dudley was drawn to "the kyngis court", he began prosecuting the king's fiscal and judicial policies to the perceived hardship of many, although the *Great Chronicle* was quick to point out that "Alle yt he dydd was doon In the kyngys name".[85] In any event, Dudley clearly enjoyed great influence in the City and he took advantage of it when it came to the king's business.

The City officials in London were constantly battling Henry VII and his councillors to maintain their ancient right to keep their books and records private, and beyond the reach of roving royal eyes such as those of Edmund Dudley and Richard Empson or their fellow councillors or servants.[86] Those privileges, many of which were spelled out in the charter of 26 October 1444 approved by parliament in the reign of Henry VI, included the right to "have whatever for the breach of any recognisaunces or securities of the peace may be found to be due to the king by the said mayor or justices". Moreover, if the king or any of his courts desired information about "any indictments of felonies or trespasses other misdeeds or any recognizance or surety taken before [the mayor, recorder, alderman or sheriffs of the city]", the only requirement on the City was "to return the tenor or copies thereof, so that they themselves may freely proceed to determination and execution according to the law and custom of the City, notwithstanding any writs, mandates or precepts of the king". The intent of any royal request was to be related to cases of error.[87]

Henry VII and his councillors did not necessarily follow the letter of the charter, and many forfeited recognizances taken in London were

---

[85] *Great Chronicle*, p. 348.

[86] During the regnal year 1505-6, Fabyan's *Chronicle* recorded that the citizens of London paid Henry VII 5,000 marks for the confirmation of their liberties, 1,000 marks in cash and 4,000 marks in yearly instalments (Robert Fabyan, *The New Chronicles of England and France*, ed. H. Ellis (1811), p. 688). Not mentioned, but hardly surprisingly, payment was to be collected by Edmund Dudley, who retained the written debt in the form of five obligations (Brit. Libr., Lansdowne MS. 127 fo. 4v).

[87] *Calendar of Charter Rolls, 1427-1516*, p. 41.

prosecuted by the king's courts and councillors. Clearly, this caused tension between City and crown. A royal writ, dated 16 May 1506, requested the tenor of a case pending in the Guildhall involving recognizances made by Bartholomew Reed, a former mayor of London, and his two sureties to an alderman. The recognizances totalled £2,606 13s 4d and were acknowledged for the keeping of orphans. The return to chancery stated only the date of the recognizance (25 October 1502) and the condition, but not the disposition of the case. Chancery had tried once before to determine a case pending between these men and another party. The results involved a long recitation of the liberties of London: the mayor and aldermen returned that by the ancient liberties and free customs of the city ("per antiquas libertates et liberas consuetudines civitates")—dating back beyond memory and confirmed by the kings of England, Magna Carta and numerous parliaments—all pleas, and the records and processes of all pleas, begun in the king's courts of the City of London should remain there.[88]

This rationale extended to all recognizances pending actions. When a writ of *certiorari* inquired into a case involving a recognizance of £100 by Alexander Arnold and his sureties, the court at the Guildhall refused to send the tenor to chancery because it would "offend the liberties and customs of the City" regarding recognizances and their execution.[89] The magistrates of London, as with most city officials in England, clung greedily to their jurisdiction and prerogatives in lawsuits. Interference by a strong monarch was always possible, especially when potential forfeitures were at stake. This could be exacerbated by petitions to the chancellor for writs of *certiorari* by disgruntled citizens hoping to obtain more lenient or objective decisions at the hands of royal justices. Chancery was also growing in popularity on the equity side throughout the 15th century, with cases for debt and trespass being sued out by parties directly, without first

---

[88] T.N.A.: P.R.O., C 244/156 no. 91(a)(b); and see Fabyan's *Chronicle*, p. 688, for Reed's mayoralty. The royal government sought to meddle in all aspects of London judicial proceedings. In 1503, a *corpus cum causa* writ was sent to the mayor and aldermen asking for a record of the matter against John and Elizabeth Dowesyng and their appearance at chancery. The reply stated that before the writ arrived, the relevant alderman heard the case before twelve men, noting "also we indite Elizabeth the wife of John Dowsing for avoutrice of hir body often tymes pᵣsented and not amended" (T.N.A.: P.R.O., C 244/152(a)(b)). "Avoutrice" was adultery.

[89] T.N.A.: P.R.O., C 244/156 no. 175(a)(b), 8 Feb. 1507.

going to the City courts.[90] Despite resistance, Henry VII and his councillors enjoyed some success in involving themselves with the various recognizances and obligations taken or pending before the City of London. When the prerogatives of the City and of the monarch clashed, the first Tudor was prepared to use his royal authority to obtain what he believed to be his due.[91]

One of the recognizances discovered in the records by the king's men was the £500 recognizance of Thomas Sunnyff. It would have been just one of many instances where individuals were summoned to pay and discharge debts that the government learned had been entered into years before, including some that the debtors thought had been cancelled or declared null and void based on the conditions.[92] This particular bond gave Dudley the excuse to demand performance of its condition in return for dropping any future suits against Sunnyff's wife for the alleged murder of a child. Camby's—or perhaps Dudley's—inability to interest Richard Empson in pursuing the bond and the case put the burden of carrying out actions against Sunnyff on them and not on Empson's "court" at the duchy chamber. It may, of course, simply have been that Empson felt Dudley, as a former under-sheriff of London with a mandate to seek out old debts owed to Henry VII, to be the best person to handle the case. Whatever his motivation, Empson did nothing to stop Dudley or Camby. The unintended hint by Sunnyff that Dudley, like Empson, may have begun to waver about prosecuting him—that Damston's story "varyed so ofte in her sayengs sayd u[n]to m[aster] Dudley yt y^ei could take no evydence by her words"—may, finally, suggest that Camby, with the aid of Richard Page, was the obsessive pursuer of this wealthy citizen of London.

---

[90] See, e.g., P. Tucker, "Relationships between London's courts and the Westminster courts in the reign of Edward IV", in *Courts, Counties and the Capital in the Later Middle Ages*, ed. D.E.S. Dunn (Stroud, 1996), pp. 117-37; M. Beilby, "The profits of expertise: the rise of the civil lawyers and chancery equity", in *Profit, Piety and the Professions in Later Medieval England*, ed. M. Hicks (Gloucester, 1990), pp. 72-90, at pp. 75-83.

[91] Searches into local records, with the aim of flushing out revenue owed the king, were ubiquitous during the reign. In a session of the peace in North Wales in 1494, justices searched the records to see if freemen were really in possession of land by freehold (J.B. Smith, "Crown and community in the principality of North Wales in the reign of Henry Tudor", *Welsh Historical Rev.*, iii (1966), pp. 145-71 at p. 164).

[92] One example of an "old bond" traced through the governmental records is in Horowitz, "Richard Empson", pp. 46-8.

The use of imprisonment as a coercive means to settle royal matters with cash payments and obligations was also viewed as trampling upon the expressed liberties of towns and cities to prosecute crimes. The summary imprisonments suffered by Thomas Sunnyff seem to have been ubiquitous during the reign, even before Edmund Dudley was actively involved in prosecuting bonds from late-1504. In March 1502, at a common council meeting in London, it was noted that through the mayor's and sheriffs' courts "div^{r}s and many p[er]sones daily been and tyme past have ben arrested atte div^{r}s mennes su[i]ts uppon div^{r}s and sev^{r}all playnts and accons". These suits were often continued by plaintiffs "and p[ro]cede not to Juggement". The result was that defendants were imprisoned for long periods of time "aswell for right finall causes or none as for false feyned and untrue causes to their grete hurt and utt^r undoying". The council decreed that sureties for bail could be taken and that the recorder, sheriff, under-sheriff "or any other p[er]sone lerned" sitting in any of the courts could "discharge all suche p[er]sones defend^{a}unts or defend^{a}unts so arrested and beyng or remaynyng prison^{r}s or yat have put sureties . . . and to comaund them to be deliv^{r}ed oute of prison and discharged of the said accions in or for default of the continuall sute of the said playntif or playntifs".[93] The exception was a legal writ or "Impediment of any suche p[ro]cess". Unfortunately, this edict did not rescue Sunnyff. Dudley and Camby moved him from the Tower to prisons used by king's bench and the duchy of Lancaster, beyond the reach of the City's jurisdiction.

Thomas Sunnyff was not the only London citizen caught in this web of ministerial malice that led to both fiscal and physical persecution. Although it is unclear to what Sunnyff was referring when he mentioned Knesworth, Shore and Grove at the end of his complaint, it was these very men who suffered a similar fate to the haberdasher, most likely at the hands of Edmund Dudley. Thomas Knesworth, a fishmonger, was mayor of London when Sunnyff signed and sealed his ill-fated bond with two colleagues for £500 each to abide by the mayor's orders and follow the law. Knesworth's two sheriffs were Richard Shore and Roger (or Robert) Grove. The nature of the offence allegedly committed by these three men is not entirely clear, but it seems to have become something of a *cause célèbre*. Fabyan's *Chronicle* recorded for 1506-7: "And this yere was Thomas Kneysworth, late mayer, & hys ij shyreffs condemned to the kyng

---

[93] C.L.R.O., JOR 10, fos. 243r-v (session held 18 Mar. 1502).

in great sommes of money, over paynfull prysonement by theym in the marshalsy susteyned".[94] Arnold's *Chronicle* expanded on this, stating:

> Thomas Knesworth, that was Mayre, and bothe his Sherefs, Wyllyam [sic] Shore and Roger Grove, by the Kyngys comaundement, was sent to the Kyngys Benche, under the kepynge of Syr Thomas Brandon, as prysoners, and there remayned unto they were put to ther fine, to pay xiiii . C. li. [£1,400] by the meane of Empson and Dudley.[95]

The *Great Chronicle* recorded that, during the period 1507-8, the three men paid "grete summis of money . . . (one annall saythe xiiij C li. [£1,400]) [and] were delyverd, which were accusid that they hadd mysusid the charge of theyr offycis".[96] Bacon, telescoping events a century later, followed the *Great Chronicle* and wrote that they were imprisoned for abuses in office and paid £1,400 for their release.[97]

What little is known outside the chronicles nonetheless points in the direction of Edmund Dudley and the king, as in the case of Thomas Sunnyff. On 25 November 1506, both Richard Shore and Roger Grove were fined eleven shillings because, "through thayre negligence", a prisoner in their keeping escaped.[98] Whether this and other missteps by the sheriffs and their mayor occurred, or as the *Great Chronicle* suggested they were involved in abuses in office, they found themselves in prison at least by 1507. Towards the end of that year, the aldermen's court broached the situation of these former London officials:

> Itm it is agreed that m[aster] Chamb[r]len [of London] shall fele m[aster] Dudley mynde wheder it will stande w[t] the kyngs pleasure that the mair & aldermen shuld maike labo[r] and sute to his gr[a]ce for m[aster] kneysworth

---

[94] Fabyan's *Chronicle*, p. 689. The Elton-Cooper articles (see above, nn. 8-9) discuss the various chronicles related to the reign, their authors and their objectivity, or lack thereof.

[95] Richard Arnold, *The Customs of London, otherwise called Arnold's Chronicle*, ed. F. Douce (1811), p. xliii. Richard Arnold, the probable author, died in 1521. He may have confused Richard Shore with William Shore, a mercer in London (*Cal. Close Rolls 1485-1500*, no. 203).

[96] *Great Chronicle*, p. 336. The annotation may have been made by John Stow.

[97] Francis Bacon, *History of the Reign of King Henry VII*, ed. J.R. Lumby (Cambridge, 1885), pp. 209-10.

[98] T.N.A.: P.R.O., E 404/86, 25 Nov. 1506. They were active as sheriffs from the summer of 1505 to the summer of 1506 (T.N.A.: P.R.O., C 245/45 no. 1; C 244/156 nos. 11(a), 54, 108-9, 116; C 244/158 no. 15(d)).

and other aldermen that been endited. And also to understande his mynde touchyng a gen^rall pardon.[99]

This was in December, about the same time that Dudley was negotiating with Thomas Sunnyff for a pardon. Moreover, it is implicit in this entry that the king was directly involved in the fate of the imprisoned London officials.

Dudley's mind and the king's pleasure soon became apparent. In February 1508, Knesworth, Shore and presumably Grove entered into three recognizances each, with different sureties, to pay £300 to the king.[100] Five days later, the same day that Thomas Sunnyff made a 50 mark payment against his obligations totalling 1,000 marks, all three men acknowledged debts to the king, taken by Edmund Dudley, in return for a pardon.[101] The total due, £1,133 6s 8d, was split between them, with Knesworth and Shore owing £500, and Grove £133 6s 8d. Each had to pay certain amounts in cash, with the rest pledged in a recognizance and an obligation. Their plight paralleled that of Thomas Sunnyff: recognizances pledged and enrolled at chancery and additional payments to obtain a pardon for their freedom. If this was the situation Sunnyff was alluding to in his complaint, he was referencing another unfair case brought against London citizens through the efforts of Edmund Dudley and Henry VII.

Sunnyff may or may not have been aware that others found themselves in similar situations, and not just the citizens of London. The *Great Chronicle* noted that many subjects "were dayly takyn In dyvers cuntrees of England & broughtht unto the Towyr and othir prysonys of london, as the marchalsy the kyngys Bench Newegate & the ij Countours, where they Remaynyd to theyr dyspleasurs long afftir".[102] In a strikingly similar case

---

[99] C.L.R.O., REP 2, fo. 35v, 14 Dec. 1507.

[100] T.N.A.: P.R.O., C 82/360 no. 1527 (*L&P*, I.i. no. 731(7); *Cal. Close Rolls 1500-09*, no. 849 (4 Feb. 1508)) for Knesworth; C 82/361 no. 1596 (*L&P*, I.i. no. 749(16); *Cal. Close Rolls 1500-09*, no. 855(iii) (8 Feb. 1508)) for Shore. *L&P* does not mention that the amounts due were £300. A search for a similar recognizance for Roger Grove (or Grene as it is sometimes read) came up empty. Both Grove and Knesworth received pardons on 22 Feb. 1508 for trade offences, which may be related both to their incarceration and to their release (*Cal. Pat. Rolls 1494-1509*, pp. 550-1).

[101] Brit. Libr., Lansdowne MS. 127 fo. 56.

[102] *Great Chronicle*, p. 343. Elton believed that the *Great Chronicle* author and other London writers were biased towards London and projected City woes as national afflictions (Elton, "A restatement", p. 3). It is evident from the thousands of bonds filed, recorded, enrolled and prosecuted during the reign involving every

with language familiar to Sunnyff, a gentleman from Norfolk named Thomas Baynard (or Banyard) found himself taking a journey reminiscent of the haberdasher from Ludgate. Baynard, along with Christopher Moy and George Clough, was to appear before Richard Empson and the councillors meeting at the duchy chamber during Hilary term 1507. Baynard had been named to several commissions for the king, including the gaol delivery in Ipswich. From 1494 he delivered the gaol in Great Yarmouth; and in 1503, Moy was on this commission as well.[103] Baynard also became a deputy to the bailiff of the port of Yarmouth. This availed Baynard little, however, and all three men were ordered to appear before the councillors again at the Easter term, when Baynard "was comytted to the flete & ther r'maigned a great space".[104]

The entry in the duchy council book relating this incident gives no reason for Baynard's initial summons before the king's councillors or the cause of his incarceration. After this long imprisonment, he was "r'moved into the Tower of lond & ther r'maigned as p'soner unto the first day of Marche in the xxiij^d yer of the king[s] reign [1508]". What happened next reflects a familiar pattern in the latter years of Henry VII's reign: Baynard "than *agred w^t the king*[s] [grace] for vj^{xx} li. [£120] & so was deliv^{r}d owte of p'son And than also m[aster] chauncello^r [Empson] commaunded me to deliv^r his said obligacon which was only for his apparence for the said matters As apperith in the term before &c."[105] The "me" in question was probably Richard Trust, a servant of Empson responsible for delivering bonds for him.[106] In this instance, yet another citizen of England was forced to "agree with the king" in order to be freed from prison.

Much like the complaint of Thomas Sunnyff, there was more going on than this recitation of events suggests. During Baynard's imprisonment at the Fleet, on 4 July 1507, he paid £100 to Dudley—£35 in cash and £65 in an obligation—for the discharge of an escape allowed by him and others at Yarmouth, this separate from the £120 that he "agreed" to pay for his non-

---

county, and persons high and low who could potentially become a "Thomas Sunnyff", that the author of the *Great Chronicle* had a much better view of the landscape beyond London than modern historians have afforded him.

[103] *Cal. Close Rolls 1500-09*, nos. 348, 476; *Cal. Pat. Rolls 1500-09*, pp. 86, 360 (with Moy).

[104] T.N.A.: P.R.O., DL 5/4 fo. 102v. Hilary term began on 11 Jan. and ended on 31 Jan.; Easter term began on 15 Apr. and ended on 8 May. The Fleet, of course, was the prison of choice for Empson and his fellow councillors sitting at the duchy.

[105] Author's italics.

[106] For Trust, see T.N.A.: P.R.O., DL 5/2 fos. 107v, 109v.

appearance (the escape was presumably the reason for his troubles in the first place). The financial arrangement with Dudley did not immediately free him from prison, however, and it was only in March 1508 that a petition by Baynard for a pardon from all concealments, escapes and other possible crimes was signed by both Henry VII and Richard Empson. He received his pardon on 8 March.[107] Baynard, like Sunnyff, was dealt with harshly over a period of time in the name of upholding the laws of the land. They both suffered the "Tudor" penalties for breaking those laws, including imprisonment, entering into bonds and the purchase of pardons, and were subject to the whims of the king's ministers. Although escapes and non-appearance were now being prosecuted on a large scale, based on Henry VII's policy of adhering to the laws, Baynard's imprisonment and multiple fines were beyond the law. If he had taken out a customary bond for his office as deputy, the only penalty accruing to him should have been forfeiture on that bond for non-performance while in office, which included escapes.

The end of Thomas Sunnyff's ordeal, and that of others like him, coincided with the death of Henry VII in April 1509. Almost immediately after the arrests of Empson and Dudley, numerous complaints were filed in returns of *oyer et terminer* held between 1 July and 1 October 1509 in thirty-six counties. These came flooding into king's bench between January and April 1510, while Dudley and Empson languished in the Tower on charges of constructive treason, no doubt to distance their behaviour from that of the dead king. The complaints carefully eschewed mentioning any wrongdoing by Henry VII, given the current resident on the throne, and most blamed their problems on Empson, Dudley and their cohorts, such as Richard Page and John Camby.[108] The reason for this outpouring was the belief that, after the arrests of the two main exponents of the shadier side of royal policy, which avoided casting aspersions on the deceased king, the young Henry VIII would be receptive to righting the wrongs of his father's reign. This the new king encouraged.

A general pardon issued on 24 April 1509, after Henry VII's death was made public, included "certeyn recognisaunces and many other offences done and comytted before the x day of Aprill last past".[109] The only

---

[107] Brit. Libr., Lansdowne MS. 127 fo. 45; T.N.A.: P.R.O., C 82/311.

[108] See T.N.A.: P.R.O., KB 9/453, *Baga de Secretis*. For commissions to flush out any grievances, see Elton, "A restatement", pp. 20ff.

[109] C.L.R.O., JOR 11, fos. 69ff.

exceptions were "detts and accompts", leaving the door open to collect on any written bond deemed a debt. As mentioned above, although no "recognizance revolts" occurred during Henry VII's reign, largely because entering and paying upon written bonds was a way of life by 1485, the pardon implied that one might have been in the offing had the first Tudor survived awhile longer and continued a policy that often included extortion, bribery and illegal activity.[110] The new monarch sought to put the realm of England "in good quietenes of mynde and out of all doubt and fere to be troubled or vexed in their bodyes or goodes" by the king or his officers because of "offences done and comytted in the king his seid faders days". Henry VIII ordered the justices of the peace and the sheriffs to stop all "misrule" and to imprison those responsible for the problems of late "w^tout bayle or mainprise" until the king was informed: a touch of irony given what had transpired with Thomas Sunnyff. The young king asked his subjects not to take the law into their own hands, "and that ev^ry man that fyndeth hym greved or wronged sue for his remedye at the co[mm]en lawe or to the kings grace and his Counsell by bill of complaint and they shall have Justice mynistred w^t reasonable spede and lawfull favour". Thomas Sunnyff, haberdasher of Ludgate, took the new king at his word and filed a bill of complaint.

Those involved directly or tangentially in the case of Thomas Sunnyff were met with justice in the new reign. A week after the death of Henry VII, John Camby, Richard Page and others—including Empson and Dudley—were excluded from the new king's general pardon, and many lost their offices and spent time in gaol.[111] On 4 September, Camby ("keper of the compter in the pultrye") and two other gaol keepers were ordered by the aldermen's court of London to be "removyd from their saide sev^rall offices and from thensforth never to enioye the saide offices nor any of theym tooccupie".[112] Camby was imprisoned with many other

---

[110] Although London traditionally kept tight vigil over possible unrest at the beginning of a new reign—as they did from 25 Apr. to 20 May 1509 with the accession of Henry VIII—business did not return to usual immediately. More than a month after Henry VII was buried, various crafts of the City were named on 25 June "to watche daily at the gates" from 6.00 in the morning to 8.00 in the evening. Soon after, the common council noted "whiche watche contynued till the iij^de day of Julij And thenne surceased the day watche kept at the gates Nev^rtheles the nyght watche contynued still &tc." (C.L.R.O., JOR 11, fos. 66ff., 81v-82; C.L.R.O., REP 2, fo. 63v.)

[111] *L&P*, I.i. no. 11(10).

[112] C.L.R.O., REP 2, fo. 71.

promoters but, to the dismay of the author of the *Great Chronicle*, he was eventually released.[113] Page was named in an indictment against Dudley detailing an alleged attempt to overthrow the government; his role was that of messenger between Dudley and other conspirators.[114]

Dudley and Empson were arraigned for treason in the summer of 1509. Dudley heard the charges against him on Monday 9 July, before the Guildhall in London. He pleaded not guilty on 16 July and was convicted two days later. Empson was taken to Northampton castle on Wednesday 8 August, where the charges were presented before a jury, which then found him guilty.[115] One of the jurors originally empanelled to hear the case against Dudley was Stephen Peacock, friend and neighbour of Thomas Sunnyff. He was unable to sit, however, because he lacked lands worth 40s a year.[116] Both ministers remained in the Tower for another year.[117]

---

[113] The *Great Chronicle* noted that the people were not happy with the release of these men, including "the enlargyng of Tofft & Canby" (p. 365). Henry Toft was another promoter operating in London.

[114] *L&P*, I.ii. no. 1548.

[115] Empson was tried and convicted on the Wednesday before the feast of St. Lawrence (10 Aug., a Friday). At Richmond palace on Sunday, 14 Oct. 1509, a payment of £12 16s was made "for the costs and charge of Sr Richard Empson and for horsse hyre from the to^r of london to Northampton and from ther to london ageyn" (Brit. Libr., Add. MS. 21481 fo. 15v; *L&P*, II.ii no. 1443, listed as £17 16s). In the same month, a future Tudor minister, who rose and fell in similarly spectacular fashion, received a grant of Empson's house, *le parsonage*, in St. Bride's, London: Henry VII's almoner, Thomas Wolsey (*L&P*, I.i. no. 218(13). Dudley first appeared at the Guildhall the Monday after the quindene ("quinzaine") of St. John the Baptist, whose feast day fell on 24 Jun. (Brit. Libr., Lansdowne MS. 511 fos. 137v, 148v-149; *L&P*, I.ii. nos. 1548-9). The list of inventory for Edmund Dudley's house included 157 bows and 35 sheaves of arrows (T.N.A.: P.R.O., E 154/2/17, not mentioned in *L&P*, I.i. no. 146). Empson and Dudley were accused of gathering armed men to overthrow the government, and perhaps this inventory was used (or fabricated) to support that allegation, which ultimately led to their convictions and executions. For the early historiography of the charges, see Horowitz, "Richard Empson", p. 45. Brodie at first believed that the treason charge should not be "arbitrarily dismissed", but later felt that "the charge seems baseless" (Brodie, "Edmund Dudley", p. 151; *Tree of Commonwealth*, p. 9).

[116] *L&P*, I.ii. no. 1549.

[117] One must wonder why Dudley and Empson, convicted of treason in the summer of 1509, were not executed until more than a year later. If the hope had been to keep alive two loyal officials who had taken a "fall" for a Tudor monarch and pardon them at some point—a strategy used intermittently through the reign of Elizabeth I—there may have been enough ongoing anger and distaste for Henry

They were executed on Tower Hill on 17 August 1510, with neither man able to raise support from friends in high places, if indeed they had any by the end of Henry VII's reign.[118]

Stephen Peacock, fellow haberdasher and resident of Ludgate, became the mayor of London in 1532, the first of his company in almost half a century. He bequeathed certain possessions to St. Martin Ludgate, where

---

VII's policy to ensure that this did not happen. The *Great Chronicle* hinted that the queen may have wanted to keep them alive, for reasons unknown. Things probably looked bad for them by Mar. 1510, when messengers with letters and writs were sent to escheators in different counties, as well as to the mayor of London, to find possible royal rights in the lands held of the late king's mother, Sir Richard Empson and Edmund Dudley (*L&P*, II.ii. no. 1445). In any case, their situation became untenable after Henry VIII's first progress through the country in the summer of 1510, when he was approached by numerous people claiming to have been wronged by Empson and Dudley. (Henry VIII was in Easthampstead on 21 July; Reading on 28 July; Romsey on 4 Aug.; Bewley on 11 Aug.; and Canforde on 18 Aug. (*L&P*, II.ii. nos. 1446-7)). During that journey, the king sent a message to the constable of the Tower "Chargyng hym that they should shortly afftir be put to execucion" (*Great Chronicle*, pp. 365-6). See also N. Samman, "The progresses of Henry VIII, 1509-29", in *The Reign of Henry VIII: Politics, Policy and Piety*, ed. D. MacCulloch (Basingstoke, 1995), pp. 59-73 at p. 60.

[118] Chrimes believed that neither Empson nor Dudley had powerful relatives or friends (S.B. Chrimes, *Henry VII* (1977), p. 317, n. 2). It would be useful to see if that holds true, especially given the land deals, office appropriations and business associations that both men cultivated. For example, in a draft will dated 12 June 1508 for Sir Richard Beauchamp, Lord St. Amand, after a list of executors the following was added: "And also I make and ordeigne ov^rsear of this my saide last will and testament Edmund dudeley esquire Whome I praye and require to se the p[ro]myssis truly executed and p[er]formyd according to this my Last Will and Testament" (Brit. Libr., Add. MS. 4521 fo. 132). His will was acknowledged at chancery on 18 June 1508 and enrolled a month later, giving Dudley, among other things, parcels of property and the governance and marriage of Beauchamp's son (*Cal. Close Rolls 1500-09*, no. 937). Dudley's role as overseer was not mentioned in the *Calendar* summary of the enrollment. Writs of *diem clausit extremum* went out on 3 July (*Cal. Fine Rolls 1485-1509*, no. 878). It has been noted that Dudley's cousin, Richard, offered Thomas, Lord Darcy, £200 to entreat Henry VIII to spare his life (Gunn, "Edmund Dudley", p. 524, citing T.N.A.: P.R.O., C 1/303/62). Brodie and Gunn suggested that Reynold Bray may have been his patron, but of course he was long dead by 1509 (*Tree of Commonwealth*, p. 3; Gunn, "Edmund Dudley", p. 523). The executions were mentioned in the various chronicles of the time, e.g., the Bradford MS.: "Audley [*sic*] & empsey behedid" (M.R. McLaren, *The London Chronicles of the 15th Century: a Revolution in English Writing* (Woodbridge, 2002), p. 220, reprinting an entry on fo. 74 for the period 1510-11).

he was buried.[119] Thomas Sunnyff received a cancellation of the debt
enrolled at chancery on 27 October 1507, but not until March 1511; he had
already paid most of it to the royal coffers.[120] As a piece of historical
irony, a John Camby entered a monastery in Oxfordshire in 1511, where
he remained until his death in 1522. A few months later, Thomas Sunnyff
began preparing his last will and testament before dying in 1523. He
requested to be buried in St. Martin Ludgate near the image of St.
Katherine, patron saint of haberdashers.[121]

The question remains of what to make of the "confession" of Edmund
Dudley. One might first ask whether Dudley had the ability or freedom to
correspond with allegedly wronged parties from the Tower. There is, in
fact, evidence that he could and did. An unnamed justice of the peace
wrote to Dudley reminding him that he had been fined £20 for "the kings
use" for not taking sufficient sureties for a man's bail. Apparently, the
justice learned that this was illegally imposed, perhaps from the
proclamation issued in the new reign offering to hear complaints against
false fines and bonds. He asked Dudley "that ye will cause the kyngs most
honorable Councell to be movyd that I may be restored to my money
ageyn for I paid yt as I am credible informed ageyn[st] all good right and
consiens". Dudley replied that "it is trew I had this xx li. & paid it to the
kings gr^ace", telling the J.P. that "in my Consiens yow o[u]ght to have it
ageyn". However, all Dudley could offer was to ask for his prayers and to
note that "if I were of power I wold restore you myself".[122] It is interesting
that the letter-writer asked Dudley to contact the king's council, which is
what the ill-fated minister said he would do for Thomas Sunnyff in his
confession. Dudley also suggested that he would repay the J.P. if he could;
in the confession to Sunnyff, Dudley noted that if he were free of the
Tower "I wolde reco[m]pence youe my selfe".

Similarly, Sir John Spencer also wrote to Dudley, "being in the Tower
of London", regarding his inability to obtain the manor of Bosworth as a
result of Dudley's unfair dealings with the current owner. Spencer asked
Dudley to "certify to the King and Lords the truth and playnes of the

---

[119] Archer, *Haberdashers*, pp. 10, 16, 34, 37. Haberdashers resided in two main
areas of London: Ludgate Hill and the parishes around St. Paul, and the parish of
St. Magnus, possibly near London Bridge.
[120] T.N.A.: P.R.O., C 82/360 no. 1540; *L&P*, I.i. no. 731(20).
[121] *L&P*, I.i. no. 924(17); III.ii. no. 2648(20).
[122] T.N.A.: P.R.O., SP 1/231 no. 167, signed "Ed dudeley". It is not known if the
J.P. ever received Dudley's reply, which appears below the letter.

premises with your own hand for my suyrte in my premises"—another request for Dudley to entreat the king's council for relief.[123] Hence, it is possible that Dudley wrote to Sunnyff, not as a confession but as a reply to correspondence from the haberdasher that is now lost.

The confession could still be dismissed as a simple forgery, written by or for Thomas Sunnyff to give extra weight to the truthfulness of his complaint at a time when Dudley was in custody awaiting trial or execution. Accusations of forgery were not new to the haberdasher. In his will, Sunnyff said that he was accused of forging documents pertaining to a land transaction, an allegation that he flatly denied.[124] This denial is also found in the star chamber proceeding noted earlier, where he accused a jury of, among other things, perjury.[125]

However, there is another source that is comparable to this admission of wrongdoing by Dudley, and it suggests that the confession stored with Sunnyff's complaint was genuine. It also provides further information about the allegation of the murdered child and Alice Damston. The information is found in the copy of a petition made by Edmund Dudley,

---

[123] Brit. Libr., Add. MS. 75308, Althorp Papers, vol. viii. See a summary of the letter in C. Richmond, "Patronage and polemic", in *The End of the Middle Ages? England in the 15th and 16th Centuries*, ed. J.L. Watts (Stroud, 1998), pp. 65-87 at pp. 85-6. In Sep. 1504, when Dudley entered Henry VII's service as a councillor and prosecutor of bonds, he and Richard Fox, bishop of Winchester, Giles, Lord Daubeney, Thomas Lovell, Richard Empson and James Hobart, knights, and several others recovered Bosworth manor and then released and quitclaimed it to Dudley and his heirs (*Cal. Close Rolls 1500-09*, no. 317, enrolled 23 Nov. 1507).

[124] G.R.O., Test. Rec., II, Register 10, fos. 27ff.

[125] T.N.A.: P.R.O., STAC 2/25/9. This is a replication in answer to the jurors. Although dealing with land deeds dating back to the reign of Henry VI, it can be dated at least to the end of Apr. 1509—Sunnyff refers to "o^r late sov^{r}eign lorde kyng hary ye vijth" (l. 35). Sunnyff seems to have been vexed by recurring legal problems in his life. He accused his adversary, a relative named Robert Sunnyff, of giving "evydens secretly & p^{r}vely to this seyd jure" (l. 11). He suggested that the jury was bribed "for on[e] grett consideracyon whiche causyd them to fynd the seid dede forged" (l. 15). Sunnyff asked for several witnesses to hear the testimony of a man on his deathbed, who swore that the documents were legitimate. One of those witnesses was his stalwart friend, the redoubtable Stephen Peacock (ll. 56-8). This case must have upset Sunnyff greatly; he talked about it at length in his will, although he asked God to "forgyve the soule off the seid Robert Sunnyff and I forgyve hym as I wold god shuld forgyve me all suche vexacious and [trouble?] as he before tyme hath [put?] me unto and in likwyse I besech Ihs to forgyve the [said?] of the meyntenaunce and supporting that he dyd ayenst me in the seid mat^r'" (G.R.O., Test. Rec., II, Register 10, fo. 28v).

mentioned above, published in 1972 by C.J. Harrison.[126] Although there are several clerical errors, including a reference to Edward Dudley instead of Edmund, the document appears to be a bona fide list of people whom Dudley felt were wronged by him and the king. It was written soon after he was found guilty of treason at the Guildhall on 18 July 1509. Harrison suggested that Dudley's petition must have been kept a secret, since he could find no reference to it during the time of Dudley's imprisonment and execution, or indeed later.[127] However, Dudley's confession to Sunnyff clearly alludes to this petition, and there may have been others, either as lists or as individual letters sent to the king's councillors for review and consideration.

In the introduction to the petition, Dudley stated that he had asked Sir Thomas Lovell and Richard Fox, bishop of Winchester, two of Henry VII's trusted ministers now advising the new king, to make amends for those wrongly treated, "forasmuch as the mynde and last will of the said late kinge, was especially that Restitution should be made to all persons by his grace wronged contrary to the order his lawes, wch thinge would in my poore mynd be specially Regarded". In his confession to Thomas Sunnyff, found with the complaint, this is, in fact, exactly what Dudley said he would do: "I shall lowly besech the kinge and hys most honorable Counsell y^t ye may be reco[m]pencyd." While clearly laying blame on Henry VII and contradicting himself in suggesting that wrongful actions were never intended to be carried out, he noted in his petition that both churchmen and laymen

> were bound to his grace or to others to his vse in great somes of money, some by Recognizance, and some by obligacon wth out any condicon, but as a simple and absolute bonde payable at a certayne day, for his grace would haue them soe made: It were against reason and good conscience, these manner of bondes should be Reputed as perfect debtes: for I thinke verily his inward mynde was never to vse them, of those there are very many.

---

[126] Harrison, "Petition", pp. 82-99. It was John Yonge, master of the rolls and an executor of Dudley's will, who copied Dudley's petition into a book (Kingsford, "London houses", p. 21). The surviving copy was made from Yonge's copy (Harrison, "Petition", p. 83). Yonge was also the recipient of the warrant ordering the cancellation of Sunnyff's 1507 bond and may have put two and two together regarding the veracity of the haberdasher's troubles.

[127] Harrison, "Petition", p. 85 and n. 1.

Dudley was in a position to know the "inward mind" of the king. The outward mind, however, was that of a monarch promulgating a policy of calling in debts, especially those related to upholding the laws of the realm and the prerogatives of the king; his ministers followed this policy with impunity. Even to his death, Dudley never strayed from this purpose, whatever remorse he may have sought to portray. In his petition, he wrote that he did not compile the list so that "all these persons hereafter wrytten should be Restored to all the paymentes" that they made on the bonds. Rather, he felt that such debts should be "Reasonablie compounded wth accordinge to the waight of the matter". The sources for the list in his petition were the various books and files of bonds that he kept, including his personal account book, signed on each page by Henry VII.[128] It is telling that, despite his major role in this royal policy, he sought to distance himself from the very actions that he pursued. In the treatise that he wrote to Henry VIII while awaiting execution, he exhorted the new king to rule by law, rather than by prerogative, and that he should not "for any cawse of his owne, enforce or oppresse any of his subiectes by imprisonement or synister vexacion, by privie Seale or lettres missyves, or otherwise by any of his particuler counsellours, but to draw them or entreate them by dew order of his laws".[129] Edmund Dudley, in offering advice on the behaviour that the new king should avoid, in return, he hoped, for sparing his life, was actually stating his own job description from at least 1504 until his arrest.

Among the eighty-four entries in the petition are two interesting references to people who had been wronged, and curiously they follow each other—curiously because the people involved are mentioned in Sunnyff's complaint.[130] The first, in referring to a previously-listed person forced to pay a large sum of money "contrary to the order of lawe", states "Item, Li[ke]wise knesworth Shore and Greene payed for a light cause". It was rightly stated in the analysis of the petition by Harrison that "Greene" was probably Grove, noting that in February 1508, three London aldermen named Knesworth, Shore and Grove paid a large sum of money in cash and bonds for their pardons (Knesworth was, in fact, mayor and the other

---

[128] Brit. Libr., Lansdowne MS. 127. Excerpts are found in Brit. Libr., Harleian MS. 1877 and Lansdowne MS. 160. For other copies, see Gunn, "Edmund Dudley", p. 517 and n. 57.
[129] *Tree of Commonwealth*, p. 36.
[130] Harrison, "Petition", p. 90, nos. 75, 76.

two men sheriffs when they allegedly broke the law).[131] Dudley suggested
that they were wrongfully dealt with, although he does not mention the
fact that he was involved with their imprisonment and negotiations for
settlement with the king.

The next printed entry is more revealing: "Item one Simmes [sic] a
haberdasher wthout ludgate payed and must pay 500^{li} for light matters
onely vpon surmyse of a lewd queane." It is difficult enough for the
modern reader to make out the name Sunnyff in the surviving records,
especially with the various interpretations of spelling and interchangeability
of "u", "n" and "f". Nevertheless, there is no doubt that this haberdasher
was in fact Thomas Sunnyff, who in his will asked to be buried in the
parish church "without Ludgate". Furthermore, this was his £500 debt for
allegations made by a prostitute, or "lewd queane". That person can only
be Alice Damston, named in the complaint as being coerced into
slandering the merchant and his wife.[132] Dudley's implication, however, is
that it was Damston who made the allegation, contradicting Sunnyff's
story of her coercion by Camby and Dudley to swear to the charge of
murder. Regardless, it was Thomas Sunnyff who unconsciously confirmed
that Dudley knew the truth about Damston when he noted in the complaint
that Damston "varyed so ofte in her sayengs sayd unto m[aster] Dudley".
It is reasonable to expect Dudley to blame Alice Damston rather than
admit to forcing her to lie, if indeed Sunnyff was telling the truth. Given
the background of John Camby, and his interaction with Damston
throughout the whole affair, it is not difficult to lay blame at the
promoter's feet, especially after the woman denied any wrongdoing by the
Sunnyffs.

The allusion to "paid and must pay" referred to the cash that Thomas
Sunnyff had already handed over to Dudley and the king, with the
remaining sum spelled out in a recognizance for twelve semi-annual
payments of 50 marks each—totalling £400—originally made on 27
October 1507 by Sunnyff and his sureties. The fact that payments stopped
in 1511 suggests that Sunnyff had, in fact, "reasonably compounded" the
obligation. Since the cancellation was countersigned by Richard Fox,
bishop of Winchester, and other councillors, it is safe to assume that either
Dudley's petition, or Sunnyff's complaint and accompanying "confession",

---

[131] Harrison, "Petition", p. 98, n. 75. A possible "light cause" for these men has
already been discussed above.
[132] Harrison could not identify this "Simmes", as he spelt it, but noted the
definition of a lewd queen (Harrison, "Petition", p. 98, n. 76).

was given credence by the new regime.[133] At the same time, Sunnyff's ongoing obligation to make semi-annual payments for two years after the death of Henry VII is an example of money still being paid in the early years of the new reign despite the proclamation to cancel illegal bonds: the councillors of the new king, knowingly or not, heeded Dudley's advice and did not simply let people off the hook. Indeed, Henry VIII and his ministers continued to take obligations and recognizances for payments to the crown, and to collect on many that were contracted in the previous reign, a continuation of royal policy not fully recognized by historians.[134] In fact, the exchequer, seeking to regain its stature (and fees) for taking bonds and cash, had to be reined in during the first few years of the new reign so that the chamber could continue to administer the policy of the old reign.[135]

Finally, there is the king. Henry VII must have known what was taking place with Thomas Sunnyff, at least from July 1507. When Dudley, according to Sunnyff's complaint, told him to "agree with the king", there was little doubt that Henry VII, who signed each page in Dudley's account book, had first-hand knowledge of what his minister was doing with the London merchant. Henry also signed Sunnyff's pardon in November, a practice he was wont to follow with Empson, Dudley and other councillors.[136] In the confession accompanying Sunnyff's complaint, Dudley expected the vexed resident of the City to believe that Henry VII was the prime mover behind this affair, referring to himself as merely the "executo^r of ye wronge", and stating that the "kinge hadde yor money, ev^{r}y grotte, and I no penny". It would hardly benefit a doomed man, who at one

---

[133] *L&P*, I.i. no. 731(20).

[134] D.M. Brodie hinted at this continuation of payments on bonds taken in Henry VII's reign, stating that "most of the recognizances for the payment of loans or fines which were cancelled at the opening of Henry VIII's reign" had in many cases "been paid up" (Brodie, "Edmund Dudley", p. 149). Elton also noted a continuation of payments (Elton, "A restatement", p. 19, n. 107). J.R. Lander's claim that a large number of bonds were cancelled without payment has been disputed in M.R. Horowitz, "Policy and Prosecution in the reign of Henry VII", *Hist. Research*, Vol. LXXXII, no. 217 (Aug. 2009), pp. 412-58. [Chapter Three]

[135] See M.R. Horowitz, "An early-Tudor teller's book", *Eng. Hist. Rev.*, Vol. XCVI (1981), pp. 103-16 [Chapter Nine].

[136] E.g., T.N.A.: P.R.O., C 82/280, Nov. 1505, signed by Henry VII, James Hobart, Richard Empson and Thomas Lucas; C 82/284 (Apr. 1506), signed by Henry VII and Edmund Dudley.

point tried to escape from prison, to blame wrongfully the father of the only person who could possibly pardon him: Henry VIII.[137] Whether Henry VII was involved earlier—and Camby's threats were given as if they came from the king—cannot be determined. The chronicles were quick to explain that Empson, Dudley and other promoters acted on behalf of the king, invoking his name to justify their actions. In the case of Thomas Knesworth and two sheriffs, it was believed that "by the kyngys comaundement [they were] sent to the kyngys Benche".[138] What can be said about Henry VII and Thomas Sunnyff is that the king knew what was going on and that the haberdasher found this hard to believe.

Henry VII was the conductor in this orchestrated attempt to bring his citizens to heel, with the resulting legitimate actions and wrongful prosecutions pursued by overzealous ministers and their servants who nonetheless took their cue from their monarch.[139] Vergil, in England since 1502, told how victims such as Sunnyff could be worn down and forced to pay money simply to end their suffering: "You could have seen daily in the halls of Empson's and Dudley's houses a host of convicted persons awaiting sentence, to whom wretchedly evasive replies were given, so that they were exhausted by the duration of the anxiety and voluntarily gave up their money".[140] Those who suffered had little recourse while the king

---

[137] Dudley's confession to Sunnyff would probably have been read by royal officials during transport, forcing him to temper his language. Regarding his attempted escape, in his will he wrote of his concern for his servants and his brother, Peter, "all whiche p[er]sons I am sure are in daunger for ony lewed demen[r] entendying to have escapid owt of the Tower how leyt they dydd as my kynesmen & srv[a]unts to have savyd my liff knowing for how false a matter I was attainted" (Preston, Lancashire Record Office, DDCL 298). The author is most grateful to Christopher Whittick of the East Sussex Record office, Lewes, for allowing him to use his photocopy of this version of Dudley's will, which supplements the many missing portions of the will preserved in T.N.A.: P.R.O., SP 1/2.

[138] *Arnold's Chronicle*, p. xliii.

[139] John Guy has observed that "minister" in Tudor times meant "servant of the king", with the responsibility of responding to what the king wanted. They were not public servants or ministers "of state" (J.A. Guy, "Thomas Wolsey, Thomas Cromwell and the reform of Henrician government", in *The Reign of Henry VIII, Politics, Policy and Piety*, ed. by Diarmaid MacMulloch (St. Martin's, 1995), pp. 35-57 at pp. 39-40). Empson and Dudley should be viewed in this light.

[140] *Anglica Historia*, p. 131. According to Hay, who translated Vergil, Empson and Dudley were treated more harshly by the author in the 1513 edition than in the 1534 version, which was softened by Cromwell (*Anglica Historia*, p. xxii). As Hay

lived. As Grafton wrote in his *Chronicle*, "learned men in the lawe . . . would say [that] to agree is the best counsayle that I can geve you".[141] The haberdasher from Ludgate was just one of many forced to "agree with the king" and later complain about his ill treatment at the hands of royal ministers following a royal policy to extreme lengths.

However, in this instance both the perpetrator and the victim jointly agreed that a citizen of the realm paid dearly for untrue allegations and false debts. When the call for redress resounded across England after the death of Henry VII, the price for justice was high for Edmund Dudley and Thomas Sunnyff: the cost of one life and the near destruction of another.

---

noted, Sir John Dudley, Edmund's son and later the duke of Northumberland, was not overly fond of tales related to his father.

[141] *Grafton's Chronicle*, p. 231. A variation of this advice is found in the *Great Chronicle*: "the Best Counsayll they coude gyve theym was ffor to ffalle to agrement, ffor they durst nott speke In theyr cawsys" (p. 335).

Appendix

Two privy seals for the use of Edmund Dudley, Northamptonshire Record Office, Stopford Sackville MSS. nos. 149, 396

Privy seals were liberally used by the king's councillors to summon parties before them or the king's courts for a variety of causes. Richard Empson made special use of them as chancellor of the duchy of Lancaster and *ex cathedra* head of a group of legal councillors prosecuting the laws of the land and the prerogatives of the king.[142] For example, at one meeting at a duchy chamber it was noted that a privy seal was to be sent to Thomas Mare to appear before the king's learned councillors during Easter term "to answere to suche things as shalbe obiected ayenst him".[143] Edmund Dudley could also move the privy seal and he made wide use of it. In the letter by a J.P. sent to Dudley while imprisoned in the Tower, discussed above, the writer reminded him that "I appered before you by privy seale and cowed not be dysmyssed till I paid xx li.".[144]

Among the Stopford Sackville manuscripts preserved at the Northamptonshire Record Office are two extant privy seals, MSS. no. 149 and no. 396, both written on behalf of Edmund Dudley.[145] The first is dated at Richmond (the rebuilt royal residence of Sheen in Surrey) on 19 February; no year is given. The catalogue states that it was sent to John Mordaunt. This is probably incorrect. Dudley came into royal service to search records and prosecute obligations in the autumn of 1504, although he worked for the king in other capacities before that time;[146] Mordaunt

---

[142] Horowitz, "Richard Empson", p. 46; T.N.A.: P.R.O., DL 5/4, *passim*, one of the two books at the duchy recording the work of the learned councillors.

[143] T.N.A.: P.R.O., DL 5/4 fo. 101v. The word "you" is crossed out and "him" written after it, as if the clerk recording the entry started to use language for the actual privy seal.

[144] See above, n. 122. (T.N.A.: P.R.O., SP 1/231 no. 167). A summary of the letter is in *L&P*, suppl. I.i. no. 92, but does not mention that the writer said he was summoned by privy seal.

[145] The author is most grateful to Mr. Charles Stopford Sackville for permission to read and transcribe these two documents.

[146] See Brit. Libr., Lansdowne MS. 127 fo. 1, for Dudley entering the service of the king on 9 Sept. 1504. He was already in the confidences of the Henry VII by the beginning of 1504, when he became speaker in parliament (26 Jan.). In Oct. 1502, he entered a recognizance with two men, including the customer from Southampton, John Dawtry, to pay the king £200 by Christmas, probably for customs duties. It was paid ahead of time, on 24 Nov. (Brit. Libr., Add. MS. 59899

died some time between September and November 1504. The privy seal is dated 19 February, so it must date from at least 1505, if not later.[147] The privy seal was authored by Robert Samson, one of the privy seal clerks and also a clerk of the council.[148] The recipient had ten days from receipt of the privy seal to appear before Dudley, presumably in London.

The second privy seal, dated 15 December from the Tower of London, was penned by another clerk of the privy seal, Thomas Robyns. It was addressed to more than one person, and the subtext of the letter implies that the recipients had previously been summoned, perhaps by chancery writs. They were ordered to appear before Dudley and other unspecified councillors. Rather than give a time limit, the message was to appear "in all goodly hast". Both privy seals suggest an ambulatory court and council. They also involved not insignificant penalties for non-appearance.[149] Finally, they are short, ambiguous yet pointed and undoubtedly unnerving for those in receipt of such royal missives.

Stopford Sackville MS. no. 149

> By the king
> We woll and straitly charge you that ye be and psonally appier befor o[r] trusty Counsayllo[r] Edmonde dudeley squier whersoev[r] we shalbe in this o[r] royame w[t]in tenne dayes next aft[r] the sight of thies o[r] l[ette]res taunswer unto suche things as at yo[r] comyng shalbe laid and obiected ayenst you in our behalf. Not faylling herof upon payne of Cc li.
> Richmond xix feb   R Samson

---

fo. 115). During the period Sep. 1501-Sep. 1502, a receiver for Reynold Bray kept a list of payments, which included 4s in expenses "to mete mayster dudley & John Ruts to schewe them the valewe of all the man[r]s by iiij days" (W.A.M., MS. 4023). Dudley had been on a commission in 1501 in Sussex to inquire into concealed royal lands (*Tree of Commonwealth*, p. 7).

[147] See Horowitz, "Richard Empson", p. 41 and n. 52, for Mordaunt's death. Steven Gunn has suggested that, if the catalogue is correct, the privy seal might have been directed to John Mordaunt, son of Sir John, who claimed to have been harshly treated by Dudley over the inheritance of his father's lands.

[148] *L&P*, I.i. nos. 20 (p. 18), 438 (3 m. 24).

[149] Privy seal summons to the council sitting in star chamber continued to be utilized well into Henry VIII's reign, with penalties varying between £100 and £500 (J.A. Guy, *The Cardinal's Court, The Impact of Thomas Wolsey in Star Chamber* (1977), p. 83).

Stopford Sackville MS. no. 396

By the king

We wol and straitly charge you that almn^r excuses and dilaies laide apart ye and ev^{r}y of you be and psonnally appere afore o^r trusty Counsaillo^r Edmond dudley squier and oth^r of o^r Counsaill whersoever we shalbe w^{t}in this o^r roy^{me} in all goodly hast upon the sight of thies o^r l[ette]res taunswere to suche things as at yor coming shalbe obiected ayenst you on oure behalf not failing herof upon payne every of you of C li.

Tow^r of London xv Dec   Robyns

CHAPTER SIX

"CONTRARY TO THE LIBERTIES OF THIS CITY": HENRY VII, ENGLISH TOWNS AND THE ECONOMICS OF LAW AND ORDER[*]

Introduction

I mentioned earlier my desire to write an article about Henry VII's attempt to control the political winds emanating from English cities and towns. These could be hotbeds for supporting rivals to the king and it was not easy to make the royal presence felt—let alone feared—by city elites running their own show.

Henry's policy of prosecuting penal statutes, the laws of the land and the various types of obligations owed the crown went into effect over time. It was not difficult for him to fold these activities into holding municipalities accountable for their loyalty at the expense of their fee farms and liberties. These are explained below. This was true for cities

[*] Reprinted with permission. The article was first published online in *Historical Research* (2009) and later in print, Vol. LXXXV, no. 227 (Feb. 2012), pp. 32-56. A paper that formed the basis for the article and an impetus for additional research was presented at *The 17th British Legal History Conference*, 4-7 July 2005, University College, London.

The initial phrase in the title, "contrªy to the libties of this Citie", is found in Corporation of London Records Office, Repertories of the Court of Aldermen, 2 (1505-13), fo. 32 (5 Oct. 1508). In referring to London, Stow used the more general phrase "in hurte, preiudice or derogation of the franchises, liberties, & priviledges of the said cittie" (John Stow, *A Survey of London* (1603), ed. C.L. Kingsford (3 vols., Oxford, 1908-27), i., p. 253). The author would like to thank John Guy and Steven Gunn for their thoughts on an early draft of this article, and Penny Tucker, Paul Cavill and James Lee for their insightful and beneficial comments on a later version. All errors and omissions are solely through his own efforts or lack thereof.

and towns outside London, as well as for London itself: the City was always fighting to preserve its inherent and ancient rights going back to William the Conqueror. There definitely could be friction between town and crown, but in the end Henry VII was able to secure loyalty and minimize potential threats from population centers when unrest bubbled up during his reign.

What Henry did was utilize bonds to place financial and judicial constraints on cities, along with constant vigilance by his trusted councilors to ferret out forfeitures from those who broke the law. Henry's men also populated commissions of the peace in every county, ensuring that the king was represented along with the laws of England. This was at the expense of local lords who traditionally viewed their county towns as their own—a situation that was slowly dissipating in the aftermath of the Wars of the Roses. The end result after almost a quarter-century of Tudor rule was a country of municipalities that had been drawn closer to a developing "national" government and law. This in turn led to a sense of "realm" as opposed to "shire", although local politics and influence remained.

The article included a brief history of the town-crown relationship along with a discussion of several cities, with emphasis on the two major ones that could be considered adversarial targets and dangerous to the king: London and York. With London, I decided to illustrate the tension taking place at the end of the reign between the City fathers and the crown and its ministers.

Although there is a separate chapter on promoters and the dark side of Henry VII's policy [Chapter Seven], I spent time here talking about aspects of this behavior in London and the reactions that occurred there. It included steps taken to protect London records from the prying eyes of royal informers. In the end, the first Tudor king developed working relationships with the cities and towns of England, but it was on his terms.

On 8 February 1507, more than twenty years after Henry Tudor acquired the English crown in 1485 as King Henry VII, a royal writ was sent from chancery to the mayor, aldermen and chamberlain of London pertaining to a merchant named Alexander Arnold. It requested information regarding a lawsuit pending in the London Guildhall involving a recognizance of £100 entered into by Arnold and his sureties.[1] A recognizance was a legal debt in the form of a bond involving a variety of promises from one party to another, recorded at a legal tribunal or court, or before a royal department such as the exchequer or chancery. It was similar in scope and application to the sealed written obligation used for centuries in England at all levels of society—including royal administration—that had developed into a "credit" instrument of exchange in an era of limited specie. The recognizance had become a ubiquitous form of administering justice and finance as a matter of policy during the reign of the first Tudor king, especially where conditions stipulated future good behaviour or appearance at a court or before a judicial body.[2] In this instance, information was most likely being sought about Arnold as a responsible party for the inheritance of the orphans of Harry Wynger, since he was an executor of their deceased father.[3]

The reply from the London officials to chancery for this request for information about a case before the Guildhall, however, was no doubt more than the king's officials bargained for, let alone desired. The court

---

[1] T.N.A.: P.R.O, C 244/156, no. 175(a)(b), 8 Feb. 1507. This is mentioned in M.R. Horowitz, "'Agree with the king': Henry VII, Edmund Dudley and the strange case of Thomas Sunnyff", *Hist. Research.*, Vol. LXXIX (2006), pp. 325-66, at p. 351 and n. 89. [Chapter Five] Arnold appears in chancery records as a merchant, mercer and "gyrdeler" (*Calendar of Patent Rolls, Henry VII, 1494-1509*, pp. 269, 381, 441; T.N.A.: P.R.O., C 244/155, no. 49(a)).
[2] H. Hall, *Studies in English Official Historical Documents* (Cambridge, 1908), pp. 246-8; Horowitz, "Thomas Sunnyff", pp. 325-6. For England as a credit society before the reign of Henry VII, see, e.g., M.R. Horowitz, "Policy and prosecution in the reign of Henry VII", *Hist. Res.*, Vol. LXXXII, no. 217 (2009), pp. 412-58 [Chapter Three]; P. Nightingale, "Monetary contraction and mercantile credit in later medieval England", *Economic History Review*, 2nd ser., xliii (1990), pp. 560-75; D. Youngs, "Estate management, investment and the gentleman landlord in later medieval England", *Hist. Res.*, lxxiii (2000), pp. 124-41, at p. 140; K. Wrightson, *Earthly Necessities: Economic Lives in Early Modern Britain* (New Haven, Conn., 2000), p. 120. Wrightson seems to view "conditional bonds" as a 17th-century invention, when in fact they were in use for centuries (p. 175).
[3] Penny Tucker suggested to the author that the case was probably resolved successfully through mediation or arbitration.

refused to send the particulars of the case to chancery—and therefore to the jurisdiction of a royal court—because it would "offend the liberties and customs of the City" from time out of mind and by the authority of the monarch, parliament and Magna Carta. Those particulars encompassed all pleas begun within the king's court in the City, and all records, processes and recognizances, including their prosecution and presumably their collection upon default.[4]

While perhaps not a typical response to a royal directive, to understand more fully the sentiment behind both this request from royal officials and the rejoinder by town magistrates it is important to place this potential confrontation in the context of both the liberties and rights of English cities at the end of the 15th century and the royal policy being implemented by Henry VII and his councillors and officials.[5] For at the heart of these conflicting interests was a desire on the part of the king and his government to establish and enforce law and order and royal authority throughout the realm, while at the same time seeking out sources of revenue to attain financial security and solvency.[6] Municipalities such as London, for their part, endeavoured to maintain their inherent customs of adjudicating and administering local disputes—and reaping the financial rewards from such activities—without royal interference. This development

---

[4] Tucker suggested that chancery writs such as *corpus cum causa* and *certiorari* seem rarely to have transferred a case to chancery, and perhaps related more to arranging bail for "strangers" to London (see also P. Tucker, *Law Courts and Lawyers in the City of London 1300-1550* (Cambridge, 2007), pp. 153-4). As will be discussed, there were both economic and "law and order" considerations for such enquiries into local cases by the first Tudor king's administration.

[5] A similar response is found in H. Hall, *Select Cases Concerning the Law Merchant*, ii: *Central Courts, A.D. 1239-1633* (Selden Soc., xlvi, 1930), no. 49 (29 Oct. 1504): the king's demand for the tenor of a case before the mayor of London's court was met with the response that cases or information could not be removed to royal courts (except in instances of error), by authority of London's charter, of former kings of England, of "Magna Carta and of very many Parliaments".

[6] Through his policies and unwillingness to alienate acquisitions after his triumph at Bosworth Field, Henry became the greatest royal landowner in England since William the Conqueror (T.B. Pugh, "Henry VII and the English nobility", in *The Tudor Nobility*, ed. G.W. Bernard (Manchester, 1992), pp. 49-110, at pp. 83-4). Charters issued in the 15th century reflect an escalating royal interest in the workings and administration of local governments, and their ability to maintain law and order (S.H. Rigby and E. Ewan, "Government, power and authority 1300-1540", in *The Cambridge Urban History of Britain*, i: *600-1540*, ed. D.M. Palliser (Cambridge, 2000), pp. 291-312, at pp. 310-11).

of "corporate identity" accelerated in the 12th century and was well established by the time Henry VII became king.[7] At the same time, town dependence on royal authority dated back before the Conquest, and except in times of royal weakness, when opportunism proffered greater town autonomy, the monarchy sought to maintain control over municipalities for support and stability.[8]

Nevertheless, any such desire for quasi-independence on the part of the urban elites became more a wish than a reality during Henry's reign. In the end, it was the king who trumped the towns at their own game by pleading the same law and custom as a way to expand royal jurisdiction, the culmination of many years of erosion of local autonomy.[9] Moreover, the resulting acknowledgement of, and adherence to, the law "of the realm" as the umbrella over local laws and customs helped to condition the inhabitants of England to resolve most conflicts with parchment rather than with pikes. In this respect, a crown-town perspective was in harmony: during Henry's reign, both local and central courts, in tandem with intermittent parliaments, sought to maintain order and to eschew local discord that affected the social, economic and political life of the realm.[10]

Furthermore, the second half of the 15th century witnessed the increasing popularity of equity law as a desirable alternative to both common law courts and local jurisdictions. This situation was not lost on the mayors, burgesses and aldermen of English towns, or on Henry VII.[11]

---

[7] D.A. Hinton, "The large towns 600-1300", in *Camb. Urban Hist.*, i. pp. 217-43, at p. 238.

[8] D.M. Palliser, "Towns and the English state, 1066-1500", in *The Medieval State: Essays Presented to James Campbell*, ed. J.R. Maddicott and D.M. Palliser (2000), pp. 127-45, at pp. 127-9, 134-6.

[9] R.B. Dobson, "General survey 1300-1540", in *Camb. Urban Hist.*, i. pp. 273-90, at p. 283. It has been suggested that the shift of power from local governments to the centre paralleled Louis IX's attempt to control and regulate French towns (J. Campbell, "Power and authority 600-1540", in *Camb Urban Hist.*, i. pp. 51-78, at p. 74).

[10] S. Gunn, "Henry VII in context: problems and possibilities", *History*, xcii (2007), pp. 301-17, at p. 310. All medieval kings—and the author would argue early modern as well—were habitually worried about law and order in towns (Palliser, "Towns and the English state", p. 136).

[11] See J.A. Guy, "Law, lawyers and the English Reformation", *History Today*, xxxv (Nov. 1985), pp. 16-22, at p. 16; Horowitz, "Thomas Sunnyff", p. 351. Although there was a decline in judicial business at the London sheriffs' courts, some of it could have been made up in the mayor's court (C.W. Brooks, *Lawyers, Litigation and English Society since 1450* (1998), p. 179). There was also a big

The recognition of the law as a viable remedy for present or future disputes contributed to the ongoing growth and importance of what had become the fount of law in England: parliament. Indeed, contrary to the long-held view that Henry VII's parliaments were rubber stamp sessions, it has become clear that debate, law reform and disagreements with the king were not uncommon occurrences.[12] Finally, the increasing perception of a "whole polity" developing in the reign between the king, parliament and city officials and elites is evident in much of the surviving documentation.[13] Bringing the accountability for local governance into the fold of "national" justice and administration was a necessary if not sufficient advance in the maturation of both a crown-town alliance of mutual interests and of the king *in* parliament, where more and more towns were represented during the 15th century as they received charters from their monarchs. Henry VII and his ministers pursued a policy of finance and order that, more for pragmatic than purposeful reasons, fortified this building block for state formation. How the policy was

---

drop in the number of complaints brought at Colchester in the 1490s and 1510/11 (R.H. Britnell, "Colchester courts and court records, 1310-1525", *Essex Archaeology and History*, 3rd ser., xvii (1986), pp. 133-40). Tucker noted that while the common law courts maintained their ability to summon city cases, the court of chancery began taking over the supervision of those cases and officials in the 15th century. She also determined that there was a marked decline in activity at both the courts of common pleas and king's bench between the mid-15th and mid-16th centuries (*Law Courts and Lawyers*, pp. 352-5). Documentation, or its dearth, is a key problem since it appears that equity law was on the rise at chancery and before the various early Tudor conciliar groupings, as it were (Gunn, "Henry VII in context", p. 303). However, the increased use of arbitration and settlement before court pleadings may skew all these observations. See, e.g., the apparently successful use of arbitration during the 15th century in Cheshire (D. Tilsley, "Arbitration in gentry disputes: the case of Bucklow hundred in Cheshire, 1400-65", in *Courts, Counties and the Capital in the Later Middle Ages*, ed. D.E.S. Dunn (Stroud, 1996), pp. 53-70).

[12] P.R. Cavill, "Debate and dissent in Henry VII's parliaments", *Parliamentary Hist.*, xxv (2006), pp. 160-75, at pp. 163-9, 175. Cavill notes that the parliamentary rolls for the reign lack a record of debates or bills not enacted, and that the early view of an autocratic "new monarchy" presented by J.R. Green over a century ago was based on a lack of understanding that evidence of most parliamentary activities does not exist. But see also Gunn's continental view (J.R. Green, *A Short History of the English People* (1874), pp. 287-97; Gunn, "Henry VII in context", pp. 305-6).

[13] Gunn, "Henry VII in context", p. 315.

implemented for the municipalities is of interest in this overall development.

While this royal policy was being charted through the course of Henry VII's reign, London and other municipalities were going through their own sea change.[14] A shifting economy, especially with a transition from wool to cloth, saw many towns crying poor as monarchs sought more and more revenue from their municipal coffers during the 15th century. Although pleading poverty was a common mantra of cities and towns round about the time the king wanted payment for fee farms, no doubt many mayors and burgesses were indeed short of money while attempting to stave off ongoing decay.[15] At the same time, city liberties were most often tied to these fees, demonstrating that by this time each successive king now required a town to purchase its charters upon accession.[16] It was therefore a balancing act to negotiate fee farms to maintain rights and customs, especially in judicial and property matters, while trying to avoid unrealistic or burdensome financial terms. Furthermore, it was important politically to establish good working relationships with the king-in-residence. These were precarious manoeuvres, considering that in the twenty-eight months between April 1483 and August 1485, the country witnessed the death of three kings and the accession of a fourth, if we can accept (as many did at the time) that the two princes in the Tower were no longer alive when their future brother-in-law became Henry VII.

---

[14] For Henry VII's overall policy as viewed in the present discussion, see Horowitz, "Thomas Sunnyff", *passim* and "Policy and prosecution". For insight on Henry VII's fiscal pursuit of the church, see the articles by S.J. Gunn: "Sir Thomas Lovell (*c.*1449-1524): a new man in a new monarchy?", in *The End of the Middles Ages? England in the 15th and 16th Centuries*, ed. J.L. Watts (Stroud, 1998), pp. 117-53, at p. 125; and "Edmund Dudley and the church", *Jour. Eccles. Hist.*, li (2000), pp. 509-26.

[15] L.C. Attreed, "The king's interest: York's fee farm and the central government, 1482-92", *Northern Hist.*, xvii (1981), pp. 24-43, at p. 26. Many complaints were real, or as Alan Dyer has observed, "It is impossible to deny that some of these wails were justified" (A. Dyer, *Decline and Growth in English Towns, 1400-1640* (Basingstoke, 1991), p. 47). The city of York, to be discussed, may have peaked in prosperity around 1400, with its population declining by one-third between 1440 and 1540. It has been estimated that cloth production fell 75 per cent between the 1390s and 1480s (Wrightson, p. 107).

[16] Palliser, "Towns and the English state", p. 137; Campbell, pp. 69, 73. By 1300, fifty towns had privileges of fee farms, providing both money and goodwill for the monarch.

Under Richard III, several cities had portions of their fee farms remitted, perhaps sending the wrong signal to local leaders about the political strength of the last Yorkist monarch.[17] Cities such as York and Gloucester—which were clearly targets for support by Richard—benefited from these remissions. Other cities petitioned the king seeking such relief. A privy seal dated in the first few months of Richard's reign alluded to the great decay of the town of Kingston-upon-Hull.[18] Lincoln had part of its fee farm remitted by Edward IV and confirmed by Richard III, as did Northampton, Oxford and Winchester.[19] This created an indirect financial problem for the royal government, since portions of these revenues were kept locally as rewards from the crown to lords, local gentry and officials.[20]

In the case of York, the exchequer apparently never got the message about remission, despite repeated bills and privy seals. When Henry VII became king, he confirmed the £160 fee farm of York, but also a £60 remission. Unfortunately for the city, nothing was done about it. This did not please the York hierarchy in search of more relief. The city fathers now communicated to the king that they had, in fact, always been loyal to the house of Lancaster and abhorred Edward IV's refusal to acknowledge their poverty—an interesting reworking of history.[21] Henry apparently was not amused. The treasurer of his household appropriated £112 13s 4d of York's fee farm for household expenses, which was confirmed in Henry's first parliament. The king noted certain circumstances but allowed that

---

[17] Weakness at the centre emboldened cities to seek remissions. Palliser calculated that between 1433 and 1482, successive monarchs remitted about £73,000 in fee farms and tax reductions, both for real relief and for political support. Large remissions could be found during a king's instalment on the throne: 1461-2, 1483-4, 1485-6 (Palliser, "Towns and the English state", p. 134). See also Dyer, p. 48.

[18] T.N.A.: P.R.O., C 81/886, 18 Sept. 1483. Richard personally visited Gloucester and Hull and may have learned of monies being moved off the books to show poverty. He nonetheless granted remissions to buy "political support" (Dyer, p. 48).

[19] Despite Lincoln's perennial complaint of a failing cloth industry, it did survive and by 1524 was the tenth largest city in England (Dyer, p. 23; J.W.F. Hill, *Medieval Lincoln* (Cambridge, 1948), pp. 270-1).

[20] Attreed, pp. 26-7, 30; P.K. O'Brien and P.A. Hunt, "The rise of a fiscal state in England, 1485-1815", *Hist. Research*, Vol. LXVI (1993), pp. 129-76, at pp. 135-6.

[21] York strongly supported Richard III and received many favours in return. The city invested £66 to cover costs for Henry VII's first visit in 1486 (D.M. Palliser, *Tudor York* (Oxford, 1979), pp. 42-3).

York would have a release of the fee "during our pleaser".[22] Henry VII's interference in local politics near the time of the Yorkshire rebellion did not improve the relationship.[23]

For the first seven years of the reign, the York magistrates sent gifts and paid a lobbyist to restore their fee farm remission, to little avail. In 1492, Henry actually took £100 of the fee farm and gave it as payments to Sir Thomas Lovell, treasurer of the king's chamber, as custodian of the estates of the young Lord Roos, whose attainted father lost the grant until it was reversed for his son. The king did the same with regard to Lincoln.[24] Henry did hold out hope to York officials, promising that the charges on the fee farm would at some point be remitted, although the city council nonetheless approved expenses for an alderman, a chamberlain and the recorder to take ten horses to ride to London "to sew and laboure unto his said Grace for the recovere and recontenuance of an c[li] [£100]".[25] However, while the king ruminated on the remission, the mayor and aldermen were enjoined by him to keep the laws and to judge men equally under them—a message Henry VII never failed to promote.[26] It was not until 1524, the year of Thomas Lovell's death, that York received the remission it had been promised almost half a century earlier. For the monarchy, it was a pointed victory in bringing a major city into the national scope of finance and law.[27]

Although it would be difficult to declare unequivocally that Henry VII was intentionally seeking stability and "law and order" through specific

---

[22] Attreed, pp. 37-9.

[23] Henry's infringement on sanctuary, plus his involvement with factional politics, is discussed in M.A. Hicks, "The Yorkshire rebellion of 1489 reconsidered", *Northern Hist.*, xxii (1986), pp. 39-62.

[24] Hill, p. 285; Palliser, *Tudor York*, pp. 207, 215-16.

[25] *York Civic Records*, ii and iii, ed. A. Raine (Yorkshire Archaeol. Soc., 103, 106, 1941-2), ii. 85 (16 Apr. 1492); Gunn, "Sir Thomas Lovell", pp. 139, 142.

[26] *York Civic Records*, ii. 87-8 (1 June 1492). The message was conveyed to the movers and shakers of York orally in the "Yeldhale within the Citie" by the alderman who had met with the king.

[27] Attreed, pp. 40-2. Attreed concluded that York's fee farm and the controversy surrounding it brought the city "into a national pattern of reward, obligation, and leadership" (p. 43). Lovell was chancellor of the exchequer in 1485 and treasurer of the king's chamber in July, 1487. In Dec. 1514, he was called to oversee the indictment against rioting by local gentry in York as well as for local murders (Gunn, "Sir Thomas Lovell", pp. 129-30, 135). Lovell did accept only a small fraction of the £100 fees from Lincoln and York annually in recognition of their poverty.

actions rather than merely indulging in the rhetoric of kings telling subjects to behave, it is clear that he held city officials accountable for unrest and for keeping the king's peace and the laws of the realm. Moreover, his actions bespeak a consistent policy for all aspects of politics, law and finance. In the case of cities and towns, Henry was wary of any possibility of dissension or discontent leading to civil strife. Not only did he put officials on notice to abide by the law and mete out justice fairly, he also became personally involved. In 1488, the king ordered the mayor and sheriffs to ensure that good rule was preserved or offenders would be punished. Although no reason was given for this censorious admonition, the York officials then reprimanded the gild searchers about the necessity of maintaining law and order in the city.[28]

Then in November 1494, a privy seal was sent to the mayor and serjeants of York to appear before the king's council "within viij daies next aftir the sight of thies our lettres", no matter where they happened to be. The reason was for "certain grete riotts and mysgouvernauncez late by you comitted and don within our Countie of York contrarie to our lawez and peax"—a reference to a dispute over commons rights between the city and York minster. Each was to be bound in £100, to be forfeited upon failure to appear: a standard amount found in privy seals used by Henry VII's "learned councillors" for appearance before them, usually in one of the chambers of the duchy of Lancaster.[29] On 15 February 1495, Henry spoke to the entourage from York at Greenwich with several lords present. The king told the assembly that he would not let "the Citie go in utter ruyne" because of their inability to govern and abide by the ancient customs and laws. Rather, Henry reproached them by saying he would "put in other rewlers that woll rewle and govern the Citie accordyng to my lawez". The king then commanded the mayor at his "perell" that he ensure that "good demeanour and peace be keped within my Citie ther and that ye mynister and execut my lawez". Failure to do so, Henry declared, meant that the mayor would be "sewrly punyshed that other shuld take ensample". To make certain that his words would have effect, the king told the mayor that he could seek assistance from "my lord of Surrey".[30]

---

[28] Palliser, *Tudor York*, p. 44.
[29] *York Civic Records*, ii. 112 (1 Nov. 1494); M.R. Horowitz, "Richard Empson, minister of Henry VII", *Bull. Inst. Hist. Research*, lv (1982), pp. 35-49, at pp. 42-3. [Chapter 4] For similar language, see the text of two privy seals created for Edmund Dudley's use, printed in Horowitz, "Thomas Sunnyff", p. 366.
[30] *York Civic Records*, ii. 115-16. Surrey had acted as the surety for the officials to appear before the king, who in turn were required to find sureties to be bound to

York was not alone in being brought further into the sphere of royal oversight and justice. Henry informed the mayor, bailiffs and burgesses of Leicester of his concern regarding commoners attending town business and government meetings, fearing "the subuersion not oonly of the gode polyce of oure seid town but lykly to the often breche of the peax".[31] During the Michaelmas 1501 session of royal councillors meeting in a chamber of the duchy of Lancaster, a privy seal was ordered to be sent to the mayor and justices of the peace of Leicester to appear at a certain date to answer matters laid against them. They in fact appeared and were "desmyssed". At the next session, the mayor of Newcastle was commanded to allow the king's tenants of Richmond to pass toll free through his city or appear before the council. He did appear to answer for the matter and was similarly dismissed.[32]

The use of privy seals by the king and his councillors was ubiquitous as the reign progressed, culminating in the 1504 Retaining Act allowing councillors to proceed against parties without information by writs of privy seal, including subpoenas. Although Empson and Dudley were accused of blatantly using privy seals in their quest for ferreting out the monies due the crown or to determine if laws were being broken, they were not alone. Many payments were made from the king's chamber late in the reign for privy seals to be delivered to citizens high and low, and they provide a clue as to their provenance. When a number of privy seals were sent to escheators throughout the realm, "m[aster] hussy"—John Hussey, the master of wards, often found as a crown representative in recognizances *ad usum regis*—was recorded in the margin as the originator of these royal missives. Privy seals for delivery to seven different people listed "[m]aster Wyatt" in the margin (see below). Robert Southwell, part of a group of royal auditors and surveyors of the crown lands that included the bishop of Carlisle, appeared as the mover of privy seals to a list of recipients.[33]

---

the earl for their appearance (p. 113). Both Surrey and the abbot of St. Mary's mediated, and award was made in 1495 in favour of the minster vicars (Palliser, *Tudor York*, p. 45).

[31] *English Constitutional Documents, 1307-1485*, ed. E.C. Lodge and G.A. Thornton (Cambridge, 1935), p. 387.

[32] T.N.A.: P.R.O., DL 5/2 fos. 15, 18.

[33] T.N.A.: P.R.O., E 36/214 fos. 75, 91v, 141, 149v; see above, n. 29, for Dudley. The 1504 act was 19 Hen. VII, c. 14.

Towns and cities believed that privy seals undermined their right to determine their own court cases.[34] They must have made a lasting impact regarding their power and authority. In 1506, Thomas Bell confessed before the York common council that he had "maid and counterfeted the Kyngs lettrez of prive seale and theym direct unto the Maire and Shireffs of this Citie commaundyng theym by the same to put Roger Bell at his large". Roger, who was imprisoned for outlawry, was Thomas's father. A search of Roger's house also turned up "a counterfete of the Kyngs signet". Privy seals were probably also feared, as when the king's councillors meeting in the duchy of Lancaster chamber noted that several men had "meddeld in deliv^{r}yng of the kings p^{r}ve seale".[35]

From the start of his reign, Henry reached out to cities to bring them into the grip of royal government and revenue generation, in part through his policy of taking bonds for the many aspects of finance and justice. On 13 September 1486, the mayor, burgesses and commonalty of Christchurch, Hampshire entered into a bond to the king for £1,000 to be paid the following Michaelmas. The condition involved covenants that both the city and the king were to perform as contained in a pair of indentures; it would be voided upon completion of the condition.[36] Similar bonds were made between the king and the towns of Hythe (one of the cinque ports), Dartmouth and Hull in the same year.[37] While mayors and other local officials were called before the king's council to answer for matters concerning the crown—a reminder that they were not independent of the royal will—at the same time Henry VII listened to their pleas and acted accordingly.[38] On 15 September 1488, a signet letter recited a situation

---

[34] Cavill, pp. 171-4.

[35] *York Civic Records*, iii. 22; T.N.A.: P.R.O., DL 5/4 fo. 117v.

[36] *Catalogue of Ancient Deeds*, iv, no. A. 6415. "A" signifies the E 40 classification.

[37] *Cat. Anc. Deeds*, iv, nos. A. 6813 (Hythe, 25 Aug. 1486), A. 6881 (Dartmouth, 22 Sept. 1486), A. 15070 (Hull, 1486-7).

[38] A petition to Henry VII from the mayor and burgesses of Gloucester concerned the "grevis fee firme of lxv li. [£65] by the yere". The petitioners claimed they were unable to levy the amount because of the "great ruyne and decay of the habitacione mansions and tenementis". Furthermore, they lacked money to repair the walls and towers which, perhaps to strike a warm royal chord, they noted were "the chief defence of great p[ar]te of that coste of this your said roialme". The city fathers also mentioned that the king had replied demanding "to attend your highnes here at London" to hear the cause, and they asked for a discharge of part of the fee farm, leaving the amount blank—suggesting this was written prior to the royal audience. They concluded that if the king signed the petition it would be a sufficient warrant and discharge "for the making seallyng and delyv^{r}yng of the

where the mayor and citizens of Chichester said they could not pay their
£52 fee farm to the king. Their reasoning was that they had no rents, lands
or possessions, "but oonly casualties of Straungers and othr of our said
Citie soo that for suche ruyn and decay as our said Citie is udre fallen"
they could not pay. Henry now granted them licence to purchase and
receive certain lands, rents and other possessions to the value of £40 per
year to help pay the fee farm.[39] Businessman that he was, the first Tudor
assisted the town in obtaining his money rather than letting them reduce
the amount that he felt was rightly due to him. It was a seller's market, and
municipalities seeking their liberties had to bend to the royal will.

The records related to various cities and counties also came under royal
scrutiny, in part to determine how to secure the lost revenue from these
various remissions as well as to reveal potential income from forfeited
bonds.[40] Henry Wyatt, one of the councillors working in tandem with key
royal personnel such as Lovell, Reynold Bray, John Mordaunt, Edmund
Dudley, Richard Empson, Robert Southwell, Thomas Lucas and James
Hobart, was also the keeper of the rolls in Surrey. He often did searches
into the records to see if old bonds were in forfeit and therefore in need of
prosecution to obtain the king's money, and to ensure that the law was
being respected and not ignored locally.[41] A commission held in York
suggests that the law was always a concern, in spite of the obvious
financial benefit of driving in forfeited bonds, both old and new.

---

same" by letters patent. (Gloucester, Gloucestershire Archives, County Council,
GBR I, 1/24.)

[39] T.N.A.: P.R.O., PSO 2/3, 5 Sept. 1488. The letter ordered the chancellor to draw
up a contract to this effect and have it validated by the great seal.

[40] S.J. Gunn, "'New men' and 'new monarchy' in England, 1485-1524", in
*Powerbrokers in the Late Middle Ages: the Burgundian Low Countries in a
European Context*, ed. R. Stein (Turnhout, 2001), pp. 153-64, at p. 156; Horowitz,
"Thomas Sunnyff", pp. 349-51.

[41] On 4 Feb. 1509 a writ went out from Thomas Routhale in chancery to Wyatt
involving an obligation undertaken by four men as sureties, in 100 marks each, for
John Saunders on 10 Oct. 1493—more than fifteen years earlier—before the J.P.s
in Surrey (Saunders was bound for £100). Wyatt was commanded by the king to
check the books, rolls and other memoranda in his custody regarding Saunders at
that session and to send a record of it to chancery. The councillor responded that a
bond was in fact taken at that session, but the four sureties were bound in £20 each
and Saunders in £40 to appear (T.N.A.: P.R.O., C 244/158, no. 46). Another record
of a bond taken by justices, including Bray, was requested of Wyatt, who reported
that it was a bond for the peace, and that the recognizor appeared at subsequent
sessions and apparently kept the peace (T.N.A.: P.R.O., C 255/8/5 no. 94(b)).

Humphrey Coningsby, a serjeant-at-law, king's councillor and close
associate of Empson and Dudley involved with implementing the king's
legal and fiscal policies, headed a commission to York in the spring of
1501. In a record he kept of his journey, he noted that from a search in the
county records he determined that there were twenty-four prisoners held
for murder and felony sentenced to be executed, but none had been "this x
yers & more in the seid Countie". Coningsby ordered the stewards and
other franchise officials to assist the sheriff and his officers to arrest
indicted felons and murderers, including those who have "stoud endicted
this x yers & more & nothyng don unto them". Land tenure inquisitions
and various indictments were also up for review, with assistance from the
bishop of Carlisle and Sir Walter Griffith, the latter an informer concerning
certain lands "whiche be in the kings honds". Coningsby also searched old
recognizances, wherein he uncovered a few surprises: "It[e]m wher it was
surmytted that one kat^{r}ine Stanley, for whom suerties were bounden by
reco[g]nysans to have appered at a c^{r}teyn day past & hath made defaute,
shuld be dede afore the day of apparans. She is alive."^{42}

Henry and his councillors often placed the burden of obtaining payment
for local bonds on the very servants and officials who would reap the
rewards coming from learning of their forfeiture. In a petition by Roger
Cook, yeoman of the crown, it was noted that two men of the county
palatine of Chester had been bound by recognizance in certain sums "befor
the Barons and other your offic^{r}s of yor Eschequier ther" for a Charles
Holford to keep the peace and appear before the palatine exchequer on a
certain day and not to depart without the permission of court officers. The
royal servant, who must have come upon this information from inquiries or
commissions, observed that Holford's bond "hath broken in ev^{r}y poynte".
Cook now asked for a privy seal to be directed to the chamberlain, barons
and other officers of the exchequer in Chester to arrest the two sureties, "ther
to Remayne unto tyme they have contented and paied their said forfaictures
unto your said s^{r}vunt orells reasonably aggree w^t him for the same"—in
other words, they could negotiate a new deal. Henry signed the order for the
privy seal.^{43} A similar situation occurred in Exeter, where two men "in oure
counte of devon were bounden before the mair of o^r said citie eithr of theim

---

^{42} Westminster Abbey Muniments, MS. 12247 (author's punctuation for the matter
of Katherine Stanley). This trip was most likely related to the work of the assizes
held in York during Lent 1501 (*Dictionary of National Biography* (2004),
Humfrey Coningsby).
^{43} T.N.A.: P.R.O., PSO 2/3, n.d. but before the end of Aug. 1492, when the king
changed his sign manual.

in the sume of twenty pounds by recognisaunce" as sureties for a third party to appear before the mayor when summoned. It was now learned that the party did not appear, and the sureties were therefore required to pay £20 each on the forfeited bond. The money was to be collected by, and assigned to, four named men as rewards.[44]

With increasing intensity during Henry VII's reign, searches were carried out to scrutinize records involving local jurisdictions, including court proceedings and bonds taken for judicial purposes such as appearance and keeping the peace. In the mind of the king and his councillors, all courts were the king's courts. Indeed, a statute in his last parliament affirmed this for the city of London.[45] Cities owed their allegiance, and their liberties, to the monarch. Henry did not seek confrontation; indeed, he and the monarchs before him required co-operation from local governments.[46] Moreover, he allowed a degree of autonomy to the municipal elites, or what one historian has called "crown-sponsored self-government"—a pragmatic approach to the realization that the royal government could not control every city and town from Westminster.[47] The first Tudor's preoccupation with micro-managing the franchises of England stemmed from his desire to maintain law and order, and to gather in what was his financial due. Although Polydore Vergil's first-hand view of Henry's policies may have suggested to him a desire to put English men and women in fear, he clearly understood that the king cast his net wide to engulf both the people and their city and town officials for a higher purpose. Vergil observed that the king "began severely to punish all offenders who had committed any crime prohibited and forbidden by the laws of the realm or municipal regulations".[48]

---

[44] T.N.A.: P.R.O., E 404/83, 1 June 1499.

[45] G. Norton, *Commentaries on the History, Constitution and Chartered Franchises of the City of London* (1829), p. 350, referencing the statute 20 Hen. VII, c. 6.

[46] G.W. Bernard, "The Tudor nobility in perspective", in Bernard, *Tudor Nobility*, pp. 1-48, at p. 23. Henry perhaps held the belief that London would remain loyal to him throughout his reign, which proved to be true (Pugh, p. 56).

[47] J. Lee, "Urban policy and urban political culture: Henry VII and his towns", *Hist. Research*, Vol. LXXXII, no. 217 (2009), pp. 493-510, for a view of Henry's balancing act of allowing local rule as a component of central control that is complementary to the present discussion.

[48] "[Q]uod legibus aut statutes municipalibus prohibitum uetitumque esset" (*The Anglica Historia of Polydore Vergil, A.D. 1485-1537*, ed. D. Hay (Camden 3rd ser., lxxiv, 1950), p. 127.

When Edmund Dudley replaced Bray more than a year after his death as the king's chief minister for taking and collecting upon old and new bonds, part of his charge involved seeking legal and financial advantage from the cities and towns of England.[49] This Dudley did with enthusiastic tenacity from the very beginning of his tenure. On 8 October 1504—a month after Dudley became the king's personal prosecutor of bonds—the city of Winchester obtained a grant of 40 marks per year (£26 13s 4d) for sixty years, to be paid from various subsidies on cloths, this a continuation of a grant made during the reign of Henry VI.[50] However, the completed transaction is not evident from the printed summaries of the patent rolls entries. An obligation for 100 marks (£66 13s 4d) was also entered into by the city and taken by Dudley for the annual fee farm—or two and a half times what the city would receive annually from the grant.[51]

Dudley also collected payments for the granting of municipal liberties, which had formerly been paid directly to the king's chamber, from early in the reign, and were historically tied to a negotiated fee farm.[52] Leicester, which paid no fee farm under Edward IV, received a confirmation of its liberties on 4 March 1505 after paying Dudley £20.[53] Doncaster in Yorkshire received its grant of liberties on 14 July 1505 for a fee farm rent of £74 13s 11½d. The city paid Dudley 20 marks in cash and £20 by obligation for the privilege, or almost half its annual rent.[54] Dudley was actually taking over a responsibility held by Henry VII, who had negotiated fee farm rents personally. In 1499, the burgesses of Yarmouth in Norfolk complained that they had paid their fee farm directly by order of the king, for which they had no discharge. The king sent a privy seal to

---

[49] See I.W. Archer, *The Pursuit of Stability: Social Relations in Elizabethan London* (Cambridge, 1991), p. 26, for law enforcement in the City by Empson and Dudley.

[50] *Cal. Pat. Rolls 1494-1509*, p. 430.

[51] Brit. Libr., Lansdowne MS. 127 fo. 1, n.d., but between 9 Sept. 1504 and 1 Aug. 1505. Dudley most likely negotiated the deal before its enrollment on 8 Oct.

[52] Dyer, p. 47. The city of Chichester in Sussex had paid its fee farm directly to the chamber. By 1499, it had made annual payments of £4 12s 4d for three years without discharge, which it requested and eventually obtained (T.N.A.: P.R.O., E 404/83, 2 Dec. 1499). By 1300, purchases for town charters were made in a lump sum ("firma burgi") for certain rights (*Eng. Const. Docs.*, p. 375).

[53] *Cal. Pat. Rolls 1494-1509*, p. 393; Brit. Libr., Lansdowne MS. 127 fo. 4. Dyer noted that the city paid no fee farm under Edward IV or Henry VII and was granted annuities for political reasons, but apparently there was a change of heart by the first Tudor late in the reign (Dyer, p. 48).

[54] *Cal. Pat. Rolls 1494-1509*, p. 431; Brit. Libr., Lansdowne MS. 127 fo. 8v.

the exchequer instructing that a discharge be forthcoming because, he admitted, Yarmouth's command to pay the king in person had been "gyven by oure mouth".[55]

Dudley, undoubtedly through the instructions of the king, often made harsh deals with various municipalities to ensure that the crown would receive a steady stream of revenue, regardless of the cry of poverty from mayors.[56] The town of Southwold in Suffolk received confirmation of an earlier patent of its liberties on 10 June 1505. It listed the town's various rights in return for an annual fee farm rent of £14.[57] However, the town had to pay Dudley 100 marks (£66 13s 4d) in cash and 200 marks (£133 6s 8d) in an obligation for its privileges: a total of £200, or more than fourteen times the actual fee farm.[58] The town of Wallingford in Berkshire received a forty-year release of its original fee farm because its fourteen parishes had been reduced to four. The release noted that the original fee farm had been £42 annually from the time of Henry III. Henry V had reduced the payment, and it was further cut to £15 for forty years by Henry VI. Henry VII now allowed a pardon of all arrears plus a confirmation of the reduction to £15. But in order to receive this remission, the town had to pay Dudley £40 in cash, or close to the amount of its original rent more than two centuries earlier.[59]

Amounts could be substantial. The liberties of north Wales cost £2,000, along with various stipulations that brought the Welsh more under the aegis of English law.[60] Moreover, a "book" on the prerogatives of the king in the region was prepared on the order of Sir John Mordaunt and

---

[55] T.N.A.: P.R.O., E 404/83, 25 Feb. 1499. Yarmouth was hit hard economically by the expansion of the London cloth trade (Dyer, p. 26).

[56] Bacon opined that Henry VII pursued a policy that confirmed "our cities, boroughs and towns, in their charter and freedoms" to his financial advantage (Francis Bacon, *History of the Reign of King Henry VII*, ed. J. Rawson Lumby (Cambridge, 1885), p. 143).

[57] *Cal. Pat. Rolls 1494-1509*, p. 429.

[58] Brit. Libr., Lansdowne MS. 127 fo. 6v.

[59] *Cal. Pat. Rolls 1494-1509*, p. 536, dated 9 Mar. 1507; Brit. Libr., Lansdowne MS. 127 fo. 39v, entered in Dudley's book 3 Mar. 1507. Wallingford was part of the duchy of Cornwall.

[60] Brit. Libr., Lansdowne MS. 127 fo. 2. See the various grants recorded at chancery (*Cal. Pat. Rolls 1494-1509*, pp. 434, 464, 534-5). Dudley, along with Thomas Lovell and other councillors of the king, formed a group responsible for the marches of Wales that ultimately became the prince's council.

sent to London "in order that the king's council might be advised".[61] The city of Chester, which rather disingenuously pleaded poverty, initially paid Dudley £50 for its liberties in early 1506. A year later, the liberties for the entire county, which included the inhabitants of Chester, involved a purchase price of £2,000 payable in six annual instalments, exempting a few named persons including the duke of Buckingham and the earls of Shrewsbury, Derby and Kent. Two months later, a large group of knights and gentlemen entered into a bond for 2,000 marks (£1,333 6s 8d) for both a blanket pardon of any past offences and further confirmation of the liberties of Cheshire.[62]

It was against this backdrop of royal policy that the steady erosion of the judicial and financial independence of cities and towns continued in early Tudor England. Local magistrates throughout England nonetheless doggedly pressed for the protection of these rights, often with small victories.[63] The charter of Chichester dated 1 August 1462 was reconfirmed in 1500 by Henry VII. It included the right of the mayor and citizens to have "cognizance" of all pleas, assizes, juries, attaints and certifications of all lands involving the freeholders of the city and its liberty.[64] The courts in Chester maintained rolls and books of recognizances entered between parties, and the records of suits initiated against those bonds. These were kept by the courts regularly up to the 17th century and provided a judicial venue for private debts to be enrolled or filed.[65] Fees for bonds, and sums from their recovery, could be a lucrative source of income for municipalities. A list of fees for Canterbury included "Itm for thentr[y] of a recognysaunce of statute staple or statute m^rch^aun—

---

[61] J.B. Smith, "Crown and community in the principality of North Wales in the reign of Henry Tudor", *Welsh Hist. Rev.*, iii (1966), pp. 145-71, at pp. 158-9. Mordaunt, a trusted minister of the king, succeeded Bray as chancellor of the duchy of Lancaster.

[62] K.P. Wilson, "The port of Chester in the 15th century", *Trans. Hist. Soc. Lancs. and Cheshire*, cxvii (1965), pp. 1-15; Brit. Libr., Lansdowne MS. 127 fos. 17v, 37v, 58v.

[63] Lee, "Urban policy".

[64] *Cal. Pat. Rolls 1494-1509*, p. 205 (14 May 1500). See a similar grant for Shrewsbury in 1445 (*Calendar of Charter Rolls 1427-1516*, vi. 45).

[65] Brit. Libr., Harleian MS. 2046 fo. 37; D.J. Clayton, *The Administration of the County Palatine of Chester, 1442-85* (Chetham Soc., 3rd ser., xxxv, Manchester, 1990), p. 240.

ijs"; "Itm for the execucion of ev^{r}y warant of suertie of peas [*sic*] of the taker—viijd".[66]

The city of London, of course, possessed a long tradition of special standing among monarchs, beginning with the brief charter of William the Conqueror, which was subsequently issued and expanded upon from monarch to monarch.[67] It elected its own mayor and aldermen, held its own courts and had ready contact with the ruler of the time, often providing loans and services as required. It took recognizances for appearance at court, good behaviour and the keeping of the peace, both between parties and within the realm. The City government kept recognizance rolls to protect orphans,[68] and maintained two sheriffs' courts (the counters) as both judicial venues and gaols, as well as the court of Hustings. It guarded its records in locked repositories and had jealously protected its perceived customs since time out of mind.

Things did not always go smoothly between the City and the crown when it came to jurisdictions and rights, often because of alleged local abuses of power. Between 1239 and 1259, the royal government took control of London governance on ten occasions—perhaps contributing to the City's support for the baronial uprising in 1258-61.[69] In 1285, Edward I took back the liberties of the City and governed by royal wardens for thirteen years. It required the payment of a fine of 2,000 marks before they were restored in 1298.[70] In 1392, Richard II withdrew London's liberties

---

[66] Brit. Libr., Stowe MS. 850 fos. 5, 5v, 6, 8v. The book probably belonged to one Thomas Rolfe (fo. 210v). See Brit. Libr., Stowe MS. 501 fo. 111 for fees in chancery.

[67] For William's terse charter for London, see *The Historical Charters and Constitutional Documents of the City of London* (1884), p. 1; Norton, p. 324. Caroline Barron suggests that it was actually a writ (*London in the Later Middle Ages: Government and People 1200-1500* (Oxford, 2004), p. 31).

[68] E.g., on 14 Apr. 1468, three London "peautrers" and one "taillour" entered into a bond for £40 to deliver to the chamber of the common council of London 10 marks plus "divers jewels and silver plate" for the four daughters of John Gugge, late pewterer, when they became of age to marry. One of the men was appointed guardian of the girls (*Calendar of Letter-Books . . . of the City of London*, ed. R.R. Sharpe (11 vols., 1899-1912), *Letter-Book L*, p. 78). On 15 Mar. 1492, the common council of London decreed that all bonds for orphans' goods should be renewed annually to determine which of those recognizors were alive or dead, and whether they were still living in the City (*Letter-Book L*, p. 286).

[69] J.L. Bolton, *The Medieval English Economy, 1150-1500* (1980), p. 124. It cost the City £13,333 13*s* 4*d* to regain its liberties.

[70] Barron, *London in the Later Middle Ages*, p. 31.

because he believed that the mayor and aldermen failed to maintain law and order—a belief that landed them in gaol. The king appointed a warden and two sheriffs, and it was largely only through the entreaties of the queen consort and London citizens that the officials were freed later in the year and pardoned for the sum of 3,000 marks. It apparently cost the City £30,000 to recoup their liberties, although the original fine was the message-sending sum of £100,000, which may have been reduced at one point to £10,000.[71] In the 14th century, English kings frequently desired London offices for members of their households. Henry III interfered in City nominations for mayor or the sheriffs, and in 1323 Edward II ousted a mayor and had him replaced. Richard II intervened as well.[72] In the following century, London officials began rejecting royal nominees, seeking to hold on to the privileges and patronage of even the most minor offices.[73]

London was not immune to the policies being implemented by Henry VII towards the cities and towns of England and it too had to arrange the purchase of its liberties and the renewal of its charter. It was a process that, perhaps to no one's surprise, involved Edmund Dudley. The procedure began in December 1503, when the mayor and aldermen agreed to let John Shaa, alderman and recorder of London, negotiate with the king to accept £5,000 for confirmation of the City's charter and the annulment of the Merchant Taylors' charter, the latter forced upon the City by the king (see below). If the king did not accept this offer, Shaa was instructed to split the payment into 2,500 marks for the annulment and 5,000 marks for the confirmation of London's charter, payable over five years.[74] Clearly, Henry could negotiate from a position of strength. Unlike Henry IV, Edward IV and Richard III, who sought London support both financially and for the legitimacy of their rule, Henry came to the throne independent of the City's help. Nor did he require large merchant loans after the first

---

[71] C.M. Barron, "London 1300-1540", in *Camb. Urban Hist.*, i. pp. 395-440, at p. 409; *Letter-Book H*, pp. 377-8, 380-1, 381 n. 1; *Eng. Const. Docs.*, p. 388.

[72] Barron, *London in the Later Middle Ages*, p. 25.

[73] Monarchs and their ministers continued to press for London offices, quite often with success. On 9 July 1510, John Ernley, the attorney-general inherited by young Henry VIII from his father, got the mayor and aldermen of London to agree to appoint his servant to be one of the attorneys in the sheriff's court if a current attorney there "be content to resign the same" (C.L.R.O, REP 2 (1505-1513), fo. 92.)

[74] C.L.R.O., REP 1, fo. 150.

few years of his reign, thanks to increasing income from both royal lands and the forfeiture of various obligations and recognizances.[75] The king would not budge on the Merchant Taylors' charter, but accepted the proposal for the City's charter. In November 1504, soon after Dudley became the king's chief financial minister for taking and prosecuting bonds, a chancery clerk received from the mayor and aldermen the London charter of Richard III, complete with the great seal. The purpose of the delivery was "to engroce and make newe l[ett]res patencs in the name of kyng henr vij[th]" for the citizens of London.[76] The charter must have been finished before spring, since at a London common council meeting held on 10 March 1505 it was agreed that five obligations would be sealed with the common seal of the City, "for the payment and contentacon of v m^l [5,000] marcs to the kyng our souv^{r}aign lord" in instalments: 1,000 marks at Whitsuntide next and 1,000 marks yearly at the same feast until the total of 5,000 marks was paid. This was the sum agreed the previous November, and negotiated by John Shaa, if the Merchant Taylors' charter could not be annulled.[77]

What was not recorded by the mayor and aldermen was the fact that the obligations were received and processed by Edmund Dudley. In his account book, he entered a notation regarding the five obligations totalling 5,000 marks due for the liberties of the city of London.[78] This book, surviving as a 17th century copy, varies in certain wording from another abbreviated copy found in the Harleian manuscripts. For this same entry, a notation is added that the obligations were for Richard Empson, knight, chancellor of the duchy of Lancaster.[79] Empson, who pursued similar

---

[75] Barron, *London in the Later Middle Ages*, p. 29; Dobson, p. 282. By 1496, Henry VII already had a reputation for avarice, and a year later the Milanese ambassador alluded to the king's "immense treasure" (*Calendar of State Papers, Milan, 1385-1618* , nos. 490, 541, 553). See M.R. Horowitz, "Henry Tudor's Treasure", *Hist. Research*, lxxxii (2009), pp. 560-79. [Chapter Eight]

[76] C.L.R.O., Journals of the Court of Common Council, 10 (1492-1505), fo. 327v.

[77] C.L.R.O., JOR 10 (1492-1505), fo. 330v. Robert Fabyan, who clearly had access to the City's records and proceedings, noted "In thys yere [1504-5] the cytezyns of London graunted to the kyng . v. M [5,000] marke, for confermacion of theyr lyberties; wherof a . M . [1,000] marke was payde in hande, and . iiii . M [4,000] mark in . iiii yeres next ensuing" (*The Chronicles of Fabyan*, ed. H. Ellis, from Pynson's 1516 edn. (1811), p. 688; also found in *The Great Chronicle of London*, ed. A.H. Thomas and I.D. Thornley (1938), p. 328).

[78] Brit. Libr., Lansdowne MS. 127 fo. 5.

[79] Brit. Libr., Harleian MS. 1877 fo. 47. It is sometimes risky to rely solely on one's transcriptions when making certain assumptions, hoping that those notations

activities to Dudley but mostly through his work at the various duchy chambers, where Dudley sometimes joined him, did not seem to have had as much involvement in the City as did his colleague.[80] Yet, it is probable that he participated to a greater extent than may be discovered from the surviving records.[81] As will be discussed, there are hints that Empson had, in fact, become a nemesis of the City on a par with Dudley.

By 1485 when Henry VII became king, London was operating on the basis of certain judicial customs approved and confirmed by parliament and the king in the reign of Henry VI, on 26 October 1444. One important right of the City involved maintaining "whatever for the breach of any recognisaunces or securities of the peace may be found to be due to the king by the said mayor or justices [of eyre]".[82] Should a king or his councillors or judges request information about "any indictments of felonies or trespasses other misdeeds or any recognizance or surety" obtained by London magistrates or officials, compliance required simply providing "the tenor or copies thereof, so that they themselves may freely proceed to determination and execution according to the law and custom of the city, notwithstanding any writs, mandates or precepts of the king". The only reason the royal government could request such an inquiry had to involve cases of error, and even then the City could respond verbally through the recorder without any obligation to reply in writing.[83] This concerned all recognizances that could potentially trigger a suit or inquiry,

---

were taken accurately and then entered correctly when using electronic devices: or, to paraphrase Dr. Paul Ehrlich, Stanford University biologist and environmentalist, and author of *The Population Bomb*, "to err is human, but to really foul things up you need a computer". The author wishes to thank Michael St. John-McAlister, curator, department of manuscripts at the British Library, for confirming that it was "Richard Emson" written in the manuscript.

[80] Bray died in Aug. 1503 and was replaced as chancellor of the duchy of Lancaster by Sir John Mordaunt. He in turn died a year later, but the wary king only named Empson "keeper of the duchy seal", waiting another year before granting him outright the chancellorship for life (Horowitz, "Richard Empson", pp. 40-1).

[81] The *Great Chronicle* spent much time deriding the "bond churle born, In Towcetry toun". The author of the chronicle hoped that Empson would be hanged, drawn and quartered, and he records one of the opprobrious poems written about him (see also Horowitz, "Richard Empson", pp. 48-9). Although Dudley seems to be the main villain for the City, Empson is also identified as offering citizens "grete trowble & vexacion" (*Great Chronicle*, pp. 334-5, 339, 344, 347-8).

[82] Horowitz, "Thomas Sunnyff", pp. 349ff.; *Cal. Ch. Rolls 1427-1516*, vi. 41-4.

[83] Barron, *London in the Later Middle Ages*, p. 37.

or a determination as to whether they were still viable. When writs of *certiorari* seeking information about recognizances taken in London courts were sent from chancery, the City magistrates could decline to provide information because it would "offend the liberties and customs of the City" regarding recognizances and their execution.[84] Moreover, they would want to prevent a change of venue from a City court to a royal one.

That these critical clauses favouring the City ever came about at all may be but a reflection of what was occurring between the London and royal governments before 1444. One incident that occurred before these rights were granted suggests that the City fathers had been flexing their jurisdictional muscles for some time. On 2 July 1441, a writ of *certiorari* was issued to the mayor and aldermen regarding an action brought against someone in the "Court of the king in the Chamber of the Guildhall".[85] The return is telling for its mirroring of the spirit and content of the 1444 declaration of City customs and jurisdictions:

> According to the ancient liberties and customs of the City existing from time immemorial, and confirmed by divers charters and the authority of Parliament, all plaints and processes begun in the King's courts of the City must there be determined. Moreover, that plaints in other courts of the City should not be removed to be heard by the King's Justices, unless something foreign be pleaded or alleged which those courts are unable to recognized, and that proceedings in error in such cases are by custom taken at St. Martin le Grand and not elsewhere.[86]

Although these rights could be acquired at a time of weak central authority, City officials were swimming against the rising tide of private citizens purchasing writs of *certiorari* seeking to remove London court cases to a royal venue. This was especially true with the growing interest in obtaining redress at chancery, which now provided equity law not found

---

[84] Horowitz, "Thomas Sunnyff", n. 89.

[85] *Letter-Book K*, p. 257. In the same letter-book, an example of a writ of error to the mayor and sheriffs on an action of trespass, and its return, was recorded on 12 Apr. 1429 (p. 97). A year earlier, a search was made in Domesday Book to see if the City of London was of the ancient demesne of the crown—which would have had serious legal, financial and jurisdictional consequences (p. 87). It was determined that London was not part of the royal demesne.

[86] In its 1327 charter, it was confirmed that royal commissions for London were to be held on a neutral ground, which was determined to be St. Martin's le Grand (Barron, *London in the Later Middle Ages*, p. 37).

at the common law courts.[87] Sometimes Londoners hedged their bets by filing in more than one court: for example, a decree in star chamber asked that a privy seal be sent to a plaintiff "to answere a contempt, because he hath sued John Ballcull in two Courts for one and the same cause".[88] Often it was the defendant who sought legal asylum from London jurisdiction in the court of chancery, especially if he was incarcerated. William Bentham petitioned the chancellor about his plight, involving a bond he entered into for £20 to pay a creditor at a certain day. That day had lapsed and the bond was "putte in exicucon and yo[r] said Orato[r] hath contynued in pryson by a long space". Bentham claimed that the creditor, who fell sick, "relesyd and dyschargyd" him of the £20 debt in the presence of three men. Nonetheless, Bentham claimed, "the Sheryffis of london will not take uppon them the dylev[r]aunce of yo[r] seid orato[r] ne delyv[r]e hym owte of prison". He now asked the chancellor to "g[r]unte a wrytte of Corpus cum causa" to be directed to the mayor and aldermen of London, commanding them to bring the body of William Bentham to chancery "to examon and here the trouth in the prmysses and th[ere]uppon to discharge yor seid Orator".[89] In another case, Thomas Bishop and other debtors were bound to a London widow for £60, but when the bond was not paid the widow took an action "onely ageyn yo[r] seyd besechour before the sheryff of London", apparently striking deals with the other men. Bishop asked for a writ of *certiorari* to remove the case to chancery.[90]

The notion of all courts being the king's courts did not sit well with the mayor and aldermen of London, who wanted to retain both their judicial rights and the fees and forfeitures associated with keeping proceedings and records within the City. Given Henry VII's policy of seeking to establish both law and order and financial solvency, and his propensity to search various records for bonds and prerogative rights related to these objectives, authority quickly blurred between City privileges and royal

---

[87] See, e.g., P. Tucker, "Relationships between London's courts and the Westminster courts in the reign of Edward IV", in Dunn, pp. 117-37. Nevertheless, the common law courts also posed a threat to the business of local adjudication. In 1454, the City sent a serjeant to inform those sitting at common pleas not to permit London citizens to sue out writs of privilege, since the proper jurisdiction lay with the London courts (p. 127). Tucker suggests that this may have been to increase the case load at the City courts, rather than being any encroachment on the part of the common law courts (pp. 136-7).

[88] Brit. Libr., Harleian MS. 305 fo. 39, 16 Nov. 1506.

[89] T.N.A.: P.R.O., C 1/289 no. 74, endorsed 5 Nov. 1504.

[90] T.N.A.: P.R.O., C 1/289 no. 4.

jurisdiction. When a chancery writ inquired of the City why Thomas Lancaster failed to appear in chancery as required, it was learned that he was in prison. The reason for his imprisonment was his failure to bring sureties to the Guildhall to enter a peace bond sued out by Elizabeth Page, a private party. It was now demanded that Lancaster come to the chancery with sureties, rather than to the Guildhall. He in fact did appear in chancery with five other men. Each surety pledged £20 and Lancaster 40 marks that he would continue to appear in chancery and not harm Elizabeth Page or burn down her house.[91]

Royal involvement in London proceedings continued unabated, and records were being scrutinized to learn what bonds might be in forfeit for breaches in their conditions.[92] A case in point relates to the judicial activities of Henry Kebell, a grocer and merchant of the staple who was elected one of the sheriffs of London for 1502-3. It is quite likely that he knew Edmund Dudley, a former under-sheriff of the City as late as December 1502 and therefore someone very familiar with local proceedings before he became a main proponent of royal policy.[93] On 8 February 1505, a privy seal noted that a mercer of London and two sureties had previously entered into a recognizance in king's bench to appear before Kebell's court to take out a peace bond promising not to harm a woman. The mercer failed to appear, and he and his sureties now forfeited the money pledged in the recognizance; it was given to royal servants.[94] Some two months later, another privy seal stated that four men were bound in a recognizance in the counter of Bread Street before Kebell for a "mynstrell" named William Donne. Donne was to keep the peace against a man named Thomas Gretham until a specified date, when he was

---

[91] T.N.A.: P.R.O., C 244/156 no. 78(a)(b)(c).

[92] This was not a Tudor invention. The crown would sometimes send royal justices "in Eyre" to inquire into how London officials administered justice and government in the City on the king's behalf (Barron, *London in the Later Middle Ages*, p. 31).

[93] "Mayor and sheriffs of London 1273-1602, Edward I through Elizabeth I" <http://www.tudorplace.com.ar/Documents/mayors_and_sheriffs_of_london.htm> [accessed 8 Feb. 2008]; C.L.R.O., REP 1, fo. 119; *Great Chronicle*, pp. 318, 321; Fabyan's *Chronicle*, p. 688. See T.N.A.: P.R.O., C 43/1 no. 59, for a return of writ from Henry Kebell and Nicholas Nyens, sheriffs of London. He is not to be confused with Thomas Kebell (*c.*1439-1500) of Leicestershire, who became a serjeant-at-law and was part of the affinity of Lord William Hastings, chamberlain of Edward IV (E.W. Ives, *The Common Lawyers of Pre-Reformation England. Thomas Kebell: a Case Study* (Cambridge, 1983)).

[94] T.N.A.: P.R.O., E 404/85, 8 Feb. 1505.

either to "yild hymsilf p^{r}sonner into thesaid Countre or discharge hym of the plaint allegged there against hym by thesaid Thomas orells fynde there newe sureties as in the said recognisaunce it is exp^{r}ssed at large". The minstrel fulfilled none of these conditions, causing the recognizance to be forfeited by all parties who had entered into it on his behalf. It was now commanded that the money be given as a reward to servants of the king.[95] Five months later, a similar situation occurred in Kebell's court, or as the privy seal revealed it, "in our Courte of the Countre in Bredestrete", initiating royal involvement and bond collection against a "wyneseller" in forfeit of his recognizance.[96]

In these and other instances, private parties were going into a London sheriff's court seeking protection from potentially belligerent people, most likely by purchasing a writ of *supplicavit* that requested the taking of a peace bond.[97] But because it was the king's peace as well that could be broken, Henry VII and his ministers believed they had the legal right to become involved in such cases and receive any cash coming from forfeitures. Kebell may in fact have been the one informing Dudley or other royal officials of these potential forfeitures on lapsed bonds before his court, since he apparently kept records of those proceedings from 1502 to 1503, more than a year before Dudley became the king's chief bond collector. Besides their overlapping offices of sheriff and under-sheriff, Kebell may have known Dudley through Richard Page, a clerk of Dudley's who was involved in some nefarious dealings when it came to prosecuting bonds or informing on fellow citizens.[98] He might have had an opportunity to know Richard Empson personally: Kebell was a former

---

[95] T.N.A.: P.R.O., E 404/85, 23 Apr. 1505.

[96] T.N.A.: P.R.O., E 404/86, 26 Oct. 1506. See other activity in Kebell's court (T.N.A.: P.R.O., C 244/151 no. 16(a)(b)(c); C 244/153 no. 58(a)(b)).

[97] E.g., a privy seal was issued about an old peace bond taken "according to the custume of o^r Citie of London" and the failure of appearance before a sheriff (T.N.A.: P.R.O., E 404/85, 2 May 1505). Another involved a peace bond to be taken "in the yeld halle", with a forfeiture going to a royal household servant (T.N.A.: P.R.O., E 404/85, 10 July 1505).

[98] Kebell entered into a quitclaim of a manor and lands in Kent recovered from Edmund Page, heir of Richard Page (*Calendar of Close Rolls 1500-9*, no. 324, 14 June 1504). Richard was most likely the father of Edmund Dudley's clerk, who therefore would have been Edmund Page's brother. For Richard Page the elder and younger, see Horowitz, "Thomas Sunnyff", n. 81.

mayor of Coventry, and Empson was that city's recorder.[99] Kebell also held lands and had the use of manors in Coventry and in Empson's home county of Northamptonshire.[100] He received a feofment for his use of the manor of Mollington in 1507 from four men, including Richard Empson's son, Thomas.[101]

Kebell was bound financially and legally to the king and his councillors, perhaps through his exposure as a grocer and merchant of the staple of Calais, a London alderman and a sheriff. Before these privy seals were being issued, Kebell and another man entered into an obligation for the large sum of £1,000, recorded by Dudley in his book, for money lent by Henry VII, although perhaps it was more of a fine.[102] Kebell required a pardon in 1503 for all offences against the customs. In February 1507, he paid Dudley 500 marks in cash and entered an obligation for another 500 marks to receive an all-encompassing pardon, which was not issued and enrolled at chancery until June.[103] Dudley later admitted, while in the

---

[99] *Cal. Pat. Rolls 1494-1509*, p. 516; T.N.A.: P.R.O., C 244/154 no. 5(b), 10 July 1503, inquisition before Richard Coke, mayor of Coventry, and "Rico Empson Recordatore".

[100] T.N.A.: PRO, C 142/32/9-10, E 150/682/4; Stratford-upon-Avon, Shakespeare Centre Library and Archives, Misc. Inq. Post. Mort., DR10/1889; Northampton, Northamptonshire Record Office, Westmorland of Apethorpe MSS. Box 2/Parcel IX/No. 2/h.

[101] Warwickshire County Record Office, CRO MS. 457/50/1 (12 Nov. 1507). All four men signed the agreement and fragments of their seals remain. The catalogue description of one of the men as "Prius" Porter should read "Richard" Porter.

[102] Brit. Libr., Lansdowne MS. 127 fo. 5; C.J. Harrison, "The petition of Edmund Dudley", *Eng. Hist. Rev.*, lxxxvii (1972), pp. 82-99, at p. 98, n. 80 for a possible explanation.

[103] Brit. Libr., Lansdowne MS. 127 fos. 5, 38, 47v; *Cal. Pat. Rolls 1494-1509*, pp. 318, 516; T.N.A.: P.R.O., C 82/300, 24 June 1507. Kebell did not suffer after Henry VII's death, if in fact he was working with Dudley. He was listed in the general pardon and became mayor of London in the reign of Henry VIII (*L&P*, I.i., no. 438 (1), m. 19); "Mayors and sheriffs of London 1273-1602, Edward I through Elizabeth I" <http://genealogy.patp.us/lordmayors.aspx> [accessed 8 Feb. 2008]). Copies of bonds and various transactions by Kebell and a fellow merchant of the staple of Calais between the years 1501 and 1517 included a letter to "Mr. Crumwell" (*L&P* Addenda, I.i., no. 345). He gave generously to the poor and left £1,000 for the renovation of the old church of St. Mary after his death in 1518. Kebell built for himself a "faire monument raised ouer him on the North side the Quier", but by mid century it was torn down and his bones were "vnkindly cast out" to make way for two deceased mayors and fellow grocers (Stow, *Survey of London*, pp. 111, 253, 263-4).

Tower awaiting execution, that Kebell paid the king "great somes vpon a smale ground".[104] It would therefore be interesting to discover if Kebell was one of many London officials working willingly (or not) with councillors to prosecute bonds, or a victim of the sometimes unscrupulous behaviour of Empson and Dudley towards London citizens and office-holders.[105]

Henry VII and his councillors were also involved in interfering with the customary procedures of the City, a not uncommon occurrence before his reign, as previously discussed. It clearly irked not a few aldermen, many of whom were members of rival gilds, when the Merchant Taylors of London paid £100 in ready money to Henry VII for his favour in having their charter approved—a move the City officials tried to annul without success.[106] Although in theory the various London companies were under the jurisdiction of the mayor and aldermen, by 1390 gilds were seeking royal charters—in effect licences to hold land in mortmain—as they endeavoured to become more independent of City control.[107] The Merchant Taylors, who had gained advantages through earlier charters, claimed a powerful ally in Sir Reynold Bray, Henry VII's chief minister and a member of their fraternity, "without charge". Undoubtedly with help from Bray before his death, and from the king thereafter (who was a brother in the fraternity as were previous kings), in 1503 they acquired the right to become fully-fledged merchants and not just cloth-traders.[108] The charter was negotiated by John Percyvale, who became the first tailor elected mayor of London, and William Fitzwilliam, another influential gild member.[109] The City government pleaded before the king's council,

---

[104] C.J. Harrison, "The petition of Edmund Dudley", p. 90.

[105] E.g., Nicholas Nyens, a sheriff at the same time as Kebell, who took a bond of the peace from several sureties on 4 May 1503 for an imprisoned man that was later forfeited to a groom of the chamber (T.N.A.: PRO, E 404/85, 2 May 1505).

[106] Brit. Libr., Lansdowne MS. 127 fo. 48v (22 Jan. 1506). See earlier discussion.

[107] Barron, *London in the Later Middle Ages*, pp. 208-9.

[108] M. Davies, *The Merchant Taylors' Company of London: Court Minutes, 1486-93* (Stamford, 2000), p. 157; M. Davies and A. Saunders, *The History of the Merchant Taylors' Company* (Leeds, 2004), pp. 73-4; Stow, *Survey of London*, p. 183. The company started a furore in 1440 when they received the right to search houses and shops for defective retail cloth, a privilege that did not bring cheer to the drapers (Davies and Saunders, pp. 76ff.).

[109] Davies and Saunders, pp. 84-6. The authors do not mention the payment of £100 to Henry VII via Edmund Dudley for their charter, nor the bifurcated negotiations for both London's charter and the annulment of the tailors' charter.

where they were enjoined to "shewe cause reasonable if anie they have whie the kinges majestie should not by authorite of his prerogative have power by lawe to graunt, unto the [art] or misterie of Taylors, the name Marchan-taylors". The mayor and aldermen were also told to make sure that no evil would come to the tailors in their various wards because of the letters patent; any aldermen inciting evil behaviour would be punished along with the perpetrators.[110]

The king's interference in the election of a London sheriff, perhaps to "plant" another possible informer such as Henry Kebell, did not go down well with the City elders either. Various London chronicles recorded that William Fitzwilliam, the London alderman who helped to negotiate the charter for the Merchant Taylors, was offered up as the king's candidate for sheriff in 1506, causing a great conflict between Fitzwilliam and the City's candidate, another alderman named Roger Grove.[111] Fitzwilliam actually lost to Grove. However, this royal rebuff may have begun a series of fines and imprisonments against Grove and his fellow sheriff and mayor by Henry VII and his ministers.[112] Fitzwilliam did become sheriff two years later, although the chronicles either did not know or failed to mention what behind-the-scenes intrigue was taking place.[113] For in

---

They note that £87 10s 6d of expenses were incurred to obtain the charter, which was granted on 6 Jan. 1503.

[110] *Select Cases in the Council of Henry VII*, ed. C.G. Bayne and W.H. Dunham (Selden Soc., lxxv, 1958), pp. 35-6; H. Miller, "London and parliament in the reign of Henry VIII", *Bull. Inst. Hist. Research*, xxxv (1962), pp. 128-49 at pp. 130ff.

[111] Horowitz, "Thomas Sunnyff", p. 347 and n. 73. Fitzwilliam was on one of the infamous commissions to find concealed lands, goods of outlaws, forfeited bonds etc. for the City of London on 26 Feb. 1505—a commission to which Dudley was appointed for Surrey and Sussex (*Cal. Pat. Rolls 1494-1509*, pp. 420-1).

[112] The story of Roger Grove, Richard Shore and Thomas Knesworth and their pursuit by Dudley and the king is found in Horowitz, "Thomas Sunnyff", pp. 352ff. and in several chronicles, e.g., *Great Chronicle*, p. 329; and Richard Arnold, *The Customs of London, otherwise called Arnold's Chronicle*, ed. F. Douce (1811), p. xliii.

[113] *Cal. Pat. Rolls 1494-1509*, p. 539, referred to Fitzwilliam as one of the sheriffs of London, 12 July 1507. The City took revenge on Fitzwilliam after Henry VII's death, electing him to the office again by declaring his earlier election invalid. Fitzwilliam refused to serve and sued the mayor—a member of the draper's company—but he was fined and lost his franchise (*Great Chronicle*, pp. 366-7). The case ended up in star chamber, where his fines were overturned. Fitzwilliam continued his career in London, working for a time in the service of Cardinal Wolsey (Davies and Saunders, p. 87).

November 1506, Fitzwilliam actually paid Dudley £100 for the king's favour in obtaining the office of sheriff.[114] Henry VII also sought to control the election of the mayor in 1508, an arm-twisting exercise that succeeded.[115]

Royal searches into the records of London seem to have taken place, with dire consequences for many citizens. The case of Thomas Sunnyff, explained in detail elsewhere, is an example of how a dormant recognizance recorded in the books kept by the mayor and aldermen of London could be used to persecute an innocent man.[116] Henry VII's councillors were blatant in their pursuit of such information, even before Dudley became the focal point for such activity. In 1499, the councillors sitting in star chamber ordered the serjeant-at-arms "to call the

---

[114] Brit. Libr., Harleian MS. 1877 fo. 47; Lansdowne MS. 127 fo. 31. Once Henry VIII became firmly established on the throne, it was not a good idea to besmirch the memory or machinations of his father. On 8 Oct. 1510, the wardens of the fellowships of mercers, grocers, fishmongers, goldsmiths, haberdashers and skinners personally appeared before the London mayor and alderman "and examined wheder my lord maire labored unto them to make m[aster] fitzwillm shiref. yee or nay. All they seid nay by the othes that they had afore this tyme made to the Citie" (C.L.R.O., REP 2, fo. 99).

[115] On 5 Oct. 1508, at the court of aldermen, it was decided that "the wardens of every fealoships shalbe sumonyd agaynst thyrsday to appere at the guyldhall a thyrsday next comyng to thentent that the kyngs letter addressid for the eleccion of m[aster] Jennyns to thoffice of maroltie shalbe redde to theyme" (C.L.R.O., REP 2, fo. 49). Whatever transpired at that meeting was probably moot: Stephen Jenyns, a former sheriff and a member of the merchant taylors' gild, was elected mayor (T.N.A.: P.R.O., C 244/145 no. 19(c); C 244/148, nos. 1, 4(a); C.L.R.O, JOR 11, 1506-18, fo. 53; Davies and Saunders, pp. 65, 87). No evidence could be found that Jenyns ever paid Dudley or the king for his office. There is an indication that he may have served time in gaol for an unpaid debt (T.N.A.: P.R.O., C 244/148 no. 4(a)(b)). He was included in the general pardon early in the new reign (L&P., I. i, no. 438 (1) (m. 19)). Five months after Henry VIII became king, there was apparently an accusation of favouritism involving Jenyns during the previous reign towards one of the informers who was punished after the death of Henry VII (C.L.R.O., REP 2, fo. 71v). A fine was paid to the new king, and Jenyns may have been one of those involved in the resolution (Brit. Libr., Harleian MS. 2252 fo. 7v). Jenyns was in fact on a commission to hold an inquest in the Guildhall for all treasons, insurrections and the like in and around London. This referred to the indictment against Dudley plus alleged crimes committed by his and Empson's cohorts (Brit. Libr., Lansdowne MS. 511 fo. 137v; T.N.A.: P.R.O., KB 9/453 no. 456).

[116] Horowitz, "Thomas Sunnyff", *passim*.

Chamberlaine of London, to appere and to bringe with him the bookes of Recognisance of suerties taken for Orphanes gooddes in London".[117] The London government endeavoured to co-operate with Henry VII and his councillors when certain information was requested. Two years earlier, in 1497, the council of the mayor and aldermen "agreed that such gru^{a}nts sta^{ts} and other records as the Cite haith to shewe for their right as touchyng the forfeato^r of fforen bying and sellyng shalbe drawn and writun in a booke and the same to be delyv^{r}d to the kyngs lerned Councell".[118] The first Tudor, however, believed it to be within his rights to have access to City records, especially when there was the possibility of forfeitures due the crown.

A conciliar action that may have taken place late in the reign possibly helped to bring London officials together to trigger some active steps against what may have been the pervasive intrusion by the king and his councillors into City affairs and records. On 17 July 1508, Henry VII signed a signet letter to the chancellor and archbishop of Canterbury. The king ordered him to put the great seal to a commission for London, reciting such articles as Sir Richard Empson, chancellor of the duchy of Lancaster, "shall devise and send unto you".[119] What those articles were has not been discovered in the surviving documentation, but it most likely involved inquiries and searches that would be intolerable to the mayor, aldermen and sheriffs of the City, to say nothing of the business community.[120] Indeed, just six weeks later a commission composed of four

---

[117] Brit. Libr., Harleian MS. 305 fo. 34v; Add. MS. 4521 fos. 113v-114; *Select Cases in the Council of Henry VII*, p. 31). At the same time, processes were to "surcease" against Richard Odiham. On 21 Sept. 1496, Richard "Odyam" was elected one of the auditors of the accounts of the chambers and wardens in arrears, and perhaps he became a source of information for the king and his councillors (*Letter-Book L*, p. 318).

[118] C.L.R.O., REP 1, fo. 13v.

[119] T.N.A.: P.R.O., C 82/315, 17 July 1508. This commission was not enrolled on the close rolls or patent rolls in chancery.

[120] Penny Tucker has suggested to the author that a commission neither enrolled at chancery nor mentioned in the City records may not have occurred, although she noted that given Henry VII's "personal" rule, with numerous examples of failure to enroll documents, there could have been an active commission. One entry on the patent rolls for 20 Oct. 1507 began listing a commission but was never finished, and later vacated (*Cal. Pat. Rolls 1494-1509*, p. 581). The author has mentioned elsewhere that "oral appointments" for offices were common in the reign, without official enrollment: an exchequer list of various officials for the woollen trade stated that it was believed that many of these appointments were made throughout

men was requested by Henry VII to make inquiries in Norfolk and Suffolk about every imaginable prerogative right of the king, similar to the list that Humphrey Coningsby drew up for York. Although there is no mention of this commission's author in the summary of its enrollment found in the *Calendar of Patent Rolls*, it is known from a surviving signet letter that Henry VII commanded his chancellor to draw up the Norfolk-Suffolk commission "according to suche articles and info^rmacions as o^r right trusty [knight] and counseillo^r Sr Richard Emson shall shew unto you".[121]

The "London commission" may have been for a similar purpose. It is also interesting to note that the 17 July signet letter for the City commission based on Empson's requirements came a little over two weeks after Empson, Lovell, Dudley and Wyatt, representing Henry VII, entered into an indenture with Edward Belknap to become surveyor of the king's prerogative with the power to inquire and seize lands in the name of the king.[122] It is therefore likely that Empson's London commission was part and parcel of this effort to determine a wide range of possible abuses of laws and prerogative rights, and any payments due upon potential violations, including those involving recognizances.This may provide a reason why the City fathers, on 5 October 1507, ordered the recorder to visit the king at Richmond and talk about the "late attemptats doon by the officers of the Towre and sundry Juries of Middlesex ch^argid to enquyre of things doon in London contr^ay to the lib[er]ties of this Citie", and it would

---

England by the king's commandment "wherof we have no Record of the kyngs l[ett]res patentes in the Escheker" (Horowitz, "Thomas Sunnyff", p. 330 and n. 18, quoting W.A.M., MS. 12248). The City journals and repertories are mute on many aspects of legal and administrative procedures and events taking place during the reign. This silence encompasses several proceedings held at various London courts regarding the undoubtedly very public matter of Thomas Sunnyff (Horowitz, "Thomas Sunnyff", pp. 330-2). The same is true with dealings involving Dudley and perhaps Empson, some of which are discussed above. It is quite likely that with the king drifting towards death and Empson and Dudley administering and enforcing royal policy, Empson did indeed move forward with a commission targeted for London, or at the very least let the mayor and aldermen know of his intention to do so.

[121] *Cal. Pat. Rolls 1494-1509*, p. 627, incorrectly printed as 1509; T.N.A.: P.R.O., C 82/315, dated 21 Aug. 1508.

[122] *Cal. Pat. Rolls 1494-1509*, p. 591. The appointment was not enrolled until 19 Aug.

be difficult to believe that a demand for looking at records was not part of those enquiries.[123]

It was not long after Empson's commission for London may have been implemented, and perhaps with the knowledge of the king's mortal infirmity, that the London officials began to deliberate and act.[124] On 23 January 1509, the aldermen swore an oath to keep the secrets of their court and not disclose them to anyone.[125] Two days later, they agreed that from that point onwards "shall no man looke nor serche any records or bookys of the Citie excepte the councell lernyd and sworn to the secrettis of the same" without the common clerk or any of four clerks being present—the "councell lernyd" here referring to the City's lawyers and legal counsel.[126] In this instance, once a clerk searched or copied any record, he was to "immediatly laye up the books or reco^rds under locke".[127] On 15 February, the aldermen took another oath and ordered that the door leading from the mayor's court to the book house "shalbe shytte and boltid on the inside" so that no one during the court's session could pass between the council chamber and the outer court except the aldermen. Any clerks or citizens having business with the mayor and aldermen were to enter the chamber

---

[123] C.L.R.O., REP 2, fo. 32. The various chronicles made note of corrupted London juries, and the role Empson and Dudley played in them.

[124] It is not certain what caused the death of Henry VII (S.B. Chrimes, *Henry VII* (Berkeley, Calif., 1972), p. 314). He was most likely ill for the last two years of his life, beginning in Mar. 1507 when he paid 40*s* for an under-clerk of the signet to write the first draft of his will and a month later when "docto^r ffyssher and m[aster] woulsey" received £180 4*s* 6*d* for the saying of 7,209 masses at 6*d* a mass, with 2,000 more in May at Oxford and Cambridge (T.N.A.: P.R.O., E 36/214 fos. 70, 73, 77v). The king was rumoured to be "in extremis" by Aug. 1508, although it might have been the sweating sickness or some other malady from which he may have only partially recovered (*Cal. St. Papers, Spanish*, suppl. to vols. i-ii, p. 23; *Cal. St. Papers, Venetian, 1202-1509*, p. 906).

[125] Such oaths were usually sworn by key city officials throughout the realm not only to uphold civil liberties but also to keep deliberations secret and information away from the royal government (J. Lee, "'Ye shall disturbe noe mans right': oath-taking and oath-breaking in late medieval and early modern Bristol", *Urban Hist.*, xxxiv (2007), pp. 27-38, at pp. 28, 32-4).

[126] E.g., when the mayor and aldermen appointed John Green and Richard Brook to render a decision in a case, "ij of the lerned Counseill of the Citie, arbitrato^rs indifferently chosen" (C.L.R.O., REP 2, fo. 31v); see also C.L.R.O., REP 1, fo. 46v, "lernyd Councell of this Cite". For the use of the terms "learned council" and "council learned" see Horowitz, "Policy and prosecution".

[127] C.L.R.O., REP 2, fo. 56.

from the outer door. The new oath, which was enrolled in their official record, stated that no books or copies of anything touching the liberties of the City could be removed without permission from the mayor, recorder and town clerk, or any two of them. This included "any custumary accions declaracions plees p[ro]cesses reall or psonell deds testaments acts or statuts of pliament" etc., and "alman^r of recognisaunce in the ffiles Books Rolls and Jo^{r}nalls w^{t}in the said Citie before this xv day of ffebruar taken entred or enrolled of record or hereaft^r to be taken entred or enrolled of record in the mayo[r]s court w^{t}in the seid Citie alwey except".[128] The "alwey except" referred to the exception pertaining to writs of error delineated in the long exception written in the 1444 charter and in other references to the City's liberties.[129]

Guarded precautions to protect records were of concern to London's elders in previous reigns. The difficulty with these extraordinary and seemingly unprecedented measures involves ascertaining how extreme these oaths and actions were compared to past confrontations between the City and the king. A major obstacle for such a determination involves the documentation itself. The repertories of the aldermen do not begin until 1495; before that, the meetings of the common council included the aldermen, as recorded in the journals. Earlier aldermen's records were their personal property, and therefore rarely survived. Most of the chamberlain's records for the medieval period were destroyed in the 1666 Great Fire, or in a fire in the chamberlain's office in the late 18th century. As for records from the sheriffs' courts, for the early Tudor period only a few rolls of actions survive from 1554.[130]

---

[128] C.L.R.O., REP 2, fos. 58v-9.

[129] The "alwey except" was short-hand for clerks eschewing the repetition of long legal sections, although the exception could follow if brief. Another journal entry regarding false imprisonment gave City authorities the power to release defendants from prison and discharge them "of the said accions in or for default of the continuall sute of the said playntif or playntiffs / *except alwey* mat^r in lawe delay by writte or otherwise be the lette or Impediment of any suche p[ro]cesse". (C.L.R.O., JOR 10, fo. 243, author's italics.) The same was true of the use of "&c", such as the recognizance taken by the London chamberlain for William Ussher and his servants to be of good abearing against the king and his liege people and to be available for appearance "afore the kyng or his Counsell or ells afore the mair and alderman &c." when warned "to answer to suche matiers as shalbe laide ayenst theym &c than &c". (C.L.R.O., JOR 10, fo. 21).

[130] Barron, *London in the Later Middle Ages*, pp. 3, 141, 179, 181; Sir J. Baker, *The Oxford History of the Laws of England*, vi: *1483-1558* (Oxford, 2003), p. 283.

There are only slight hints of similar actions before those taken late in Henry VII's reign. However, they appear quite tame by comparison. One example occurred on 7 May 1462, during Edward IV's reign, when an ordinance by the mayor and aldermen decreed that all rolls and records in the custody of the chamberlain or under-chamberlain should be delivered by indenture to the common clerk. These would remain in his custody in the upper chamber, "and he in future be responsible for them, and not deliver any Record without his responsibility". However, this may have simply been a statement of procedure, since the common clerk began to share the chamberlain's authority to provide access to records or to make copies of them. Penalties were forthcoming if the common clerk allowed unauthorized persons to view the records. No oath-taking was involved in this decree.[131]

The powerful volley of oaths and actions at the end of Henry VII's reign strongly suggests a reaction to the policy of the king and his councillors against what was perceived as the rights and customs of the City. It was now apparent that a major confrontation between the City and the king was potentially in the offing. Events, however, not only conspired to avoid a conflict but also shifted the policy of the first Tudor and his ministers. On 21 April, Henry died. His two main proponents of royal judicial and fiscal policy, Richard Empson and Edmund Dudley, were arrested on a charge of constructive treason because of their sessile relationship to a king whose soul had to be protected.[132] Many of their informers and henchmen were arrested or lost their franchise in the City, and the young Henry VIII was quick in denouncing the reign of recognizance terror perpetrated on many of the citizens of London and throughout England by his father's evil ministers. Of course, missing from this wave of arrests and finger-pointing was the fact that Henry VII was the main patron behind the policy, and that many of the new king's inner

---

[131] *Letter-Book L*, p. 17.

[132] See Horowitz, "Thomas Sunnyff", pp. 357-8; "Richard Empson", p. 45; S.J. Gunn, "The accession of Henry VIII", *Hist. Research*, lxiv (1991), pp. 278-88, at pp. 283ff. Although there were discrepancies as to whether he died on 21 or 22 Apr. 1509, his death was apparently kept secret until 23 Apr., with a general pardon going out on 24 Apr. (Gunn, "Accession", p. 279). The populace may well have been kept in the dark: a deed written at Henlow, Bedfordshire on 25 Apr. 1509 still referred to Henry VII as the king (Bedford, Bedfordshire and Luton Archives and Records Services, LJeayes/Intro/2, no. 579). However, if Henry died on the 21st and it was public knowledge, it could still have taken four days for word to reach Henlow some 45 miles away.

circle of councillors had worked closely with Empson and Dudley in taking and prosecuting bonds.[133] However, it was Empson and Dudley who were singled out as the worst abusers of suing upon bonds for spurious reasons—or no reasons at all—and searching the files and records of various repositories to ferret out potential violations of the law. It would not be the last time that governments pursued such an activity.

The city of London and other towns throughout the realm now had a fresh start with a king seemingly bent on righting the wrongs of the past reign. Many of the recognizances and obligations taken or "discovered" and put in prosecution were vacated, although quite often after a full or partial payment was made.[134] Parliament condemned the activities of those representing the old regime and legitimized both the new reign and the rule of law, although a bill to rescind the use of privy seals contrary to the common law was vetoed by Henry VIII.[135] Commissions went out across the country offering redress of grievances, many of which had been longstanding during a long reign. Six months after the new king ascended the throne, the London charter approved by Henry VII was delivered to chancery, most likely for review and reworking. A committee of eleven men was also convened by the mayor and aldermen to decide what should be presented for the new charter.[136] Although Henry VIII continued his father's administration of bonds for both judicial and financial business— despite an attempt by the exchequer to regain its direct involvement in obligations and recognizances, usurped with other financial responsibilities by the Tudor chamber—the blatant misuse of power and its intrusion into the lives of the citizens and cities of England did not return, or at least not in this form.[137]

Nonetheless, after almost a quarter of a century of strong central rule the cities and towns of England had been brought more closely into the sphere of royal administration, if not always royal jurisdiction. The local

---

[133] E.g., Gunn, "Sir Thomas Lovell", p. 127: "For debts great and small, payable and suspended, reasonable and outrageous, Lovell took bond after bond on the king's behalf".

[134] Horowitz, "Thomas Sunnyff", n. 134; "Policy and prosecution".

[135] Cavill, pp. 173-4.

[136] C.L.R.O., JOR 11, 1506-18, fos. 87, 89.

[137] M.R. Horowitz, "An early-Tudor teller's book", *Eng. Hist. Rev.*, xcvi (1981), pp. 103-16 [Chapter Nine]; D. Grummitt, "Public service, private interest and patronage in the 15th-century exchequer", in *The Fifteenth Century III: Authority and Subversion*, ed. L. Clark (Woodbridge, 2003), pp. 149-62, at p. 160.

liberties and customs that since time out of mind had signified the state of England were morphing into the concept of a centralized English state. Reining in London was a key development toward "national" law, and late-medieval commentators concerned with royal infringement could point to Henry VII's reign and its aftermath.[138] At the same time, the City's customs and procedures had an impact not only on the laws and judicial administration of other cities but also on the common law of the realm.[139] Arbitration in London and throughout England was becoming a cost-effective tool for dispute resolution in opposition to the ponderous, expensive common law proceedings. Conditional bonds were often part of an arbitration, in effect leading to "binding arbitration" to discourage one side from defaulting on its pledges. Such remedies may have threatened customary local courts—even London lawyers complained of losing cases and fees to arbitration between members of gilds.[140] But such remedies, which were on the rise through the course of the 15th century, also demonstrated a growing respect for legal solutions.

The first Tudor most likely did not work this out in pursuing a royal policy based on bonds for debts, behaviour and appearance at various courts or conciliar tribunals. But this policy, which deployed the accepted laws and customs of England, nonetheless helped him to establish a more stable, financially-sound monarchy than his predecessors. By the end of his dynasty, it would perhaps be appropriate to refer to a "national" system of law courts.[141] However, that could only occur with a shift in perspective that allowed national law to supplant or envelop local custom or the particular rights claimed by cities and towns. Furthermore, it had also become evident that the angst often created by royal commissions of the

---

[138] P. Tucker, "Reaction to Henry VII's style of kingship and its contribution to the emergence of constitutional monarchy in England", *Hist. Research*, lxxxii (2009), pp. 511-25. With regards to London, Tucker notes that "whereas in the fourteenth century the pressure from below was sometimes as great as the pressure from above, under Henry VII it was evidently the pressure from above which was greater, or at least the more strongly felt, by the last few years of his reign."

[139] Christian Liddy has an interesting take on the metaphor of the "royal chamber" as a reference to London and emulated by York and Coventry in the 15th century, especially when seeking favourable charters (C. Liddy, "The rhetoric of the royal chamber in late medieval London, York and Coventry", *Urban Hist.*, xxix (2002), pp. 323-49).

[140] Miller, p. 132. Arbitration was widely used in the later middle ages by the various trade companies (Davies, pp. 25-8). For Thomas Lovell and arbitration, see Gunn, "Sir Thomas Lovell", pp. 132-3.

[141] Tucker, *Law Courts and Lawyers*, pp. 6-7, 362ff.

peace or special commissions established a reign of legal, not martial, conflict between the centre and the localities under the first Tudor. Nevertheless, these commissions were peopled more and more by both landed gentry, who were shifting their political sights from local magnates to the royal government, and by ministers seeking to look into the records of counties and municipalities to protect and prosecute not only the king's prerogative but also the laws of the realm.[142]

After Henry VII's death, the notion that a new king, his councillors and parliament could legally right the wrongs of a past government demonstrated that there truly was recourse against bad or dubious aspects of royal policy. Moreover, it had become clear by this time that legal solutions to disputes were readily available and forthcoming in the courts of the king, which had become the courts of the people. Tensions between the towns and the monarchy would continue to ebb and flow, and neither would entirely cease from pursuing competing interests.[143] Posturing would also continue between city elites and their own citizens.[144] But there was a real sense developing of a central government, and not just a royal centre of power. The first Tudor contributed to that development through a policy that went beyond rhetoric and proclamations when it came to law and order and the financial wellbeing of his government and monarchy.

---

[142] Gunn, "Henry VII in context", p. 307. The commissions of the peace held throughout the reign usually included one or more of the king's trusted councillors to infuse central government interests and policies as a counterweight to the local gentry who traditionally served on them (Gunn, "Sir Thomas Lovell", pp. 133-5). Conciliar participation also meant pursuing the king's interests in law and order as well as finance. A 1496 statute allowed the indictment process to be bypassed by the J.P.s, who could present felonies solely based on information (Horowitz, "Thomas Sunnyff", p. 331 n. 21).

[143] "The Crown conceded urban self-government but insisted on ultimate control. The rhetoric of borough charters shows that monarchs gave privileges in return for assistance to groups of people who were willing to be amenable to royal direction". (S.M. Jack, *Towns in Tudor and Stuart England* (Basingstoke, 1996), pp. 120-1). See also Lee, "Urban policy".

[144] R. Tittler, *The Reformation and the Towns in England: Politics and Political Culture c.1540-1640* (Oxford, 1998), pp. 293-4.

CHAPTER SEVEN

HENRY VII AND THE DARK SIDE
OF ROYAL POLICY*

Introduction

I spent much of 2009 developing a course syllabus with primary and secondary readings. I also created attention-grabbing (I hoped!) PowerPoint presentations and video "field trips" to relevant English castles, towns and such—I didn't think it reasonable to ask the History Department for air tickets to England to help students visualize what we were discussing! This was all done for a course I titled The Tudor Kings, *previously mentioned, which I began teaching in the spring of 2010. It covered the reigns of Henry VII, Henry VIII and Edward VI, with the bookends of briefly exploring the Wars of the Roses and the reign of Queen Mary.*

Due to time constraints in a fifteen-week semester, I knew that certain topics could not be discussed or explored at length. One of those that I thought might pique class interest centered on the corruption and shady dealings taking place in Henry VII's reign, which had intrigued me as a student [Chapter Four]. For one, it was important for the reputation grafted onto this king for greed and harsh behavior towards English men and women. "Greedy" is probably the wrong word choice for any king, especially a medieval or early-modern one. It is, in effect, the sine qua non *of kingship—monarchs needed money to maintain their monarchy. A preoccupation with seeking money, independent of other sources from rival power bases such as parliament, was expected. Henry VII was no different except for his other commitment that often took precedent: enforcing the customs and laws of England.*

Indeed, the contemporary observer Polydore Vergil could be wishy-washy in trying to decide which course of action the first Tudor king was

---

* Essay completed and made available to students Dec. 2009 for Spring Quarter 2010 and each spring through 2013.

pursuing. In my work and in the classroom I have expressed my belief that Henry's prosecution of penal statutes and of those in breach of legal obligations did bring him wealth, but law and order was paramount. No one told him the Wars of the Roses were over.

It was also significant to know what illicit activities were taking place in Henry VII's reign and by whom beyond the two men who lost their lives to contain the anger permeating the populace once the king was dead: Sir Richard Empson and Edmund Dudley, Esq. Just as key was how Henry VIII, his government and the city of London reacted to this "dark side".

I therefore decided to write something on the topic for the class, make it available for reading and touch upon it if and when feasible. Most of the research had been completed but not used for an article I had published on English towns, which is Chapter Six. The "dark side" essay was written with the knowledge that students would have already read four of the articles that are now found in the present book as Chapters Three through Six. As it turned out, over the four years of teaching the class I observed a keen curiosity in Empson, Dudley and the sinister aspect of the reign—behavior that nonetheless did not impinge on Henry VII's resolve to keep the peace and build a financially sound monarchy. I found their fascination interesting—I guess corruption sells, too.

Henry was committed to enforcing the laws of the realm, which he did with impunity. He and his ministers held people of all stations in life accountable for any judicial or financial obligation they might have with the crown that had lapsed or had simply been ignored. The king made it patently unambiguous that all courts were the king's courts, as were the obligations to pay debts or keep the peace. The essay hoped to scratch the surface of how things got out of hand, so to speak. It addressed how corruption and extortion set in, as it is wont to do, when money is involved and political or financial power is available to wield. These are not unfamiliar concepts today.

I made the decision to spend a little time discussing the attributes of the informer, hoping to impress upon the students that this was an ongoing activity long before and after the first Tudor king gained the throne. Scholarship on the topic for Henry VII's reign up to that time usually focused on the evil deeds and perpetrators in the waning years of the first Tudor king, often without context for the entire reign. Finally, I wanted to remind students that a government could both prosecute and violate the law at the same time! Again, that is hardly a foreign situation in our present world.

It has been argued elsewhere[1] that Henry VII sought both financial security and financial independence—he let it be known in parliament in 1504 that he hoped it would be his last one, and it was. He also wanted adherence to law and order for civil stability and the avoidance of a continuation of the Wars of the Roses.[2] These objectives have been blurred since his death in 1509 by the perception that he used old laws and unfulfilled or neglected contracts (bonds) simply to funnel cash from those allegedly in default of those bonds into the royal coffers in the form of fines, fees for pardons or renegotiated debts. Moreover, he used officials and ministers to discover such breaches in contractual obligations to prosecute them. While much of this was done quite legally, if not popularly, it became apparent that many who pursued this royal policy in his name also did so unethically and illegally to profit themselves as well as the crown.

What follows is an exploration of a few of those who actively engaged in this undertaking. It is important to realize that their activities were not new nor were they a Tudor invention for good or for evil. Hence, some historical background will also be provided. While it is evident that Henry VII was aware of at least some of the illicit behavior of many of these "promoters" of his policy, it is also evident that the king wanted justice and stability and did not tolerate in his subjects some of the very behavior accomplished by these men who nonetheless benefitted him. This may seem contradictory. It can be argued with no great burden that in the realm of finance and law and order, such opposite behaviors often go hand in hand, if not from one hand to the other.

The occupation of the reward-seeking "informer" probably grew along with civilization and codified laws, going back in time long before Judas identified Jesus for thirty pieces of silver. A widespread reason for informing on someone to the benefit of the government usually involved bringing to bear those who allegedly broke the law, and it continues into the present in the form of "whistle-blowers". Recently, in the Dodd-Frank Bill first proposed in June 2009 by the U.S. Congress, whistleblowers could receive a 10 to 30 per cent bounty for exposing million-dollar

---

[1] [Chapters Three through Six]

[2] *The Parliament Rolls of Medieval England 1275-1504*, Vol. XVI, Henry VII 1489-1504, ed. Rosemary Horrox (London, 2005), p. 332. Other than requesting two non-war aids—expenses for the knighting of Prince Arthur and the marriage of his daughter Margaret to James IV of Scotland—there was no effort to seek money from parliament. (p. 316.) Henry VII was doing quite well on his own by 1504.

securities fraud.[3] Whistle-blowers today, and their historic ancestors the informers, are usually seen in favorable light, although their work involving searches into records and private lives can be unnerving, especially if innocent people are caught up in any investigation.

The acceptance of the informer was true in England where it was viewed as a profession. Indeed, they were seen as pursuing an important activity to help uncover abuse. A 1335 statute allowed an informer, "who will sue for [the king] against those that commit any Fraud" against an ordinance prohibiting the import of counterfeit coinage, "to have the fourth penny of that that shall be so achieved at his Suit to our Profit."[4] In the 1420s, a statute provided informers with from a third to a fourth part of the goods forfeited for, among other reasons, trespasses from evading the customs on wool. An act passed in the reign of Henry VIII gave half the penalty for exports of brass or bell metal overseas "to the party that will sue for the same by writ, bill, plaint or information."[5]

Sometimes referred to as "common informers", they plied their trade through the judicial system at the national and local levels or worked through government officials.[6] In the Essex Quarter Session in 1615, one informer accused a party of poaching; another for an unlicensed alehouse and for breaches of the peace; another for working as a brazier (brass worker) without first going through an apprenticeship.[7] Upon conviction, informers at those sessions often received half the fines or confiscations ordered by the court. At the city of Chester Assembly in November 1536, to prevent price hikes in barley due to unfettered brewing of malt, a law was passed limiting such activity. The penalty was forfeiture of the malt with half going to the informer and half to the sheriffs.[8] A proclamation in 1602 against the use of "decried (depreciated) moneys" by anyone in England except certain goldsmiths carried penalties of seizure and fines, half of which went to the informer.[9]

---

[3] The bill was in revision in both houses as of Dec. 2009 and took the name of its legislative sponsors.
[4] 9 Ed III, c. 5.
[5] Alan Harding, *Medieval Law and the Foundations of the State* (Oxford UP, 2002), p. 246.
[6] Blackstone discussed the "common informer". (Sir William Blackstone, *Commentaries on the laws of England* (1769), 4.III.
[7] Essex Record Office, Quarter Sessions, Q/SBA 1/19, 1/21.
[8] Cheshire and Chester Archives, First Assembly Book, ZA/B/1/65-6.
[9] Lambeth Palace Library, Carew MS. 617, p. 264.

While the informer was seen as legitimate and a means of both rooting out corruption and discouraging it, greed often got in the way of investigating violations of the law. This could easily lead to the very corruption it sought to dampen or eliminate. The informer could trump up charges or even blackmail potential victims with false accusations through forgery, or misrepresentation of documents, or perjury, whether before a magistrate or government official. At those same Quarter Sessions in Essex for 1623, two examinations included information about a "corrupt common informer".

At the same time, fixing juries to obtain a favorable ruling by one of the parties was a separate but related law-related offense throughout the medieval period. The action of influencing a judicial outcome by corrupting jurors was part of a broader set of illegal actions known as "maintenance", whereby money could buy someone willing to lie against a party in a court of law. The litigant who pursued fixing a jury could thus unfairly win in court and be awarded money, goods or lands depending on the lawsuit. Statutes were passed periodically to discourage the practice.[10]

Corruption was ubiquitous. The 14th century Dominican friar John Bromyard warned that money perverted justice: "like weather cocks, jurors, lawyers and judges turn instinctively towards every wind of silver."[11] Abuses at the time were rampant, including the imprisonment of people until they were forced to pay fines, or empanelling jurors who would be paid off to favor one of the litigants. One historian of the period provided examples and noted that it was "only the tip of a rather unsavoury iceberg."[12]

Henry VII's first statute against maintenance early in his reign possessed a bit of irony.[13] While recognizing and seeking to root out these continuing illegal activities, by the end of his reign the corruption of jurors had become so pervasive that, along with shady informers, it contributed to his reputation as purposefully mulcting the populace through legal chicanery. It also hastened the arrests of the two most visible exponents of such

---

[10] E.g., 3 Ed I, c. 28 (1275); 1 Ed III, c. 14 (1327); 1 Ric II, c. 7 (1377). See also J.R. Lander, *English Justices of the Peace, 1461-1509* (Alan Sutton, Gloucester, 1989), p. 9.
[11] G.R. Owst, *Literature and Pulpit in Medieval England* (Oxford, 1961), p. 317, citing from Bromyard's *Summa Predicantium*, a book of sermon topics.
[12] Richard Gorski, *The Fourteenth-Century Sheriff, English local administration in the late middle ages* (Boydell, 2003), p. 112.
[13] 3 Hen VII, c. 1; S.B. Chrimes, *Henry VII* (U. of California, 1972), p. 155.

corruption, Richard Empson and Edmund Dudley, soon after the king's death.[14] Nonetheless, Henry followed in the footsteps of his royal predecessors, seeking to stamp out corrupt jurors with the help of some of those very men who promoted such activity.

Turning first to juries and perjury, the so-called Star Chamber Act passed in Henry VII's second parliament (1487) included prosecuting jurors who perjured themselves.[15] Councilors meeting in star chamber or in other venues or jurisdictions were diligent in upholding the law. On 22 May 1500 several of the king's counselors heard a case and reached a decision,

> It is decreed, Thomas Hall, and other Jurors with him, to be punished for perjurie committed by them in their aunsweares, here given, to their examinacon, made upon Interrogatories by the kinges Atturney ministred unto them.[16]

Entire juries could be summoned for appearance before the council on a charge of perjury.[17] The king strived to make the law reach far beyond London, to the inconvenience of many. A writ was sent to twelve jurors in Leicester to appear in star chamber for perjury; non-appearance would cost each £100. Henry was directly involved in this case.[18] A jury in Suffolk was ordered to appear before councilors in the duchy of Lancaster chambers for reasons unspecified.[19] This was a parallel policy adhered to by cities and towns across England, who meted out justice against perjurers in local legal venues. London had no taste for the crime, as when

---

[14] Empson was accused of fixing juries. In a letter to Sir Robert Plumpton, Empson was referred to as "the great man E" and it was inferred that he paid off jurors for favorable verdicts. (*Plumpton Correspondence*, ed. Thomas Stapleton (1839), Letter CXIX (18 May 1501), pp. 150-52).

[15] 3 Hen VII c. 1.

[16] *Select cases in the council of Henry VII*, ed. C.G. Bayne, Selden Society Vol. LXXV (1958), p. 33.

[17] E.g., Bayne, pp. 75-77, writ for summons under penalty of £100 each, dated 26 Oct. 1501. This is discussed below.

[18] T.N.A.: P.R.O., C 244/144 no. 20(a)(b)(c)(d). The first writ went out 23 May 1498 and subsequent correspondence included recognizances taken for their appearance and a signed warrant by Henry VII to members of the council in star chamber. The jurors did appear "to answer unto div'se poincts of periurye surmised against thaym." The king eventually ordered the chancellor to discharge the jurors and annul their bonds filed in chancery.

[19] T.N.A.: P.R.O., DL 5/4 fo. 119v (Hilary term, 1508).

four men were banned from sitting on future juries "for detestable and haynous p[er]iury."[20]

Henry VII also went after those who would intimidate juries. A signet letter from the king dated 6 September 1506 recited an incident in a sessions of the peace in Cornwall before the justices of the peace where a Bodmin gentleman named Thomas Trotte, upon hearing the indictment of felonies and trespasses read against him, "in suche wise faced and thretened [the jury] that thay ne durst present any Verdi[c]te of the p[r]misses to thaire grete trouble and fere." Trotte also threatened one of the J.P.s! He was fined £10.[21] The king continued to support the prosecution of perjured jurors. In his last parliament, a statute rehearsed previous laws from the 1495 and 1497 parliaments against false verdicts, stating their continuance as "necessarie to be contynued for the punysshment of the horryble vice of perjury."[22]

The use of informers was a common vehicle for discovering people who might have broken the law or reneged on any written obligations. First and foremost, all of the king's ministers took on that responsibility, searching rolls and files of the royal and conciliar courts, chancery, the exchequer and local judicial venues personally as J.P.s, on special commissions or with the help of their subordinates. The objective was to find out who broke the law by not paying debts, keeping the peace or allegiance, appearing in court or skirting the royal prerogatives such as wardship, marriage and entry into lands. Again, this had the dual results of maintaining strict adherence to the law and filling the coffers of the king.

But Henry VII also encouraged third parties not suffering from any alleged offense to sue upon it on behalf of the crown.[23] A 1490 statute spelled this out and it helped create a growing group of people who would gain access to possible infractions in statutory or contractual law either via a particular office they might hold or through assistance from one or more of the king's ministers or officers. Henry continued to push for information to prosecute those in breach of the law "to the derogacioun

---

[20] Corporation of London Records Office, Repertories of the Court of Aldermen 1 (1495-1504), fo. 38v.

[21] T.N.A.: P.R.O., E 404/86, also found in PSO 3 with the same date.

[22] Parliament Rolls, p. 337 (19 Hen VII c. 8). The statute ended with the formulaic "Le roy le vault" (the king wills it).

[23] P.R. Cavill, *The English Parliaments of Henry VII 1485-1504* (Oxford, 2009), pp. 95ff.

and losses of our rightes and prouffites and vnto the great lette and hurte of the said comune weal."[24]

While no doubt a shock to society, it was legal and there were many people involved besides those in Henry VII's government. Henry Kebell has been discussed elsewhere as a probable informer and promoter for the crown.[25] Moreover, he could use his office as sheriff in London to inform royal officials of potential forfeitures due on bonds. In a suit filed in chancery by a tradesman against the mayor, aldermen and sheriffs of London, the plaintiff alleged that Kebell imprisoned him because he would not accept sureties for bail.[26] Dudley may have been known to him and would have been a likely connection.

Some informers surface briefly and only in passing. Sir Walter Griffith was an informer who sought out lands held by others that rightfully were part of the royal demesne "whiche be in the kyngs honds."[27] It is difficult to determine when he was involved in personal matters or for the king. In a variance between Griffith and Richard Rokeby, the latter was sent a privy seal to appear before Empson, Dudley and other councilors sitting in the duchy chamber. No reason was given for the matter.[28] Earlier, when Henry VII ordered Griffith's arrest by the sheriff of York for certain "contempts" and misdemeanors committed against the king, Griffith was forced to find sureties and take out a personal bond for £500 to appear before the same councilors. Was he therefore forced to become an informer to avoid a large fine or gaol time?

It seems that is exactly what happened with Gregory Caus of Norwich in a case described elsewhere.[29] It was Richard Empson who summoned Caus by privy seal to appear before the king's councilors for failing to pay shipping duties, and who soon after was "turned" to become an informer against others in his city. Richard Odiham, one of the auditors of the accounts of the chambers and wardens in arrears in the city of London, may as well have provided information to the government in return for avoiding legal consequences.[30] Others in league with promoting the royal policy were customers, controllers and searchers.

---

[24] Quoted in Cavill, p. 96. This is part of an excellent discussion about Henry VII's concerns for upholding the laws of England and the use of informers.
[25] [Chapter Six]
[26] T.N.A.: P.R.O., C 1/433/15; [Chapter Six]
[27] Westminster Abbey Muniments, MS. 12247.
[28] T.N.A.: P.R.O., DL 5/2 fo. 91v.
[29] [Chapter Four]
[30] [Chapter Six for Griffith and Odiham]

This commitment to ongoing and all-encompassing searches into records for such bonds was encouraged by a statute in 1495 allowing information to be brought before a court of law by any informer without evidence.[31] Although passed in the wake of Perkin Warbeck's first attempt at invasion in July 1495 along with concern about internal support of his claim to the throne[32], it caused citizens much grief on two fronts. The first was being held accountable for legitimate debts or promises owed the crown or the courts that had never been collected upon. The second was the possibility of falling victim to corrupt officials who would change or misinterpreted the conditions in those obligations to coerce people into paying money they did not owe, or forcing them to purchase a pardon to escape legal jeopardy.[33]

Hence, an obligation to keep the peace could be turned into an actual debt owed the king by unscrupulous people. Informers did much of the dirty work to find or prosecute old bonds. Interference by royal officials and their minions in court proceedings by using corrupt jurors added to this persecution of people. Collectively, they were referred to as "promoters" and they were vilified during Henry's reign by the chroniclers.

Given his close association with Dudley and his careful review of all his actions, it is fairly certain that Henry VII was aware of the situation with Thomas Sunnyff and the promoters John Camby and Richard Page, described in detail in the article about that case.[34] Whether he thought the prosecution of the haberdasher from Ludgate was justified may never be ascertained. In his will, Henry asked that "any p[er]sone of what degree soevir he bee, shewe by way of complainte to our Executours, any wrong to have been doon to hym, by us, oure commaundement, occasion or meane." However, included in the list of examiners of such wrongdoings were "Sir Richard Emson Knight our Chaunceller of our Duchie of Lancastre [and] Edmund Dudley Squier our Attourney," insuring that those harmed by these ministers and their followers, including Thomas

---

[31] 11 Hen VII c. 3. Blackstone noted that the statute was of great use to Empson and Dudley, "the wicked instruments of king Henry VII" (4.III). It was repealed at the beginning of Henry VIII's reign (1 Hen VIII c. 6).

[32] Cavill, pp. 16, 75-6.

[33] J.P. Cooper believed the statute opened the way for forged information. ("Henry VII's last years reconsidered," *Historical Jour.,* Vol. 2, no. 2 (1959), pp. 103-129 at p. 125.

[34] [Chapter Five] For Camby and Page, see below.

Sunnyff, would remain without remedy for their misfortunes.[35] Henry may
or may not have sensed before his death that his request for justice would
in fact be pursued after his passing, and that his "chancellor" and
"attorney" would be removed to the Tower of London.

Henry VII's knowledge of the various promoters was most likely
extensive, and he inevitably had a direct hand in their activities. He
employed several of them in his household, including William Smith of
the wardrobe, and he could see their names appear in Dudley's accounts.
The king also may have protected many of those who perhaps perjured
themselves to his benefit. In 1506 a petition for pardon by Thomas Henley
and the rest of a jury for false judgment at king's bench was granted. It
was signed by the hands of Edmund Dudley and Henry VII.[36]

However, it is difficult to tell if the king was righting alleged wrongs
or supporting certain perjurers to suit his needs. James Hobart, the attorney
general, brought a suit on behalf of the king against an Oxford jury on 20
July 1498 before the justices at the Oxford gaol delivery. The jury had
presented a non-guilty verdict in a case and Hobart claimed that the
defendant was in fact guilty and that the jurors perjured themselves. The
jurors were now summoned to appear before the chancellor. It is hard to
know if this was royal interference or the king upholding the law against
false jurors.[37]

For half a millennium it is Empson and Dudley who have taken the brunt
of the charges of corruption and extortion in Henry VII's reign. Their
reputations long outlived the notoriety heaped upon them since Henry VIII
became king. A century later in the reign of James I, their names were
used in the House of Commons as examples of everything from sedition
and the prosecution of penal laws by commission "under the great seal" to
excessive fines and bribery and indicting people without judicial consent.[38]
In a discussion of an act against "certain troublesome Persons, commonly
called Relators, Informers, and Promoters," Sir Edward Coke said it was
an excellent although defective bill, with other articles added to it to
address "forfeitures, upon penal Laws, granted to some Noblemen; who

---

[35] T. Astle, *The Will of Henry VII* (1775), pp. 11-12.
[36] T.N.A.: P.R.O., C 82/285, May? 1506.
[37] Bayne, pp. 74-5.
[38] *House of Commons Journal*, Vol. 1 (1802), pp. 499 (26 May 1614), 530 (27 Feb.
1621), 540 (6 Mar. 1621), 577 (27 Mar. 1621). [See also Chapter Four]

use Knaves, such as Empson and Dudley had. These terrify.—To have these Terrors taken away."[39]

During the trial of Sir Henry Vane in 1662, a mention of the act in Henry VII's reign allowing indictments to proceed without evidence resurrected the names of Empson and Dudley, stating that they

> had an Act of Parliament for their Warrant, made the 11th of [Henry VII's] reign . . . being against Equity and common Reason, and so, no justifiable ground or apology for their infinit Abuses and Oppressions of the People.[40]

This was not quite accurate. The 1495 statute referred to was passed long before Edmund Dudley entered Henry VII's service as chief bond officer. Reynold Bray, not Richard Empson, was the chancellor of the duchy of Lancaster and at this time apparently just began to hear extra-duchy cases with other learned counselors. Later on it clearly did facilitate their activities and those prosecuting cases in the name of the king. Richard Overton cited Coke in his 1646 "An arrow against all tyrants", noting that the statute was used by Empson and Dudley and others for "many sinister, crafty, and forged informations . . . against divers of the king's subjects, to their great damage and unspeakable vexation."[41]

Their infamy trickled into the 18th century by two unlikely observers of Henry VII's reign, one on each side of the Atlantic Ocean. Jonathan Swift's essay arguing against abolishing Christianity talked about old laws being resurrected in his time as if Empson and Dudley were alive.[42] But Swift also got his jabs in against informers in his *Gulliver's Travels*, apparently continuing his interest in the first Tudor's reign. In comparing the laws of Lilliput with England, he offered a wish that the laws in his own "dear Country" were as well executed. The first Lilliputian law he discussed involved informers. In noting that all crimes against the state

---

[39] *House of Commons Journal*, 1, p. 514 (8 Feb. 1621).

[40] *The Tryal of Sir Henry Vane, Kt., at the king's bench, Westminster, June the 2d. and 6th 1662*, (1662), p. 537. Under Cromwell's Commonwealth, Vane called for religious tolerance and a new constitution, believing that the source of sovereignty in England was the people. Refusing to adhere to the Restoration in 1660, he was put on trial for high treason. In an irony due to the referencing of Empson and Dudley in the trial proceedings, Vane had to take out a bond to keep the peace and do nothing against the government. He was executed 14 June 1662.

[41] Richard Overton, "An arrow against all tyrants (12 October 1646)," *Cambridge texts in the history of political thought*, eds. Raymond Geuss and Quentin Skinner (Cambridge, 1998).

[42] [Chapter Four]

were punished in Lilliput "with the utmost Severity", he observed that if a defendant accused of a crime demonstrated his innocence at trial,

> the Accuser [the informer] is immediately put to an ignominious Death; and out of his Goods or Lands, the innocent Person is quadruply recompensed for the Loss of his Time, for the Danger he underwent, for the Hardship of his Imprisonment, and for all the Charges he hath been at in making his Defence.[43]

It is as if Swift had read the strange case of Thomas Sunnyff and what he went through at the hands of the king's informers! Furthering his criticism of what seems to be Henry VII's lack of concern about such injustice, Swift said that if the informer could not pay these penalties, "it is largely supplied by the Crown." Moreover, the government then made a proclamation of the defendant's innocence "through the whole City." For Tudor England, restitution was not always forthcoming once Henry VIII became king, and there were no public proclamations of innocence, only public condemnation of the guilty informer.

John Adams, the second president of the United States, recalled Empson and Dudley in his diaries with regards to the statute allowing "bare information" only to be able "to hear and determine all offences and Contempts." Because of this law, "horrible Oppressions and Exactions were committed by Sir Richard Empson and Edmund Dudley." Adams noted that the statute was repealed early in Henry VIII's reign. He also added a little of the macabre, perhaps to show his distaste for the king's ministers as well as that law. He was "reminded of the Fate of Empson and Dudley, whose Trunks were exposed with their Heads off, and the Blood fresh streaming after the Ax."[44]

Contemporary observations at the time suggested that it was Empson and Dudley who established a group of informers and "fixers" of juries around 1504 when both were given responsibilities to prosecute penal statutes and drive in debts old and new.[45] However, there is evidence to suggest that such activities were already in progress.

---

[43] Jonathan Swift, *Gulliver's Travels* (1726) (Airmont Publishing, 1963 ed.), p. 55.

[44] <http://www.masshist.org/digitaladams/archive/index> [accessed 11 Nov. 2009], Diary 11, 25 Dec. 1765 (p. 19); Diary 20, 7 Mar. 1774 (p. 8).

[45] *Hall's Chronicle* records 1504-05 as the time frame when the king, Empson and Dudley along with "a companye of accusers (commonly called promoters)" prosecuted old laws. (p. 499.) The *Great Chronicle* seems to put it in the fall of

In a memorandum of a writ dated 13 May 1501 to the sheriffs of London, it was ordered that a group of men, under penalty of £100 each, were to appear before the chancellor, treasurer, chief justices of both benches and the clerk of the rolls at chancery at a certain date "to answer concerning certain articles of perjury to be objected against them." These men included William Simpson, John Wright and Richard Smith, three of the promoters who later worked closely with Empson and later Dudley, and who were arraigned and punished after the accession of Henry VIII in 1509.[46] They had been summoned to sit on a jury by the king himself in a suit against a foreign merchant to be heard by the barons of the exchequer regarding the illegal import of cloths. The jurors found in favor of the merchant and were now accused of "manifest perjury". The attorney general now asked the king to have them appear before the council—those councilors to be in attendance suggest the star chamber—to receive their due justice.[47]

Although it is not clear what happened to them following the summons, it is evident that they continued to practice their trade of perjury in courts of law to the end of the reign under the auspices of royal ministers.[48] What is not certain is whether they perjured themselves in 1501 or they simply reached a verdict counter to what Henry VII had in mind.

Either way, the chief judges and administrators of the realm knew what these men were about in 1501, and it is a stretch to think that the omnipresent first Tudor remained uninformed that they were still at it after this suit. These promoters constantly worked their trade in the name of the king, and one can only wonder how many times the king or his ministers may have instructed them to do so. Indeed, Henry may have had a hand in getting them out of trouble at court in 1501 considering those adjudicating the case were all the king's men and members of star chamber

---

1506 (p. 334). (*Hall's Chronicle*, collated with editions of 1548 and 1550 (1809); *The Great Chronicle of London*, ed. by A.H. Thomas and I.D. Thornley (London, 1938.)

[46] *Calendar of Close Rolls 1500-1509*, no. 67. Another man named in the 1501 writ, Thomas Checheley, came before the court of aldermen on 8 June 1509 and "presented to the maire and aldermen the kyngs letters of pardon for his discharge of periury." (C.L.R.O., REP 2 (1505-13), fo. 68v.) This list of 1501, therefore, may represent one group of promoters already at work more than three years before Dudley entered royal service.

[47] Bayne, pp. 75-77a.

[48] For the fates of Simpson, Wright and Smith, see below.

proceedings. It was this court that handled, among other things, cases of perjury.[49]

Henry and his councilors could have even recruited them, something that Empson and Dudley did frequently. In fact, it was Empson who conscripted John Baptist Grimaldi, discussed below, after he was convicted by a court to be set in the pillory for three days in different markets and then banished from the City. The *Great Chronicle* flatly states that Grimaldi was rescued by Empson in return for becoming a promoter.[50]

Polydore Vergil painted a portrait of a king in search of peace and obedience to the laws by his subjects. He saw a policy shift after 1500 because the first Tudor monarch was determined to make English men and women, high and low, aware of the consequences of disobeying the law— a policy construed as greed because of the large amounts of money collected from those allegedly breaking those laws.[51] Vergil believed it was Henry who instigated the policy, and his ministers who actively and enthusiastically pursued it.[52] In a passage regarding the *modus operandus* of Empson and Dudley, it is not difficult to envision Thomas Sunnyff as one of those citizens caught up in this form of royal policy taken to extreme:

> You could have seen daily in the halls of Empson's and Dudley's houses a host of convicted persons awaiting sentence, to whom wretchedly evasive replies were given, so that they were exhausted by the duration of the anxiety and voluntarily gave up their money.[53]

Hall followed Vergil and believed that after two decades on the throne the king realized his subjects were not observing the laws, and that they were escaping penalties for legal wrongdoings and against various statutes.

---

[49] Cora L. Scofield, *A study of the court of star chamber* (University of Chicago, 1900), p. 29. In at least one instance, Henry VII was present in star chamber as well (p. 25), and both Empson and Dudley attended sessions.

[50] *Great Chronicle*, p. 360. For the reasons to be set in the pillory, see below.

[51] See Horowitz, "Henry Tudor's treasure," *Hist. Research*, Vol. LXXXII, no. 217 (Aug. 2009), pp. 560-79. [Chapter Eight]

[52] *The Anglica Historia of Polydore Vergil, A.D. 1485-1537*, ed. D. Hay, Camden 3rd ser., lxxiv (1950), pp. 127, 129.

[53] Vergil, p. 131. According to Hay, who translated Vergil, Empson and Dudley were treated more harshly by Vergil in the 1513 edition that the 1534 version, which was softened by Cromwell. (p. xxii.) As Hay noted, John Dudley, later the duke of Northumberland and Edmund Dudley's son, was not overly fond of tales related to his father.

If inquisitions were made into these areas, Hall said "there shoulde be fewe noble men, merchauntes, fermers, husbandemen, grasyers nor occupyers, but they shoulde be founde transgressours and violators."[54] Who these promoters and fixers were became more evident to historians once the first Tudor died.

Soon after Henry VII's death on 21 April 1509, a general pardon was issued throughout England by the seventeen-year-old heir to the throne, Henry VIII. Its purpose was not only to protect the majority of government officials and important political figures in support of the upstart dynasty, but also to make amends for the criminal activity and subterfuge perpetrated by Henry VII's "evil ministers" since the late king could do no wrong as God's appointee on earth. The document is telling in that it offers a glimpse of what was taking place with greater frequency during the reign.

It proclaimed that those who were to be prosecuted included "any p[er]sones calling theym self promoters." Even as complaints poured into king's bench, which the pardon encouraged wronged parties to pursue, those involved with the activities spearheaded by Richard Empson and Edmund Dudley were rounded up, imprisoned and brought to justice.[55]

The reaction began swiftly. Empson and Dudley were taken to the Tower of London soon after the first Tudor's death. A few days after their arrests they were excluded from the general pardon. On 5 June, men not generally known to the history of the reign but well-known at the time in London were conveyed to the City's common council. Besides the three promoters and perjurers mentioned earlier—John Derby (*alias* Wright), bower; Richard Smith, carpenter; and William Simpson, fuller (wool cleaner)—they included Henry Stockton, fishmonger; Thomas Young, saddler; and Robert Jakes, sherman (shearer of woolen cloth).

These men were confronted with their crimes and handed out punishments. They were to be disenfranchised "for ev[r] from the lib[er]tie

---

[54] *Hall's Chronicle*, p. 499. [See Chapter Five]

[55] C.L.R.O., Journals of the Common Council 11 (1506-18), fos. 68ff. G.R. Elton minimized the entire flood of exactions on Henry VII's subjects as postulated by the chronicles, suggesting that even when the new regime recommended that grievances be filed at court it was "much more noise than substance in the complaints." ("Henry VII: A Restatement," *Hist. Journal*, Vol. 4, no. 1 (1961), pp. 1-29 at p.21.) The evidence found in the plethora of chancery writs; memoranda and enrollments of bonds; warrants and privy seals; filed complaints; and recorded activities of the working councilors suggests otherwise.

of this Citie." Derby, Smith and Simpson were singled out for being the worst offenders of perjury.[56] They additionally were ordered to ride backwards on saddleless horses to the pillory in Cornhill, "their hedds in the holys tyll [a] Jugement and p[ro]clamacion be redde and made."[57] The other three men were to remain on horseback. All six were then to be conveyed to the standard in Fleet Street where they were to leave the City forever upon pain of further punishment and imprisonment.[58] Henry Stockton was sentenced to be pilloried but escaped this fate because of illness; he died soon afterwards.[59] Many other promoters lost their offices and spent time in gaol.[60] For example, ten days later (15 June), George Jackson, plumber, and Christopher Rothery, fuller, were disenfranchised from the city "for their greate p[er]jurye . . . agaynst the kyngs subiects."[61]

The author of the *Great Chronicle* clearly had first-hand knowledge of these promoters and provided more information about them than can be gleaned from the common council and aldermen records of London. He wrote that in the case against Sir William Capell, former mayor of London,

---

[56] Richard Smith was a London sheriff who incarcerated people allegedly in debt to the king. Sir Laurence Aylmer, former mayor of London, was confined to Smith's house in 1508, where he remained until Henry VII's death. (Brit. Libr., MS. Vitellius A.XVI, printed in *Chronicles of London*, ed. Charles L. Kingsford (Oxford 1905), p. 262.) While on a jury, Derby was accused of taking a bribe consisting of 10 shillings "and a q[ua]rter of ffisshe for his howsehold." (C.L.R.O., REP 2, fo. 67 (21 May 1509). In the Common Council records, Derby, Smith, Simpson, Stockton and Jakes were called "evill disposed p[er]sones" who, beside perjury, took money "for to conceyle felonyes and other enormyties." (C.L.R.O., JOR 11 (1506-17), fo. 74v.)

[57] The pillory was punishment for numerous offenses, including forging a false bond, perjury, sorcery, kidnapping and selling stinking fish.

[58] C.L.R.O., JOR 11, fos. 74v-78 (fos. 76 and 77 pagination missing). In the proclamation to be recited publicly, there is no mention of letters missive or any royal involvement in their crimes.

[59] *Great Chronicle*, p. 339. Hall's Chronicle noted that "Canby", Richard Page, Smith and "diverse other, as Derbie, Wright, Sympson and Stockton" were sentenced to "the Pillorie." (p. 506)

[60] *L&P*, I.i. no. 11(10). Pardons continued for some time. On 31 Mar. 1510, three of Henry VIII's councilors, including his father's almoner, "Master Woolsey", were given £57.12.4 to free various people still remaining in prison within and near the city of London. (Brit. Libr., Add. MS. 21841 fo. 28.)

[61] C.L.R.O., REP 2, fo. 70. In the margin a note states that both were exonerated. For Jackson, see fo. 83.

he was by derby Symson & othir of theyr company which as than the hool Jury of theym was ffastly boundyn to the gyrdyllis of dudley & Empson soo that as they wold the veredict passed, and soo was he by theym endytid, and afftyr by dudley at the kyngis Commandement put In prison as soom whyle In the Countour.

Capell was then transferred to one sheriff's house, then another,

> ffor soo much as he wold not agre to paye unto the kyng MM li. [£2000] was by the fforenamyd dudley commaundyd unto the Towr where he laye tyll It was nere whytsontide afftyr [& then let go free].

The charge against him, sued on behalf of the king by the informer Henry Toft, was for usurious loans.[62] Here was another example of a misadventure similar to the matter of Thomas Sunnyff, with more evidence of culpability on the part of the king's ministers and possibly Henry VII himself and the methods used to force people to agree with the king.

As an Act III to his ordeal, Capell may have sought revenge once Henry VII was dead. He was elected mayor of London and on 28 February 1510 the court of aldermen noted

> that all suche p[er]sones & Juro^s as in the last kyngs dayes indyted the maire and certeyn alderman of ffelonye and treason and be not yet disfraunchesed shalbe disfraunchesed at the next comon Counsell.[63]

---

[62] *Great Chronicle*, p. 336; T.N.A.: P.R.O., C 1/227/45. For the regnal year 24 Hen VII, when this was recorded in the *Great Chronicle*, Whitsontide was the week following 3 June 1509. Capell therefore had been in the Tower at the same time as Sunnyff's imprisonment there. Sometime between 9 Sept 1504 and 1 Aug 1505, Dudley recorded bonds and cash payments totaling £2000 for Capell and his son, Giles. (Brit. Libr., Harl. MS. 1877 fo. 46; Lans. MS. 127, fo. 3v.) Capell separately had to pay for a pardon for "skavaye," which may refer to shaving coins: 100 marks in ready money to Dudley for the king, £30 to "Tofte," or Henry Toft, one of the promoters who may have tipped off Empson or Dudley and was rewarded for his effort. (Brit. Libr., Lans.MS. 127, fo. 9.) For more on Capell, see *The History of Parliament: the House of Commons 1509-1558*, ed. S.T. Bindoff (1982) art. on Sir William Capell. For Toft, see below.
[63] C.L.R.O., REP 2, fo. 83.

Similar fates awaited the nemeses of Sunnyff: Richard Page and John Camby, and two gaol keepers. Page had been recently named in an indictment against Dudley in an alleged attempt to overthrow the government; his role was that of messenger for Dudley to the other conspirators.[64] On 4 September, Camby along with Robert Hall ("keper of ludgate" gaol) and Thomas Bate ("bayly of Billyngsgate" prison) were ordered by the alderman's court of London to be "removyd from their saide sev^rall offices and from thensforth never to enioye the saide offices nor any of theym tooccupie."[65]

Among Hall's travesties was his role in an obligation falsely sued upon. Crimes involving obligations were not new although they seem to have reached an apex during the reign. Forged obligations sometimes took years to uncover: on 7 September 1502 a case against a forger alleged that the false document, created through "subtill Imaginacion", was written 30 September 1486. Bribery was a common motive. In July 1501 a party was paid £5 to swear that an obligation was legally entered although it allegedly never existed.[66]

One case against Hall before the court of aldermen on 25 October 1509 involved an obligation of £40 recovered by the chamberlain of London from William Cornysshe of the king's chapel, with "half to th[e] use of Robt Hall merch^aunthab[er]dassher And late keper of ludgate." The other half went to the chamber of London. It was learned that Hall sued on the obligation "by Crafty meanes and of pure malice," for which the chamberlain was unaware. It involved a bond taken out on 5 October 1504 to keep the peace against Hall. According to the condition, the breach of the peace could include "unfittyng langage or words of any sclaundre" against Hall, and it is possible that Hall fixed a jury to find against Cornysshe.[67] In this instance, only Hall and the city of London profited, not the king.

John Camby has been discussed elsewhere regarding his extensive role as a promoter in pursuing Thomas Sunnyff. The *Great Chronicle* spent a

---

[64] *L&P*, I.ii. no. 1548.

[65] Horowitz, "Thomas Sunnyff,"; C.L.R.O. REP 2, fo. 71. For Hall, who was known to sue out old obligations to receive half the amount due, see fo. 73; T.N.A.: P.R.O., C 244 no. 76(a). He was pardoned 1 June 1510. (*L&P*, I.i. no. 438(3), m. 13.)

[66] C.L.R.O., REP 1, fo. 109; JOR 10 (1492-1505), fo. 260.

[67] C.L.R.O., REP 2, fo. 73. The peace bond may have been a *supplicavit*, which was not uncommon to obtain between parties. The common council heard such cases of alleged breaches of the peace, e.g., JOR 10, fo. 262v.

lot of time castigating this henchman of Edmund Dudley. It noted that he bribed people and was well-versed in "crakkys" (lies), using his position as an officer in the sheriff's house to incarcerate people. He came close to losing that office after accumulating substantial money, but then fell in with Dudley "a yere space or two." This relationship helped him obtain the office of weigher of wools and they became business associates as well, entering land deals.[68] He subsequently became a keeper of one of the two sheriff's gaols, the counter "in the pultry".

His activities involved going after people with false accusations and bribing jurors to obtain verdicts favorable to the crown.[69] Along with other promoters, Camby was thrown in prison after Henry VII's death: the *Great Chronicle* referred to them as "many of [Empson's and Dudley's] dyscyplys promoters of all [ill]." It recorded that the defense of their actions offered by the promoters was that "they were servyng men and Did noo thyng but as they were commaundyd of theyr superior w^t othir many excuses"—an early Nuremberg defense. The author of the *Great Chronicle* was less than thrilled that many of the promoters were eventually released from prison, and that Londoners were especially unhappy "ffor the enlargyng of Tofft & Canby."[70]

According to indictments, these promoters "many and sundry tymes have comitted detestable p[er]iury aswell in enquests or offices as between p[ar]ties and p[ar]ties." They took money "for to conceyle felonyes and other enormyties by div^{r}se evill disposed p[er]sones" when they had been "sworne to eny enquests or Juries." These men were empanelled "by l[ett]res myssives and otherwise by drede full comaundements"—a suggestion of the involvement of royal authority such as by Empson or Dudley. Included in their list of crimes were the false indictments of "sume of the late maires shireffs and aldermen . . . of treason felonyes and misprisions." It was perhaps these men who precipitated the imprisonment of Knesworth, Grove and Shore, possibly with the help of "letters missive" from Dudley or his henchmen, if not the king.[71]

---

[68] E.g., Cheshire and Chester Archives, DCH/B/43 (8 Dec. 1506); DCH/B/44 (23 Jan. 1507).

[69] He often found himself on both sides of a suit in the court of chancery, e.g., T.N.A.: P.R.O., C 1/121/13; C 1/351/32.

[70] *Great Chronicle*, pp. 337, 345, 349, 365. For Toft, see below. Camby died in 1522. An Ellen Camby, "late the wife of John Camby", died 24 June 1516 and is buried in St. Michael's church, Stanton Harcourt, Oxfordshire.

[71] [Chapter Five]

Other promoters with high profiles in London and elsewhere were linked directly to Empson, Dudley and the king. Henry Toft worked for Dudley and filed lawsuits on behalf of the crown; he also informed on possible violators of the law and sued on actions of debt.[72] Toft filed a suit against someone named Crowmer, which cost the defendant £40 by obligation to Dudley.[73] He also brought suits against Sir Henry Tey and William Pirton "for the king's part", both of whom settled by paying for pardons to Dudley in obligations of 100 marks and £40 respectively.[74] Pirton later sued Toft for extortion in order to receive that pardon.[75]

Toft held the office of warden of the mint and was undoubtedly known to the king long before Dudley's service.[76] On 23 February 1493, two sureties entered into bonds enrolled at chancery totaling £450 for Toft, who also was bound for £500, on condition of Toft's "loyalty and appearance before his highness, whenever summoned."[77] Dudley, therefore, may have inherited the services of Toft when he became the chief bond collector in 1504. It is possible Toft was granted access to London records to search for old bonds, most likely over the protests of the City fathers. He sued the chamberlain of London, William Milbourne, for refusing to bring an action against numerous men for breaking the conditions of a recognizance as sureties. Unless he sat in on proceedings in the London courts and kept track of bonds, how did he know about this recognizance and its status?[78]

John Baptiste de Grimaldi (or Brymaldi), a merchant, was described by the *Great Chronicle* as the worst of the lot and in the service of Richard Empson. However, in a grant given by letters patent to his son, Louis Grymald, on 10 February 1509, John Baptiste was referred to as the

---

[72] E.g., T.N.A.: P.R.O., E 404/85, 10 Nov. 1504.

[73] Brit. Libr., Lans. MS.127 fo. 15. It may have been William Crowmer, who was named to a commission on 14 Oct 1507 for Kent to inquire into "alman^r our wards, Intrusions, Reteyndo^rs, felonyes" and other possible breaches of the law "concernyng o^r interesse proffit and avauntage." (T.N.A.: P.R.O., C 82/304.) He and three others had recognizances taken late in Henry VII's reign for £160 each and due in the king's chamber. They were cancelled 21 Nov. 1509. (C 82/335 no. 685; *L&P*, I.i. no. 257(68).)

[74] Brit. Libr., Lans.MS. 127 fo. 20; *Great Chronicle*, pp. 337, 365. For other promoters, see C.L.R.O., REP 2, fos. 67, 68v, 70, 71v.

[75] T.N.A.: P.R.O., C 1/346/32.

[76] T.N.A.: P.R.O., STAC 1/2/124, E 101/302/14.

[77] *Cal. Close Rolls 1495-1500*, no. 728.

[78] T.N.A.: P.R.O., C 1/255/50.

"king's servant".[79] He received rewards from the king and Dudley for uncovering alleged crimes or potential sources of income for the king, such as when he helped in the forfeiture of merchandise to Henry VII and received a reward "for the spying and seasure of the said forfeiture."[80] After the death of the king, Grimaldi fled to sanctuary at Westminster.[81] He was nonetheless arrested as complaints were filed against him in king's bench, including one that accused him along with Empson and Camby of illegal activities in London.[82] His pardon by Henry VIII in January 1510 could not have been popular.[83] The *Great Chronicle* even recorded a poem about him and his actions as a perjurer.[84]

Benedict Davy, from Towcester in Northamptonshire near Empson's county manor, was another promoter who found himself mentioned in complaints filed at king's bench at the beginning of the new reign. He worked with both Empson and Dudley.[85] He was the bailiff in Towcester and one of the receivers of the king at Kenilworth castle.[86] The *Great Chronicle* cited a poem that lumped him with Camby and Grimaldi as a triad of trouble for the City, pursuing people

> by theyr ffals surmysys / of many a ffals matier, wold they the compace ffecch / To bryng In trowble, trewe men offt Sythys / Puttyng to theym, ffals cawsys many wysys / Whereoff to the was browgth the Jugement / Whych alle with brybery, & couytyze was blent.[87]

A man named Smith, not to be confused with the carpenter pilloried for his offences, was recorded in the *Great Chronicle* as being a former official in Henry VII's wardrobe who was arraigned at the Guildhall as a

---

[79] *Great Chronicle*, pp. 337, 343, 345, 352, 355-65; *Calendar of Patent Rolls*, 1494-1509, p. 625.

[80] Brit. Libr., Lansdowne MS. 127 fo. 36 (24 Jan. 1507). See fo. 56v (13 Feb. 1508) for another reward from the king for a matter he discovered.

[81] *Hall's Chronicle*, referring to Grimaldi as "the moste craftiest knave of all," recorded that he "escaped and came to Westminster, and there toke Sanctuarie." (p. 506)

[82] T.N.A.: P.R.O., KB 9/453 no. 456.

[83] T.N.A.: P.R.O., C 82/345 no. 848 (*L&P*, I.i. no. 381(6)).

[84] *Great Chronicle*, pp. 355-65.

[85] E.g., T.N.A.: P.R.O., KB 9/453 nos. 125, 140, 144.

[86] Northamptonshire Record Office, Hicks' Charity, Deeds, Towcester no. 640; Shakespeare Birthplace Trust Records Office, Ferrers of Baddesley, Clinton, Warwickshire, DR 3/651 (10 Nov. 1506).

[87] *Great Chronicle*, p. 345.

promoter. The author again knew his players in this royal policy of prosecuting the laws and ferreting out old bonds. The reference was to William Smith, a page of the wardrobe, a collector of leases on crown lands and an escheator in Lancashire. He also gained the offices of searcher in various ports and bailiff in a liberty of the duchy of Lancaster. Smith became yeoman of the standing wardrobe in the Tower of London and did well by the king. Although excluded from the general pardon along with other promoters, he was eventually pardoned at the same time as Grimaldi but lost his offices.[88]

Then there is the curious and telling entry in the London court of aldermen repertory book dated 8 October 1510, less than two months after the beheadings of Empson and Dudley. It referred to a man named Wilford: "The sayeng of the mair was 'Wilford. Su^m men have loste their heds that have not doon somoche harme to this Citie as ye have doon.'"[89] James Wilford, along with other merchants, shipped large quantities of cloth abroad. He apparently was not in competition with mercers and cloth workers or it might have explained this obfuscating declaration about him. More likely it involved his activities in other areas.[90] Besides being a master tailor, he was also a sheriff (1499-1500), an alderman (1500-11), an auditor (1506-08), and a notary.[91]

Notaries were in a good position to do some shady dealings with contracts and sworn testimony should they be so inclined. The many accusations against promoters included "ffals fforgyng of lettyrs of byllys, and sundry acquytauncis [acquittances]," the latter leading people to believe they had been discharged of a bond.[92]

It is not known if Wilford was connected with those working for the royal government. He clearly had a harsh side to him that would have suited the role. A Mrs. Newman claimed that she and her husband were

---

[88] *Great Chronicle*, p. 365; *L&P*, I.i. no. 54(86), 438(4m.26), pardoned 4 Feb. 1510 (T.N.A.: P.R.O., C 82/345 no. 869); S.J. Gunn, "The Courtiers of Henry VII," *Eng. Hist. Rev.*, Vol. CVIII, no. CCCXXVI (Jan., 1993), pp. 31-3.
[89] C.L.R.O., REP 2, fo. 98v.
[90] Matthew Davies and Ann Saunders, *The History of the Merchant Taylors' Company* (Maney Publishing, Leeds, 2004), pp. 65, 270.
[91] Fabyan's *Chronicle*, p. 687, sheriff 1499-1500; *The Merchant Taylors' Company of London: court minutes 1486-1493*, ed. Matthew Davies (Stamford, 2000), p. 304; *The Aldermen of the City of London*, by the Rev. Alfred B. Beaven, Vol. II (London, 1913), pp. 20, 168. For alderman, see *Cal. Close Rolls 1500-1509*, no. 470; *Calendar of Patent Rolls 1494-1509*, p. 275.
[92] *Great Chronicle*, p. 360.

unjustly thrown into prison and deprived of their property in 1500. This was accomplished, along with further ill-treatment, by the two sheriffs of London at the time, one of them being James Wilford.[93] In 1503, Wilford was suspended from coming to the court of alderman on "account of contumelious words openly spoken in full Court to the Mayor and Aldermen."[94]

While deeper knowledge of illicit activity was perhaps meant by this enigmatic entry in the repertory book, it is interesting to note that Wilford crossed paths with none other than Thomas Sunnyff. When Sunnyff was arrested in 1500 for a debt, one of the arresting sheriffs was James Wilford. And in the surviving star chamber case involving Thomas Sunnyff, a "Wilford" was listed as a notary who accused Sunnyff of forgery, which the haberdasher vigorously denied.[95]

Edmund Dudley realized that all kinds of accusations against him and others implementing royal policy would occur after Henry VII's death to protect the name and legacy of the late king. In his will he wrote,

> if any other [per]sons will [disturb the executors of my will] or lett them or ony of them thus to doo by power, myght or awctorytie, or ells by fyndyng of untrew offices or by ony other [un]due, un[j]uste and colorable meane, then therwith I [plea to] their concyences that so doo as they will aunswer byfore god at the dredfull day of [J]udgement, & trustyng then in the greate m[r]cy of god & therby my sowle shalbe saved & discharged.[96]

It was left to the young king and his councilors to sort out the harm caused by the first Tudor king and his ministers, and those who promoted royal policy beyond the fringe of legality. Laws continued to be upheld and old obligations pursued, but the dark side of Henry VII's reign seems to have dissipated amid the dawn of a new king and the promise of righting the wrongs of the past. But such justice did not quell the developing legend of Empson and Dudley that would enter the story of early-Tudor England.

---

[93] T.N.A.: P.R.O., STAC 1, 1/1.
[94] *The Aldermen of the City of London*, p. 168, citing C.L.R.O., REP 2, fo. 129.
[95] T.N.A.: P.R.O., C 244/147 no. 171(c); STAC 2/25/9, lines 56-62. Wilford continued to practice as a notary in the new reign. *(London Consistory Court Wills, 1492-1547*, ed. Ida Darlington (London, 1967), p. 16, no. 25, 13 Mar. 1514.)
[96] T.N.A.: P.R.O., SP 1/2 fo. 7.

CHAPTER EIGHT

HENRY TUDOR'S TREASURE[*]

Introduction

When reading the various chronicles and histories that were either contemporary or close to the reign of Henry VII, it is easy to picture the first Tudor sitting in his tower (or Tower) sifting coins through his fingers onto a velvet-covered table and perhaps voicing a sinister cackle for good measure. Not only was he usually viewed as avaricious—which I would argue is endemic to the job of king and therefore a bit disingenuous—but also very wealthy during his time on the throne. For argument's sake and foregoing the motives behind his methods, let us suppose Henry VII was as rich as reported. It begs a question: where did the wealth come from?

It was after a long period of time learning about Henry's finances and his commitment to driving in debts and accounts that I started to wonder about that question. Some rather assiduous historians over the last century have grabbed abacus and adding machine to try to ascertain how much money he had, where it came from and even where it went over time. One consensus arising from these exercises concluded that, from the ordinary and extraordinary traditional income for an English monarch, he did increase it over the course of his reign. But he did so incrementally, and not to a point where historians could see the coins running through his fingers.

My study of obligations and recognizances recorded and collected suggested that these sources alone could have provided a large source of

---

[*] Reprinted with permission. The article was first published in *Historical Research*, special 500th Anniversary issue on the death of Henry VII, ed. Mark R. Horowitz, Vol. LXXXII, no. 217 (Aug. 2009), pp. 560-79. A very early "trial balloon" on the subject in the form of a short presentation was floated at the *10th Annual Arizona Center for Medieval and Renaissance Studies Conference*, 12-15 Feb. 2003, Arizona State University. Tables 8.1-4 were tabulated by Mark R. Horowitz from data found in all the printed entries in the *Calendars of Close Rolls 1468-1509*.

income. That led to two further questions: How much? And how could we ever know what percentage of it was in fact collected?

Sometimes looking ahead helps one look backwards better, although it can be dangerous. (Looking back from the English revolution of the 1640s and 50s can conjure up actions and ideas in previous years that really do not "pre-ordain" the revolution.) In the case of Henry Tudor's treasure, one did not have to look too far ahead to see that something large had happened to the royal treasury. Within the first five years of Henry VIII's reign, the young king spent well over one million pounds, the majority of it for war with France. Yet his revenues were not much more than his father's, and perhaps even less. Where did he get the money?

For me, putting two and two together was not difficult with the caveats of conjecture and possibility in full view. If Henry VII collected on a large number of those obligations, he left an enormous amount of money to his son. This flies in the face of more recent historians who believed that Henry VII in fact had little money in his coffers—although none talked about how his son was able to go on a military shopping spree. I believed that the contemporary observers were correct regarding his wealth, and that those bonds were the source of his very good fortune.

There are thousands of memoranda of recognizances and obligations found in the chancery and exchequer records and warrants, along with the surviving account books of Henry VII's government. While it would have been untenable to try to figure out which ones were paid, there was one source that offered the opportunity to use those conjectures and possibilities to come up with a number: the printed Calendar of Close Rolls *for the reign. In fact, as a graduate student these two volumes began my interest in Henry VII, so it was fitting that I returned to them for some assistance. By determining the number of recognizances enrolled at chancery related to the king and his government, for what purpose and involving how many people, I could see a pattern emerge: more money was owed as the reign progressed, and more of these bonds were enrolled.*

To broaden the scope of what was taking place, I looked at enrollments going back to 1468 as a "control" to see if the Yorkists were doing anything different, or anything at all. The caveats mounted with this approach. They included the possibility that Henry VII simply ordered bonds to be enrolled with greater frequency than did Edward IV or Richard III. But by focusing on the question of potential revenue for Henry VII, it became clear that indeed the bonds recorded at chancery alone could have provided him with an enormous income had all or a majority of them been collected. We may never know how much money Henry VII accumulated. But we can safely say it was enough for his son to squander.

Henry VII amassed "an immense treasure" that he "continues to pile up" (1497, 1499, Milanese ambassador).

"Henry is rich, has established good order in England, and keeps the people in such subjection as has never been the case before" (1499, sub-prior of Santa Cruz).

Henry VII "has upwards of six millions of gold [£1.3 million], and it is said that he puts by annually 500,000 ducats [£104,000], which is of easy accomplishment, for his revenue is great and real, not a written schedule, nor does he spend anything" (1499, Milanese envoy).

"The King of England has the reputation of being very rich"; "His riches augment every day . . . he has no equal in this respect. If gold coin once enters his strong boxes, it never comes out again" (1499, 1507, Spanish ambassador).

The king has "accumulated so much gold that he is supposed to have more than well nigh all the other Kings of Christendom" (1509, Venetian ambassador).

The king "mervelously enriched his realme & him selfe, & yet left his sub[j]ectes in high wealth and prosperitie. The pro[o]fe wherof is manifestly apparau[n]t by ye abou[n]daunce of golde & silver, yerely brought into this realme, both in plate, money & [bullion] . . . " (Edward Hall, 1548).

His treasure was reputed to be "near eighteen hundred thousand pounds sterling [£1.8 million]" (Francis Bacon, 1621).

Four years before his death, Henry "had on hand in money, as the excess of receipts over expenditures up to that time, only £22,729" (F.C. Dietz, 1921).

"At the end of the reign [treasurer of the king's chamber John] Heron's issues exceeded the charge against him" (B.P. Wolffe, 1964).

At the death of Henry VII "the chamber cash balance was exhausted, and the issues of the new reign had to be used to pay the debts of the old" (S.B. Chrimes, 1972).[1]

The author would like to thank David Grummitt, Steven Gunn and Penny Tucker for their helpful comments and empathy on a draft of this article.

[1] *Calendar of State Papers, Milan, 1385-1618*, nos. 541, 601, 618; *Calendar of State Papers, Spanish, 1485-1509*, nos. 204, 1239; *suppl. to vols. i and ii, no. 14;*

Henry VII's fortune has been steadily dwindling ever since his death in 1509, and through no fault of his own. Putting aside earlier beliefs about the king's riches, the main difficulty in any realistic assessment of his fortune has been the reliance on drawing conclusions from the surviving financial records—which point directly to traditional revenue coming to the crown—and from surviving documentation of expenditure made during the years the first Tudor ruled England. This might have surprised Henry. Although he left posterity with the image of a meticulous record-keeping, cash-seeking king perhaps sitting in a tower (or *the* Tower) counting his gold, he in fact did not account for every groat, nor did any one specific councillor, committee or department.[2] Moreover, there are

---

Calendar of State Papers, Venetian, 1202-1509, nos. 751, 944; *Hall's Chronicle*, ed. H. Ellis (1809), p. 505; Francis Bacon, *The History of the Reign of King Henry VII and Selected Works*, ed. B. Vickers (Cambridge, 1998), p. 195; F.C. Dietz, *English Government Finance 1485-1558* (1st edn, Urbana, Ill., 1921; New York, 1964), p. 87; B.P. Wolffe, "Henry VII's land revenues and chamber finance", in B.P. Wolffe, *The Royal Demesne in English History: the Crown Estate in the Governance of the Realm from the Conquest to 1509* (1971), p. 225, reprinting the article in *Eng. Hist. Rev.*, Vol. LXXIX (1964), pp. 225-54; S.B. Chrimes, *Henry VII* (1972), p. 217. A Venetian ducat was worth between 48 and 50 English pence in the London market place in 1505-6, down from about 52 pence in 1497, making Henry VII's annual hoarding of specie in excess of £104,000 according to the ambassador, which is very close to Wolffe's estimate (see below). (R.C. Mueller, *The Venetian Money Market: Banks, Panics, and the Public Debt* (Money and Banking in Medieval and Renaissance Venice, ii, Baltimore, Md., 1997), pp. 346, 348-9; P. Spufford, *Handbook of Medieval Exchange* (1986), p. 206; *Cal. State Papers Milan*, no. 53 (18 Dec. 1497): "Everything costs incomparably more in [England] . . . and one cannot spend even for the very smallest thing less than a penny, fifty-two of which go to the ducat"). The hiatus in the above quotes from 1621 to 1921 is largely from historiographical circumstances, or as Sydney Anglo has concluded "Bacon remained the loftiest single authority on Henry VII right up to the end of the 19th century, when he was suddenly dethroned" (S. Anglo, "Ill of the dead: the posthumous reputation of Henry VII", *Renaissance Studies*, i (1987), pp. 27-47, at p. 39).

[2] Henry's reputation was intact after only a dozen years on the throne. Ambassador Don Pedro de Ayala wrote to King Ferdinand and Queen Isabella of Spain that "he spends all the time he is not in public, or in his Council, in writing accounts of his expenses with his own hand" (*Cal. State Papers Spanish 1485-1509*, no. 210 (25 July 1498)). This was quite true. By his own hand he wrote of various amounts of money delivered to his treasurer of the chamber, John Heron, in "souv[er]ains of gold", "dyv[r]s coyness of gold", "olde weighty krownes", "good krownes", "ducatz"

several difficulties that at times receive short shrift when declarations on Henry's accounts are made: missing or unknown accounts; major sources of revenue not cultivated before his time and far beyond traditional royal income; and a misunderstanding of what the king and his ministers were writing down when they were administering and collecting upon those sources.

One might also question the need to ascertain the wealth (or poverty) of Henry Tudor in the first place. After all, it would be an enormous task even to attempt to account for every known source of income and somehow determine if money was actually received, while at the same time addressing both the duplication of debts found in the records and missing documentation altogether.[3] It also begs a question: would such knowledge add anything to the discussion about his legacy and impact on what was to follow after his death and for the rest of his dynasty? The answer is most likely no and yes. At the very least, it would be an intriguing bit of trivia to know the actual amount of fortune (cash, assets and accounts due) that he accumulated by the time of his death in April 1509. Nonetheless, that exercise in isolation is not essential to the study of Tudor history, although it would be helpful to clarify to what extent the king was either overleveraged—as the Yorkist kings were when they relinquished certain customs and subsidies to support the finances of Calais and redeem the crown jewels—or highly solvent beyond the dreams and envy of his successors.[4] However, the firm knowledge that he left his heir either a fortune or in debt might have ramifications for how historians view subsequent events, including foreign policy and parliamentary-constitutional development. Furthermore, if Henry VII were consciously pursuing activities and policies to bolster the royal bullion, one way to measure his success might be to determine the amount of money he obtained from his efforts. Finally, it is clear that young Henry VIII spent a

---

and "Spaynysh gold", worth many thousands of pounds (T.N.A.: P.R.O., E 101/413/2/3 fos. 1-4).

[3] Wolffe criticized Dietz for not taking into account the duplication of revenue income between the exchequer and the chamber (Wolffe, "Land revenues", p. 217).

[4] For Edward IV's redemption of the crown jewels, see *Calendar of Close Rolls 1468-76*, nos. 1053, 1236; *Cal. Close Rolls 1476-85*, no. 1104 (Richard III's reign); and a final confirmation of payment for their redemption in *Cal. Close Rolls 1485-1500*, no. 9. Edward IV did not leave sufficient funds to pay for his funeral, a marked contrast to Henry VII's lavish tomb and ceremony (M.A. Hicks, *Edward IV* (2004), p. 161).

fortune on his early war with France—where did he get the capital to do so?

It might therefore suffice for the time being to focus on one source of Henry VII's possible wealth: his bond policy of prosecuting and collecting upon written obligations and recognizances for all aspects of finance, law and order.[5] It is possible at least to view his bond policy in terms of intensification and potential income, the latter suggesting that the king pursued an untapped source of money beyond customary royal revenue to his benefit and that of his heir. If indeed Henry VIII was wealthy the day he became king, it is tempting to ponder whether the new ruler squandered a rare opportunity for the English monarchy to become independent of parliamentary financial support. Some suppositions may be offered regarding the first Tudor's ubiquitous use of bonds as it related to his potential treasure and that of his son's.

It has been known for some time that the loss of the chamber books for the period 1495-1502 is but one reason why any definitive statements about Henry's fortune become moot. Furthermore, the various entries in the rolls and books of accounts that do survive suggest that many other repositories for debts on bonds, and the keeping of actual cash, were utilized beyond the traditional exchequer and the fiscally dominant chamber. Not the least of these were boxes, coffers, rooms and buildings containing coins, plate and bullion as well as a plethora of documentation in the form of rolls, books, sealed obligations and memoranda.[6] The king was clearly accumulating specie that required many storage facilities capable of holding prodigious weight. On just one day alone—5 February 1509, near the end of his life—Henry made payments from his chamber to eleven individuals totalling £5,000 *in pence*, or 1.2 million pennies weighing at the low end approximately 837 kilograms, or more than 1,800 pounds.[7]

---

[5] See M.R. Horowitz, "Policy and prosecution in the reign of Henry VII", pp. 412-58 [Chapter Three]; and S. Cunningham, "Loyalty and the usurper: recognizances, the council, and allegiance under Henry VII", pp. 459-81, both in *Hist. Research*, Vol. LXXXII, no. 217 (Aug. 2009).

[6] Lisa Ford's paper on the subject lists some of these (L. Ford, "Books, boxes and signatures: authority and accountability in Henry VII's council and administration", paper delivered at Yale University, British Studies Colloquium, 16 Nov. 2007). Henry VII purchased eight "greate coffers" to carry his silver (T.N.A.: P.R.O., E 36/214 fo. 145).

[7] T.N.A.: P.R.O., E 36/214 fo. 159. Another payment in pennies—240,000 of them—was made on 25 Feb., with an additional 480,000 given as two loans on 27

Although Francis Bacon is not a reliable source for the reign—F.J. Levy noted that the disgraced chancellor, when writing his history of Henry VII, "invented the past as well as reporting it"—he at least understood that there were many sources related to finance beyond the traditional methods of reckoning.[8] He alluded to a book kept by Richard Empson, a main proponent of the bond policy, which was presumably similar to his cohort Edmund Dudley's book of obligations and recognizances, although Bacon may have confused the two.[9] More problematic was his recounting of a "merry tale" of Henry VII's pet monkey tearing the king's "principal note-book all to pieces"—merry at least for those in attendance because they "liked not those pensive accounts". It is not known what happened to either Henry's account book or the monkey.[10]

Feb. (fo. 161). The above weight calculation was made by the author after weighing a sample of 10 pennies from Henry VII's reign preserved at the British Museum with the least amount of clipping, the average weight of the coins being 0.6977 grams. The weight of a pure penny was set at 12 grains (0.7776 grams) in 1464, then reduced to 11.2 grains during the period 1489-93 (H.A. Grueber, *Handbook of the Coins of Great Britain and Ireland* (1899; 1970 edn.), p. 71; C.E. Challis, *The Tudor coinage* (Manchester, 1978), pp. 48, 277). If pennies in Henry's possession were all new then the weight of the coins would have been about 933 kg., or approximately 2,053 pounds for the £5,000 in pennies. D.M. Metcalf stated that Henry held no old pence or half-groats (*Sylloge of Coins of the British Isles*, xxiii: *Ashmolean Museum, Oxford, pt. iii, Coins of Henry VII* (1976), p. xix, n. 1). David Grummitt has noted payments of old silver coins from the exchequer to the master of the mint, Bartholomew Rede, in 1504 in return for thousands of pounds sterling in new coins to the king (D. Grummitt, "Henry VII, chamber finance and the 'New Monarchy': some new evidence", *Hist. Research*, Vol. LXXII (1999), pp. 229-43, at. p. 236). John Heron, treasurer of the chamber, also received old coins and had them sent to the mint for recasting into new coins during the period 1504-5: payment of £2,000 "in olde money" to be repaid in new; delivered to "my master" at the Tower of London "in grots pens & gold"—£646 18s 5d; delivered to the Tower at least £6,000 in gold and groats (T.N.A.: P.R.O., E 101/415/6 fos. 1, 1v, 2, 16). Reynold Bray, the king's trusted minister, delivered pennies directly to the chamber from early in the reign, e.g., £666 13s 4d "in penes" (160,000 coins) received in the chamber 10 Dec. 1488 (T.N.A.: P.R.O., E 101/413/2/1 fo. 20).

[8] F.J. Levy, *Tudor Historical Thought* (San Marino, Calif., 1967; Toronto, 2004), p. 257. Levy proffered that Bacon used very little material for his history besides the chroniclers.

[9] M.R. Horowitz, "Richard Empson, minister of Henry VII", *Bull. Inst. Hist. Research*, lv (1982), pp. 35-49, at p. 35, n. 2. A copy of Dudley's account book is Brit. Libr., Lansdowne MS. 127.

[10] Bacon, p. 202.

There is enough evidence to demonstrate that bonds were not only taken with increasing regularity from the beginning of the reign but were also being forfeited and paid through a conscious effort by the king and his councillors, although it is not apparent where all the money actually ended up.[11] For example, using Dudley's account book covering the period September 1504 to May 1508, F.C. Dietz totalled the annual amounts due on fines, obligations and recognizances. Because some were cancelled, he made the assumption that cancelled equated to no payment received, and therefore estimated that three-quarters or less of the amounts due eventually came to the king. W.C. Richardson used Dietz's annual totals and arrived at the figure of £219,316 6s 11d due the crown for the time period. Dudley, as both an informer and collector, received a percentage of the amounts obtained, but as Richardson rightly observed "that total does not show how much money was actually collected during any given period, since most payments were made in installments, part of which was received during the ensuing reign".[12] Moreover, many of those bonds were renegotiated (compounded) but not always recorded by Dudley, or were duplicated in other places where they may have been cancelled after being paid.

Regardless, this attempt to ascertain income from bonds kept in one book by one councillor should be viewed as a sobering exercise. The king's annual gross revenue from all traditional sources near the end of his reign (including £40,000 in "ordinary" revenue) has been calculated at £104,863—an amount extremely close to the estimate, mentioned above, by the Milanese envoy in 1499.[13] If that is the case, Dudley was potentially responsible on average for an additional 50 per cent per annum over and above the king's expected income from traditional sources—and this from activities recorded in just one of Dudley's several books.[14]

---

[11] Horowitz,"Richard Empson", pp. 41-2; Horowitz, "Policy and prosecution", *passim*; S. Cunningham, "'To keep all Englishmen obedient through fear': Henry VII, the council and rule by recognizance, 1485-1509", paper read at the University of Oxford (2000) regarding T.N.A.: P.R.O., C 54/375-6, a recognizance roll; and S. Cunningham, "Loyalty and the usurper". Bacon said that at Henry's death most of his treasure was "in secret places under his own key and keeping at Richmond" (Bacon, p. 195).

[12] Dietz, p. 39; W.C. Richardson, *Tudor Chamber Administration, 1485-1547* (Baton Rouge, La., 1952), p. 158.

[13] This was calculated by Wolffe, "Land revenues", pp. 217, 223.

[14] Horowitz, "Policy and prosecution". Dudley wrote that, while in the Tower, he had access to "my books" (C.J. Harrison, "The petition of Edmund Dudley", *Eng. Hist. Rev.*, lxxxvii (1972), pp. 82-99, at p. 86).

Indeed, another of his surviving books involved money due on 280 obligations, mainly for appearance in a court from years earlier. A majority of likely collectible sums in this book were stipulated at £100 or less, with a large number between £20 and £40, for a total of almost £31,000.[15]

But what has loomed large in the minds of early Tudor historians for almost half a century regarding bonds has been the second volume of the *Calendar of Close Rolls* for Henry VII's reign, published in 1963. K.B. McFarlane was so taken by the large number of recognizances summarized in the *Calendar* that he suggested the first Tudor was ruling by recognizance on a separate plane: neither medieval nor modern but *sui generis*.[16] Recognizances were similar to written obligations for debt or the promise of a future behaviour, but they were specifically recorded at an official local or royal court or tribunal without the necessity of a seal. Sureties were usually required to guarantee the bond.[17] This large number of recognizances on the close rolls seemed to signal an intensification of a bond policy after 1500 or so. However, it has been demonstrated that these increased enrolments were part of a new administrative process initiated by Henry VII to follow through on bonds for discharge, with or without payment, as part of a policy that began soon after 1485.[18]

The close (*clausarum*) rolls dated to 1204 and contained entries of the closed and sealed documents that were written and exchanged between parties. Although similar to the patent rolls, which copied open (*patente*)

---

[15] T.N.A.: P.R.O., E 101/517/11, a book of obligations given "by the kings comaundment" through an indenture dated 1 Feb. 1505 with Edmund Dudley and his clerk "for to kepe and p[ur]sue unto thuse and behove of our forsaid souveraigne lorde". Of the 280 obligations, one was listed as a recognizance. This book was created from actual sealed bonds—one entry noted that four men from Kingston-upon-Hull were bound in £100 for the true allegiance of John Crouche "w^t a writyng sealed w^t the mayer of hulls seall of his office anext fast to the said oblig[ation]" (fo. 8v). John Heron ticked off each entry in the list and signed the bottom of each page. The bonds were mainly from 1495 to 1502 until 25 Oct. 1504 (fo. 14); the earliest listed was 15 July 1487. A number of entries are crossed out or have a line through them, for a total of £6,138 6s 8d, suggesting they were already collected upon or recorded elsewhere. Those not crossed out total £24,604 7s, giving a total amount of £30,742 13s 8d for all obligations due.
[16] K.B. McFarlane, review of *Calendar of Close Rolls 1500-9*, in *Eng. Hist. Rev.*, Vol. LXXXI (1966), pp. 153-4, at p. 154. The first volume of the *Calendar* for Henry VII's reign (1485-1500) was published in 1955.
[17] Horowitz, "Policy and prosecution"; Cunningham, "Loyalty and the usurper".
[18] Horowitz, "Policy and prosecution".

documents with affixed seals, the closed letters were often of a personal nature and dealt more with family affairs than with patents for office.[19] The concept of enrolling recognizances on the close rolls was not new; nor was it strictly for government activity. Since the 13th century, obligations in the form of a recognizance continued to be entered on the back (dorse) of the membranes making up the close rolls. Enrolment procured by individuals took place at chancery "apud Westmonasterium", or wherever the chancellor was, unless contracts or bonds were taken outside London and forwarded to Westminster by writ of *dedimus potestatem*. Obligations were also advanced to chancery from the royal exchequer, other royal treasuries (for example, duchy of Lancaster, palatinate of Chester), local and royal law courts and royal officials. Although the front of a membrane ceased to be used for royal writs and missives by 1533, the dorse continued to function as a record of private deeds until 1903. It also served as a place to enrol recognizances until the reign of Queen Anne when these contracts formed a distinct category at chancery.[20]

Early examples of these enrolments engender precedents for how the close rolls were used by the time Henry VII became king; indeed, many bear evidence of the same procedures that Henry and his councillors utilized as part of a bond policy. After the de Montfort rebellion (1263-4), sureties were found and enrolled to guarantee the appearance of rebels in the king's court. Around the same time, it was ordered that the rolls be inspected to determine who owed the crown money.[21] Many private debts acknowledged on the rolls were subsequently marked "cancelled" *upon payment*, demonstrating that the notation should not be viewed as synonymous with null and void without payment.[22] A list of debts to the king enrolled in 1276 to be paid at certain times included many that appear to be old—a scrutiny of lapsed payments that Henry VII and his councillors raised to a high art form.[23] Other procedures would be emulated by the first Tudor and his councillors. In 1279, Edward I kept a chest of bonds, tallies, charters and other documents, for which a command was enrolled that they should all be delivered to the

---

[19] See the introduction to *Knights of Edward I*, ed. C. Moor (Harleian Soc., 5 vols., lxxx-lxxxiv, 1929-32), i, p. viii..
[20] *Guide to the Contents of the Public Record Office*, i: *Legal Records* (1963), pp. 14-24.
[21] *Cal. Close Rolls 1264-8*, pp. 129, 52, 366.
[22] *Cal. Close Rolls 1272-9*, pp. 238-9; Horowitz, "Policy and prosecution". This is discussed below.
[23] *Cal. Close Rolls 1272-9*, pp. 340-1.

exchequer.[24] The next year, the chancellor ordered the enrolment of debts, including a recognizance, and in Edward II's reign eighteen recognizances taken in the presence of the king were received by the keeper of the chancery rolls and enrolled by the king's order.[25] Peace bonds in the form of recognizances were also recorded on the close rolls, such as those in 1319 as debts owed to the king for £2,000 taken in York, which were partially paid.[26] And in a procedure reminiscent of what was to occur on a regular basis in Henry VII's reign, on 6 April 1322 an enrolled debt of 100 marks owed to the crown by recognizance was ordered cancelled by the king through his privy seal since the money was paid "into his chamber" by the hands of a clerk of the receipt at the exchequer.[27]

Using the *Calendars of Close Rolls* in Henry VII's reign for the purpose of calculating potential income to the crown from enrolled bonds is fraught with problems, not the least of which is whether they should even be viewed as true sources of accounts receivable. Indeed, while it can be instructive to compare both the number of recognizances and the number of people enrolled on the close rolls over time, it is not feasible to try to obtain an accurate view of how much money was owed to the king or collected using the summaries. Conditions for these contracts between the king and his subjects run the gamut of possibilities: allegiance to the king or good behaviour, either as an individual or as an officer of the crown; keeping the peace, individually or as part of an arbitration or statutory law such as livery; paying revenues to the king generated from lands or trade; appearance in a court or before the council; or other reasons not listed in the *Calendar* summaries.[28] The amounts could be small or climb into the thousands of pounds, the latter usually more of a warning to remain loyal, keep the peace or perform competently in a royal office. Although such large sums might be viewed as uncollectable, the work of Edmund Dudley and other councillors related to bond income shows that any non-compliance of a condition could trigger the forfeiture of a bond and allow the king's officers to compound moneys owed the crown for a

---

[24] *Cal. Close Rolls 1279-88*, p. 41.

[25] *Cal. Close Rolls 1279-88*, pp. 51, 63; *Cal. Close Rolls 1313-18*, p. 477 (1 June 1317).

[26] *Cal. Close Rolls 1318-27*, pp. 204-5.

[27] *Cal. Close Rolls 1318-27*, p. 205.

[28] A few examples are given here from *Cal. Close Rolls 1485-1500*: allegiance-good behaviour (nos. 52, 70, 126-7, 686, 735, 907); peace (nos. 228, 492, 974); revenues (nos. 617, 908, 989); appearance (nos. 744, 900, 950).

new, often lesser amount and in instalments.[29] Dudley suggested in his petition from the Tower while awaiting execution that many bonds were made, often without conditions, simply to keep people in line without any real thought on the part of the king to collect upon them.[30] Conversely, Dudley did compound large amounts, binding people in new bonds that were collected. Lord Clifford's recognizances totalling 1,300 marks net were first enrolled at chancery and then compounded by Dudley for £1,000 and additional bonds in return for a pardon.[31]

Moreover, there is also little doubt that Henry VII and those councillors involved with royal finance had a clear view of potential income, collectible or not, scrutinizing the original close rolls as much as historians do with the *Calendars*. Parliamentary grants were never paid in full throughout the medieval period—in fact, it would not be difficult to argue that grants (that is, taxes) approved in today's modern budgets rarely if ever generate the desired revenue. Although the first Tudor seems to have been successful in his collection of tenths and fifteenths approved by parliament, similar grants of money were not always paid in full.[32] This was true of the directly-assessed subsidy in 1489 for £75,000 from parliament: only between £21,500 and £27,000 was actually collected.[33] Henry would want to know the sources of all potential income, and poring over the king's current accounts and moneys due on bonds was a hallmark of his reign. John Heron kept weekly or periodic totals of expenditures and revenues in his account books, and it is quite likely that once the close rolls became a main record for recognizances taken in favour of the king they were also viewed as possible income in varying amounts. The deciding factors for projected revenue would have been the nature of the bonds and whether the large ones were viewed as subsequently

---

[29] See, e.g., Dudley's account book (Brit. Libr., Lansdowne MS. 127) and warrants at The National Archives in the C 82 and E 404 series for Henry VII's reign when compared to amounts enrolled at chancery or filed as memoranda.

[30] Harrison, p. 87: "for I thinke verily his inward mynde was never to vse them, of those there are very many".

[31] Horowitz, "Policy and prosecution".

[32] Roger Schofield calculated that between 99 and 100 per cent of parliamentary grants for tenths and fifteenths were collected in the early Tudor period with the exception of Henry VII's first years. The average gross yield after grants and exemptions was £29,800, which Schofield noted would have been a predictable amount from an accounts receivable perspective (R. Schofield, *Taxation Under the Early Tudors, 1485-1547* (Oxford, 2004), pp. 70, 176, 182).

[33] Schofield, pp. 78-9.

renegotiable amounts to remain loyal to the monarch, while actual debts owed the king would be paid in full, most likely in instalments.[34]

Another difficulty involves the nature of the *Calendar* summaries: they are incomplete.[35] Many recognizances marked "cancelled" or "vacated" do not indicate if they were paid first or cancelled before payment. Conditions for bonds are not always listed—a situation that sometimes occurs in the original documentation or in entries to account books—making it difficult to ascertain the nature of the bond and its viability as a true source of revenue. People named in the summaries are often recorded in multiple bonds for a variety of reasons and sums. The issues mount with the analysis. To obtain a better determination of the amounts involved in the entries of recognizances for possible collection would entail a reading of all the original rolls and cross-referencing the entries with the chamber books, chancery and exchequer warrants involving payments and receipts and the myriad writs and memoranda of recognizances preserved in The National Archives, as well as individual obligations taken out by the various revenue officials of the realm for their payment on farms, rents, customs and other royal sources of income. Sean Cunningham notes as much,[36] and it is hoped that some day a major project could be undertaken and defined to provide a closer approximation of Henry VII's success in generating income from bonds.

One example of both the shortcomings of the *Calendars* and a means to determine moneys actually collected involves two recognizances to the king by Sir Nicholas Vaux and Sir Thomas Parre enrolled 10 July 1507.[37] The summary states that the bonds were for £800 each for the payment of 1,000 marks at two designated times and that they were cancelled. No reason is given for the bonds or the cancellation, nor can it be determined if money was paid. However, a bill signed by Henry VII three months later recited one of these recognizances and noted that 1,000 marks had been paid, for which that bond was now to be cancelled.[38] Moreover, these recognizances were most likely part of an indenture between the two men and councillors of the king. Entries in Dudley's account book soon after 14 July 1507 acknowledged that both Vaux and Parre owed the king 9,000

---

[34] For references to the various chamber account books, see Richardson; and Cunningham, "Loyalty and the usurper".

[35] T.B. Pugh, "Henry VII and the English nobility", in *The Tudor Nobility*, ed. G.W. Bernard (Manchester, 1992), pp. 49-110, at pp. 58-9.

[36] Cunningham, "Loyalty and the usurper".

[37] *Cal. Close Rolls 1500-9*, no. 745.

[38] T.N.A.: P.R.O., C 82/306, Oct., no date.

marks for their marriages to the two daughters and heirs of Sir Thomas Grene and discharge of various intrusions and suits regarding his lands: 2,000 marks by recognizance and 7,000 marks by indenture, along with two obligations for payments of rents due.[39] Dudley later felt that this was unjust, for after Henry VII's death he petitioned his former conciliar colleagues to recognize that both Vaux and Parre "payed 9000 markes vpon a very light ground".[40] A signet letter written early in the new reign referenced the indenture for 9,000 marks (2,000 by recognizances) made between Vaux and Parre and three of the late king's councillors: Thomas Lovell, Henry Wyatt and Edmund Dudley. Perhaps because of Dudley's admission, it further declared that 2,400 marks had been paid and ordered the cancellation of the balance due, suggesting that Dudley may have been referring to the 9,000 marks as money due but not actually paid in full.[41] Regardless, the 2,000 marks summarized in the *Calendar* was cancelled because it had been paid. This example also demonstrates that large sums of money described in the summaries as cancelled without any reason given could in fact have been paid to Henry VII.

With all of these caveats and hazards in mind, certain measurements based on the *Calendars* can be compared and contrasted with both Yorkist and early Tudor enrolments. They reveal not only a change in the way the close rolls were being used but also the potential income that might have been due the crown just from this one source (See Tables 8.1 and 8.2).

This is highly imperfect, but as noted earlier it is a start and, it is hoped, an inducement to launch a full-blown investigation into the bond policy of Henry VII and its success from a financial standpoint. At present, this article hopes to provide a snapshot of what was taking place at the chancery with regards to enrolments of these real or potential debts, much as Henry Tudor would have wanted to know who was bound to the king, why and for how much. Therefore, calculations should not be viewed as accounts due, but rather as figures comparative to those before his reign and throughout. The fact that Henry VIII seems to have had a large amount of cash on hand to launch his war with France suggests that his father's pursuit of driving in both old and new bonds literally paid off.

---

[39] Brit. Libr., Lansdowne MS. 127 fos. 45v, 50, 52v, 57v.

[40] Harrison, p. 88.

[41] T.N.A.: P.R.O., C 82/341 no. 600, Oct. 1509; see also no. 602 for an additional pardon of payments related to this indenture.

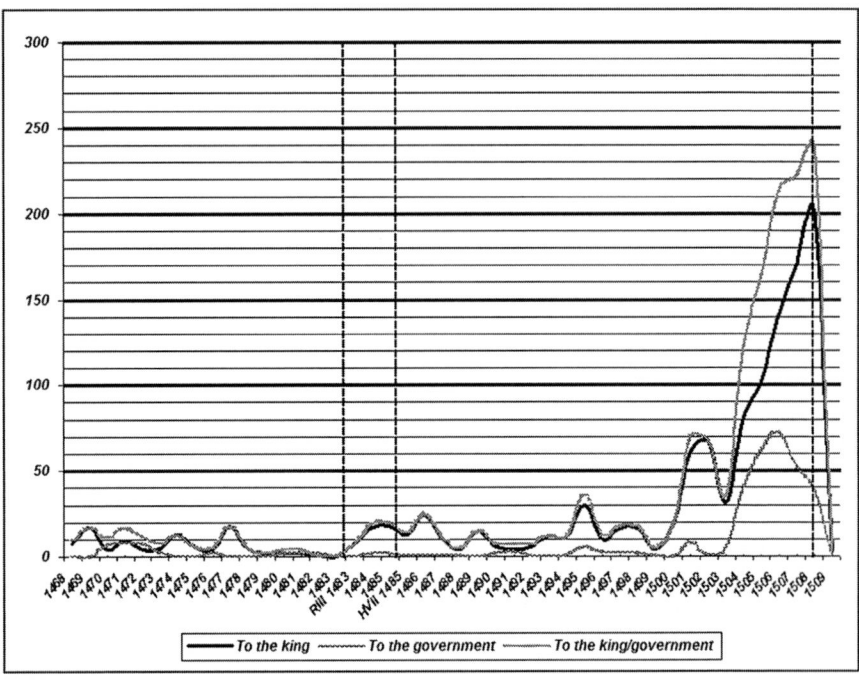

Table 8.1 Number of recognizances enrolled at chancery per year.

To understand Henry VII's reign from the perspective of recognizances enrolled at chancery and a clear break from past procedures, it is instructive to view a period of time prior to his reign. Although any timeframe is arbitrary, subject to risky interpretations beyond the previous issues raised, the sixteen years of Edward IV's reign from 1468 to 1483 saw the king struggling with, and then establishing control of, his government, mirroring similar problems facing Henry VII in his first sixteen years of rule. Edward also had rebellions, plots, a possible "phony" war with France and a hand in the murder of his predecessor.[42]

---

[42] It has been suggested that Henry VII's version of invading France in 1492 was not half-hearted but a serious attempt to end French rule in Flanders and Brittany and to stop the support of Perkin Warbeck (J.M. Currin, "'To traffic with war'? Henry VII and the French campaign of 1492", in *The English Experience in France c.1450-1558: War, Diplomacy and Cultural Exchange*, ed. D. Grummitt (Aldershot, 2002), pp. 106-31).

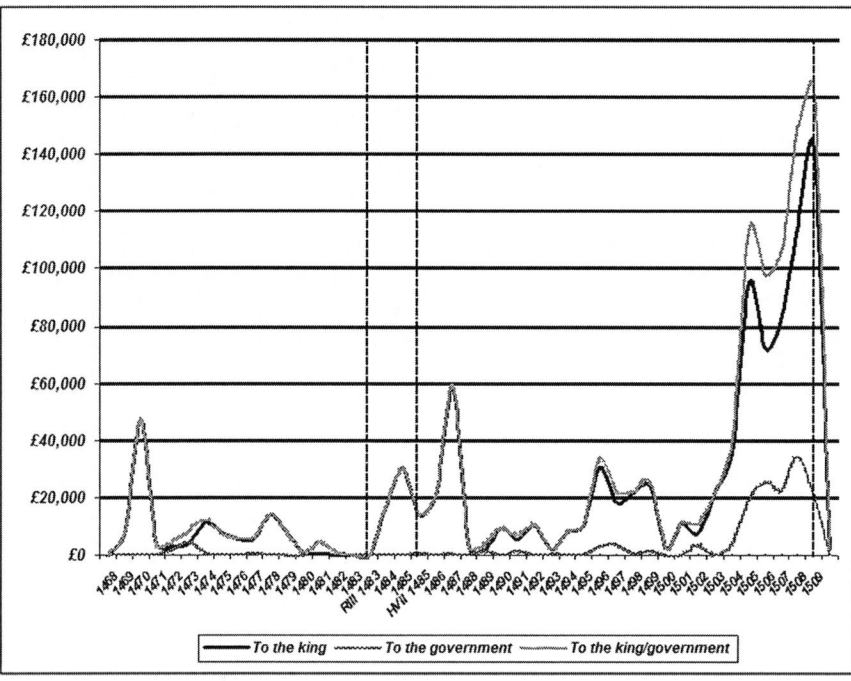

Table 8.2 Potential gross revenue from recognizances per year.

What follows are some observations and estimates based on an analysis of the use of the close rolls for recognizances and their enrolment during this period as summarized in the *Calendars*.[43] Those "due to the king" were specifically stated as such; those "due to the government" as defined in this present study were recognizances owed to ministers, councillors and officials of the king for his use. Amounts calculated are for potential forfeited bonds—in other words, the best case scenarios for revenue enrichment. Adjustments were made to make a best determination as to what the liability was for each participant in a recognizance (see appendix).[44] The reign of Edward V, such as it was, is not included in the discussion because no recognizances due to the king or his councillors

---

[43] Two volumes of the *Calendars* were used for the reigns of Edward IV and Richard III: 1468-76 and 1476-85.

[44] Some recognizances are duplicated on the close rolls, which are taken into account. All totals are rounded to the nearest pound.

were recorded in those short months. Finally, adding up the number of summary "entries" involving recognizances by their designated number was avoided because it does not equate to the number of people under such bonds, or even to the number of bonds. So in the *Calendar* for 1500-9, entry 377 is actually twenty-one recognizances involving eighty-two people; entry 955 is a summary of sixty-three recognizances involving 170 people. Tables 8.3 and 8.4 show the actual number of people in recognizances, by year and by selected timeframe.

Of the 100 bonds due to Edward IV from 1468 to 1483, just fourteen were annotated as cancelled, with a mere two noted as paid, one of them partially.[45] There were only a few royal bonds for allegiance. If other bonds were taken for such, they were not enrolled.[46] A few bonds stipulated that money was due to the treasurer of the chamber, evidence that royal revenues were paid directly to the king, bypassing the exchequer. (The earliest reference is from 1471.) The total number of recognizances enrolled for the period to either the king or his councillors on his behalf was 135, with eighteen being the largest number due to the king and his government in one year (1477). During this timeframe, 262 people were bound by recognizance, some more than once. Of these, 136 were bound directly to the king and 126 to the king and his councillors. Only two years saw a total of more than twenty people in bonds (1473, 1477) except for one anomaly when seventy-six individuals were bound to the king and his government (1471). However, of those, forty-six took out recognizances for oaths to Edward, prince of Wales, skewing the trend line.[47]

---

[45] Those annotated as cancelled in the *Calendars* were *Cal. Close Rolls 1468-76*, nos. 403-4, 541-2, 824, 851 (100 marks paid although 200 marks were due), 1039, 1520 (£5,000 paid by Louis XII on a 1475 bond of 20,000 crowns, most likely related to the pension due to Edward IV), 1535; *Cal. Close Rolls 1476-85*, no. 396. One recognizance was listed under the reign of Henry VI in 1471 (*Cal. Close Rolls 1468-76*, no. 676.).

[46] Two were enrolled in late 1469 for the allegiance of Henry Percy, son of the late earl of Northumberland. (*Cal. Close Rolls 1468-76*, nos. 403-4.) Several bonds for allegiance were enrolled in Apr. 1470. (*Cal. Close Rolls 1468-76*, nos. 539, 541-2).

[47] *Cal. Close Rolls 1468-76*, no. 858.

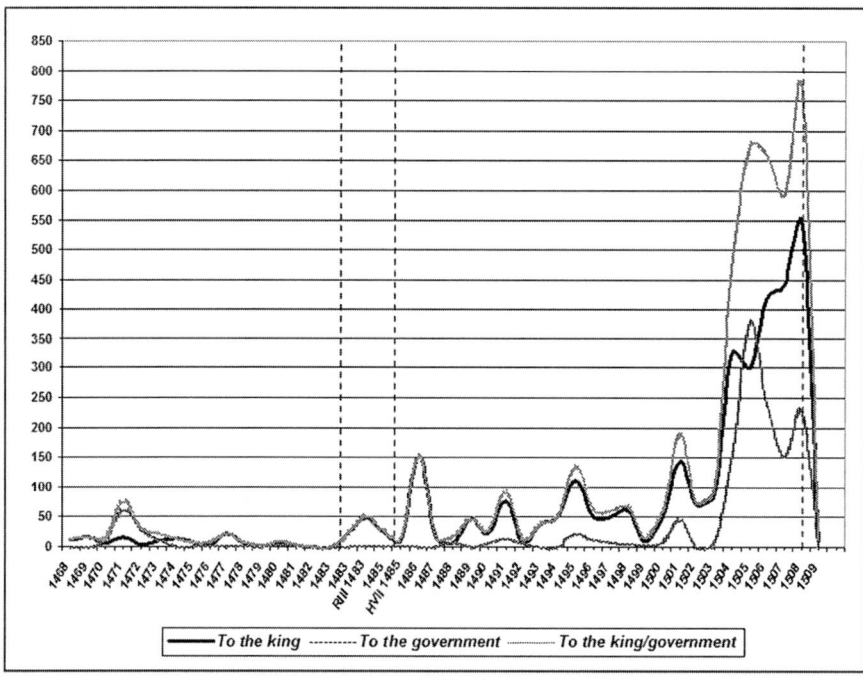

Table 8.3 Number of people in recognizances per year.

If all revenue were collected from moneys due on recognizances to the king and his councillors—keeping in mind that several were for enormous sums to keep the peace or a specific contract and would never have been paid in full—it would have totalled £131,501.[48] In any given year, potential revenue never exceeded £14,000. The annual number of enrolments bore little relation to the amounts payable on recognizances to the crown. For example, the two bonds enrolled in 1480 totalled £260, while the five for 1473 amounted to over £11,000, most of it due largely to the bonds of the countess of Oxford and her sureties for her appearance before the king and council.[49]

---

[48] This is obtained from adding £118,503 due to the king and £12,998 due to the king and his councillors ("the government").

[49] *Cal. Close Rolls 1468-76*, no. 1103.

These observations from the *Calendars* suggest that although a significant amount of income was potentially available from default on bonds, averaging £8,219 per annum, it was never vigorously pursued by Edward IV or his councillors. The exchequer and various administrative bodies (for example the duchy of Lancaster), and most likely the chamber, were the active places for record-keeping and revenue pursuit. Even the paucity of bonds for allegiance suggests a lack of interest in this form of binding behaviour, at least as they relate to enrolment at chancery.[50] If the king or his ministers ever realized the potential income or governmental control from debts on record for all possible conditions, there is little evidence from the close rolls at chancery that it was a policy to be pursued. This does not preclude the possibility that such bonds were kept or recorded elsewhere.

If Edward IV's last sixteen years represent a long period of time beset with a variety of disruptive events affecting administration and policy, Richard III's reign of twenty-six months hardly provides a more stable venue for analysis. Nonetheless, the *Calendar of Close Rolls* for the reign does suggest that Richard's government enrolled recognizances on the close rolls to a greater extent than his brother. For one, recognizances due to the king on an annualized basis averaged more than a threefold increase over Edward IV's last sixteen years: from more than six to almost twenty-two (a total of forty-seven recognizances due to the king or his councillors during the reign). Nine bonds were enrolled for appearance before the king and council, including one before "star chamber". This was a large figure in a short timeframe considering that about the same number were enrolled for such appearances during the entire sixteen-year period under Edward IV. During the more than two years Richard spent on the throne—and 1484 was his only complete year—total recognizances due to the crown or the government were eight, nineteen and twenty respectively for 1483-5. Although thirteen bonds to the government were cancelled, a proportionately larger number than under Edward IV, seven of them involved Edward Grey, Viscount Lisle, for keeping the peace, upon which nothing was apparently paid.[51] There were 102 people under recognizance,

---

[50] See J.R. Lander, "Bonds, coercion and fear: Henry VII and the peerage", in *Florilegium Historiale: Essays Presented to Wallace K. Ferguson*, ed. J.G. Rowe and W.H. Stockdale (Toronto, 1971), pp. 327-67, at p. 338. For a rejection of Lander's view that the nobles were harshly treated through the use of recognizances under Henry VII, see Pugh, pp. 49-110.

[51] *Cal. Close Rolls 1476-85*, no. 1317.

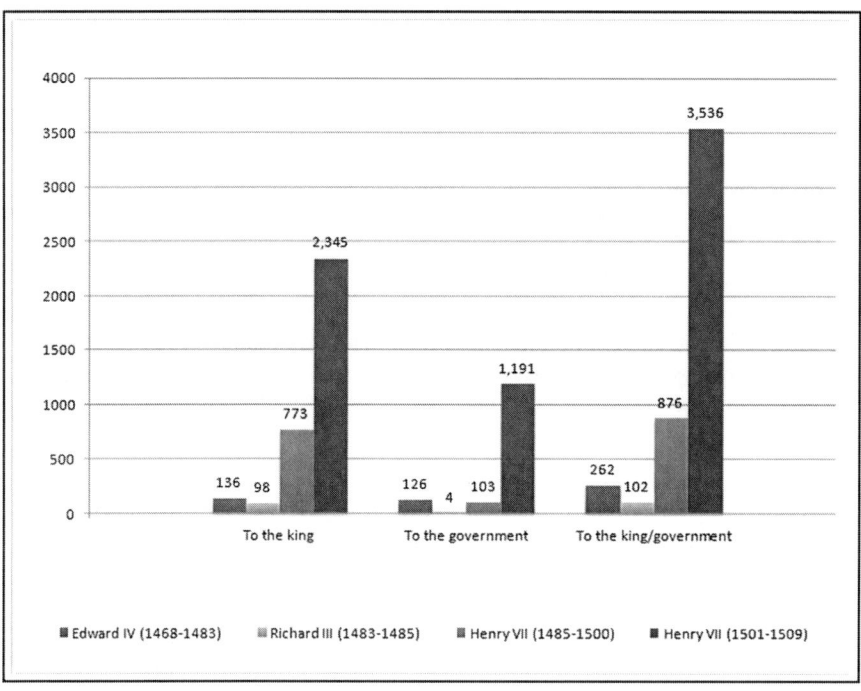

Table 8.4 Number of people in recognizances by time frame.

almost all directly to the king (ninety-eight). About half were taken in 1484 (fifty-one), with the majority for allegiance to the king, which would come as no surprise given Buckingham's rebellion in the autumn of 1483.[52]

Had Richard III collected all sums of money due on enrolled bonds during his reign, the total would have been £61,019, a little less than half the amount due to Edward IV in sixteen years and with almost half (£30,106) enrolled in 1484. Most of the totals stipulated in the conditions involved large bonds for allegiance, making potential collection on their full amounts doubtful, although the intent was evidently to threaten financial exaction for disloyalty. However, there is no indication that Richard, like his brother, saw any advantage—financial or otherwise—in

---

[52] *Cal. Close Rolls 1476-85*, nos. 1242-5, 1258-9 and Viscount Lisle's just mentioned.

prosecuting delinquent recognizances enrolled on the close rolls. Alternatively, they may not have thought it feasible or politically astute to do so.

The last Yorkist king utilized the close rolls for recording recognizances due to the crown more frequently than his brother. While the number enrolled increased steadily during Edward IV's reign, it jumped markedly under Richard III. But it is not clear if a trend or policy was in motion or if there was something else at work during this time of uncertainty. The majority of the bonds due the government were for direct payment to the king on default: only four of the forty-seven governmental bonds involved the king's councillors. What is evident is that the close rolls at chancery were being used to record bonds entered into for conditions involving the government with greater incidence. Henry VII did not invent the idea; he took advantage of it and intensified it.

The period 1485-1500 broadly corresponds with the last sixteen years of Edward IV's reign. It is also a convenient, although admittedly arbitrary, historical marker. Since the days of Polydore Vergil, one indictment against Henry VII has been his apparent change in policy and procedure near or after 1500, one that involved prosecuting the laws of the land ruthlessly to financial advantage. It was an accusation addressed over four decades ago in three articles debating the king's alleged rapacity during his last years, and his possible remorse.[53] Using the same analytical methods applied to the Yorkists for the *Calendars*, the only shift on the close rolls during this period involved an increased number of bond enrolments over time. For the first sixteen years of Henry VII's reign, the number of recognizances due to the king doubled when compared to the reign of Edward IV: from 100 to 200. Bonds to the king's councillors and officials for his use totalled twenty-five, less than the thirty-five enrolled under the first Yorkist king. In one of those recognizances, enrolled in 1490, the actual bond was to Reynold Bray, Thomas Lovell, James Hobart, Oliver King and Andrew Dymmok for the use of the king—the earliest example on the close rolls of what was to become a regular practice of the king's working councillors administering bonds on his

---

[53] *The Anglica Historia of Polydore Vergil*, ed. D. Hay (Camden 3rd ser., lxxiv, 1950); G.R. Elton, "Henry VII: rapacity and remorse", *Historical Jour.*, i (1958), pp. 21-39; J.P. Cooper, "Henry VII's last years reconsidered", *Historical Jour.*, ii (1959), pp. 103-29; G.R. Elton, "Henry VII: a restatement", *Historical Jour.*, iv (1961), pp. 1-29. Elton and Cooper barely addressed recognizances during their discourses.

behalf.[54] But at this juncture, Henry VII was binding people to him directly through recognizances at a greater rate than his father-in-law Edward IV. The major stipulation for recognizances between 1485 and 1500 was the nebulous area of good behaviour, coupled with allegiance and keeping the peace. Such bonds were not strictly reserved for the high and mighty.[55] John Hayes recognized a debt of £1,000 for his allegiance; his seventeen sureties were bound in the recognizance for £3,000.[56] Given his usurpation in 1485, and the rebellions in 1487, 1489 and 1495-7, Henry was in frequent need of allegiance.

Other observations suggest both continuity and contrast with Yorkist practice. While the few bonds due to the Yorkist treasurers of the chamber were in fact debts owed the king, these now took the form of debts due to Thomas Lovell, treasurer of the chamber to Henry VII. That there was little difference between these entries to various governmental officials and those of the Yorkist period further bolsters the belief that both Edward IV and Richard III had active chambers collecting money for the king. Several bonds owed to the crown involved the king's feudal prerogatives, such as wardships, which were not found under the Yorkist enrolments. The number of people placed in bonds escalated in the first sixteen years of Henry's reign: 773 to the king and 103 to his councillors for a total of 876 people—more than three times the number under Edward IV. Revenue potential was also larger, as would be expected from an increase in recognizances: all moneys owed to the king and his government if bonds were in forfeit amounted to £250,165. In comparative terms, Henry VII averaged £15,635 per annum on potential bond revenue versus Edward IV's £8,219. But like the situation with Richard III and large amounts for allegiance, Henry probably would have compounded such debts if he prosecuted them for default of their conditions.[57] Conversely,

---

[54] *Cal. Close Rolls 1485-1500*, no. 541. For the working councillors involved in the bond policy, see Horowitz, "Policy and Prosecution".

[55] See the discussion on such bonds across socio-economic lines in Horowitz, "Policy and Prosecution".

[56] Lander, "Bonds, coercion and fear", pp. 339ff.; *Cal. Close Rolls 1485-1509*, no. 686. Hayes was implicated in the Warbeck conspiracy in late 1491. He was captured, attainted in parliament, lost his offices and eventually received a pardon in conjunction with this bond. Eight of the sureties were eventually released; it is not known if they paid their penalties. (Chrimes, *Henry VII*, p. 91.)

[57] This would have been true for Lord Beaumont's £10,000 bond to keep the peace or the £8000 worth of recognizances by Anthony Brown and his sureties to keep Calais castle. (*Cal. Close Rolls 1485-1500*, nos. 52, 1006; Pugh, pp. 60-1.)

many were collectible. The spike in both the number of recognizances and their amounts in 1486 largely involved payments due on tollage to the crown in Wales, with 114 people placed in those bonds.[58]

Of the 200 recognizances to the king twenty-five were cancelled with little indication of payments made, a situation similar to the *Calendar* annotations for Edward IV and Richard III. While other sources such as lists in the chamber books and the various warrants found in chancery and exchequer records in fact suggest that bonds were being effectively prosecuted for payment, the close roll summaries give little indication of their final disposition. In fact, the success of such collection led not only to a more intensely pursued bond policy but also to a shift in administrative practice which saw the close rolls become, along with the records of individual councillors, a main record of bonds owed the king.[59] This change in procedure, however, would begin later in the reign.

After 1500, the front of the close rolls was all but abandoned as a place for entering records; from 1504 to 1509, there are only nine entries to be found there. The close rolls were now becoming almost exclusively a record of deeds and debt on the dorse of each membrane, most likely induced by a directive from the king to enrol bonds for treason and misprision beginning at the end of 1499.[60] Recognizances specifically owed to Henry VII numbered 858 from 1501 until his death in April 1509; that averages out to 101 annually. Although this is only a period of a little over eight years, the average enrolment was sixteen times higher than the six bonds per annum during Edward IV's last sixteen years; nearly five times the almost twenty-two bonds per year under Richard III; and almost eight times the thirteen bonds per annum during Henry VII's first sixteen years of rule. For recognizances due to the government, the increase was dramatic: 279, with a large number due to the working councillors involved in taking and prosecuting many of the bonds. The number of people entering recognizances also increased precipitously: 2,345 to the king and 1,191 to his councillors, for a total of 3,536 people.[61] It is no coincidence that in the latter part of 1504, when Edmund Dudley became the king's personal bond administrator and Richard Empson the de facto

---

[58] *Cal. Close Rolls 1485-1500*, no. 129.

[59] Cunningham, "Loyalty and the usurper"; Horowitz, "Policy and prosecution".

[60] *Cal. Close Rolls 1485-1500*, no. 1199; Horowitz, "Policy and prosecution"; Pugh, p. 94, n. 29.

[61] For the entire reign of Henry VII, 4,412 people entered into one or more recognizances to the king and his councillors as summarized in the *Calendars* of the close rolls.

head of the duchy of Lancaster where many bonds were taken, there commenced a discernible jump in enrolments involving the king's councillors. Many of them were actually taken elsewhere and enrolled at chancery. The money paid on them was destined for the king's chamber.[62] Indeed, when the chamber books are compared to the close rolls, it becomes clear that a chancery-chamber connection was developing to record and obtain debts due to the king.

For recognizances due to the king and government, of the 1,137 enrolled the total amount due was a staggering £704,625, almost three times that for the period 1485-1500 and five times that for 1468-83, yet covering half the number of years. On an annualized basis, potential income from these bonds was £84,555, more than twice the revenue from ordinary income in the last years of Henry VII's reign. But the possible amounts due per given year—debts real or otherwise that his early detractors claimed Henry and his ministers endeavoured to collect with vigour—indicate the direction of his bond policy from a possible revenue-generating perspective: in 1506, the total due on bonds was £106,382— more than Henry's entire annual revenue; for 1507 it was £148,377 and for 1508 it was £163,443.

It cannot be stressed enough that realistically a number of these recognizances were non-collectable in full, especially the larger ones meant more as a threat than a real source of revenue. Furthermore, large debts owed to the crown could be reduced or renegotiated by the king upon his command. Nevertheless, as mentioned above, there is enough evidence from the chamber books and other financial and judicial sources to suggest that Henry and his councillors were quite successful in collecting on bonds, old and new. There was a deliberate effort on the part of the government to collect on debts and penalties owed on obligations and enrolled recognizances as the reign progressed, and there was a plethora of records of such bonds to determine which might be in default.[63] The fact that bonds *ad usum regis* increased dramatically on the close rolls in the last years of the reign suggests that Henry's financial councillors were bent on enforcing the payment of written debts and needed to keep track of them. While it can be maintained that something "different" was happening after 1500, it was more in the persistence of

---

[62] One of the close rolls had sewn to it the warrant of acquittance for three recognizances due five councillors because the money was duly received by the treasurer of the chamber (*Cal. Close Rolls 1500-9*, no. 456).

[63] Dudley's petition is replete with examples of this vigorous pursuit of money from bonds (see Harrison).

policy than in any shift in direction. Henry VII and his councillors understood the role and workings of the written obligation and enrolled recognizance in society, and they could use them to political and financial advantage with little worry of protest. Henry also succeeded in part because, as Rosemary Horrox has observed, his leading subjects wanted him to succeed as king.[64] The first Tudor did not invent the bond; he simply realized that it could be an efficient way of managing his monarchy to great effect.

It has been suggested that Edward IV's lavish spending was disproportionate to his income, and that perhaps one way in which he closed the gap was through forfeitures on recognizances.[65] Lack of evidence for this conjecture, including enrolments on the close rolls and the paucity of recognizance memoranda in the chancery files, suggests that this may be but a projection backwards from the *modus operandi* of Henry VII, although it would be worthy of exploration. Where Edward IV managed to pay his own way, it was through cost-cutting and credit, and not from "new revenues and new systems of financial administration".

The same dilemma of addressing expenditure exceeding income exists when studying the finances of Henry VIII, who succeeded his father at the age of seventeen and soon engaged in an invasion of France. If Henry VII had indeed been broke, or had left little ready money for his son to inherit and spend, how was the latter able to commence a lavish lifestyle while waging an expensive war? Money beyond traditional sources must have either been flowing to the crown or discovered in cash among those "strong boxes" mentioned by the Spanish ambassador that Henry continually filled. Some time ago, an account notebook covering the period 1512-19 used by John Hasylwood, one of the exchequer tellers, was shown to contain entries of almost £36,000 in obligations, with only about two-thirds of that money actually accounted for at the king's chamber or delivered there.[66] Before Henry VIII's reign, three account books kept by exchequer tellers under his father involved large amounts of money paid to the chamber, the single biggest source being unspecified obligations and

---

[64] R. Horrox, "Yorkist and early Tudor England", in *The New Cambridge Medieval History*, vii: *c.1415-c. 1500*, ed. C.T. Allmand (Cambridge, 2005), pp. 477-95 at p. 489).

[65] Hicks, p. 163.

[66] M.R. Horowitz, "An early-Tudor teller's book", *Eng. Hist. Rev.*, xcvi (1981), 103-16, at pp. 104, 114-15.

debts to the king. Moreover, many of the cash transfers to the king's coffers in the Tower were not entered in the king's book of receipts.[67]

The amounts of money and fungible assets accumulated by the time of Henry VII's death most likely relate to the profitability of the bond policy, which in turn provided his son with the ability to make large expenditures. In the first years of the new reign, Henry VIII obtained revenues from the royal lands in the neighbourhood of £40,000 per annum. However, the reversal of attainders and grants of his father's lands, plus the loss of his mother's estates to jointure for Katherine of Aragon, left the young king with less ordinary revenue than his father. By the 1520s, Henry VIII may have only had between £80,000 and £90,000 from his own resources.[68] How did he finance his early war with France, especially if, as some modern historians have suggested, he inherited either little money or actual debt? John Heron's books of payments for 1509-15 show that in 1512 he paid £181,468 for military purposes, which increased to £682,000 in 1513 (along with an additional 10,040 crowns) and £92,000 in 1514: a total of just under £960,000 in three years.[69] Adding in the £4,515 in military expenditures for the period 1509-11 and perhaps other payments not accounted for, the almost £1 million for war and war preparation cannot be traced to any traditional royal income during this period that would have remotely covered these costs.[70] Indeed, when in 1512 Wolsey asked the commons for a grant of £600,000 for the invasion of France, they refused and responded with just over 20 per cent of the requested amount: £126,745 gross on tenths and fifteenths and a subsidy, which then had to be collected.[71] This led Richard Hoyle to observe: "Henry was extremely liquid, but where this money came from remains a mystery".

Borrowing (and paraphrasing) from Conan Doyle's sedulous sleuth, once the impossible is ruled out, whatever remains—no matter how

---

[67] Grummitt, "Henry VII, chamber finance and the 'New Monarchy'", pp. 233-5.

[68] R.W. Hoyle, "War and public finance", in *The Reign of Henry VIII: Politics, Policy and Piety*, ed. D. MacMulloch (1995), pp. 75-99, at pp. 76-7. Another estimate for Henry VIII's revenue in the 1520s is £110,000 (D. Potter, "Foreign policy", in MacCulloch, pp. 101-33, at p. 112).

[69] Hoyle, pp. 74-85.

[70] Totalling all expenditures from the king's chamber beginning in Feb. 1512 (John Daunce given £6,000 "for the army") through to May 1515 (when Daunce received £6,000 "for the late wars in France, and on sea against the Scots"), the amount paid out during these 40 months was £1,162,214 1s 11d (*L&P*, II.i., pp. 1441-90: summary of king's book of payments, 1-10 Henry VIII, 1509-18).

[71] Schofield, p. 16.

improbable—is the truth.[72] In this case, what remains is much more conceivable than improbable: the first Tudor left his son a vast fortune. From the close rolls alone, potential revenue from enrolled recognizances during Henry VII's reign was £954,790. This was separate from but sometimes linked to the bonds for collection kept by Edmund Dudley, Richard Empson and the working councillors, who also took bonds as justices of the peace and collectors of money due to the king for his various prerogative rights (wardships, marriages, outlawries) and those of justice (appearance, keeping the peace and allegiance to the king).[73] All of these revenue sources were again separate from the £104,000 estimated annual gross income that Henry received in the last years of his reign, which of course he used in part to run the realm. Even with the knowledge that some bonds were cancelled without payment or renegotiation, the sheer number of debts owed and conditions pledged by myriad sureties represented revenue unfathomable to his predecessors going back to the Conquest. Henry VII's accumulated wealth in actual specie, plate and bullion and his acquisitive nature ensured that his son would inherit a prodigious fortune, including a large "accounts receivable" list of bonds due to the crown after his death that were collected upon or compounded for lesser amounts.[74] In noting that Henry VII paid the Habsburgs at least £260,000 in the last years of his reign as a *quid pro quo* for controlling the

---

[72] Maitland might have concurred, suggesting that one source of Henry VII's treasure emanated from the work of Empson and Dudley "for the purpose of swelling the revenue" (F.W. Maitland, *The Constitutional History of England: a Course of Lectures* (Cambridge, 1908; repr. by The Law Exchange, 2001), p. 183). Dietz also admitted that besides jewels and plate there were large sums owed to the first Tudor in the form of obligations, although he does not suggest how much might have been collected that remained unaccountable: "It was these jewels, plate and bonds of various sorts which made up the bulk of the wealth left by Henry VII to his son" (Dietz, p. 87).

[73] David Grummitt has noted that much of the revenue to the king was not recorded, and that there were several repositories where cash was being stored (Grummitt, "Henry VII, chamber finance and the 'New Monarchy'", pp. 238ff.).

[74] Horowitz, "Policy and prosecution". The National Portrait Gallery has little doubt of the king's fortune. In describing Henry VII, portrayed in several gallery works of art, the website tersely notes in one sentence his lineage, defeat of Richard III and establishment of the Tudor dynasty, and then his accomplishments in a second sentence: "A notably clever king, he amassed enormous wealth for the Crown and established relative peace in England" (National Portrait Gallery, <http://www.npg.org.uk/live/search/person.asp?linkID=mp02144> [accessed 1 Oct. 2008]).

volatile Edmund de la Pole, T.B. Pugh suggested that in the light of such heavy demands on the king's revenues in the early 16th century "his reliance on bonds and recognizances as part of his governmental system in the latter half of his reign should be reconsidered".[75] The fact that Henry could easily muster such payments suggests the success of a bond policy bent on increased revenue generation.[76]

It was for Henry VIII to spend his father's money and resort to extraordinary taxes to finance his reign, making the English crown dependent on parliament, especially when waging future wars.[77] Unlike the father, the son was not focused on becoming solvent and therefore financially independent. Even with a second chance—the dissolution of the monasteries—Henry alienated those lands, ensuring that the king in parliament would be the constitutional path followed, one that contributed to the establishment of the modern English state. Henry VII's treasure provided his son with the means to seek out Lancastrian glory abroad and royal pageantry at home. The price was modest in the beginning since cash was available for his every need. However, from the perspective of a Fortescuesque self-sustaining, unencumbered ruler, the price was very high. In the end, it might be said that the final disposition of Henry VII's fortune helped to change the fortune of his dynasty and the monarchy.

---

[75] Pugh, p. 65. Pugh says that these amounts paid to Maximilian I and Archduke Philip were in the guise of loans with no intention of repayment.

[76] There was also a critical "law and order" *raison d'être* to the bond policy, discussed in Horowitz, "Policy and prosecution"; and Cunningham, "Loyalty and the usurper".

[77] Hoyle, p. 96.

Appendix

Determining individual liability in a bond

An important issue regarding recognizances internal to the *Calendar* summaries, and often to the memoranda of those stored at chancery, involves exactly how much a surety (or mainpernor) and the principal party put up as a monetary pledge for a recognizance. The condition is the determining factor and can render a seemingly large denomination (ten people in £100 each for a total of £1,000 pledged) into a relatively minor one (ten people in a £100 bond, each pledging £10 for a total of £100) depending on interpretation. Language is the key to understanding liability. In one series of chancery memoranda of recognizances,[78] sureties were bound in a sum either *utrumque (uterque)* or *quilibet eorum*, the first term ("either" or "both") usually describing two persons and the second ("any or every of them") more than two.[79] The "either or both" depends on the condition; thus, if one person was bound for the other's performance, the sum referred to the total payable by both *collectively* for default. In this case, for example, John was bound in a recognizance for William to perform a condition, with the default penalty of £100 owed by both of them together, or £50 each. If both John and William were required to perform the condition, each owed the sum due *individually*, for a total of £200.

A warrant in the chancery files provides a guide to help determine the exact meaning of liability in a bond.[80] Two men, Thomas Thoresby and John Bele, entered a recognizance in chancery "either of them [*uterque eorum*] upon pain of a 1,000 marks that they and either of them should stand and obey the decree ordinance and judgment" of two royal councillors for controversies existing between them. Each man "observed not . . . the said undertaking and recognisance" and forfeited the sums. Thoresby was now granted a pardon for his 1,000 marks, which was "remitted unto him". He received a pardon under letters patent as well.[81]

---

[78] T.N.A.: P.R.O., C 244 series.

[79] The author owes much of this discussion to the late Revd. Joseph R. Frese, S. J., of Fordham University for his thoughts on the issue.

[80] T.N.A.: P.R.O., C 82/201, 16 Feb. 1500, modernized spelling. The original recognizance is in a writ of *scire facias* (C 245/44 no. 19.)

[81] *Calendar of Patent Rolls 1494-1509*, p. 188. The summary in the *Calendar* agrees with this interpretation. Note here that cancellation involved voiding a

Bele's fate was not recorded on either the patent or close rolls, but since the recognizance was not enrolled but placed on file, he may have received an acquittance of his bond and the remittance of his 1,000 marks. This example is decipherable only because of the stated condition: both parties to obey arbitration, and each ("either of them") responsible for 1,000 marks. When Edward Lord Howard and his wife were bound in £1,000 for a similar condition, they represented one party, with Walter Hungerford bound in £1,000 as the other party. The lord and his wife were therefore responsible for the total £1,000, and not £1,000 each.[82]

The same problem exists for groups of people bound in recognizances. Four men were bound "every of them" in 40 marks for the appearance of a man at the sessions in Kent.[83] That information alone affords no means of establishing the financial responsibilities of the sureties: either one sum of 40 marks due by all four (10 marks each) upon default, or a total of 160 marks due, with 40 marks payable by each surety. The warrant for pardon, however, stated that "the said pledges have well and truly contented and paid unto us in our Chamber the sum of 100 marks and the residue of the said forfeitures, which is xl li. [60 marks] we . . . have pardoned remitted and released unto the said pledges". (And note that "pardoned" and "remitted" meant only for the remaining amounts not paid.) The *Calendars of Close Rolls* often omit the translation for *quilibet eorum*, leaving additional guesswork beyond any lack of stated conditions. Of the several recognizances summarized in one section of the printed close rolls for 1500-9, the *Calendar* records William Scargyll and seven other men in a bond with the amount of £100 placed in parenthesis.[84] The actual entry on the original close rolls explained that the men were bound "se et quilibet eorum per se recognovit", suggesting that each was responsible for £100, or a total of £800.[85] Unfortunately, the printed *Calendars of Close Rolls* for the Yorkist period and Henry VII's reign add to the confusion by summarizing recognizances in such a way as to leave the question of liability open, making any calculation of moneys due on bonds imprecise. As stated earlier, only the original rolls and ancillary evidence in the form of rolls, books, filed recognizances and warrants can give a better reading of what is meant with regards to liability.

---

forfeiture; it therefore represented cancellation of the original condition, not of the subsequent sum to be paid.

[82] *Cal. Close Rolls* 1485-1500, no. 407.

[83] T.N.A.: P.R.O., E 404/84, 13 Nov. 1502, modernized spelling.

[84] *Cal. Close Rolls 1500-9*, no. 454.

[85] T.N.A.: P.R.O., C 54/266, m. 26d.

CHAPTER NINE

AN EARLY-TUDOR TELLER'S BOOK*

Introduction

After passing the Oral Exam to become a PhD candidate in February 1976 [Addendum 3], I began writing a dissertation proposal on the reign of Henry VII, which was accepted in June. The University of Chicago's impressive Regenstein Library housed all the catalogues of documents stored in the British Library (then at the British Museum) and in the Public Record Office (then down Chancery Lane in London). I asked my adviser how I might narrow my search since I hoped to leave for England the following year and I had only scratched the surface of documents to review in England—the catalogues took up an entire long wall! His reply was rather terse: "Read every entry about early-Tudor history—you might discover something."**

I read them all over a seven month period, creating hundreds of index cards with many of the single entries representing dozens or hundreds of documents or folios—this was the pre-computer era but none of the cards crashed or were accidentally deleted. In January 1977—the Queen's Jubilee Year—I arrived in London for a year of research on my

---

* Reprinted with permission. The article was first published in *The English Historical Review*, Vol. XCVI, No. CCCLXXVIII (Jan. 1981), pp. 103-16.

** That adviser was Mark A. Kishlansky, newly arrived at the university with a professional interest in 17th century England, concentrating on the Civil War and the New Model Army. Clearly he was far afield from my chosen era of study, which he admitted was foreign to him. Nonetheless, Mark was extremely helpful in the ways and wiles of thorough historical research, and we became friends. Both of us and our spouses once traveled through Wales in part to seek the oldest red post boxes—imprinted on them were the initials of the reigning monarch when they were made. I still have a picture of him in front of one from Victoria's time. Mark finished his career at Harvard University.

dissertation topic, which I had published in a listing with the stodgy but alliterative title "Recognizance and Rule in the Reign of Henry VII".

One day at the British Library, I checked out an entry on one of those index cards: Egerton Manuscript 986. It was described in the catalogue as a 19th century copy of obligations for debt to the crown covering the years 2 Henry VII to 10 Henry VIII (c. 1486-1519). While reading the manuscript I realized the description was suspect: the writing looked contemporary, not Victorian. It was not a copy. There were also letters patent entered that I could not find in their original form at the Public Record Office; hence, these were missing additions to the record of the early years of Henry VIII's reign.

Before leaving for England I had met the leading (at the time) Tudor historian G.R. Elton visiting the U of C. He suggested I contact him after I arrived in London. I did regarding this manuscript, sending him excerpts and a letter asking his opinion. He replied that he would be in London in July for the Anglo-American Conference and we could look at it together. After our joint review of it, he believed I was correct and that it was the genuine article. Soon after, I received a card from him suggesting that he write an article on it—he would put me in a footnote as the discoverer.

Some British diction entered my head: "Bloody hell! Just what Elton needs: another bloody publication! And me a lowly grad student with a total of zero publications!" I fumed for a day. Then I dropped him a card thanking him for the gesture but explaining that I would write the article and I would be pleased to thank him in a footnote for reviewing a draft, if he would be so kind. Rather than ending my career a bit early, which was now a strong possibility, Elton wrote me back agreeing to my proposal. We actually became good friends and correspondents.

"An early-Tudor teller's book" was my first scholarly article, published in The English Historical Review. *It was a fortuitous find because it demonstrated some of the continuity between the reigns of Henry VII and Henry VIII at the administrative and financial levels of government. But it also showed a purposeful reversion to some of the medieval practices the royal treasury (exchequer) of old pursued before the first Tudor committed to administering finance through the king's personal chamber. Moreover, it confirmed the ubiquity of bonds and the exchequer-chamber connection for recording them and collecting upon them, in effect financing the Tudor government more efficiently.*

Finally, the manuscript illustrated how the treasurer of the chamber accounted for, and renegotiated, debts due the crown—a peek at the process of revenue collection. It clearly succeeded well enough to provide Henry VII with a lot of money in hand and on the books.

Henry VIII began his reign in 1509 with an inherited chamber administration directing national finance, a continuation of developments under the Yorkists and Henry VII. The king's chamber constituted a national treasury, receiving royal revenues and leaving to the exchequer its ancient administrative functions and the collection of customary rents and farms. The chamber acquired statutory recognition under Henry VIII which confirmed procedures for the administration of finance; these procedures in turn required the services of both the exchequer officials and the department of receipt. But by no means was there a static, accepted method for obtaining the king's money, and a further attempt to standardize procedures can be seen in one special form of finance: the processing and collecting of debts "by obligation", a written contract for payment.

Evidence of a system for recording and collecting these written obligations for debt in the early years of Henry VIII's reign exists in one revealing manuscript in the British Library, a workbook kept by one of the tellers at the exchequer of receipt. The volume contains entries of debts by obligation and enrolments of royal commands and letters patent.[1] Its survival allows the reconstruction of a method used for contracting and paying debts to the crown and affords a clearer understanding of the long lists of obligations filed in the chamber books of Henry VIII's reign. Many letters patent either lost in the original or not recorded elsewhere are preserved in this manuscript. It is therefore both a supplement for the *Letters and Papers* of Henry VIII's reign and a source for comprehending the financial administration in the early years before the reorganization of the chamber and the advent of Thomas Cromwell.[2] It also shows that,

---

I would like to thank G.R. Elton and Mark Kishlansky for their helpful comments on drafts of this article.

[1] The manuscript is Brit. Libr., Egerton MS. 986 (133 fos.). All references to folios placed in parentheses refer to this manuscript.
[2] *Letters and Papers, Foreign and Domestic of the Reign of Henry VIII,* Second ed. (1965). Of the six letters recorded in the book for the years 1-2 Hen. VIII, four are missing from *L&P*: (1) 29 June 1509: General warrant to pay the costs of the household and courts (fo. 41); (2) 8 Aug. 1509: John Hasylwood confirmed as teller (fo. 43); (3) 30 Feb. [*sic*] 1510: All revenues of Henry VII to be delivered to John Heron (fos. 45v, 46, Original found in T.N.A.: P.R.O, E 404/87; (4) 2 Jan. 1510: Grant for David Owen (fo. 50v). The remaining two, grants, to Cornelius Johnson (fos. 54v, 55) and Richard Babham (fo. 106v), are in *L&P* (I.i. nos. 632(67); 651(9)).

despite the royal desire to make the chamber the focal point of fiscal activity, the exchequer of receipt continued to collect on written debts—a sphere of administration reserved for the chamber during Henry VII's reign. The general view that the exchequer was in a state of atrophy after the onslaught of chamber administration cannot withstand the evidence found for the first decade of Henry VIII's reign.

The ownership of the book can be ascribed to John Hasylwood, one of the four tellers of the receipt at the exchequer. Numerous notations for delivery of obligations to him are recorded in the book and his name heads several folios of obligations listed in the back of the chamber books kept by John Heron, treasurer of the chamber under both Henry VII and Henry VIII. It was Heron who eventually received these written contracts from the exchequer and the money due upon them. Unfortunately, the hand recording these notations in the workbook cannot be identified positively with that of Hasylwood's.[3] The only other reference supporting ownership by him is his patent of confirmation as teller of the exchequer, the third entry in the letters patent section of the manuscript (fo. 43, 8 August 1509).

External evidence, however, points to Hasylwood as the custodian of the book, if not the owner. An extract from the pell records entitled *Recepta Scaccarii* declared the charges of Hasylwood at the receipt from roughly 1512 to 1519, about the same dates covered by the entries in the manuscript:[4] £34,092 15s 7½d in his charge, of which Hasylwood delivered £24,315 4s 3d in obligations to Heron. Although it is fruitless to juggle totals in the workbook to match these figures, the sum of the entries for this same period amounts to £35,923 9s 3d (discounting three repeated debts)—a figure surprisingly close to the declaration since any totals are estimates based on scribbled entries whose official status remains uncertain. Hasylwood undoubtedly based this declaration on information contained in the workbook, and the manuscript will be referred to as Hasylwood's book.

Two other men had access to the workbook: John Lewis (Lewys) and Hugh Fuller. Lewis was clerk of the pells in 1486 and writer of the tallies

---

[3] Taking a sample of fourteen warrants for issue endorsed "sol *p* hasilwod", all resemble each other but none appear to be of the hand recording entries in the teller's book. (T.N.A.: P.R.O., E 404/87.) Nonetheless, Professor G.R. Elton has suggested to me that the endorsements on the warrants may be by a clerk and not by Hasylwood.

[4] *L&P*, Addenda, I.i. 229.

three years later.[5] A debt owed by him to Sir John Cutte, undertreasurer of the exchequer, was entered in the workbook in first person at about the time the record begins (fo. 10v). Moreover, a description of the office of gentleman-usher at the exchequer of receipt, which Lewis probably held, appears on the first folio page and includes the duty "to square and make the tallies, to provide all manner necessaries to the court [of exchequer], to lock and unlock the coffers where the king's records be".[6] If Lewis did not write the entries in the workbook he at least kept it safe and perused it for recording a private debt.

Hugh Fuller's name is found in a notation on the top of a folio which attributes to him the role of delivering to the exchequer written obligations entered on that page (fo. 14v). Fuller was a clerk of the undertreasurer of the exchequer and kept an account of receipts and payments obtained from John Golding, another clerk to Sir John Cutte, involving artillery and ordinance during 1513: the first year in which entries of obligations appear in Hasylwood's book with any frequency.[7] He also delivered money from John Heron, treasurer of the king's chamber, to Cutte at the exchequer. Since Lewis and Fuller acted as messengers between the two departments, both would undoubtedly use a book of obligations due the crown for their work. Because Fuller was a clerk at the exchequer, he, too, may have recorded entries in the workbook as the need arose.

Besides the enrolment of obligations for debt, Hasylwood's book contains a section of 197 letters patent of which two were signets, four indentures and the remainder privy seals (fos. 41-132v). They were entered not only as a permanent record of payments due to individuals by the tellers of the receipt, but also as a working list of grants with their status annotated. Thirty-four of these were marked "morte" (*mortuus, mortua*), indicating the decease of the prospective recipient; ten were noted as vacated by act of resumption, an incomplete copy of which appears at the beginning of the workbook. Most privy seals were for annuities but the few involving official orders or licences from the crown are important for the light they shed on the administration of obligations and their role in the interaction between exchequer and chamber.

---

[5] G.R. Elton, "The Elizabethan Exchequer: War in the Receipt", in *Elizabethan Government and Society: Essays presented to Sir John Neale*, etc. (London, 1961), p. 218, n. 5. In 1518, Thomas Danyell held the office of one of the officers of the receipt in place of Lewis. (Brit. Libr., Add. MS. 36675 fo. 7v; *L&P*, II.ii. no. 2736 (p. 877).)

[6] (My commas) Spelling is modernized for all quotations from documents.

[7] *L&P*, I.ii. no. 2604.

For the purposes of this discussion, an obligation was a written debt, incurred by the laws and customs of England and based upon a stated condition (loan, duty, payment). There could be a penalty written into the condition for late payment, non-payment or non-performance. They were real debts yet listed separately in the chamber books from other debts owed to the Crown because of their contraction by consensus, payments falling due at certain dates, often by instalments. In this way a loan or debt on record could be transformed into an obligation with stated conditions for payment, payable to named officials or to the creditor directly. Obligations were used at all levels of society to conduct everyday business transactions.[8]

An example of an obligation entered in Hasylwood's book will serve to illustrate the form many of these contracted debts acquired (fo. 22). Next to the entry was written "anno vj", indicating the regnal year (in this case 1515). What followed was the date and month (*penultimo die Februarii*), to whom the debt was owed (Sir John Cutte) and the amount due (£75 2s 2d). In this particular obligation, instalment dates were recorded, half the amount due in 1515 and half one year later. In the left-hand margin the persons obliged to pay the debt were entered: John Calwodeley of Padstow, Cornwall, gentleman, and John Clyf of the city of Exeter. No reason was given as to why the debt was contracted.

This entry is similar to obligations entered in the chamber books, but in Hasylwood's account they might be considered in "long form", yielding more information than the "short form" ones of the chamber which only stated the debtor(s) and sums due, usually without specific date of contract. The greatest difference is that the payee was recorded in Hasylwood's book: Sir John Cutte, undertreasurer of the exchequer. This allows a glimpse of the intermediaries between the debtor and the actual accounting of the money received. Cutte may never have been involved personally in taking written debts, but his department was responsible for processing and recording them.

---

[8] The immense subject of obligations and recognizances cannot be appreciated fully by using one or two manuscripts for examples. There were enough differences between these two debts for Heron to distinguish them in two separate lists. Often they were convertible: "John Treguram and Pieter de Opuciis are bound in an obligation to pay [100] li. by Hallowtide next coming or else to find sufficient sureties by that day to be bound in a recognizance to pay the same [100] li." (Brit. Libr., Add. MS. 21481 fo. 290). An analysis of those written contracts in the late medieval period and their basis for statecraft under Henry VII is found in my Ph.D. thesis (University of Chicago).

The entries of obligations run unevenly throughout the workbook, their number totaling 168 with all but two dated in the reign of Henry VIII.[9] Over 80 per cent of the recorded debts were contracted between 1513 and 1517. Of these, five were listed as recognizances—for no stated reasons—four of which each included a fine or penalty: 80 marks were due if the sum of £50 was not paid on time (fo. 27).[10] Most of the obligations were owed by merchants, payable to the treasurer or undertreasurer of the exchequer, one or more of the king's councilors or the collectors of the customs and subsidies at the various ports in England. The sums involved varied from a few pounds to £1500, and when these amounts are totalled for each year obligations were contracted, they create a curve which at first glance suggests intense financial activity between the years 1513-17 at the exchequer of receipts for debt on trade. This curve or the sums due, however, cannot be construed as a reflection of national activity but are simply the activity in one teller's book concerned with recording obligations for debt.[11]

The obligations entered in the book are, in themselves, divided into two groups, here designated A and B.[12] Group A, which contains sixty-six entries, can be called "working" obligations because most of them were annotated *lib[er]at' hasylwod* and most were also listed in John Heron's chamber book.[13] John Hasylwood often delivered sums of money and written obligations directly to the chamber; this first group involved obligations delivered to him at the exchequer where they were recorded in the present book before being conveyed elsewhere. Group B contains entries which, with a few exceptions, were not duplicated in Heron's chamber book.

The procedure for recording an obligation at the exchequer of receipt can be gleaned from entries in Hasylwood's book and the corresponding

---

[9] Those of Henry VIII's reign were contracted between 2 Feb. 1511 and 18 July 1519, with many payments falling due after 1519.

[10] A recognizance was usually enrolled before a court of law such as chancery or the exchequer. They often had fines attached; in this instance, the fine was extremely low (£3 6*s* 8*d*, or 6.67 percent over the amount due).

[11] The revenues from customs decreased slightly after 1516, whereas the teller's book shows an expected increase. (Frederick C. Dietz, *English Government Finance, 1485-1558* (New York, 1964), p. 89.)

[12] Group A runs from fos. 9-18; Group B from fos. 21-36.

[13] Brit. Libr., Add. MS. 21481 fos. 336-7v. The contraction "libat" is found on many of the chancery warrants delivered to the Great Seal (T.N.A.: P.R.O., C 82 series).

records of the king's chamber. A signet letter (23 January 1513), addressed to the collectors of customs and subsidies in the ports of London and Southampton, was enrolled in Hasylwood's book (fo. 53). It contained a license for John Baptist de' Caponis (Capponi), merchant of Florence, to ship goods from those two ports totalling £500 worth of customs and subsidies, "taking of him sufficient land and surety for the same customs by obligation to be paid to us within four years next after the shipping of the said merchandise". The license alerted the collectors of the customs at the two ports to take the written obligation, which they did over a year later. It was sent to the exchequer of receipt and entered at the bottom of the enrolled license: two obligations contracted on 4 May 1514 by John Baptist and his sureties, one for subsidies totalling £500, the second for customs. A penalty was written into this debt, demanding £600 in the event of default, a 20 per cent fine (fo. 53v). If any of the sureties died in the interim or if the debt was not paid, other sureties were to be found and bound to either the treasurer or the undertreasurer of England.

The debt was also recorded in the obligations entered at the beginning of Hasylwood's book (Group A, fo. 14v), and was later duplicated in the chamber accounts of John Heron after the original written instrument was delivered to him.[14] Payment was due at the chamber, but as Heron did not record it as paid it is probable that money was received at the exchequer; a notation of payment was, in fact, written in Hasylwood's book next to the obligation. This was the procedure for taking written debts, using the exchequer for the administration of the records while the actual cash was to be collected by the king's chamber. The system, however, was not inflexible, and the officials at the exchequer of receipt often reverted to their usual responsibility of following a debt through to its payment, as seems to be the case with the obligation of John Baptist. This problem was recognized by the king and his financial ministers, and an attempt was made to standardize the procedure for recording and collecting debts, with the chamber as the financial nerve-centre for the receipt of obligations and monies due on them.

Part of this attempt may be seen in a privy seal recorded in Hasylwood's book (fos. 43v, 45, 45v). It was dated 4 June 1513 and was addressed formally to the treasurer and chamberlains of the exchequer and specifically to the undertreasurer, Sir John Cutte.[15] It began almost as a reprimand: "Where as we be informed that the treasure of our revenues

---

[14] Brit. Libr., Add. MS. 21481 fo. 337.
[15] The original privy seal is found in T.N.A.: P.R.O., E 404/89. It is not in *L&P*.

being in your keeping remains in the hands of the tellers at the receipt of our said Exchequer. . . ." The "informer" was undoubtedly John Heron, treasurer of the chamber, who realized that after Henry VII's death—or shortly before it—the tellers at the exchequer retained money and obligations intended for the chamber.[16] The privy seal ordered the tellers to deliver "all such sums of money of the treasure and obligations of our revenues as remain in the[ir] said hands and that hereafter shall come to their hands from term [to] term to the said Sir John Cutte by Indent[ure] to our use".

Cutte, a trusted Tudor servant since the victory at Bosworth Field, was now assigned the task of controlling both money and obligations. This was to eliminate any capricious hoarding or spending by the tellers and to implement a system for processing and collecting debts. The tellers were to specify (record) "the receipt of all such sums of money and obligations as the same Sir John Cutte shall receive of them" for the use of the king; this in effect was accomplished with the entries of obligations written in Hasylwood's book. The warrant further commanded Cutte to declare his accounts of revenues received at the exchequer yearly, "before us or our council", as sums of money and obligations kept by him. The privy seal coincided with the statutes establishing the court of general surveyors as the auditing department of royal revenues due the crown.[17] Cutte was being brought into a concerted effort to tighten up chamber administration. This was a continuation of the procedure developed by Henry VII, Sir Richard Empson and Edmund Dudley, scrutinizing all sums of money and written debts owed the king.

The first clause of the privy seal also established chamber control for collecting debts: "then he [Cutte] to deliver *or cause to be delivered* from year [to] year all those sums of money and obligations as shall be found

---

[16] Tellers often used the king's money for private transactions and steps to transfer these reserves out of their hands continued into the reign of Elizabeth. I would like to thank Professor Elton for this point.

[17] The general surveyors received statutory recognition in 3 Hen. VIII, c. 23. This recited the system under Henry VII whereby receivers declared their accounts orally before Reynold Bray, Robert Southwell and other councilors "for the more speedy payments of his [Henry VII's] revenues to be had and for the accounts of the same more speedily to be taken than his Grace could or might have been answered after the course of his Exchequer. . . ." This was further clarified under 4 Henry VIII, c. 18 and 6 Hen. VIII, c. 24. This last statute was repealed and updated a year later (7 Hen. VIII, c. 7); Part xxxiii provided the surveyors with the power to take recognizances for payment.

remaining in your custody and keeping to our trusty and well-beloved servant John Heron treasurer of our chamber". Not only was Cutte promoted to the position of formal financial liaison officer between the exchequer of receipt and the chamber, he was also instructed to work directly with the tellers, and the wording "deliver *or cause to be delivered*" confirms the role of Hasylwood as an agent for delivery to the chamber. Hasylwood's name headed several pages in Heron's accounts for obligations received by the teller and delivered to the chamber. John Heron was now the head of a financial junta involving the tellers of the receipt and the undertreasurer. It was Heron's task to drive in the unpaid debts; the exchequer provided him with the records.

The tellers were the key personnel for both recording and delivering obligations to the chamber. John Daunce, appointed teller at the receipt on 14 May 1505, referred to himself as clerk to John Heron.[18] By September 1511, Daunce was the king's treasurer of war and his accounts, beginning 1 July 1511, listed receipts of money, obligations and specialties.[19] Daunce acted as both general surveyor and receiver for the chamber, handling written obligations and sums of money. The debts listed in the back of his book included memoranda of bonds to pay money to the king's use, with notations concerning either payments or the delivery of the written debts to John Heron. One entry in Heron's book shows this process: "delivered by Sir John Daunce, knight, unto John Heron . . . one oblig[ation] contain[ing] the sum of [2500] li. . . ."[20]

These were similar to the obligations entered in Hasylwood's book and show a continuous procedure of record-keeping at the exchequer of receipt. In 1513, however, all obligations were to be delivered to the chamber, and the manuscript reveals that this command extended to those debts for customs and subsidies. The royal order had to be reissued three years later; a privy seal entered in Hasylwood's book dated 10 January 1516 commanded that all obligations of the customs—and all other obligations—from Michaelmas last should be delivered to Heron, including those debts still due to Henry VII (fos. 46, v). The king and his treasurer of the chamber had to keep a constant watch over exchequer administration and reiterate the needs of personal royal control and expenditure. Upon reading these two privy seals, the *raison d'être* for

---

[18] T.N.A.: P.R.O., E 404/85; B.P. Wolffe, *The Royal Demesne in English History* (Ohio, 1971), p. 214, n. 75.
[19] W.C. Richardson, *Tudor Chamber Administration* (Baton Rouge, 1952), p. 227; *L&P*, I. ii. no. 3608.
[20] Brit. Libr., Add. MS. 21481 fo. 340.

Hasylwood's book becomes apparent. Whether or not the tellers followed these procedures may be seen from Groups A and B in Hasylwood's book.

The obligations in Group A begin on folio 9 in trickles; on folio 11 at the top appears the heading *Obligaciones in Recepta Scaccarii Remanen'*, announcing the beginning of a record of obligations kept at the exchequer of receipt. The first one listed under this title was contracted on 8 November 1508 for £22 by Edmund Jenny and Robert Clere, this for partial of a debt for £88 10s 11d owed by Jenny for his office of sheriff in Norfolk and Suffolk.[21] A list of debts to Henry VII kept by Henry VIII in 1509 "till our mind and pleasure be further known in that behalf" included this one by Jenny, condemned in the court of common pleas "upon diverse misdemeanors and attempts contrary to the statute being late sheriff of Norfolk and Suffolk".[22] The debt was originally payable to Edmund Dudley, minister of Henry VII: £80 as discharge for being sheriff for two years.[23] Henry VIII now had a copy of the unpaid debt; so did the exchequer of receipt in the form of a compounded obligation recorded in Hasylwood's book. This debt was crossed out in the workbook at some unknown date and annotated as cancelled and paid at the exchequer of receipt.

Eleven obligations follow on fos. 11-12, seven involving debts contracted by William Grene with one or more co-debtors. They were made between February and September 1511 and totalled £1100. All were due to Thomas, earl of surrey, treasurer of the exchequer, and other unnamed members of the king's council. William Grene was a collector of the petty customs in London and his co-debtors were most likely guarantors or sureties for his collection and payment of the customs.[24] A

---

[21] In the last decade of Henry VII's reign, Jenny sat on several gaol deliveries for Ipswich and Great Yarmouth, the latter one occupied jointly with Clere. Both were knighted by the first Tudor and served on commissions of the peace in 1515, Clere for Norfolk, Jenny for Suffolk. Clere was thus well acquainted with Jenny and consented to be a surety for his debt. (*Calendar of Patent Rolls, Henry VII, 1494-1509*, pp. 86, 118, 559; *L&P*, II.i. 207.)

[22] T.N.A.: P.R.O., SP 1/1 fo. 105. The condemnation came at the end of Henry VII's reign: an exchequer warrant dated 1 June 1508 related the amercement of the sheriff of Norfolk and Suffolk in common pleas because he failed to return writs against Jenny and others (E 404/86).

[23] Jenny paid Dudley £40 in "redy money" and £80 by obligation 9 Mar. 1506. Clere discharged a recognizance to Dudley three months later for £80 as sheriff of the same counties. (Brit. Libr., Lansdowne MS. 127 fos. 17v, 22.)

[24] *L&P*, I.i. no. 312. In the memoranda roll for Trinity Term, 3 Hen. VIII (T.N.A.: P.R.O., [LTR] E 368/285 fo. 14), William Grene was recorded as owing money for

note next to these debts indicates that the sums were to be delivered to the serjeant of the king's cellar by instalments from 1513 to 1516. Grene had previous experience in delivering money directly to royal officials, bypassing the exchequer.[25]

All of the foregoing obligations have several things in common: they are not found in Heron's chamber book; all were conceived in the first few years of the new reign or at the end of the old reign; none were "delivered" to Hasylwood. They were either paid directly into the exchequer or assigned elsewhere and cannot be traced through the chamber system of accounting although the money may have ended up there. The exchequer sought to collect on written debts throughout the rise of chamber administration in the 15th century and usually had its greatest success when the monarch was preoccupied with rebellions or soon after his decease. A re-assertion of this function by the exchequer also occurred at the beginning of Henry VIII's reign as is evident from these first few written debts and the subsequent privy seals to deliver all obligations to the chamber.[26]

Twenty-six of the sixty-six obligations in Group A are not found in the chamber books. While it might be tendentious to explain each away as reasonable omissions during a customary increase in exchequer activity at the beginning of a new reign, this is the plausible explanation and it is strengthened by subsequent debts and the eventual need for the privy seal issued in 1513. Four of the next six obligations entered are not found in Heron's lists. One was owed by Francesco de' Bardi, merchant of Florence, and William Buttry (Bottry), mercer of London, due to Thomas, earl of Surrey; the second was made by William Lytton and two others,

---

24 Hen. VII and 1 Hen. VIII; Thomas Grene and Robert Barker came before the barons of the exchequer and mainprised 1000 marks for William to appear in the court of exchequer. Grene failed to escape the scrutiny of Edmund Dudley as well (Brit. Libr., Lansdowne MS. 127 fos. 10v, 31v).

25 Grene and several customers delivered sums and merchandise to the chamber in Henry VII's reign and received discharge on 2 Mar. 1511 (T.N.A.: P.R.O., E 404/87).

26 "Though in the new reign John Heron, Henry VII's treasurer of the Chamber, was at once confirmed as collector and paymaster of crown monies, the general surveyors were subjected to audit as the Exchequer (as it usually did as the death of a king when Household government was at its weakest) sought to re-establish its lost control". (G.R. Elton, *Reform and Reformation, 1509-1558* (Cambridge, Mass., 1977), p. 30.)

due to the collectors of the subsidy in London.[27] That of de' Bardi differs from all others by having in the margin a note of delivery to Hasylwood and payment received at the exchequer.

The other two absent from the chamber books were not of Hasylwood's concern and their fate is unknown. All of the "exchequer" obligations so far were contracted between 1508 and 1512-13; they involved the complete administration of written debts at the exchequer of receipt. Chamber influence or concern cannot be detected and if any of these written debts reached the chamber, Heron failed to record them.

These initial entries explain the need for the privy seal in 1513 ordering the delivery of obligations to the chamber. The exchequer of receipt had been collecting on the written debts and the money remained with the tellers, causing an administrative delay before money could actually be forwarded to the chamber. When the privy seal was issued, Hasylwood or clerks responsible to him began the present workbook in compliance with the royal command. But the first nineteen entries were a *fait accompli* as far as collection was concerned: they were old obligations stored at the exchequer. Heron undoubtedly received the money, but Hasylwood had long before collected on the debts. This made their duplication at the chamber redundant. Heron was only concerned with written obligations yet to be paid, and he now wanted all of those resting at the exchequer of receipt to be delivered to the chamber.

The last two obligations on folio 13 of Hasylwood's book were contracted in 1513 and appear in Heron's book under the heading "Obligations received of Sir John Cutte, knight, undertreasurer, of his remain of the proffers (28 March 1515)"—a belated response to the privy seal.[28] These two obligations common to both books were made by four men and totaled £1000. The first was due to William Tyler and Nicholas Waryng, collectors of the subsidies (tonnage and poundage) in London; the second to Sir William Compton, collector of the customs at the same port.[29] Both debts were annotated in Hasylwood's book as delivered to

---

[27] Both de' Bardi and Buttry were involved in numerous obligations for debt, to be paid in cash or set against the customs duties. Buttry was an attorney for the merchants and denizens of London (T.N.A.: P.R.O., E 404/86, 31 Jan. 1507). William Lytton was the son of Sir Robert, the former undertreasurer of the exchequer.

[28] Brit. Libr., Add. MS. 21481 fos. 336, 336v.

[29] Tyler and Waryng received their patents early in the reign (*L&P*, I.i. nos. 357(7), 94(73)). Tyler was also a groom of the chamber and probably delivered cash there. Compton is a more curious Tudor creation. G.R. Elton, using Brit. Libr., Cotton

him and exemplify the procedure of a teller receiving obligations and delivering them to the undertreasurer for conveyance to the chamber as per the privy seal warrant. Heron's entry in the chamber book was similar to that in the teller's book except that Tyler, Waryng and Compton were not listed as the payees of the debt. This should be expected since the exchequer remained the department of records for contracts of customs and subsidies; the treasurer of the chamber merely recorded the sums due for the scrutiny of the monarch, since Henry VIII began his reign signing the chamber books in the tradition of his father. When Heron wanted to collect on a debt, he had the original before him stating all the vital information.

Thirteen obligations listed on the first folio in the chamber book with Cutte's heading were entered in Hasylwood's account, four of which explain one way the chamber administrated written debts owed the crown after receiving them from the exchequer. From Hasylwood's book, it is known that these four debts, due by merchants, were payable to Compton, Tyler and Waryng (fos. 14v, 15). In Heron's book, the marginalia indicate

---

MS., Titus B.I fos. 188-90v, stated "it appears that Sir William Compton was responsible for privy-purse money and accounted for it" (*Tudor Revolution in Government* (Cambridge, 1953), p. 38). He quotes the document—a remembrance written under the aegis of Wolsey—concerning Compton's duties: for accounting "aswell all such somes of money as the said sir william Compton shall Receyve as also by the kynges commaundment ley oute and pay". The assumption is that Compton held no office in which royal treasure was administered (p. 38, n. 2). W.C. Richardson noted that from 1511 onwards, Heron regularly advanced money to Compton as the chief gentleman of the royal bedchamber for the king's use in denominations averaging £1000. (*Tudor Chamber Administration*, pp. 227-8.) Hasylwood's book clearly shows Compton as an important customer of London, in charge of receiving sums from 500 to 1000 marks (fos. 13v, 14v, 15, 16), although he probably did not collect them personally. He received his patent 6 June 1509, obtaining the same fees as William Grene, the customer mentioned above. He was appointed usher of the receipt, wages, necessaries, etc. for life with a fee of £26 13s 4d per annum. Compton owned or controlled ships and was given several grants, some by statute. (*L&P*, II.i. no. 2736 (p. 877), I.i. nos. 94(27), 1748; I.ii. nos. 1844, 3502; *Statutes of the Realm*, 3 Hen. VIII, c. 18; 14-15 Hen. VIII, c. 24; T.N.A.: P.R.O., E 163/10/3.) He was held accountable to both chamber and exchequer scrutiny. Indeed, near the end of Heron's account book, five obligations for 12 July 1517 were noted as received of "m[aster] Compton". (Brit. Libr., Add. MS. 21481 fo. 352.) Henry VIII signed this folio. No doubt Compton had great influence with the king, as when he was paid by a sheriff to secure a royal warrant for £70 as reward for the shrieval office (Brit. Libr., Stowe MS. 850 fo. 212v).

that the debts were vacated and rewritten on other folio pages in the same account book as the results of new negotiations.[30] Once the treasurer of the chamber held a record of debts, he was free to negotiate new obligations to facilitate payment to the chamber. He could summon the payees to inform them of new transactions or meet with the debtors and take new written instruments.

The second folio headed with Sir John Cutte's name in the chamber accounts as well contain debts recorded in Group A (fos. 16-18).[31] Although the payees are not recorded by Heron, Hasylwood's book contains the names of many people involved in processing debts: half were due to Tyler, Waryng and Compton; three to Thomas "Norfolk", Sir Thomas Lovell and Cutte;[32] one to the last three plus Sir Henry Marney, chancellor of the duchy of Lancaster; one to John Palmer, customer of Southampton. The two marked "paid" by Heron show that payment to the chamber was not long in coming by 16th century standards. The teller's book listed one debt as due 7 December 1516 (Heron marked it paid 24 July 1517); the other due by two installments in 1516 and 1517 (the total was paid 17 June 1516).

Hasylwood's book portrays a diverse group of collectors responsible for obtaining the king's money, not because they were part of a committee or agency but because of the trust the king had in them. This was personal finance directed by the chamber, and the notations in Hasylwood's book show exchequer responsibility for receiving written debts. That the workbook was called into existence illustrates the royal desire for a pervasive chamber system—a system nonetheless dependent on the established machinery of the exchequer and the personnel involved with taking obligations.

---

[30] The first two of these debts were renegotiated on what Heron denoted as "folio xvj" for a recognizance. The last two were vacated for "folio xxx" where they were combined in a large debt of £60,000 owed by many merchants (T.N.A.: P.R.O., Add. MS. 21481 fos. 304v, 349).

[31] T.N.A.: P.R.O., Add. MS. 21481 fo. 337.

[32] Sir Thomas Lovell was a major financial minister under Henry VII, treasurer of the household and chancellor of the exchequer. Thomas Howard, earl of Surrey, became duke of Norfolk by letters patent on 1 Feb. 1514 (*SR*, 5 Hen. VIII, c. 9; *L&P*, I.ii. no. 2684(1)). Because of either a delay in recording the debt or the anticipation of Surrey's laurels, the clerk recording obligations in Hasylwood's book listed him as *Norf* on 7 Dec. 1513 (fo. 18). Flodden Field was fought two months earlier.

Most of the remaining "working" obligations of Group A in Hasylwood's book have a similar fate of duplication in Heron's account. Several, however, show that the exchequer maintained control in collecting certain debts. One missing from the chamber book—a debt for £8 due by one Bassett—was annotated in the teller's book as paid to Hasylwood at the receipt and the obligation returned to Bassett and cancelled in the presence of the undertreasurer (fo. 14). William Ever(s) and a co-debtor contracted for two obligations of £50 each to Sir John Cutte, payable in two successive years (fo. 15v). The first was marked as being delivered to one William Selyok, an exchequer official, and the money obtained by Hasylwood for the king.[33] The second obligation to Ever had no notation and no mention of Hasylwood: hence, both remained at the exchequer without chamber duplication.[34]

Information from debts recorded in Group B of Hasylwood's book rounds out both the explication of the administrative process for obligations and the unsuccessful attempt at complete chamber fiscal control of them. None of these entries have the *liberat' hasylwod* notation which usually corresponds with entries kept in Heron's account. Many indicate debts for licences to trade, and after a few folios they are mainly due to Norfolk, Marney, Cutte and Lovell *ad usum regis*. One exception, a debt due by Sir Richard Cholmeley and William Bulstrode, collectors of the customs and subsidies in London, has a notation indicating money paid to the hands of Hasylwood and the date received—evidence of direct

---

[33] Ever was one of the controllers at Berwick. (*L&P*, II.i. no. 973.) William Selyok could not be located in *L&P*; he received debts due the Crown and was referred to as "of the exchequer" (Westminster Abbey Muniments, MSS. 16082-3).

[34] "Traditional" obligations such as for appearance before a court continued to be processed and collected at the exchequer. An obligation of £100 for Henry Myles and two mainpernors to guarantee his appearance before the court of exchequer was taken by Geoffrey (Blythe) bishop of Coventry and Lichfield, Charles Bothe, clerk, Sir William Uvedale, Sir Griffith Rice, Peter Newton and George Bromley. It was recorded in Hasylwood's book and remained on file at the exchequer (fo. 17v). Bothe (Booth), Uvedale and Bromley were granted letters of commission in Aug. 1509. These three plus Newton were on the council of the marches of Wales, which probably took this debt. All but Rice and Blythe were on a commission in Mar. 1510 to conclude recognizances, tallages and other dues. These commissions were continued in subsequent years with Blythe added in July 1512 and Rice in June 1513 (*L&P*, I. i. nos. 142, 1174, 414(48, 52), 1123(20), 1316(9); I.ii. no. 2055(42)).

payment to a teller of the exchequer on an obligation.[35] This debt was then itemized by nine separate obligations listed as delivered to Hasylwood by bill and by tallies of cash payment (fo. 25v). They were entered in a neat hand and refer to actual money received and not an assignment by tally. These debts and many subsequent ones were of normal exchequer business, without any apparent delivery of obligations to the chamber.

The entries in Hasylwood's book represent an established exchequer procedure with a new addition—a chamber structure concerned with recording debts and collecting money owed to the crown. The treasurer of the chamber strove to obtain all obligations involving payments of money to the king, and any relaxation of this commitment would allow the officials at the exchequer of receipt a return to their traditional course of receiving payments. This, in turn, would lead to the lethargic system of checks too slow for the close scrutiny of the first Tudor and the martial needs of the second.

Sir John Cutte was employed to tighten the gap between the two departments because of his trustworthiness and his office of undertreasurer of the exchequer. The tellers, who delivered money and obligations personally to the chamber, were aware of this push for chamber supervision yet did not always comply with the letter of the royal command. Indeed, the declaration of Hasylwood's charges cited above stated that only some £24,000 in written obligations were delivered to the chamber; yet Hasylwood's workbook records over £35,000 in obligations, implying that one-third of these written debts remained at the exchequer. Cutte sought to improve the situation by personally ordering the delivery of obligations to the chamber as attested by lists of these debts under his name in the chamber books. Hasylwood and his fellow tellers abided by the privy seal command of 1513, but as seen in his workbook, compliance was not forthcoming on a regular basis.

Henry VIII's reign thus commenced with the king's necessity to perpetuate his father's chamber system and standardize procedures for expedient financial administration in obtaining royal revenues. John

---

[35] Bulstrode, a gentleman-usher of the chamber under Henry VII, was paid £100 to convey ordinance with Queen Katharine northward against the Scots and was a frequent agent of the crown (T.N.A.: P.R.O., C 82/256, 31 Mar. 1504 (mistakenly filed under C 82/260, July); *L&P*, II.ii. p. 1462). Cholmeley, esquire and knight for the body, deputy lieutenant of the Tower, customer of London, surveyor and treasurer of Berwick, steward of the duchy of Cornwall, supervisor-general of the lordship of Richmond and target for a lampoon by Gilbert and Sullivan in their *Yeomen of the Guard* was a most loyal and versatile Tudor servant.

Hasylwood's book demonstrates this assertion in the form of debts contracted and recorded at the exchequer of receipt and delivered to the chamber for collection. It also reveals a reluctance on the part of the tellers in delivering all obligations, many of which were paid directly to the exchequer. Once Henry VIII—and his energetic treasurer of the chamber—determined to continue the fiscal policy of Henry VII, steps were taken to gather up the reins of debt-recording and debt-collecting. This was reflected in privy seal letters to the exchequer and statutes of the realm, elevating the chamber to its lofty status as financial overseer.

There can be little doubt that John Heron, and not simply his office, became the cornerstone of financial activities. He was a member of several committees in charge of taking, cancelling and transacting obligations and recognizances of the old and new reigns.[36] Such conciliar control over debt collection is visible in two obligations contracted by Thomas Empson, son of the ill-fated minister of Henry VII. Thomas and three sureties (one being his brother John), owed debts totalling 2000 marks, payable to Compton, Tyler and Waryng on 11 February 1513 as recorded in Hasylwood's book (fo. 13v); Thomas already owed 1000 marks to the king by a recognizance enrolled in the king's chancery a year earlier. In 1515, Thomas Empson appeared before Thomas Wolsey, archbishop of York, Richard Fox, bishop of Winchester and John Heron, royal commissioners settling with persons indebted to the king or to others for the king's use.[37]

The commissioners agreed to divide the total debt into an installment plan of 100 marks bi-annually until the 3000 marks were paid, all due to John Heron or his successor at the chamber. A further security of various manors and lands were required of Empson, and by 1530 he had paid 1100 marks; the remaining 1900 marks were to be paid by Richard Fermor in exchange for numerous properties of Empson. Here a private transaction entered the realm of public finance and the treasurer of the chamber was guaranteed payment.

Heron pursued the collection of debts vigorously: one merchant complained to Wolsey of being so hard-pressed by the treasurer of the chamber for the payment of £290 owed to the king that he feared leaving

---

[36] *L&P*, I.i. no. 1493; Richardson, *Tudor Chamber Administration*, p. 224; *L&P*, I.ii. no. 3226(8).
[37] Northamptonshire Record Office, Fermor-Heskith MSS., MTD/D/15/7. This indenture, dated 20 Aug. 1530, states the entire proceedings held before the commission on 10 June 1515, including all the debts owed by Empson.

his house, which as well was not a safe place to abide![38] This treasurer of
the chamber was the master of his king's house, and the trust given him by
the first two Tudors allowed a chamber system to flourish and function as
the national treasury. The exchequer remained an administrative
department for processing debts; the treasurer of the chamber tried to
secure these written obligations and drive them in, often with success but
seldom with great haste.

---

[38] *L&P*, III.i. no. 501; Richardson, *Tudor Chamber Administration*, p. 226. That
Heron was a central figure for debt collection can be seen in the introduction to
Edmund Dudley's notebook. After stating the date of inception for the book
involving obligations and money due the king. Dudley added "All the which
obligations and sums of money and every of them I the said Edmund have
delivered to our said sovereign lord and to John Heron to the use of his highness"
(Brit. Libr., Lansdowne MS. 127 fo.1).

CHAPTER TEN

"LIKE FATHER, LIKE SON"? EXPLORING THE ACTIONS OF HENRY VIII THROUGH THE LENS OF HENRY VII*

Introduction

For many years, when historians wrote about Henry VII and Henry VIII there seemed to be a pause from the death of the first Tudor king in 1509 until about 1513 or so when the second Tudor king went to war with France. In my graduate student days, I liked to call this hiatus of sorts "Waiting for Wolsey". It appeared that the anticipation of the arrival of Thomas Wolsey as the first influential minister of Henry VIII overshadowed what was occurring in the new reign during these first years. Fortunately, this gap began to fill up over time.

Wolsey notwithstanding, at the start of his monarchy the teenage Henry VIII may have had thoughts in his head not only about reviving the quest for conquering France from the days of Henry V, but also succeeding where his father failed in the attempt. It is debatable whether Henry VII was serious about his short-lived invasion of France in 1492, which ended with him being "pensioned" off by the French king to go home. Charles VIII also promised Henry that he would not support any pretenders to the English throne while trying not to appear giving up too much to the king of England. In fact, the pension was a resumption of the one given to Henry VII's father-in-law, Edward IV, to call off an earlier invasion of France.

For me, this segued into a larger discussion about father and son and how much the former influenced the latter in ruling England. Pop psychology has been a favorite if at times facetious exercise when talking

* A shorter version of this paper was presented at *The Southern Conference on British Studies*, 1-2 Nov. 2013, St. Louis, Missouri.

about Henry VIII. It ranged from his bevy of wives and a superego emerging in wars with France, to vengeful executions and playing ministers and supporters against each other on royal whim if not pathology.

It was while reading about Henry VIII's building and renovation of manors and castles that I came across the Whitehall Mural. As might be expected, much discourse about the mural had centered on Henry VIII's overpowering image in this Holbein work that adorned the king's privy chamber at Whitehall Palace until it burned down in 1698. It was the portrayal of a king that relegates the other three figures in it—his third wife, father and mother—almost to the shadows.

Today we speak of leaders and politicians striving to project positive, strong images through various media to gain support and hold onto their power bases. Henry's mural, which gazed at the domestic and foreign visitor to the king's inner sanctum, clearly meant to send a message of power and authority. From his stance and facial expression to the sheer disproportionate size of his frame, the king let it be known he was a force to be reckoned with and a literally larger-than-life symbol of might and strength.

When discussing the mural, the inscription on it has generally taken a minor role. It is usually seen as complementing Henry VIII's image by speaking of his accomplishments and greatness as king. What struck me in reading it was the fact that the inscription obviously was put in the mural with the approval of Henry, who perhaps had a hand in writing it. This meant that the king was broadcasting his feelings and beliefs about himself first-hand: it was not a message from a chronicle or a supporter doing an editorial or "fluff piece" on Henry VIII. It therefore opened a window into his view of himself as king. Furthermore, one theme that ran through the inscription was his place in history versus his father and founder of his dynasty, Henry VII.

While Freud might have had a field day with this confessional, my thoughts about it moved towards certain actions by Henry VII and how they may have influenced his son to the point where the inscription, in Henry VIII's mind, was necessary. It seemed to me that Henry VIII not only put his father in the mural to show continuity in the Tudor dynasty, but also to take the opportunity to compete with him. This he did both visually and through his own "voice" in the inscription.

In writing the paper for the 2013 conference, I kept in mind that my audience was a diverse group of historians in various fields of study. I therefore decided to forgo a historiographical survey of state development through these two reigns or ongoing scholarship about how different or alike father and son were as rulers—there is a body of work in both areas. Instead, I wanted to concentrate on father and son, and how Henry VIII viewed himself in light of the significant accomplishments of Henry VII.

To me the inscription is a narcissistic self-portrait rife with great insecurity, self-aggrandizement and taking more credit than was deserved—attributes of often accidental leaders found before and after his time. We can speculate and guess and psychoanalyze from afar. Regardless, the Whitehall Mural provides a moment that offers Henry VIII's beliefs about his kingship, his place in history and his obsessive concern with measuring up to, if not surpassing, his father Henry VII. Historians will continue to pass judgment on that count. We already know how Henry VIII weighed in on the subject, both visually and in his own thoughts.

On 12 October 1537, Jane Seymour, the wife and queen of Henry VIII of England, gave birth to a child who would become the king's only legitimate, surviving son and heir—an event that was three wives and nearly three decades in the making. To celebrate what was perhaps his greatest achievement in keeping his Tudor dynasty viable, Henry commissioned the German court painter, Hans Holbein the Younger, to create a colossal mural in Whitehall Palace of himself and his wife, with the founders of his dynasty placed in the background: his parents, Henry VII and Elizabeth of York. When Holbein completed the mural, Jane may or may not have been alive to see the final creation. The palace burned down in 1698 but there survives a poorly-executed Dutch copy of the mural commissioned by Charles II in 1667 as well as part of the original cartoon Holbein used to stencil the images to the wall.

Of the four figures, Henry VIII alone stared at the onlooker. He was portrayed in a menacing stance with impossibly broad shoulders. In his left hand he held an entwined rope attached to a dagger, and he completely overshadowed his father. The mural adorned the king's privy chamber in the palace where the great, the mighty and the influential from at home and abroad would see it prior to entering the presence chamber of the monarch. As has often been noted by modern historians, although perhaps with more amplification than accuracy, Henry's portrait left a late-sixteenth century spectator of the enormous portrait of the king feeling "abashed and annihilated".[1]

While it might seem an appropriate if ostentatious means of commemorating this auspicious birth and the promising continuation of Henry's line that was so long in coming, there was something much more compulsive, perhaps even pathetic taking place. Henry VIII, for his mental well-being and for the benefit of Europe's princes, emperor, pope and his own English nobility, needed to prove a point, one that has plagued the sons of leaders and successful men for millennia: "I am far greater and better and more worthy than my father." Henry would attempt to fulfill this purpose both visually and in the written word in Holbein's mural. He knew that to back up any claims of primacy over his father he would need to render declarations from actual deeds if he hoped to be taken by his princely peers and rivals as a king surpassing the accomplishments of his dynasty's founder. This he did in a lengthy inscription next to his portrait, proclaiming his superiority over the first Tudor king.

---

[1] Roy Strong, *Holbein and Henry VIII* (London, 1967), p. 39.

It is therefore both significant and telling to discuss and assess several of Henry VIII's actions as king to explore whether the second Tudor did in fact measure up to the first one according to his own words, and if there truly were marked differences in how he ruled England from his father, which has often been averred by historians.[2] Indeed, it will be argued that Henry VII and his achievements, beliefs and behavior had an enormous impact on Henry VIII. It affected how he acted and reacted as king of England to the point where rather than becoming his own man he often tried to emulate his father, with mixed results. In this context, the mural will be discussed in terms of its purpose and how the "message" of its inscription possibly had a deeper meaning—one that was clearly understood by an onlooker but was perhaps misinterpreted over time.

Finance and Administration

It has been regularly repeated that Henry VIII reversed much of the financial and administrative pursuits of Henry VII, which had appeared capricious and arbitrary to both contemporaries and later commentators.[3] These included his father's various committees or courts overseen by councilors charged with administering debts owed the crown and the king's prerogative rights. Such rights included the remunerative advantages gained from the control of wardships, marriages and entry into lands held by the crown *in chief*. The king's chamber had also become the repository for much of the royal treasure, bypassing many of the traditional auditing and collection procedures practiced by the antiquated exchequer.

That Henry VII was successful in scrutinizing and improving the various functions of government reflected a pragmatic approach to achieving solvency and stability, in large part from his reliance on competent, learned men and financial experts. Most of these officials had worked for his mother, step-father or their servants or officers before the first Tudor became king of England after he defeated and killed Richard III at Bosworth Field on 22 August 1485.

---

[2] For example, Lucy Wooding, *Henry VIII* (London, 2009), p. 17. Numerous contrasts have been posited since Stanley Bindoff's important overview of the Tudors. (S.T. Bindoff, *Tudor England*, The Pelican History of England, Vol. 1 (London, 1950), pp. 66-7.

[3] E.g., David Starkey, *Henry VIII, Man and Monarch*, 500th Anniversary Exhibition, British Library, with various authors, Intro. by D. Starkey (British Library, 2009), p. 15.

Henry VIII, however, did not part from these approaches but in fact enhanced them and built upon them.[4] Nor did he simply abandon the men who helped administer them.[5] When Henry VII died on 21 April 1509, he left a seventeen-year-old son as the heir to his throne. The young king did the prudent thing by keeping on most of his father's councilors. The exceptions were Richard Empson and Edmund Dudley, two of the most visible ministers who had conducted their king's unpopular financial policies with impunity in the last decade of the reign, although other councilors were as deeply involved and remained in office.[6] These two men were arrested soon after the king's death and sent to the Tower of London.

Henry VIII was well-aware of the popular discontent sowed by their actions, which had included putting people in financial obligations, or bonds, for their good behavior, keeping the peace or paying alleged debts to the crown that were sometimes entered into or collected upon without just cause. It was why his first action as king—issuing a traditional general pardon to gain popular favor—included an apparent cancellation of most of these bonds and the promise of rounding up the henchmen who prosecuted them. It led one historian to review the summaries of the disposition of these bonds for the first few years of the new reign in the printed *Letters and Papers* of Henry VIII. He concluded, with general acceptance by others studying the period, that a large number of them were indeed canceled without payment ever being made.[7] Henry VIII was therefore starting off on the right foot and in a different direction from his father.

---

[4] Henry VIII's first Great Seal was the same as that of his father, created in 1485, with the addition of a lion and a fleur-de-lis in the field. (Pamela Tudor-Craig, "Iconography of the painting," in *King Arthur's Round Table, an archaeological investigation*, Martin Biddle *et al* (Boydell Press, 2000), pp. 285-334 at p. 304; Brit. Libr., Seal XXXVI.7.

[5] Mark R. Horowitz, "Policy and prosecution in the reign of Henry VII," *Hist. Research*, Vol. LXXXII, no. 217 (Aug. 2009), pp. 412-58. [Chapter Three]

[6] Horowitz, "Policy and prosecution"; Sean Cunningham, "Loyalty and the usurper: Recognizances, the council and allegiance under Henry VII," *Hist. Research*, Vol. LXXXII, no. 217, pp. 459-81.

[7] J.R. Lander, "Bonds, coercion and fear: Henry VII and the peerage," in *Florilegium Historiale*, essays presented to Wallace K. Ferguson, ed. J.G. Rowe and W.H. Stockdale (Toronto, 1971), pp. 328-67; Wooding, *Henry VIII*, p. 17.

Or was he? The general pardon exempted "debts and accounts", which could be taken as any bond the government decided to prosecute.[8] Furthermore, when the actual original warrants for those canceled bonds are read, rather than just their printed summaries, it becomes clear that far from reversing his father's financial policy he continued it, and with many of the same councilors who pursued them in the previous reign. Missing from the printed summaries were two words after the word "canceled", namely "upon payment".

Henry VIII recognized rather quickly the large income these bonds generated since he found his treasury overflowing with cash thanks to his father's efforts.[9] For the next twenty years and more he was to continue collecting upon or refinancing old bonds from his father's reign while recording new ones. Even Thomas Cromwell, the architect of the Henrician Reformation and better efficiency in government, was involved in their collection.[10] It would be the son who would squander his father's fortune in futile wars and lavish building projects—he had fifty-five palaces renovated or built during his reign. If he was greater than his father in the area of finance, it was through his prodigious spending and his nearly bankrupting of the government.

The new king also kept many of his father's administrative practices intact. The chamber remained the core repository of the king's revenue and gained statutory footing despite attempts by the exchequer to resume its traditional role. John Heron, Henry VII's treasurer of the chamber and general receiver of bonds and cash, remained in his office.[11] Henry also began his reign emulating his father's proclivity of signing pages in his account books—an exercise he eventually abandoned in favor of a dry stamp. In 1518, Henry established the privy chamber to handle his personal needs, appointing new officers who had his ear directly, such as the master of the stool—a position nonetheless originally created by his

---

[8] Corporation of London Records Office, Journals of the Common Council 11 (1506-18), fos. 69ff; Mark R. Horowitz, "'Agree with the king', Henry VII, Edmund Dudley and the strange case of Thomas Sunnyff," *Hist. Research*, Vol. LXIX, no. 205 (Aug. 2006), pp. 325-66, at p. 356.
[9] Mark R. Horowitz, "Henry Tudor's Treasure," *Hist. Research*, Vol. LXXXII, no. 217, pp. 560-79.
[10] Brit. Libr., Cotton MS., Titus B.I fos. 157v, 427, 436.
[11] Mark R. Horowitz, "An Early-Tudor Teller's Book," *Eng. Hist. Rev.*, Vol. LXXXXVI, no. 378 (Jan. 1981), pp. 103-116. [Chapter Nine]

father.[12] This is thought to have politicized the chamber although Henry VII as well ruled through a small group of officers who had access to the chamber.

The "council learned in the law" headed up by Empson, which was more probably a group of "learned counsel" prosecuting bonds and the kings prerogative rights rather than an actual council, did not disappear as is often stated.[13] Cromwell's papers note that a "council learned" was alive and well decades after Empson and Dudley were executed in 1510—most likely in the form of councilors pursuing similar activities but with less graft and corruption.[14] Both Henry VIII and Cromwell built upon the old king's willingness to invent as situations dictated, such as creating the court of augmentations to handle the revenues generated from the dissolution of the monasteries. But they also borrowed. The court of wards and liveries folded in the responsibilities of Sir John Hussey under Henry VII; the court of general surveyors had its origins in the auditing responsibilities of Reynold Bray and Robert Southwell in the old reign.

Advisers to the king

Where there was a shift in relationships between king and close advisers, it was more from circumstance than choice although the results went full circle. Henry VII became king at age twenty-eight in 1485. Although his father, Edmund Tudor, died before he was born, he was nonetheless surrounded by relatives and close family ties to guide him as a new monarch with no governing experience. These included his mother, Margaret Beaufort, the countess of Richmond and Derby; his uncle Jasper Tudor; his step-father and step-uncle Thomas Lord Stanley and Sir William Stanley respectively who helped him win the crown at Bosworth Field; and his uncle John Viscount Welles. His mother's chaplain, Bishop

---

[12] Michael A.R. Graves, *Henry VIII, A Study in Kingship* (London, 2003), pp. 54-5; David Loades, *Henry VIII, Court, church and conflict* (National Archives, 2007), p. 36; Eric Ives, "Henry VIII: The Political Perspective," in *The reign of Henry VIII. Politics, policy and piety*, ed. Diarmaid MacCulloch (London, 1995), pp. 16ff.

[13] For example, R. Somerville, "Henry VII's 'Council learned in the law,'" *Eng. Hist. Rev.*, Vol. LIV (1939), pp. 427-42.

[14] Horowitz, "Policy and Prosecution," p. 452; M. Condon, "From caitiff and villain to *pater patriae*: Reynold Bray and the profits of office," in M.A. Hicks, ed., *Profit, Piety and the Professions in Later Medieval England* (Gloucester, 1990), pp. 137-68.

Richard Fox, became Lord Privy Seal and a key adviser to the king. Fox was followed by Margaret's former chief financial adviser, Reynold Bray, who became Henry's chancellor of the duchy of Lancaster, treasurer of the exchequer and important minister and confidant.[15] The first Tudor thus had family members and familial friends and officers who had either lived with him in exile or supported him at Bosworth Field, or were known to him through his mother.

When Henry VIII became king in 1509 he was a decade younger than when his father seized the throne. He had his two sisters—one living in Scotland married to James IV—and only one other living relative: his aged grandmother, Margaret Beaufort, who continued to keep a watchful eye on her grandson, and not passively. She was known to sign documents "Margaret R", no doubt raising eyebrows as to whether the R referred to the countess of Richmond, or Regina.[16] Yet two months into the new reign the countess died, leaving Henry on his own and without a father figure or older family member for support. Nor did he ever get over the premature death of his mother when he was eleven: several years after her passing he wrote that "news of the death of my dearest mother" was "hateful intelligence."[17]

It was therefore hardly unexpected that he would seek such parental proxies, beginning with his father's royal chaplain, Thomas Wolsey. This would begin a thirty-year succession of individuals charged with carrying out the king's whims and commands, all at their peril as it turned out: Wolsey, Thomas More and Thomas Cromwell. Although Henry viewed Wolsey as a father figure and More perhaps as a big brother, neither could deliver what the king required: a papal marriage annulment from

---

[15] Horowitz, "Policy and Prosecution," pp. 423ff; John Guy, *Tudor England* (Oxford, 1988), pp. 53-6.
[16] Michael K. Jones and Malcolm G. Underwood, *The King's Mother: Lady Margaret Beaufort, Countess of Richmond and Derby* (Cambridge, 1993), p. 292.
[17] D.R. Starkey, *Henry, Virtuous Prince* (London, 2008), pp. 169-7; Julia Fox, *Sister Queens, Katherine of Aragon and Juana, Queen of Castile* (London, 2011), p. 44. John de Vere, 13th earl of Oxford, was Henry VII's lifelong supporter whom the king referred to as my "most dear cousin". (*Materials for a history of the reign of Henry VII*, ed. William Campbell, Vol. 1 (Cambridge, 1873, 2012 ed), p. 412 grant from Henry VII to the earl, 9 April 1486.) He fled captivity by the Yorkists to join Henry in exile, led the vanguard at Bosworth Field and fought at the battle of Stoke—loyalty that brought him fortune, a seat on the privy council, a premier knighthood (Knight of the Garter) and the Lord Great Chamberlainship. He outlived the first Tudor king and would have been a natural mentor for Henry VIII. But at the start of the new reign in 1509 the earl was well over 66. He died in 1513.

Katherine of Aragon. It led to the destruction of both and the rise of Cromwell as a facilitator, not a family figure. Cromwell, like More, was a lawyer who used the law—and customs and precedents to justify laws—to bring about Henry's Reformation and annulment much as Henry's father relied on lawyers to manage and prosecute the laws of the land in the same manner. After Cromwell's fall, Henry resorted to the same conciliar administration in his last physically-debilitating years as his father did during his own physical decline.

It is important to note that Henry VIII was aware that his father had surrounded himself with lawyers or learned men well-seasoned in the common law and statutory law: four of the king's close confidants were speakers in the seven parliaments held during his father's reign. He could witness first-hand how Henry VII expanded and enforced the law, and that for the most part it was accepted by a people tired of uncertainty, corruption and lawlessness after the throes of civil discord and intermittent warfare during the Wars of the Roses.

It is therefore no great revelation that by 1529, the thirty-eight-year-old Henry VIII went from relying on a paternalistic churchman (Wolsey), who failed to resolve his Great Matter by obtaining an annulment through Roman church law and process, to English lawyers (More and Cromwell). It was Cromwell who assisted Henry in making the various legal and historical arguments in the 1530s about royal supremacy over the church and the king's right to run his own country unimpeded by foreign influence.

Sovereignty and war

Not surprising, the notion of an independent sovereign nation, summarized in Cromwell's preamble to the Act of Appeals that "this realm of England is an empire", was influenced by the first Tudor and thereafter reinforced by Henry VIII.[18] In 1489, Henry VII commissioned a new gold coin with the telling name the *sovereign*, England's first one pound currency. It portrayed the king sitting on a throne wearing an Imperial closed crown.[19] As the masterful progenitor of Tudor propaganda, Henry

---

[18] 24 Hen. 8, c. 12 (1533).
[19] <http://www.royalmint.com/discover/sovereigns/history-of-the-goldsovereign> [accessed 26 Oct. 2013]; D'Arcy Jonathan Dacre Boulton, "Henry VII and Henry VIII," in *Princes and Princely Culture: 1450-1650*, 2, eds. M. Gosman, A. MacDonald and A. Vinderjagt (London, 2005), p. 157.

VII was disseminating a very clear message to his subjects and Continental observers: he was not simply a king, but an emperor.

This emphasis on might, power and prestige through images and words was not lost to Henry VIII; it was expanded throughout his reign. He kept his father's image on the coin for sixteen years, later replacing it with his own.[20] Cromwell was not so much innovating a concept of empire as continuing a perception promoted by Henry VII and accepted by his son.

When it came to war, it has often been thought that Henry VIII was merely participating in the sport of kings pursued by his rivals in France, Spain and the Holy Roman Empire while abandoning his father's cautious stance on costly military incursions. However, it perhaps had more to do with the realization that he was the son of an English warrior king who won the crown on the battlefield. Two years after Bosworth Field, Henry VII led armies on English soil to defend it. He would also muster the largest military force in English history up to that time and cross the Channel in October 1492 to invade France.[21] He besieged Boulogne, taking the lower town, and forced Charles VIII of France to sign the Treaty of Etaples. This treaty extracted a promise from Charles not to support a pretender to Henry's throne; pay for the cost of the invasion; and renew a lapsed annuity since the days of Edward IV, Henry's father-in-law.[22] Undisputed was the first Tudor's active, personal involvement in war and battle, and no one at home or abroad could doubt his bravery or his commitment to defending his realm and his honor.

Henry VIII became the heir to the throne in 1502 at age eleven after the death of his older brother, Arthur. His life for the next seven years would be far removed from any battlefield. This sudden and unexpected shift from his role as second son was compounded by his mother's death less than a year later. Where Arthur had his own household and lived at Ludlow near the Welsh border, the concerned father of his only surviving male heir kept young Henry under the royal wing. He was schooled with a

---

[20] Christopher Lloyd and Simon Turley, *Henry VIII, Images of a Tudor king* (London, 1990), pp. 32-3.

[21] John M. Currin, "To Traffic in War'? Henry VII and the French Campaign of 1492," in *The English Experience in France, c. 1450-1558. War, Diplomacy and Cultural Exchange*, ed. David Grummitt (London, 2002), pp. 106-31; "To Play at Peace: Henry VII, War against France, and the Chieregato-Flores Mediation of 1490," *Albion*, 31, No. 2 (Summer 1999), pp. 207-37.

[22] David Potter, "Foreign policy," in MacCulloch, *Henry VIII*, pp. 125-6; Colin Pendrill, *The Wars of the Roses and Henry VII: England 1459-c.1513* (London, 2004), pp. 169-70.

sister and raised by his pious and tenacious grandmother, Margaret Beaufort—hardly an environment for royal manly development.[23] He was not allowed to partake in tournaments and despite careful practice sessions in weaponry he would be crowned the first king of England in fifty years never to have fought in a battle.[24]

This was a perceived shortcoming for a Renaissance prince, along with his youth, no queen or heir, and a father known for his military successes. It pushed Henry VIII into a belligerent stance as soon as he became king. Four days after his father's death, the Venetian ambassador reported that Henry was the great enemy of the French, which may have come as a surprise to many, including the French. The next day, the ambassador wrote that immediately after Henry's coronation the king swore to make war on the king of France.[25] His father would not be buried for another two weeks nor would his betrothal treaty to Katherine of Aragon be confirmed until May. This was a monarch on a mission.[26]

Henry VIII anachronistically portrayed himself as the hero of the Hundred Years War, Henry V, and the one English king who could reconquer France by creating his own Agincourt victory. He commissioned a book on Henry V and made it known from the onset of his reign that war was to be his preoccupation. After becoming king and planning what would be the first of three invasions of France during his lifetime, Henry had much to prove to the Continental princes, his own citizens and especially himself. Honor was the elusive grail sought by contemporary rulers, and for Henry it could be found in battle, where his father had won and kept his throne.

Largely by squandering Henry VII's treasure, the twenty-two-year-old monarch invaded France in 1513 with an army three times the size of his father's. He left Katherine of Aragon, his wife six years his senior, as regent of the realm. Henry had earlier joined a newly-constituted Holy League with the Pope, Spain, the Emperor Maximilian and England to

---

[23] Starkey, *Henry VIII, Man and Monarch*, p. 13.

[24] Technically, the exception would be the twelve-year-old uncrowned king, Edward V, who ruled for two months in 1483 before disappearing in the Tower with his younger brother while their uncle, Richard III, claimed the throne.

[25] *L&P*, I.i. no. 5 <www.british-history.ac.uk/report.aspx?compid=102615> [accessed 26 Oct. 2013]

[26] Graves, *Henry VIII*, p. 10. Henry VII was buried on 10 May 1509. (Brit. Libr., Harleian MS. 3504 fo. 264v.)

depose Louis XII of France—a League his father finessed so well twenty years earlier.[27]

On 30 June, Henry VIII landed in Calais and arrayed himself in armor. The next month the main force set out for Thérouanne and Henry galloped around the camp encouraging his men just as one of his role models, Henry V, had done a century earlier. Then on 16 August, a small French cavalry force accidentally ran into the main English army. They fled the scene with the English and allied Burgundian cavalry in hot pursuit. There was no fighting, just a lot of galloping to the east of Thérouanne. Most of the French escaped except for a few prisoners that included a duke, a marquis, and the vice-admiral of France.[28] Henry immediately declared a victory and had paintings and engravings made of the "battle". History has referred to it as the Battle of the Spurs, since the fleeing French utilized their spurs as their battle strategy.[29] The English king's capture of Thérouanne was short-lived as the emperor asked for it back.

While Henry regaled in his victory, despite his absence from the rout, his wife Katherine had her own challenge back in England. She was not merely a regent in name. The chamber accounts show that she signed a warrant to Sir John Cutte, the under-treasurer of the exchequer, informing him that he was now working directly for her and the council, and she gave him £100 to make the point stick.[30] Since an English king going abroad always presented an opportunity for the Scots to invade, that is exactly what happened despite the fact that their king, James IV, was married to Henry VIII's sister, Margaret.

Katherine helped muster the troops, which were put under the command of the aging earl of Surrey: he was over seventy years old. She rode north in full armor and fully pregnant, rallying the soldiers. On 9 September the English forces met James IV and his army at Flodden Field, where 10,000 Scots were slain along with their king. Surrey and his troops captured twelve earls, two abbots, two bishops and the archbishop of St. Andrews. In jubilation, Katherine wrote to her husband in France informing him of the great victory against the Scots and perhaps rubbing it

---

[27] John Currin, "Henry VII, France and the Holy League of Venice: the diplomacy of balance," *Hist. Research*, Vol. LXXXII, no. 217, pp. 526-46.

[28] J.J. Scarisbrick, *Henry VIII* (California, 1968), 35.

[29] Wooding, *Henry VIII*, 72-3.

[30] Brit. Libr., Add. MS. 21481 fo. 132v (1 Aug. 1513). An example of her authority over the exchequer is found in T.N.A.: P.R.O., E 404/87, 4 Feb., n.y., a disbursement order to Cutte sealed with her signet at Richmond Palace and signed "Katherina the queene".

in when speaking of "the great Victory that our Lord hath sent your subjects in your absence."

She also sent him the bloody coat worn by James IV "for your banners".[31] If Henry had not lingered in France during the autumn, he might have brought his troops to Scotland and conquered it. It would not be the first time Henry VIII may have felt emasculated by one of his wives. Indeed, the treason charges of adultery against Anne Boleyn and Catherine Howard (numbers two and five), and the fervent, often vocal religious opinions of Catherine Parr (number six) left the explosive king of England less than amused.

Henry launched two more invasions of France during his reign, the last yielding him Boulogne, which his father had captured but wisely relinquished in exchange for a large pension. The son, however, did not want to let go and it all but bankrupted the government to keep it provisioned; it was returned to France after his death. Although failing at war throughout his reign, Henry VIII never stop trying to prove his manhood in the martial arts, especially since such prowess was suppressed in his youth.

To show onlookers that he was the essence of a warrior king, he held tournaments as his father and grandfather, Edward IV, had done but in greater number. This did not always work out well. In March 1524, Henry's close friend and brother-in-law, Charles Brandon, duke of Suffolk, nearly killed him in a joust. Twelve years later, at the age of forty-four, Henry was unseated by an opponent, crashed to the ground in full armor under a horse, and remained unconscious for two hours.[32] As he well knew, none of that ever happened to his father.

The church

Henry VIII knew his father had a complicated relationship with the church. As usurper to the throne, Henry VII sought papal approval for his legitimacy—he had already won God's consent on the battlefield. He also supported the pope in his decrees and actions as long as they did not

---

[31] Letter from Katherine of Aragon to her husband, King Henry VIII (16 Sept. 1513), <http://englishhistory.net/tudor/letter-katharine-aragon-husband-king-henry-viii-16-september-1513> [accessed 26 Oct. 2013] For a summary of Flodden Field that includes issues related to Katherine's role, see <http://www.distant-clansman.com/queen-catherine-middle-ages-warrior-myth> [accessed 26 Oct. 2013]

[32] Graves, *Henry VIII*, p. 62.

require direct military involvement or inhibit his basic control of the church in England. He thus followed in the footsteps of previous English kings, making—and selling—church appointments; forbidding transfer of cases to Rome if they impinged on secular jurisdiction; and restricting benefit of clergy and sanctuary to bring most clerical criminals to justice under English common law, avoiding canon law courts.

Henry VII allowed his ministers, and his mother, to dissolve decaying monasteries, replacing them with more worldly edifices, such as Corpus Christi College, Oxford. He was undoubtedly aware of the historic unmasking of the Donation of Constantine as a forgery in1440, dispelling any notion of a pope's supremacy over an emperor, or any prince.[33] Indeed, the king fostered the new Renaissance learning that often conflicted with or satirized church practices and doctrine—as a student of history who impressed Erasmus, the first Tudor would know of the previous clashes of English kings and popes, most often to the advantage of England and its monarch.[34]

He might even have turned a blind eye to matters involving church desecration. When the earl of Kildare—accused of burning down the church at Cashel in Ireland—replied that he would not have done so except he thought the archbishop was inside, he received both approval from Henry VII and the governance of the island.[35] Yet he remained faithful to church dogma and purchased dispensations for the marital needs of his family and thousands of masses for his soul when on his deathbed.

No doubt young Henry VIII adhered to many of his father's religious beliefs and ecclesiastical practices, perhaps with his own personal trepidations about the church since, as a second son of the king, he might have had an expectation of taking the cloth, perhaps as the archbishop of Canterbury.[36] In 1512, Henry VIII's parliament abolished benefit of clergy

---

[33] Wooding, *Henry VIII*, 12.

[34] For a good summary of the tumultuous events of the 12th century between England and the church, see John Guy, *Thomas Becket, Warrior, Priest, Rebel, Victim: A 900-year-old story retold* (New York, 2012).

[35] A version of the story is related by Sir Richard Cox, *Hibernia anglicana, or, the history of Ireland...* (1689).

[36] This possibility was first mentioned by Lord Edward Herbert of Cherbury, *The Life and Raigne of King Henry the Eighth* (1672), p. 2, and widely accepted, for example Scarisbrick, *Henry VIII*, p. 4; Alison Weir, *Henry VIII, the king and his court* (London, 2001), p. 5; Loades, *Henry VIII*, p. 202. Cherbury seems to be the only source for this specific suggestion some 180 years after Henry VIII's birth, although he may have been using documents since lost.

for those in minor orders, defying the church as his father had done.[37] The
Richard Hunne case involving the jurisdiction of ecclesiastical courts in
potentially secular affairs saw Henry against church involvement.[38] He
allowed Wolsey to dissolve monasteries as in the previous reign,
furthering precedents that led to the massive monastic dissolution in
England beginning in 1536 under Cromwell.

Henry VIII may have been personally religious, but the outer trappings
of zeal were of greater importance than his actual support of papal
jurisdiction. His treatise defending the sacraments against Martin Luther in
1521 earned him the title Defender of the Faith from the pope. But the
obvious impetus to compose the piece in the first place, with the help of
Thomas More, was his competition with Charles V, who owned the papal
title the "Most Catholic King of Spain", and with Francis I, known as the
"Most Christian King of France".[39]

Nonetheless, he held fast to certain Catholic doctrine, including
intercessory prayer. That involved helping those deceased souls who were
directly responsible for his crown to a speedy departure from purgatory,
especially his father. On 4 July 1512, he confirmed a grant by letters
patent for a parcel of land on the manor of Savoy in London to all his
father's executors to found a perpetual hospital with five chaplains. These
men were charged with praying for Henry VIII, his wife and the souls of
his father, mother, and the intended heir to the throne, his late brother
Prince Arthur. It was to be called the hospital of Henry VII of Savoy.[40]
Clearly, the father was always on the mind of the son.

All those wives

It would be remiss not to address a topic that has fascinated historians
and the general public for centuries: Henry VIII and all those wives. From
movies showing the lusty king tossing a chewed chicken leg over his
shoulder, to portrayals of his roving eye and need for bedroom conquests
in fiction and non-fiction alike, Henry was even mocked in his own time
by Continental observers who marveled at his various marital machinations.

---

[37] Loades, *Henry VIII*, p. 33.
[38] For a summary of the case and particulars against Richard Hunne, see
<https://sites.google.com/site/richardhunneandthereformation> [accessed 26 Oct.
2013]
[39] Loades, H*enry VIII*, pp. 205-6.
[40] *L&P*, I.i. no. 1316 [11] <http://www.british-history.ac.uk/letters-papers-
hen8/vol1/pp592-609#highlight-first> [accessed 26 Oct. 2013]

But a different image emerges when placed in the context of his life as the second son of an English monarch who had anemic claims to the throne, and then as an unexpected heir watching his widowed father's frantic behavior to secure the throne and then the dynasty. It is one of a frightened, sometimes helpless ruler in fear of becoming the last Tudor king for lack of a legitimate male heir.

Henry VIII saw first-hand the dual catastrophes for a king failing to secure a spare male heir or a wife to conceive one. On 2 April 1502, only months after his marriage to Katherine of Aragon, the fifteen-year-old Prince Arthur died, perhaps from the sweating sickness or tuberculosis.[41] Henry VII had little time to grieve or protect his remaining son and heir, whom he quickly created duke of Cornwall. Some ten months later, his wife Elizabeth of York died on 11 February 1503 while giving birth to a short-lived daughter—the queen's eighth child of which four died young and now only three remained, with young Henry the sole male.

The first reaction has been previously discussed: Henry VII sought to protect his only male offspring by keeping him close. It was recently suggested that this smothering was done because Henry saw his son as a threat and a rising star compared to "the elder and rather drab figure of Henry VII."[42] This is probably unlikely. Besides the implausibility of worrying about a publicly-hidden eleven-year-old prince's popularity, the deaths of his eldest son and wife made the future Henry VIII a priceless dynastic commodity given the fickleness of fate when it came to royalty and their success at producing adult males.

It is hardly coincidental that the over-protectiveness of the remaining male heir to the throne would be mirrored by none other than Henry VIII himself after the birth of his own son, Edward. For while some historians have suggested that Henry's cloistering of Edward was done to avoid the growth of factions at court, it was most likely for the same reason his father had protected him: a precaution to keep the sole male heir from harm while the king began seeking a new fertile queen and another son.[43] In fact, that is what his father did after the death of Elizabeth of York, combing the Continent for a new bride. It is not difficult to see why the son behaved the same way as his father in similar circumstances.

---

[41] Scarisbrick, *Henry VIII*, p. 4; Starkey, *Henry VIII, Man and Monarch*, p. 14.

[42] Loades, *Henry VII*, p. 18.

[43] Charles Beem, "Preparing for Josiah: Henry VIII and the minority of Edward VI," presented by Charles Beem at the annual meeting of the NACBS, Nov. 2006, in Boston, MA.; Chris Skidmore, *Edward VI: The lost king of England*, (London, 2009), pp. 22-9.

Henry VII invested his surviving son as prince of Wales and earl of Chester one week after Elizabeth's death and immediately began seeking a queen to bear a son should young Henry go the way of his older brother.[44] Time was of the essence. The old king was indeed old before his time in 1503 at age forty-six, having fought off illnesses for several years and weary of internal plots by pretenders to his throne and the ever-present potential hostilities from abroad and from the north. He first considered marrying the wife of his dead son, Katherine of Aragon.[45] Strange and grotesque as it may sound, it would have solved several problems at once: keeping her dowry, retaining an alliance with Spain and, hopefully, bearing a second male child.

This idea was soon dropped and in 1504 Henry VII began to pursue the Dowager Queen Joanna of Naples. He asked to see a portrait of her along with explicit information about her height, the shape of her face, her breasts and other attributes.[46] But delays pushed him to begin negotiations with the daughter of Emperor Maximilian, Margaret of Austria. The emperor sent Henry two portraits of her and it is possible that the famous likeness of Henry VII attributed to Michael Sittow was painted in reciprocation.[47] The exercise came to nothing. There was even talk of Henry marrying Katherine of Aragon's sister, Joanna of Castile, after the unexpected death of her husband, Philip of Burgundy, in 1506. But possible questions about her sanity—real or politically concocted—and prevarication by Ferdinand of Aragon ended any thoughts of a union. The old king would spend his last three years ill, often to the extreme, without a second son or a wife to produce one.[48]

This was undoubtedly a lot to take in for an unexpected heir to the throne of England during the ages of eleven to seventeen. But however the future Henry VIII chose to internalize what he saw at court with his father, his youth allowed him to give his wife and brother's widow, Katherine of Aragon, a chance to do her duty to the crown once he became king and married her. It was the eventual realization that, after turning thirty-six and waiting eighteen years for a son that would most likely never be conceived by his forty-two-year-old wife, he needed to act. A second catalyst was the promise of that son from a young, flirtatious and ambitious lady-in-waiting to the queen, Anne Boleyn. Through unpredictable events, including a

---

[44] Scarisbrick, *Henry VIII*, p. 4.
[45] G. Mattingly, *Catherine of Aragon* (1950), pp. 52ff.
[46] Fox, *Sister Queens*, p. 146
[47] Lloyd and Turley, *Henry VIII*, p. 16.
[48] Fox, *Sister Queens,* pp. 146-49.

pope held hostage by Katherine's nephew, the Emperor Charles V, Henry's path to annulment and desperation for a male heir led to the break with Rome.

The need for a viable male heir and a spare—the latter a role to which he was born—plagued Henry VIII his entire life. His first two wives failed their charge, and in 1537 with the birth of young Prince Edward to his third wife the king was half way to dynastic security. All he needed to insure the continuation of his dynasty was a second son, as he knew too well. After Jane Seymour's untimely death in childbirth, Henry embarked on the same game plan pursued by his father: a search for a queen among the royal houses of Europe.

In March 1538, a portrait of Christina, duchess of Milan was delivered to Henry. The king was pleased and he ordered masques and feasts to be held in celebration.[49] When that match failed to materialize, he went to his mural and portrait painter, Hans Holbein, to bring back a painting of Anne of Cleves, a bride promoted by Thomas Cromwell in search of Protestant alliances against potential invasion overtures by Catholic France and Spain. The finished portrait once again pleased Henry, but not the reality of the lady when Anne arrived in England for her wedding. Referred to variously as a Flanders horse or Flemish mare, Henry discreetly annulled the marriage and less quietly beheaded Thomas Cromwell for the indignity of it all, among other political reasons. One wonders if it should have been her flattering portrait painter, Hans Holbein, who went to the block.[50]

Henry VIII would marry twice more but by 1540 he was too infirmed to perform and too involved in navigating his rocky Reformation and planning another war with France to hope for another son. The dynasty depended on a young Prince Edward—the same situation his father faced on his death bed. In the case of Henry VIII, the heir would only outlive his father by six years.

The Whitehall Mural

But in 1537, Henry VIII could only feel joy and satisfaction at creating the next Tudor heir. At this time he might have remembered when his father restored Shene Palace and renamed it Richmond in 1501 in honor of the earldom of his grandfather, Edmund Tudor. It was here that his older sister, Margaret, was betrothed to James IV of Scotland to help secure

---

[49] Graves, *Henry VIII*, p. 88.
[50] [Addendum 1]

Henry VII's reign and rule through a foreign alliance, or at the very least the hopeful neutralization of a potential enemy. He might also recall that his father had a mural painted of himself at Richmond as a warrior king.[51] This Henry VIII now imitated in grand fashion. But he also let it be known in a revealing Latin inscription that the viewer of his mural was seeing and experiencing a king far greater than his father:

> If you find pleasure in seeing fair pictures of heroes,
> Look then at these! None greater was ever portrayed.
> Fierce is the struggle and hot the disputing; the question
> Does father, does son—or do both—the pre-eminence win?
> One ever withstood his foes and his country's destruction,
> Finally giving his people the blessing of peace;
> But, born to things greater, the son drove out his councils
> His ministers worthless, and ever supported the just.
> And in truth, to this steadfastness Papal arrogance yielded
> When the scepter of power was wielded by Henry the Eighth,
> Under whose reign the true faith was restored to the nation
> And the doctrines of God began to be reverenced with awe.

A recent biographer wrote that the inscription demonstrated Henry VIII's "healthy respect for his father's skills and success."[52] However, when viewed through the lens of his father, a very different conclusion may be drawn. For these words belie an insecure, competing son in fear of not living up to his father's achievements and in need of telling the world that he was the better of the two. He could not boast of killing a king to win his crown as his father had done, or of his victories in battle—by the time the mural was created the greatest victory was one led by his first wife. Henry's army chased away French cavalry, and he was in fact a no-show.

Getting rid of his "ministers worthless", which could refer to his father's councilors, Empson and Dudley, was an easy decision given their unpopularity, but he nonetheless kept them alive for sixteen months, possibly at the behest of Katherine of Aragon, before executing them. If Henry was referring to Wolsey and More, it would be in the context of the next line about his personal triumph over the pope. He could not mention defending his throne in battle, as his father had done several times, since by 1537 there had been no real threats: the Scottish invasion ended quickly in 1513, and the Pilgrimage of Grace in 1536, his only major internal

---

[51] John Timms and Alexander Gunn, *Abbeys Castles and Ancient Halls of England and Wales South* (London, 1890), p. 134.

[52] Wooding, *Henry VIII*, p. 34, from where the full inscription is taken.

rebellion in a reign of thirty-eight years, was more about religious and economic grievances and not about Henry VIII or his dynasty.

It was in fact his removal of the pope from everyday life and his supremacy over the English church that he could point to with satisfaction, restoring "the truth faith" as he said in his mural. No doubt this was an accomplishment, however unintended a consequence from his obsessive desire for a legitimate male heir and a queen to provide him with one. But it also came about through the long erosion of faith in and respect for Rome from an English populace who had access to the Bible in English for more than a century. Henry was the recipient of a long tradition of English kings making their own ecclesiastical decisions, not the least of whom was his father, Henry VII.

What of the intimidating stance, almost coming out of the wall in front of a less-imposing mother and father in the background? The obvious purpose was to convey strength, power, fearlessness and physical dominance: attributes a Renaissance king sought to portray to rival and ruled alike. But beyond impressing visitors to the king's privy chamber with this initial visual presence, there were also the accompanying assertions from the inscription to support the emotional response to the portrait and to justify its impact and purpose. But was there something more to the image in relation to the words?

Carel van Mander, a Flemish painter and art historian, published a book in the Dutch Republic in 1604 entitled Book of Painters (*Het Schilder-boek*), offering numerous autobiographies of artists. In speaking of Hans Holbein, he made reference to the Whitehall Mural, including the reaction by someone who actually visited the Palace and stood before it. When van Mander's book was translated from Dutch into French by Henry Hymans in 1884, that reaction in the relevant passage took on a different meaning, which in turn underwent additional shifts in implication when modern historians turned it from French into English.[53]

Roy Strong noted in his book on Holbein and Henry VIII that van Mander said the viewer of the mural was "abashed and annihilated" upon observing the overbearing portrait of Henry VIII. This was echoed by an art historian who wrote "this image was said to have stricken with terror

---

[53] Carel van Mander, *Het schilder-boeck* (Haarlem, 1604), p. 222; C. Van Mander, *Livre des Peintres*, trans. by Henri Hymans (Paris, 1884), p. 218. The original Dutch passage is online:
<http://babel.hathitrust.org/cgi/pt?id=nnc1.0029875978;view=1up;seq=62>
[accessed 26 Oct. 2013]

all who saw it."[54] Others have repeated the "abashed and annihilated" Dutch-to-French-to-English response of the unknown observer.[55]

But this appears to be more interpretation than translation as others have noted, which has detracted from the more important inscription.[56] In delving backwards to van Mander's original statement there is perhaps more than meets the eye of the beholder and it may relate to the actual objective of the portrait. For context, the entire French passage by Hymans using the Dutch version translates as follows:

> [Holbein] painted a magnificent life-sized portrait of Henry VIII standing, and so lifelike that everyone who sees it are awestruck, for it seems as if the subject of the portrait lives on the canvas and that his head and arms and legs move as in nature.[57]

"Awestruck" is a far cry from "abashed and annihilated" by any measure. In this version, which was closer to the Dutch passage, the viewer is in awe of the king and the reality of his image, not emotionally destroyed by him. Indeed, Henry's intent was not to frighten observers of the mural or drive them away. He wanted first to overwhelm them and draw them into his visual representation; then learn of the justification of his power as "spoken" in the Latin inscription. The key point here is that the image seemed to *move*—in a modern sense a hologram so lifelike it could be mistaken for the real thing: "for it seems as if the subject of the portrait lives on the canvas and that his head and arms and legs move as in nature." Those in attendance of the mural could almost hear and see the

---

[54] Strong, *Holbein and Henry VIII*, p. 39; Lorne Campbell, *Renaissance Portraits* (New Haven, 1990), p. 84.

[55] For example, Kevin Sharpe, *Selling the Tudor Monarchy: Authority and Image in Sixteenth-Century England* (New Haven, 2009), p. 67, writing that Carel Van Mander reported in 1604 that a contemporary said "the spectator felt abashed, annihilated in his presence."

[56] Tatiana C. String, "Henry VIII and Holbein: Patterns and conventions in early modern writing about artists," in *Henry VIII and the Court*, eds. Thomas Betteridge and Suzannah Lipscomb (London, 2013), pp. 131-141, who emphasizes the portrait over the inscription.

[57] "*Pour en revenir aux œuvres que Holbein fit pour le roi, il peignit un magnifique portrait de Henri VIII, en pied, grand comme nature, et si animé que tous ceux qui le voient en sont frappés, car il semble que le personnage vit sur la toile ete que sa tête et ses membres remuent comme dans la nature.*" I would like to thank Ellen McClure, Associate Professor of French and History at the University of Illinois at Chicago, for her translation from French to English.

king speaking the words as the eyes moved back and forth from the king to the inscription. The message conveyed the superiority over his father.

The relevant Dutch words printed in black letter in 1604 that described the reaction of the viewer further the purpose of the image: *soo gheheel levendigh / dat een yeder wei't siet verschrickt*. The phrase "soo gheheel levendigh" in modern Dutch would be "zo geheel levendig", or possibly "levensecht", which would translate to "so (completely) alive/lively/lifelike". The second part is slightly more challenging and more significant. There is no modern Dutch equivalent for "yeder" although what was most likely meant was "ieder", or "any/every". "Verschrickt" is the archaic past tense of "verschrikken", which is the verb "to be surprised/shocked".[58] "Wei't siet" would be modernized as "die het ziet", or "would have been". Putting it together, the modern phrase "Zo geheel levendig/levensecht dat een ieder die het ziet, schrikt" would read "[the portrait of Henry VIII is] so alive/lifelike that anyone who sees it would have been surprised/shocked."[59]

If this was the response of the 16th-century visitor to the Whitehall Mural as noted by van Mander, then it is exactly what Henry VIII desired for anyone viewing this prodigious work of art and written declaration upon entering his privy chamber: "you will experience first-hand my superior majesty in full view as if alive; and you will learn from me *personally* why I am greater than my father." Such a message was created by a volatile monarch with an inferiority complex who knew he was never destined to be king and thus had to prove himself to the living and—in this instance—to his dead father, each day of his life.

Although hardly planned, Henry VIII perhaps would have even hoped to overshadow the birthday of his father and founder of his dynasty—28 January 1457—when he died on that very day and month in 1547, ninety years later. This unexpected heir would never have accepted the opposite result.

---

[58] String noted that *verschrikken* in its modern spelling means "to get a shock" as an intransitive verb, rather than past tense ("surprised/shocked"), which has a different meaning more in line with jaw-dropping than frightened or almost physically receiving a shock. ("Henry VIII and Holbein," p. 135.)

[59] I would like to thank Christopher van den Berge, MA, an independent Dutch scholar, for his analysis and translation from Dutch to English.

Father and son

Perhaps Henry VIII greatest triumph, one he would never acknowledge, was in absorbing what took place during the reign of his father and emulating those things that made him a strong if impulsive monarch who for his first twenty years of rule brought him great popularity at home and abroad. The Henrician Reformation and his own inner conflicts produced confusion and sometimes fear for English men and women grappling with new religious practices and dogma and a secular head of the church *of* England. But from his coronation to the birth of his own legitimate son, many of his actions were in line with what his father had done to establish a viable dynasty and a strong monarchy.

There would be less concern over many of his financial and administrative policies prior to the painting of the mural, or even his early searches for a wife to bear a male heir. His break with Rome was also a necessary requirement for the development of an inchoate nation state independent of a foreign entity. However, it was triggered in part through the pursuit of preserving a dynasty and the customs, traditions and laws of England since "time out of mind", and not from purposeful state planning.

Henry VIII was different from Henry VII, in personality, deeds and foibles. Their similarities, conceived through the policies and decisions of the father, influenced the son in ways he may not have understood well, although they shaped much of his reign and the actions he pursued as ruler of England. Achieving less than his father was something Henry VIII could never accept, and he hoped to ensure that his imagined superiority would be proclaimed to the world through the lifelike portrait and words on a palace wall. It was a wall that burned to the ground more than a century and a half later, along with some of the memories of the inner turmoil of the second Tudor king.

Addendum 1

The Many Faces of Thomas Cromwell[*]

Introduction

I was invited to compare and contrast two books, both taking as their subject Henry VIII's principal minister, Thomas Cromwell. One was a scholarly book by Geoffrey Elton, the other a work of historical fiction by novelist Hilary Mantel. The review appeared online as part of a special conference on academic writing and historical fiction sponsored by the Institute of Historical Research. It also was printed in Reviews in History, *published by the Institute.*

I have always been a big fan of historical fiction and from time to time threaten myself with writing one. More times than not, truth can indeed be stranger than fiction as Mark Twain observed. There are numerous events and people involving stories that bear out that observation. Melding the two into a novel can result in a memorable story that is believable because its premise really happened. Moreover, I am often impressed by the research that such authors undertake to portray people, places and plots as accurately as possible. It not only gives credence to the author's grasp of the era and characters in question, it also can provide an entry point for the general public to read non-fiction history and gain further insight and knowledge.

My early readings of such authors as James Michener and Anya Seton did just that: they heightened my interest in various topics and eras of

[*] Reprinted with permission. The article was first published online as part of a virtual conference sponsored by the Institute of Historical Research: *Novel approaches: from academic history to historical fiction*, 21-25 Nov. 2011. <https://ihrconference.wordpress.com/2011/11/21/the-many-faces-of-thomas-cromwell-mark-r-horowitz> [accessed 3 May 2012] It was also published in *Reviews in History*, No. 1168, Nov. 2011: <http://www.history.ac.uk/reviews/review/1168> [accessed 3 May 2012], Institute of Historical Research, School of Advanced Study, University of London.

history. We are fortunate that the tradition of well-researched and well-written works of historical fiction continues today, most recently by Ken Follett and Hilary Mantel, the latter one of the authors in this review. The same is true with movies, although some do stretch accuracy a bit for what is believed to be a better dramatic result. I would argue that sticking with what happened and being clever about how best to portray it on the screen will have a better emotional impact.

Movies about Queen Elizabeth I and Mary Queen of Scots where they have some confrontation "for effect"—even though in real life they never met—would not be necessary if the screenwriter figured out how to create an arc of tension between the two cousins.

The historian, of course, cannot use dialog in his or her work unless it actually existed in the documentation, which it usually does not for the period of time I study. Once in a while a record or chronicle from early-Tudor England will note something that was said—or purportedly said—that brings to life people long dead. In my discussion of the dark side of Henry VII's policy [Chapter Seven], I mention a notation in a court book in London that quotes what a mayor allegedly said about James Wilford. I also titled an article based on words allegedly said by Edmund Dudley: "Agree with the king!" [Chapter Five]. When read in the context of how they were voiced, both are chilling statements and it would be advantageous to have more such discourse from these men. The novelist can provide that readily and dramatically; the historian can only try to determine the meaning of what was said, its context and its veracity.

As I note in the following review, Thomas Cromwell is a good subject for fiction, in part because of the scholarship by Elton during his career. I talk briefly about his connection to Cromwell in the next chapter, but for those familiar with his work there is a purpose to what Elton hoped to prove: that Thomas Cromwell was the driving force behind the development of the modern English state. Although largely disproven by scholars—and it took a very long time to do that!—Elton let the proverbial cat out of the bag about a minister few people knew about even in the scholarly world.

Mantel thus had a rich landscape to tread upon concerning Cromwell thanks in part to Elton's lifelong preoccupation with him. In her novel, she brought Cromwell and other characters to life and, from my perspective, heightened curiosity about this minister of Henry VIII that could encourage her readers to pursue historical writings about him. In an age where less and less history is read or studied, this would be a good thing.

Reform and Renewal, Thomas Cromwell and the Common Weal by G.R. Elton
Cambridge University Press: Cambridge, 1973; ISBN: 9780521098090;
188pp.

Wolf Hall by Hilary Mantel
London: Harper Collins, 2009; ISBN: 9781861975966; 672pp.

Reviewer: Professor Mark Horowitz
University of Illinois (Chicago)

When a late-medieval or Tudor historian is asked to compare and
contrast a historical novel with a scholarly book that both take as their
subject Thomas Cromwell, and the latter work has been written by the late
G.R. Elton, the inevitable disclaimer becomes compulsory unless that
historian has spent several decades inhabiting a historiographically-
isolated cave during the rise and fall of the Tudor revolution in
government. In the present case, I must submit that I knew Sir Geoffrey
during his last fifteen years at Clare College, Cambridge and I still retain a
cache of our letters. I read his publications and the numerous reviews of
them, and I on occasion disagreed with the perspicacious Regius Professor
verbally in conversations and once in print with regard to his view that
Henry VIII's principal minister, Thomas Cromwell, was the mastermind
behind the inchoate modern English state as first described in Elton's
magnum opus on a Tudor revolution.[1]

That written wallop, relevant to this present assessment, occurred when
I was asked to write an article on a book he co-wrote with the future Nobel
laureate, Robert Fogel. I began by briefly summarizing each authors past
work. I ended Elton's by positing the query of whether it was Thomas
Cromwell behind the Henrician revolution in government or G.R. Elton
behind the Cromwellian revolution in history. Upon completing the piece,
I asked both authors to read the final draft before submission in case of
any factual errors and with the understanding that in effect the article itself
was cast in stone. Although neither found any glaring mistakes and
thanked me for the endeavour, I must believe that Elton displayed a bent
eye as he read my Cromwell quip. With this in mind, I have approached
the present dual review from the narratives and conclusions offered by the

---

[1] G.R. Elton, *The Tudor Revolution in Government: Administrative Changes in the
Reign of Henry VIII* (Cambridge, 1953).

respective authors, and not from what others have thought of them or written about their books.[2]

Thomas Cromwell is a good subject for fact and fiction. He was and remains somewhat of an enigma both as a visionary for government efficiency and as an ambitious "new man" rising from the obscurity of a blacksmith's son to perhaps the most powerful man in England save his king, Henry VIII. Moreover, much like his mentor Cardinal Thomas Wolsey—the son of an Ipswich butcher—Cromwell's descent was as spectacular and dramatic as his climb. For both men, historians have tried to untangle how much influence they had over Henry VIII and whether they were the puppet-masters or the puppets in the monarch's affairs of state and of the heart. Regardless, the arcs that were their lives remained dependent on the whims and commands of a Tudor king.

Mantel pursues segments of the lives of Wolsey and then Cromwell, beginning in 1527 amid the rising turmoil of the Great Matter (Henry's annulment of his marriage to Katherine of Aragon to make Anne Boleyn his queen and progenitor of a male heir) and leading up to the execution of Sir Thomas More in 1535. Elton focuses on Cromwell and his legislative roots and actions during the 1530s within the environment of Protestant evangelicalism, humanistic writings and verbal discourse. The authors necessarily pursue different genres and disciplines for their accounts. Mantel constructs lives, images and conversations from what is known about her characters; Elton seeks to establish Cromwell as a thoughtful, purposeful and results-oriented minister based on interpretation of surviving documentation. It is therefore perhaps best to discuss three topics where the paths of the authors intersect. The first centers on the personality of Thomas Cromwell. The second involves the religious and humanistic nature of Cromwell's beliefs and their effect on his actions and life. The third entails his accomplishments and acumen at survival as the chief minister of Henry VIII. However, the style, format and themes followed by the respective authors will be addressed first to understand better where they are coming from and, if it might be suggested, where they intended to go.

---

[2] For a good summary of Elton's thesis and a revision of his conclusions, see Ethan H. Shagan, "*The Tudor Revolution in Government* fifty years later: rethinking Geoffrey Elton's vision of political modernization", paper presented at The University of Chicago Nicholson Center for British Studies Conference: Modernizing Politics? (21-2 May 2005). [The actual article about the co-authored book referred to is found in Addendum 2.]

Elton decidedly positions himself as the master of the manuscripts, in this case contemporary documents and parliamentary records from the statutes and the journals of the House of Commons. He comes close to chastising those historians pursuing the history of ideas—he is not a fan—believing that all is for naught unless such ideas can be traced to actions beyond the mental exercise. Indeed, he has little time for More's Utopia because no proposals were put forth to better the commonwealth, only "remedies in the fictional realm of the unattainable". Elton's goal is to demonstrate the translation of "aspiration into achievement" and how "thought yielded results in deed". This of course provides a theme and path for his discussion of Thomas Cromwell as the exemplar of a Tudor action hero of sorts, and he takes his readers on a legislative journey portraying a practical minister's transition into a proficient planner stoked by the reformist fervour of the day.

Elton accomplishes this first by examining three members of Cromwell's reformist *group*—Stephen Vaughan, Thomas Starkey, and Richard Morison—although he takes pains to convince that none were part of an official body but rather a "company of like-minded men" who were "haphazardly brought together and always on their own initiative". This may seem to some as flying in the face of the adage that coincidences take a lot of planning. Nonetheless, Elton insists they were not recruited by the minister but simply thought much as he did, although they are labeled "Cromwellians" by the author because they believe Cromwell would reform England along humanistic, Protestant thinking. Then true to Elton's mission, any contemporary rivals to the man behind reform and renewal are summarily dispatched. He quickly marginalises Cromwell's predecessor and mentor Wolsey as never doing anything, completely "useless" to a generation of intellectuals and reformers, and the poster child for the old clerical order they deplored. He then finds time to stomp on Thomas More as missing the boat to becoming the Erasmian humanist reformer in favour of concentrating on heresy and the maintenance of the church. This provides a segue to the actions of the minister who got it right—Thomas Cromwell—and what he did during the parliamentary sessions of the Henrician Reformation. Because the book is a compilation of Elton's Wiles Lectures presented at Queens University, Belfast in 1972, they fall under topic headings although Cromwell's legislation agenda is placed in somewhat chronological order.

The tone and style exhibited by Elton are that of a constitutional scholar in the know, lecturing other historians (often by name) on where they were misled—or failed to lead at all—while forcefully demonstrating Cromwell's *modus operandi* through the use of parliamentary documentation.

The general public might not grab on readily to the scholarly story being told, but Elton has a self-assured way with words that are understandable and on occasion clever and humorous: Cromwell as the "pragmatic prophet" who receives letters in Latin "with Greek bits in them"; propagandist preambles to parliamentary bills embodied with "standard commonwealth stuff". Few would argue at the time of his lectures that Elton contributes to a clearer understanding of how bills were initiated, their chances of passing based on origin (Commons, Lords or support from the king) and the nuances involved in the role of politics and religion, which from a modern perspective were hopelessly intertwined. It remains not so much winning a legislative initiative, which will be addressed later, but the intent and purpose that is at the heart of Elton's narrative and thesis. The medium Cromwell utilizes, with far-reaching effects for the development of the modern English state, is parliament, through which the laws of England are guided with his steady if not always successful hand.

Mantel proffers a Thomas Cromwell confident in his own thinking and actions regarding the law, a posture developed early on through the reactions of a young boy to his physically-abusive father. This situation is introduced on the first page when as a fifteen-year-old Cromwell is almost throttled to death—occurrences that later shape his views towards legal reform to protect the helpless. Through intermittent flashbacks and intriguing dialog with key players in the era of Henry VIII, the author constructs a self-made, self-educated man unafraid to face the unknown: living and learning business in Northern Europe, fighting in Continental wars. Both Mantel and her Cromwell are cynical about Roman Catholicism, which she views as a corrupt business founded on practices not mentioned in the New Testament—for this is the time when translations into the vernacular by the likes of Tyndale and Luther unmask the deceptions of the popes and their biblical foundation for authority and practice.

So when in 1527 Wolsey's trip to France includes granting throngs of people remission for their sins, the author throws out an observation by no one in particular: "That's a few thousand Frenchmen free to start all over again". Mantel also confides Cromwell's knowledge that to obtain the right scriptural interpretations or permissions from the pope for marriages or divorces, every "opinion" must be paid for in cash. It is this disdain for the church and its reliance on cash payments from countries in need of capital—such as England—that fuels Cromwell's search for reform and solvency for his king and country. However, to dispel the irony of a future principal minister cutting his political teeth in the household of a cardinal, Mantel's Wolsey—a very rich character in the story and in many respects more interesting than Cromwell—shares some of the cynicism of the day against Rome.

It is Mantel's dialog between Cromwell and major characters and the development of their personas that drives her story. Because of the abundance of personages, a glossary is provided for those unfamiliar with the period. This is not a bad idea because in many respects the reader waits in anticipation for the next tête-à-tête between Cromwell and a variety of people besides important figures such as Anne Boleyn, Henry VIII, the duke of Norfolk (an avowed enemy turned self-interested ally), Thomas More (portrayed as more of a Torquemada-on-the-Thames when it comes to heretics than even Elton suggests), Bishop Stephen Gardiner, and Jane Seymour and Mary Boleyn (targets of Cromwell's affections and perhaps more). Historians do not have the luxury of making up dialog—although mental attempts often occur once years are spent studying an individual— and Mantel is wonderfully adept at coloring her characters with attributes well-known to aficionados of Tudor history. Hence, when Anne Boleyn speaks the reader is already aware that when Cromwell gives her a present of silver forks with rock crystal handles one Christmas he notes that "he hopes she will use them to eat with, not to stick in people". To make the point stick further, so to speak, on another occasion when thinking about Anne he confesses "you wouldn't trust her near a sharp knife". It is largely through these conversations, and the musings of Cromwell, that the theme of a rapidly-ascending powerful and shrewd minister amid court intrigue develops.

While such interplay between people helps advance the story of the rise of Cromwell, the stylistic use of the pronoun "he" when referring to him is both confusing and momentum-halting. Indeed, on several occasions it was necessary to reread a few lines just to determine who was speaking. This uncertainty of voice is compounded by an occasional shifting into first person singular or plural: Cromwell, after being referred to as "he", suddenly says "I dry my eyes"; an abrupt shift from being "he" to a new scene beginning "October, and we are going to Calais"; a conversation between Cromwell and Henry VIII includes the narrative "He watches Henry's face. He is alive to anything that concerns honour". Presumably it is Henry alive with the notion of honour. Presumably, if in fact the reader is aware of the king's obsession with honour as explicated in such historical works as Lacey Baldwin Smith's book on Henry VIII.[3] While experimentation in writing style is the artist's prerogative—from

---

[3] Lacey Baldwin Smith, *Henry VIII: The Mask of Royalty* (London, 1971).

Dorothy Parker's "stream of consciousness" dialog with oneself to the frenzied episodes that comprise James Joyce's *Ulysses*—it serves little purpose to push Cromwell away by becoming "he" through most of the book just as the reader tries to get closer to him.

Mantel is intent on staying fairly true to what is known about Cromwell and his life, such as information gleaned from Cavendish's book on Thomas Wolsey.[4] She also hints at events or attributes that the knowledgeable reader will enjoy but the neophyte might miss unknowingly. So when it is suggested that Anne Boleyn has a "deformity", many readers may be unaware that she has been attributed to having, among other things, six fingers on one hand—an improbability given Henry's superstitious nature that nonetheless has brought about much discussion, including an essay in a medical publication.[5] The king of England's trip to the Field of Cloth of Gold near Calais in June 1520 to meet with the king of France is mentioned several times but without the visually-interesting story of Henry VIII being thrown to the ground in a wrestling match by his regal cousin Francis I: fodder for further character development of a Tudor king Mantel portrays as paranoid, constantly hunting and bedding, and doubting of his abilities and his future. Those aware of these inside stories will gain a greater embellishment of the world of Thomas Cromwell and how he acts and reacts within it.

Elton's Cromwell is a far-horizon thinker and it is through the minister's surviving papers that the reader encounters a man jotting down ideas for future actions: improving the system of taxation (clearly an age-old problem for king and commoner alike); addressing the enclosure of pasture and farmland by sheep owners at the expense of farmers. While ignoring Wolsey and the possibility that many such reforms were first addressed by the cardinal without follow-through or result—a circumstance similar to many of Somerset's non-starters under Henry's son, Edward VI—Elton sees Cromwell as a visionary bent on converting ideas into actions that succeed. Part of this image stems from an innate work ethic

---

[4] George Cavendish, *The Life and Death of Cardinal Wolsey*, ed. Richard S. Sylvester, Early English Text Society, 243 (London, 1959). Cavendish was a gentleman usher in Wolsey's household.

[5] Félix Martí-Ibáñez, M.D., "The Anne Boleyn syndrome", *MD Medical News Magazine*, 18, 10 (Oct. 1974), pp. 11-16. There are no contemporary descriptions of Anne's deformities. The notion of having six fingers (polydactylism), a goiter and "moles" occurred years after her execution and most likely by anti-Anglicans seeking to portray the attributes of a witch who enchanted Henry VIII into his divorce from Katherine and the papacy.

and drive, and Elton relates that Stephen Vaughan tells his friend Cromwell that he is overworking as the king's minister. Moreover, to support the idea that having what we would call a Type A personality and being a workaholic are forces for Cromwell's personal mission, Elton paints a portrait of an erudite analyst with an eidetic gift that allows him to memorize Erasmus Latin version of the New Testament—no mean feat. He is also represented as an intellectual equal to the Oxford man and humanist Thomas Starkey, for whom Cromwell obtains a position as a chaplain to Henry VIII. Indeed, Elton argues that Starkey's writings are influenced by discussions with Cromwell, more often at the minister's house with other reformers at what is referred to as a "learned salon". Cromwell's view of pursuing a middle way (*via media*) is part and parcel of the like views held by these men. The minister thus avoids the extremes and this possibly is a reason he was able to survive throughout the 1530s amid social and religious upheaval in England.

Perhaps the most important aspect of Cromwell's personality and political outlook is, according to Elton, a belief and reliance in the efficacy of the law and its use to reform and transform England. Cromwell's vision of a self-contained realm—the phrase "this realm of England is an Empire" illuminates the preamble to the 1533 Act of Restraint of Appeals that removed papal authority from England—becomes a focal point for laws that encourage growth and stability internally and commerce with Europe. In spite of his often grandiose schemes, Elton notes that Cromwell is nonetheless a realist aware of the opposing forces to change: the church, the nobility, the gentry and often the king himself. This is perhaps why Cromwell relies on couching bills in rhetoric pointing to precedents and age-old practices: a means to demonstrate what has always been, not what must now become.

Curiously missing from Elton's portraiture is a discussion of the Great Matter or even Cromwell's involvement with the monumental affair. This is perhaps because the core concerns of Elton's Cromwell are reforms through parliamentary action, rather than the larger issues of cause and effect during the break with Rome. However, Cromwell could hardly ignore the fact that his mentor Wolsey fell from grace over his failure to achieve the "Divorce". Nor could he fail to understand that much of the legislation he proposed dealt with the severing of financial and religious relations with the vicar of Christ, once Henry VIII moved from a wayward Roman defender of the faith threatening papal authority to an independent head of his own church and state. One can say that keeping all the money destined for the church or making the bible more accessible to the populace were reforms long overdue (or more likely long in the making).

But it is difficult to ignore the trigger for this flurry of legislation in parliament: Henry's desire to marry Anne Boleyn. It takes away little to realize that Cromwell and his king could each have their cake and eat it too by abandoning Rome—one seeking to reform age-old or emerging iniquities, the other desperately in need of an unquestionable male heir.

Mantel, of course, can paint broad strokes on a large canvas that is the Cromwell in her mind's eye, and it is most enjoyable to view. She does an admirable job of bringing in contemporary stories and historical sketches concerning Cromwell's traits, including much that is in common with Elton. When Cromwell talks about a book of mathematics and its lesson of balance, Mantel is echoing the *via media* views often expressed about the minister. She notes that when Cromwell writes "this realm of England is an empire", he does so almost in passing—it is obvious to him and it is a means to an end. As Cromwell reflects on parliament and drafting bills, he says "like spells, they have to make things happen in the real world". Nevertheless, because the minister realizes that it is difficult to implement "new things in England", he says "there can be old things freshly presented, or new things that pretend to be old". Mantel carries this English viewpoint to other characters: when Cromwell tells Katherine of Aragon and her daughter Mary Tudor that Henry's rule over the English church is based on ancient precedents, Mary replies such precedents were "invented these last few months".

Where her tones and colors for individuality resonate are in the personal qualities of Cromwell. For one, he is a clever, ambitious man with a quick mind bordering on the cynical and the brazen. When a self-righteous Thomas More tries to bait him into heresy, Cromwell dodges and parries verbally with great effect. Mantel uses his famous portrait by the court painter Hans Holbein (also a character) as a means to reference the "hard Cromwellian stare—the equivalent of a kick" that many fear once he becomes the king's chief advisor. This goes hand-in-hand with a self-assuredness not often seen in a Tudor courtier. His first long conversation with Henry VIII reveals an almost flippant Cromwell, and although his stark honesty no doubt brings him into Henry's trusted graces one wonders if he truly sparred with words in his meetings with the combustible king. Mantel, like Elton, recognizes Cromwell as the chief architect of many statutes of the realm. When Katherine of Aragon introduces him to her daughter, Mary, she says "This is Master Cromwell. Who now writes all the laws". Near the end of the book it becomes clear that ambition is part and parcel of Cromwell's persona. In thinking of his various properties he muses "all this is small stuff. It's nothing to what he intends to have, or to what Henry will owe him".

Cromwell is also a vindictive man with a long memory and the patience to wait for the right time to bring down an enemy—Mantel says he keeps a mental enemies list of those who have crossed him. When his mentor Wolsey is arrested by Henry Percy, the author writes of Cromwell: "God need not trouble, he thinks: I shall take it in hand". On another occasion, when he hears rumors of Anne Boleyn having an affair with Tom Wyatt, Cromwell overlooks it but notes that he will "bear it in mind" for the future. He also places people in his debt, running the gamut from merchants and clerks to nobles and queens and the king himself. He pays for the installation of his nemesis, Stephen Gardiner, to become the bishop of Winchester, creating a future accounting for the prelate.

There is a sensitive side to Mantel's Cromwell not usually considered by historians of the period. Cromwell cries in talking about the loss of his wife and two daughters to the periodic sweating sickness that killed those of low and high birth with impartiality. He is compassionate for the poor, feeding vagrants at his gate and bringing a poor mother and her two children into his household—but telling her she must learn to read. He also has an affair with Johane, the sister of his dead wife, and he is portrayed as possessing strong feelings for the likes of Anne's sister, Mary Boleyn and the king's future wife, Jane Seymour—two very risky attractions considering they at various times are placed in Henry VIII's bed during the story.

Cromwell's religious beliefs and humanistic opinions are of import to both authors and are seen as driving forces in his actions. Elton tells of a Cromwell who is patron to scholars and a "man of the gospel". Reformers wanted new laws, and Elton describes a process where experts in Cromwell's employment discuss reforms, draft them as laws and encourage their master to bring them to the king and council for promotion to parliament. A slight glitch in this analysis is noted: Elton admits it is difficult to ascertain if Cromwell was annotating a private petition to reform something he believed in, or whether he was merely helping a private interest. Although unemployment is identified as the main target for reform (high rents, enclosures, loss of trade opportunities), Elton sees four areas Cromwell pursues for his reformist program: the church, removing special privileges and constitutional diversities such as in Wales and Ireland, overhaul of the central administration of state to make it less personal, and socio-economic problems. However, while these areas are targets for both commonwealth reformists and Protestant adherents, many of them had been addressed in varying degrees before—Elton observes that impeding enclosures dated back to a statute in Henry VII's reign and the subsequent 1517 Enclosure Commission spearheaded by Wolsey. The impression given is that Cromwell hopes to succeed where others failed, and he could attempt to do so within the maelstrom of the retreat from Rome and a willingness for parliament to take bold actions for the king and their own self-interests.

Mantel places Cromwell and his beliefs in a world where Christianity and pagan practices are balanced to hedge one's bets. Henry VIII is a good Christian son who believes he rules by divine right and is in touch with the Supreme Being. But he also keeps astrologers close at hand and listens to the rantings of a so-called holy woman who predicts the future. Cromwell is religious in the sense that he compartmentalises what may be divine from what may be politically useful. He can therefore seek religious reform, including getting rid of the non-biblical concept of Purgatory, yet at the same time pay for seven years' worth of masses for his deceased wife while his nieces pray with rosary beads. Where there is no compromise to him is the law. To Cromwell, Christ did not bestow lands and property on people—that is done through earthly authority and none higher than parliament. Indeed, Cromwell believes that the king derives his power from the people and the laws of parliament—if Henry VIII did not at least recognise this in practice, Cromwell would not follow him.

When it comes to accomplishments and the art of survival, each author takes a different route with varying results. Elton seems to see the act of proposing legislative reforms as both an end unto itself and an achievement. Yet he is hard-pressed to show that Cromwell overall was successful during the Reformation Parliament up until his execution in 1540. It is clear that this was a very busy minister, but the success rate getting reformist bills passed was not earth-shattering. The 1536 Enclosure Act he shepherds through the commons loses much of its teeth along the way. Cromwell's attempt at a Poor Law, part of the reformist agenda, is eventually watered down and fails. His efforts to limit sanctuary and benefit of clergy—the latter where men could easily claim the privilege to avoid common law prosecution—was addressed by Henry VII and subsequent statutes without Cromwell's imprint. When Cromwell attempts to restrain sanctuary in a 1540 bill, it is defeated after his fall. Much of the legislation in the last years of the Reformation Parliament involve law enforcement, not law reform; those law reform bills initiated fail, including a bill to prosecute rigged juries. In all of this, Elton makes clear that Cromwell can only do so much to push through a bill, and fairly little if the king is against it.

Ironically, Elton undercuts his argument after outlining Cromwell's legislative reform failures by noting that in the last four parliaments after Cromwell's fall, twelve, thirteen, seven and fourteen acts deemed commonwealth bills actually pass. Nevertheless, Elton entitles his last chapter "The achievement", although admitting that most plans for the common weal through Cromwell's endeavors "came to little or nothing". Some that succeed were for terms, lasting until the next parliament or the death of the king. One is left with the impression that a hard-working minister, undeterred by defeat and opposition, doggedly pushes bill after bill through an institution without result. Thomas Cromwell perhaps believed in parliament more than it believed in Thomas Cromwell and his purpose. His survival through these turbulent times is not directly addressed by Elton, nor are much of the politics beyond parliamentary procedures. Nonetheless, it is clear that Cromwell had the trust of the king during the uncertainty of Continental responses to the Henrician Reformation and the demise of three wives until both court intrigue and an unfortunate painting of Anne of Cleves cost the minister his life.[6]

Time and again, Mantel portrays Cromwell as adept at manipulating Henry VIII. There are many examples throughout her story: instructing Henry that it is the king who is now head of the church of England in place of the Roman church in England; "teaching" the king to call the pope the bishop of Rome; interpreting Henry's dream in the middle of the night as a call to take charge of the realm; telling Henry that the monasteries are corrupt and useless, and thus ripe for dissolution. It is, after all, the caprice of a ruler—yesterday and today—that determines the rise or fall of a minister. Cromwell is a master of his master, and therefore of survival amid court plotting, back-stabbing and the volatile nature of a king losing his youth, his health and his hold on a viable dynasty. Mantel has Cromwell play the game as well as anyone in the Tudor orbit. Moreover, because of his ability to accomplish what his monarch wants—and here she only mentions those laws that passed—this unlikely minister through tenacity and ruthlessness was able to survive and thrive until, ironically, the Reformation was legislatively complete and England was, indeed, its own realm.

Mantel's book as a whole sets itself up for a sequel, and those familiar with the period have a sense of what will happen to many of the characters presented, including Anne Boleyn, Jane Seymour and Thomas Cromwell.

---

[6] It has always been my feeling that once Henry VIII viewed the unfortunate lady in person and recognised the disparity between pictorial rendition and reality, it should have been the artist, Hans Holbein, who went to the block and not Cromwell. After Cromwell's demise, Henry lamented the execution of his minister and might have come to the same conclusion. Holbein died in 1543, possibly from the plague.

A word should be mentioned about the title, *Wolf Hall*, since it is more descriptive of what it portends than what it has to do with the present book. The Seymours live at Wolf Hall, and it will be Jane Seymour who succeeds Anne Boleyn as Henry VIII's next wife and the one who fulfills his quest for a male heir. Other than mentioned in passing, it is only discussed briefly on the last page and in fact the last sentence. Cromwell, whom we know is emotionally attached to Jane Seymour, intends to visit her and the Seymour family. The book ends thusly: "Early September. Five days. Wolf Hall." To the reader waiting for the relevance of the title, it is a long wait indeed and perhaps without any meaning for the entire story. It is the author, in her notes published at the end of the novel, who admits as much: "Wolf Hall, the Seymour house in Wiltshire, is where we're going at the end of the book. But, of course, I chose it primarily for its metaphorical resonance: who could resist it? The whole of Henry's court is Wolf Hall".

It might prove useful to read both books, beginning with Elton's, if the reader desires to understand first what it was that preoccupied most of Thomas Cromwell's time before entering the social and political world he dealt with on a daily basis during his rise to become the chief minister of Henry VIII as narrated by Mantel and Cromwell himself. It is sometimes difficult to comprehend a life solely through a fictionalised account, no matter how well researched, without becoming grounded in how things worked, or why they did not. Both authors have a great respect for their subject, and together they have taken a lesser-known Tudor figure in the popular mind and created a major component in one of the great events of English history: the Henrician Reformation, with its cast of famous characters caught up in this uncertain time.

ADDENDUM 2

WHICH ROAD TO THE PAST?*

Introduction

In 1980, I worked at the University of Chicago's Business School full-time while writing my thesis and publishing. I stayed in touch with Geoffrey Elton at Cambridge, who by 1983 was the Regius Professor of Modern History and who would receive a knighthood three years later. [Chapter Nine] In the meantime, economic historian Robert F. Fogel was at Harvard. In 1981, he came to Chicago to oversee the Center for Population Economics in the Business School as a chaired professor. By then, both scholars were at the top of their respective fields of study.

I met Fogel—after reading his controversial book Time on the Cross *so I would have something to talk about—and we struck up a friendship. He was familiar with Tudor history and asked to see my "Teller's" article. That surprised me until he said he was friends with Elton, who told him about it. I sent him a copy and soon after he sent me a draft article he had prepared for a book, asking if I would review it. I had no idea why he asked me until I saw a discussion about Tudor England. I did have a few thoughts and sent them back. I later found out he graciously thanked me in a footnote in the article . . . along with fifty-three others, including Elton. I was thrilled—graduate students take whatever they can get!*

Soon after I received a call from Yale University Press asking me if I would review a book that Elton and Fogel had written. It would appear in History Today. *I said yes and then wondered the wisdom of screwing up in front of two Big Guys in their fields. I actually asked the editor "Why me?" and he said the authors recommended me. That just made it worse.*

I read the book and its title gave me an idea for a drawing: Which Road to the Past? *I asked the editor if I could include an illustration stylizing the scene from the movie* The Wizard of Oz *where the scarecrow*

---

* Reprinted with permission. The article was first published in *HISTORY TODAY*, Vol. 34, Issue 1 (Jan. 1984), pp. 5-10.

pointed to two different roads that could be taken by Dorothy. I had no idea whether "Yale" had a sense of humor. "Chicago" often did as a matter of surviving a rigorous curriculum—one of the T-shirts worn by undergraduates read "The U of C: Where fun comes to die". As it turned out, the editor liked the idea. All I had to do was get it done.

That old saying "be careful what you wish for" now became clear.

In the early 80s, the new innovative gizmo was the VCR and no one I knew could afford one. Fogel had one. My wife, Barbi, has an art degree and is quite good at drawing cartoons. I rented a VHS tape of The Wizard of Oz and brought it to his house with our two young children. The only challenges we encountered were keeping the little ones occupied (Fogel bounced them on his knees); and freezing the frame for Barbi to sketch the scene: it kept starting up again after five minutes. I told her where I wanted labels as a metaphor for the book. She signed it with a pseudonym: nepotism is sometimes frowned upon, except apparently in government.

Much later on, my children were thrilled to learn that they were bounced on the knee of a Nobel Laureate: Fogel won a Nobel Prize in Economic Sciences in 1993.

The book was important to me and to historians not exposed to large amounts of statistical data, let alone the attempts to draw historical meaning from them. Although like Elton I viewed history in terms of human behavior that follows patterns but not necessarily predictability, I was appreciative of efforts by those who crunch numbers. Cliometrics eventually fell upon hard times. Conclusions based on numbers were often flawed, missing what was actually taking place, much as models of how nations evolve were similarly coming under fire.

However, I believe data can be helpful if the "history" is understood from the onset, so to speak. For example, I have spent many years trying to comprehend how Henry VII used bonds to collect revenue and to put a population in peril should they refuse to keep the peace or rebel against the king. That research began with the Calendar of Close Rolls *entries of recognizances for his reign, and decades later I returned to them and decided to add them all up to see if they fit my ideas about them! That painful exercise, found in Chapter Eight, not only confirmed and expanded my thinking about what was taking place but also went further in helping me compare and contrast his reign with those of his Yorkist predecessors. It was an exploration I could not have accomplished without the numbers.*

Elton and Fogel presented views of these two "roads to the past" in a surprisingly objective way, and my hope at the time was that the profession of history would be the better for it. I definitely benefitted from their respective perspectives.

Add 2.1 Dorothy's Dilemma.

DOROTHY:
Follow the Yellow Brick Road. Follow the Yellow . . . Now which way do we go?
SCARECROW:
Pardon me. That way is a very nice way.
DOROTHY:
(*Confused*) Who said that?
TOTO:
Arf! Arf-Arf! Arf-Arf-Arf-Arf! Arf!
DOROTHY:
(*Skeptical*) Don't be silly, Toto. Scarecrows don't talk—
SCARECROW:
—It's pleasant down that way, too.
DOROTHY:
(*Rhetorically*) That's funny. Wasn't he pointing the other way?
SCARECROW:
Of course, people do go both ways.
DOROTHY:
(*Enlightened*) Why, you did say something, didn't you? Are you doing that on purpose, or can't you make up your mind?

(*The Wizard of Oz*, MGM, 1939)

G.R. Elton and R.W. Fogel intervene in the vital current debate of
historians: are there two separate species of history, scientific and
traditional?

Although seeking historical truth may not be as clear-cut a journey as
Dorothy's trek to Oz, a fork in the road has emerged that has historians—
and those who read history—barking as noisily as the mindful Toto. For
where once the "historical method" implied a rigorous investigation of the
documents and the application of an open, subjective mind to reconstruct
the past, a new approach has undermined the notion that history was an art
that could not be reduced to scientific analysis. Born of the computer age,
this new "scientific" history, with its practitioners often referred to as
cliometricians, seeks both to reduce the human error involved in
rediscovering the past from historical documents, and to subject such
evidence to statistical analysis on a par with the social sciences.

Whether Clio, the Greek Muse of history, is pleased with her new
offspring or loath of it may reach resolution in a new book by two
proponents of these apparent "schools" of history. Both scholars are
leading representatives of their *modi operandi*, and both have laid down
pathbreaking interpretations of their subjects of study, leaving controversy
and new methodology in their wake. It is therefore an event unto itself that
two such professors of history should pause for a moment to meet at the
fork in the road and debate the roads to the past.

The title of the book, quite appropriately, is *Which Road to the Past?
Two Views of History* (Yale University Press, 1983). Its authors are G.R.
Elton, Regius Professor of Modern History at Cambridge University; and
Robert W. Fogel, Charles R. Walgreen Professor of American Institutions
at the University of Chicago. It would not be an overstatement to say that
both are well-known, respected historians who have contributed greatly to
our knowledge of the past. How they reached their pre-eminence explains
the very roads they have followed, and what their "meeting" in this book
portends for the future of historical study.

G.R. Elton's contributions to the field of Tudor history began with his
1953 book, *The Tudor Revolution in Government*. The very title suggested
that the author was painting a new picture of history, and it turned out to
be a carefully documented landscape showing how wrong our thinking had
been about Henry VIII's reign, or the previous reign of Henry VII. Where
Henry VII had been viewed as the progenitor of a "new monarchy" which
set the scene for the modern state, Elton's picture showed a continuation
of medieval England into the 1530s. In that decade, Thomas Cromwell,
Henry VIII's principal minister, began to construct the modern state—a
revolution in government.

The anticipated volley of reply and retort usually following a sweeping revision in history was slow to materialize, largely because of Elton's methodology. He had analysed innumerable documents to support his thesis, and argued it so convincingly that any detractors would have to roll up their trousers, hold their breaths, and plunge into the sea of documentation Elton had so masterfully sailed through without mishap.

When the scholarly report was finally heard, it came predictably from the two areas dealt heavy blows by Elton: the Elizabethan period (for was not that the beginning of the modern state?), and the late medieval period (for was not that . . .?). The arguments sought to show that Elton was either too soon or too late in his assessment of the bureaucratic reality of the modern state. Moreover, there was some suspicion about the "discovery" of Thomas Cromwell as the chief architect of this Tudor revolution, and the seemingly docile, almost semi-comatose behaviour of Henry VIII through it all. Was Thomas Cromwell behind the Henrician revolution in government, or was it G.R. Elton behind the Cromwellian revolution?

Elton was undaunted and unconvinced by the criticism, which he answered with the cool efficiency of master Cromwell. Further, there was more work to be done to explain this intriguing view of Tudor history. To the key question, If a modern bureaucracy was in the works, how was it planned and implemented?, Elton answered with his book *Reform and Renewal*, showing Cromwell's careful state planning. To explain the important problem of enforcement, Elton replied with *Policy and Policy*. Along with a large body of scholarly articles and papers, Elton had restructured and redefined the long-held images of the Tudor state, and forced historians—young and old—to reassess their thinking and their prejudices. Perhaps most important, his meticulous use of historical records established an unwritten creed that thoroughness, care, and a disciplined understanding of the documents was to become the standard for reconstructing the past. G.R. Elton is now the symbol of that standard.

Robert Fogel's splash on the blotter of historical research came two decades after Elton's momentous book with the publication of *Time on the Cross* in 1974. Although an accomplished economic historian before this work, *Time on the Cross* gained international attention—and notoriety— both for its subject and its methodology. Simply put, where once the institution of American slavery was viewed as a stagnant economic aberration peopled with lazy, promiscuous blacks and cruel, sadistic slaveowners, Fogel and his co-author Stanley Engerman proffered an entirely different picture. The economic system of slavery, they said, was not only profitable but more efficient than the free farms of the North.

Slaves were well-fed, tenacious workers, and as Victorian in moral outlook as their white owners.

The proof of this revisionist pudding lay in the cliometric, or "scientific", approach to the surviving data of the period. With the aid of computers and graduate students, Fogel utilised the myriad lists and numbers found in records such as slave market invoices and plantation documents. Equipped with statistics and social science models, Fogel enraged traditional historians, and not a few fellow cliometricians, with a view of slavery that many Americans had great difficulty reconciling with their inherited belief in a "land of the free and the home of the brave". Worse, Fogel went public with his findings; that is, he made them available in a non-technical volume. He also appeared on television and spoke to reporters of major newspapers.

Fogel's book prompted immediate reaction. The controversy appeared before the public in newspaper and television interviews by rival factions, and a three-day conference was held in the autumn of 1974 at the University of Rochester, USA, to discuss *Time on the Cross*. Over 100 historians, economists, and sociologists from America and abroad came to exchange academic blows and take Fogel to task over his research methods and results. One scholar said that their analysis was based on "selective data and dubious assumptions." Others recognised that, because of this book, it would no longer be possible to blame a ruling Southern class, dead a century and more, for all of the woes blacks share today. Fogel and Engerman parried each jab at their work skilfully, and continued to do so for the next few years in papers and articles. (Three volumes by Fogel and Engerman will soon appear detailing their findings and the entire scope of the controversy.) Their basic assumptions have weathered the storm. If cliometricians were a splinter group off the main line of historical research before 1974, they were clearly in the forefront of a debate on historical methodology after that year.

That the *cause célèbre* of "scientific" history was the emotionally-charged subject of American slavery added to the argument over how to "do history". Traditional historians of the Elton ilk feared that history would get lost among the numbers. Lord Bullock, referring to the *Annales* school of social scientific history in France, told an audience at Cambridge University, "History would no longer be seen as the drama of human existence, recreated by the historian's imaginative powers, but as a series of interlocking structures, independent of personal experience but penetrable by thought and capable of rational explanation." More cynical traditionalists scoffed at the notion that the social sciences, and the models created for such sciences, could be implanted in the body of historical study. One detractor referred to the makers of the cliometric revolution as "cliomagicians"; another suggested that "if you ask them to do a study of the Crucifixion they'd start by counting the nails." On the other side, the "Young Turks" of cliometrics viewed all historical work before their time as incorrect and hopelessly biased. Only the numbers themselves were objective witnesses of the past, and only statistical analysis could eschew the prejudices that historians bring to their synthesis of history.

This state of affairs has prompted the exchange between Elton and Fogel. They begin their book by acknowledging that these two approaches to history exist, that they are different, and that they are both legitimate. Fogel then gives an historical sketch of how historians have practised their craft since the nineteenth century. He notes that with the advent of the scientific revolution ("steamboats, railroads, telegraph"), new disciplines emerged using scientific applications: economics, demography, anthropology, sociology, and statistics, the latter a sub-field of mathematics. These disciplines in turn made up a corpus of fields administering scientific methods to study social behaviour, the social sciences.

History was not to be left behind. "Scientific", to the founders of the profession, means objectivity, and such early professionals as Leopold von Ranke (1795-1886) adhered to the rule that the historian must immerse himself in the sources and subject them to internal and external criticism. Footnotes now began to sprout like poppies, spoiling the vivid scenery evoked by the narrative, but pinpointing the sources consulted and analysed. These early "scientific" historians were criticized by the traditional scholars who believed that constructing general laws of behaviour—a goal of the social sciences—was not possible. People, it was argued, or their observable behaviour, could not be reduced to statistics. By the 1930s, historians such as Carl Becker and Charles Beard completed the assault against the old brand of scientific history by seeing historical writing as temporary appraisals of what happened, not fundamental knowledge. This line of thinking continues today: in the preface to S.B. Chrimes' biography of Henry VII, he states the limitations of his study, and of the evidence, and writes, "The present work therefore is to be regarded as a report—an interim report—on the existing state of knowledge on these matters."

Elton agrees with Fogel's general assessment of how the study of history "evolves" (if we might pinch a scientific term). He believes with Fogel that divisions do exist so long as "nobody supposes that 'scientific' historians have no traditions and 'traditional' historians no science." Elton also identifies an element of *déjà vu* upon observing the cliometrician's search for discovering laws governing human behaviour, since their early "scientific" ancestors—some of whom were traditional historians—also attempted this task: "This latest manifestation is young enough not to have yet suffered the disillusionment that came to its predecessors." Fogel's mention of one cliometrician's message to traditional historians, however, suggests that disillusionment may be long in coming: "Retool, rethink, conform, or be ploughed under."

Fogel's assessment of traditional historians valuing the "literary art" of history finds little support from Elton, who does not see this as a major characteristic of his colleagues. Both agree, however, that the two schools approach an historical problem differently, and Fogel offers an example: the death of John Keats. Traditional historians would want to know why Keats died at the time, in the place, and under the particular circumstances that he did. Cliometicians desiring to analyse mortality among the English will see Keats' death as "less interesting than those circumstances that contribute to an understanding of why deaths due to tuberculosis were so frequent during the first half of the nineteenth century." These are not mutually exclusive, but Fogel remarks that the two schools of history behave as if they were.

Fogel is adamant in his belief that cliometrics is not only useful, but integral to understanding the past: "In virtually every field to which it has been applied, . . . the cliometric approach has not only yielded substantive findings that are strikingly different from the findings of older research but also called attention to important processes that previously had escaped notice." He describes the work of Peter Laslett and his colleagues at Cambridge as an example of such successes. In 1965, Laslett and his group began a study of the family and the household structure. Initial results are indeed "strikingly different" from previously held conceptions of the household. For one, there was greater mobility among residents of pre-industrial English villages than thought, with a turnover of more than 50 percent per decade. The so-called "nuclear family" (parents and children) was not the result of the Industrial Revolution, but had predominated in Northwest Europe and the United States for at least 300 years.

Fogel sees these results as significant for obtaining a more accurate picture of the past, but he is not encouraged by the resistance to cliometric methodology. Despite the important results of such studies as the project at Cambridge, traditional historians continue to obstruct the teaching of behavioural models and statistics, and often block changing the curriculum in history departments. Elton, hardly an obstructionist, infers that cliometrics is here to stay and will not doubt validate itself. He would nonetheless be happier if the models cliometricians use "were derived from the study of the evidence and not borrowed from supposedly scientific work in the social sciences."

Fogel breaks downs the differences between scientific and traditional historians into several categories. While admittedly not a complete set of topics for comparison, they provide a forum for discussion. The following examples reveal not only their own differences and similarities in the study of history, but do much to explain the continuing methodological controversies.

He believes that cliometricians concentrate on the study of collectives, while traditional historians tend to concentrate on individual behaviour. Traditional historians tend to emphasise the unique aspects of events while cliometricians tend to search for the common elements in repetitive events. Despite these differences, he notes that both schools have analysed certain topics, including the origins of the New South and the decline of feudalism. Although traditional historians are interested in general forces and their impact on human behaviour, according to Fogel they would never explain the reason for Louis Napoleon's decision to go to war with Prussia from the statement "that under such and such circumstances monarchs are likely to go to war."

Elton feels that Fogel's descriptions of subject matter are misleading and suggest an implication that cliometricians are looking for "some kind of statistical law based upon their study of collectivities." Further, if Fogel sees traditional historians being unable to accept as an explanation the existence of certain conditions that make it likely for a monarch to go to war, Elton feels that neither would cliometricians. Elton also believes that the differences run deeper; he sees cliometricians slighting the major part of what the traditional historian studies—the event—and he rejects "the concept of forces as identifiable agents creating or conditioning historical events." Preoccupation with background forces, he insists, may not only be misleading; by themselves they are insufficient to explain the behaviour of individuals in specific times and places. Using Lawrence Stone's work on the family as an example of a "pattern-maker" who got carried beyond the evidence, Elton says "Critics have had no difficulty in producing real people in shoals, involved in love, marriage, procreation, and the bringing up of children, who quite simply refused to behave in the manner postulated by the pattern-makers."

Elton believes that Fogel's definitions are short of their mark for still another reason: the examples proffered, Elton argues, relate not to traditional history, but to "bad history". One example used by Fogel is feudalism and its decline. Elton declares that there was no such thing as feudalism, a term invented to make discourse easier: "Only those historians who have fallen victim to the tendency to submerge the individual in the collectivity, or to clothe the abstract in a semblance of concreteness, have been able to speak of such things as the decline of feudalism."

Elton identifies another difference between the two schools: the responsibility of the traditional historian not to eliminate any question about the past in his research, even if it is unanswerable. Cliometricians, he says, must necessarily dismiss large areas of inquiry and "confine themselves to the production of large-scale analyses and schemes touching certain events only." How this relates to human beings at first mystified Elton, who wondered "how cliometric methods can handle human thought." He has come to see, however, that behaviour and artifacts might be construed as the products of thought, subject to quantitative analyses. But ever cautious, Elton posits two caveats: first, the results of cliometricians are based on products not intended to describe ideas; second, the treatment affords no means of entry into the individual mind.

Fogel has hardly made Elton a believer in the new scientific methodology, but the latter feels that traditional historians in England are becoming more tolerant of the upstarts, more so than traditional historians in the United States: "Traditional historians in England are liable to ask where all that investigation of, say, fertility rates will get us, but they do so in a spirit of hope that it will get us somewhere."

Fogel sees a clear division in the types of evidenced perused by the two schools. Traditional historians, he says, prefer literary (by which he means non-quantitative) evidence; the cliometricians prefer quantitative evidence. While noting the incompleteness or flawed condition of much surviving data, he believes that "even proven defects in a given body of evidence do not necessarily deprive it of usefulness," and he says that traditional historians come down hard on such evidenced. Fogel offers the example of the cliometrician's collection of data on the characteristics of slave households to assess theories about the bond of affection within such households, while traditional historians have used Harriet Beecher Stowe's *Uncle Tom's Cabin* to show love and affection in the slave community. But Fogel warns against using either method exclusively: "The worst of all errors is to assume that either literary evidence by itself or quantitative evidence by itself is sufficient, when they are not." Theories will collapse if they are not based on a "rock of evidence" as to what was typical and what was aberrant.

Elton agrees that cliometricians must do more than analyse evidence deemed open to mathematical interpretation. He cannot agree with Fogel's emphasis on literary evidence for traditional historians and states that strictly literary evidence (imaginative writing or *belles lettres*) "ranks very low." With reference to Fogel's illustration of how to determine the marital relationships of slaves, Elton reiterates a flaw in the example: someone using *Uncle Tom's Cabin* as a reliable source is not a traditional historian, but a bad historian. He completely agrees that all sources, regardless of their defects, are useful. Both men are in agreement that quantitative evidence or literary evidence alone are insufficient for thoroughness, and that both groups of historians must analyse their documents carefully. Says Elton, "Both kinds should, as Fogel agrees, accept that they labour in the same vineyard and that any form of mutual exclusiveness will spoil the wine."

Fogel identifies the traditional historian's method of proof: "The traditional historian's model for proving his case or disproving an opponent's case is the legal model." It involves the employment of witnesses to the past to reconstruct what happened. These witnesses, taking the form of documents, are tested for their veracity and then cross-examined, all as part of a judgment on the sources in question. This "critical re-examination" of the documents carries over to an evaluation of the historian's interpretation of the evidence, the end results being a repudiation or vindication of the conclusions reached.

Fogel also believes that traditional historians often view "established authority" as sacrosanct for proof of historical interpretation: those who conclude differently from the recognised authority are often presumed to be in error.

Elton says flatly that the legal model is a wrong one for the traditional historian, and he finds it difficult to believe that he practises the kind of history "enshrined in that peculiar compilation, the *Harvard Guide to American History of 1954*." He notes that the *Guide* divides evidence into primary (first hand testimony about an event) and secondary (descriptions of events based on primary sources), and says that secondary sources are not sources at all. In fact, they may be little more than the sources for a study of the author of that source! True sources, states Elton, "are all the deposits of past human action, observed or not, in all its forms." Few surviving documents are so simple that "all one needs to know about them is whether they tell a truth or a lie." Further, evidence is not tantamount to a series of witnesses, and Elton feels that the model is based on a limited notion of historical evidence. Financial accounts, records of court, legislative enactments, city ordinances—all constitute evidence that defies the interrogation envisaged in the law model. Elton concludes with the blunt statement that "real historians, traditional or not, do not assess their evidence or construct their proofs in the manner of a court of law."

Established authority finds little meaning for Elton in identifying standards of proof: there simply is no authority. The historian, says Elton, must keep an open mind when surveying the evidence. And since past dictums are not etched in marble, a term like verification "has virtually no usable meaning in history." Elton explains that historians deal with interpretations, not verification of propositions. The truth is unattainable by the very nature of the historians' search: it lies in the past. Moreover, the past is so complex that merely writing about it creates certain distortions through omission or emphasis. Elton wishes that historians of either persuasion would take cognisance of this limitation to historical research: "It would help in all these debates if people could accept that the only 'model' for explaining historical method is that of the historian himself: he is not a philosopher or a scientist or an imaginative artist but simply an historian working by the rules and standard of his own craft."

Fogel discusses the empirical-scientific model used by the cliometrician for testing the validity of historical interpretations. "The strategy is to make explicit the implicit empirical assumption on which many historical arguments rest and then to search for evidence, usually quantitative, capable of confirming or disconfirming the assumptions." Unlike the traditional historian who uses non-quantitative material that can be documented in the footnote, the scientific historian relies on large bodies of quantitative information that are stored on computer tapes and summarised in charts, graphs and in equations. While presenting little problem to cliometricians who are used to working with these tapes and the lengthy technical guides needed to read them, Fogel notes that traditional historians "are often appalled by the effort that is required to verify cliometric research."

Since Elton has little sympathy for those claiming to have found ultimate truths, he sees cliometrics as no more scientific or compelling than the work of good traditional history. History "aims at explanations which approximate to an unverifiable truth"; it is exhaustively investigated and presents "Contructs of persuasive probability." That is all. Since quantitative evidence is never complete, Elton states that cliometricians cannot produce "strictly verifiable proofs."

Before walking their separate methodological ways, the two scholars part company with certain conclusions and observations. Fogel notes the excitement cliometrics has caused, with many young historians struggling to master scientific methods for historical research. But he offers warnings regarding what the scientific historian should consider about his craft. Cliometricians have had to admit that traditional history is better suited for certain studies, painful as this admission might be. Perhaps more important, Fogel says that few generalisations cover all aspects of human behaviour, and that behavioural models must be "place- and time-specific." He believes that while cliometricians have contributed to the elaboration of the narrative, "Cliometrics has not made traditional history obsolete." Finally, in the spirit of détente, Fogel allows that both schools "supplement and enrich each other", and that the two methodologies are neither "mutually exclusive nor intrinsically antagonistic." Fogel's hope for *rapprochement* between the two groups may yet see the day when the lion lies down with the lamb. Which group is the lion will probably never be agreed upon, but one thing is certain: the lamb won't get much sleep.[1]

Elton pauses to reload and reflect on the usefulness of cliometrics. "We are all historians," he says, "differing only in what questions interest us and what methods we find useful in answering them." He agrees with Fogel that the achievements of scientific historians lie in two areas: the study of long-term trends and developments, and the investigation of broad phenomena like the economic effects of slavery or the demographics of large populations. Because of their use of quantitative data, Elton sees the scientific methodology as not very useful before the year 1700, and impossible before 1500 because of the nature of the historical record. Cliometrics, he says, can only operate by suppressing the individual in favour of the aggregate, which can prove valuable for concepts and structures, but not for "the story of people." Elton also warns that "the method is so mathematical that is process a false sense of security." But he nonetheless accepts the new methods as valid and promising.

Both historians agree on certain fundamentals of historical research: the need for thoroughness in the search for evidence; taking precautions against subordinating details to interpretation; searching for better investigative methods. They note the popular view that each age rewrites its own history of the past because each age is conditioned by values and judgments of that age. This can be seen today with the increased interest in black history, female history, and the history of certain third-world countries. Such ideological changes, however, are not the only reasons—or the primary reasons—for rewriting history. New evidence and better methods are more likely to lead to new interpretations. How one "does history" is at the heart of the debate.

The two roads to the past may never cross, but they will undoubtedly wind over hill and vale in close proximity to each other. The traditional

---

[1] Paraphrasing a quote attributed to American writer, comedian, actor and director Woody Allen.

historian may wonder if the cliometrician's method to his madness of counting up seemingly incongruous numbers really reflects but a madness to the method. The cliometrician may marvel at the traditional historian's preoccupation with documents relating to individuals or events that somehow allow for the construction of a government or the policies of a monarch.

When the Scarecrow pointed to one road, then another, Dorothy asked "Are you doing that on purpose, or can't you make up your mind?" Historians have apparently made up their minds: both roads lead to the past. But unlike the hapless little girl who had to make a choice, we can follow the progress of the travellers to the past. Discoveries abound along both routes.

ADDENDUM 3

FEAR OF FAILING:
THE TAKING OF THE ORAL EXAM*

Introduction

On 6 February 1976, some five months before the U.S. Supreme Court ruled that the death penalty was not inherently cruel and was therefore a constitutionally-acceptable form of punishment, another ominous event occurred with a possibly similar outcome—at least to me. On that day I met with five professors of history at the University of Chicago to participate in a two-hour session known as the Oral Exam. Its purpose was to determine whether I would move forward in my graduate school studies as a newly-minted PhD candidate, or be relegated to that inglorious scarred landscape found at colleges and universities worldwide I call The Land of You Failed—Goodbye. *I was peppered with questions by The Five in three broad areas of history behind closed doors. Thus, no one could come to my rescue even if I cried for help.*

Both the Exam and the years of studying that preceded it were so traumatic and emotionally-crippling to me that I decided to impose a cathartic self-therapy by actually revealing to the world the oft-hidden, inner-workings of what a graduate student endures to reach this point of no return. Moreover, I surmised that if misery does enjoy company, there was an abundance of company out there who needed to know about this line in the sand between a doctorate and a career-ending disaster. The least I could do was give them ample warning.

The eventual article I wrote was published, and not without a little irony, in The University of Chicago Magazine *(Winter 1976). I entitled it "Fear of Failing" as a dubious play on a very popular book published three years earlier by Erica Jong called* Fear of Flying. *Her work was*

---

* Reprinted with permission. The article was first published in *The University of Chicago Magazine* (Winter 1976), pp. 18-20.

about female sexuality and it sparked debates and controversy. My confessional as well was provocative and eye-opening—if you were a graduate student contemplating the journey to a PhD in the humanities and social sciences. It also shed light on the entire process for a friend or relative of one such lost soul—they might wonder why that soul looked so lethargic, feeble and depressed all the time, and actually paid for the privilege.

The article has elicited many responses from students and professors alike over the years. I have also had requests for copies, either through word of mouth or possibly because a brief description of it remains on the Internet. (As of this writing it is still there: https://magazine.uchicago.edu/0112/class-notes/ourpages.html)

What follows is the article, which divulges all the gruesome details of the taking of the Oral Exam. It reminds me that whenever I am stuck on a historical problem or analyze a document that makes little sense, it still pales in comparison to passing through the metaphorical and treacherous gates of Dante's Inferno on that fateful February day—the gates with the sign admonishing the unwary graduate student to "Abandon All Hope Ye Who Enter Here".

We have forty million reasons for failure, but not a single excuse.
—R. Kipling

A graduate student has three basic tasks to complete before he or she admits privately that a PhD is, in fact, attainable: (1) Actually deciding to go to a graduate school; (2) surviving the years of course work, research papers and various and sundry written examinations; (3) the Oral Exam.

The first two parts are well-known to parents, friends and confessors; the third remains a mystery to all but the initiated—and they are generally in too much shock to divulge their ordeal to a curious world. What *are* the Oral Exams? What does one do to prepare for them? Has anyone lived to tell the tale?

I have, and the countless nightmares before the Exam continue to haunt me. It has been just a few weeks since the Orals, and I have decided to reveal the gory details of this event. Edgar Allan Poe would be green with envy—he missed this one.

A graduate student takes from nine to twelve courses per year and passes some form of examination for a Master's degree (along with the writing of a research paper or thesis). He then continues in course work, exams, writing, etc., and when he and his professors believe he is prepared, plans are made to take an Oral Exam. Many graduate schools require a preliminary written examination in one's fields which usually forms a basis for the Oral Exam.

The Drama Begins

I came to the University of Chicago with an M.A. degree from another university and continued my work in three fields of history. After completing the requirements of a second year student, I entered the Fall Quarter as a "third year student": the most pitied and honored of creatures on campus. They were the ones no longer involved with course papers and exams. They were the ones who survived two years of poverty and obedience—chastity being incompatible with their survival.

By October, I had a major field in Tudor history (Henry VIII and family) and two minor fields: ancient Greece in the sixth century B.C. (early philosophy, early government and early Greeks in general) and medieval England, 1066 to 1485 (events between William the Conqueror and the so-called War of the Roses). After careful consideration, I decided to declare myself a candidate for the Oral Exam and visited the history secretary.

I listened nervously as she told me to fill out a form indicating my three fields, the professors examining me in each and a fourth professor (known as "the fourth"). I was also informed that, of course, the professor overseeing British history would be present. Of course.

The exam was to be two hours long.

I went home in a light-headed daze and asked my wife, Barbi, if Walter Cronkite had said anything I needed to know; my only free time involved watching Walter.[1] Then I sat at my desk wondering what a lemming feels like at the edge of a cliff. My decision had been irrevocable; I could not change my mind and postpone the Exam. To do so was to let five professors know I wasn't sure of my competency. The problem was I wasn't sure.

*

What follows is a somewhat unknown series of events that graduate students keep close to their hearts and occasional martinis. And since the University of Chicago is a renowned institution of knowledge and learning, I must declare that these experiences are solely my own. Nevertheless, show this to any third year student and I'll give odds he winces.

After submitting the perilous parchment, I requested late January as the date of execution. From October through November, I continued attending classes and reading several books and scholarly articles a week. Barbi tiptoed through the mountain of notes and books in the living room. (We lost our Persian cat for six hours—she was under a "book bridge" comprised of the Oxford Histories of England.) Our social life consisted of brushing our teeth together.

---

[1] Walter Cronkite (1916-2009), at one time referred to as "the most trusted man in America", was the managing editor and anchorman (newsreader in the UK) for the CBS Evening News. He signed off his newscasts "And that's the way it is," and we all believed him. Ironically, although he never knew how helpful he was as a distraction during my Oral Exam ordeal, I had the good fortune of meeting him when he visited the University of Chicago. We actually corresponded for awhile regarding the importance of history to contextualize the news, and he kindly offered his thoughts on a few of my early opinion pieces for newspapers using an historical perspective.

Add 3.1 "Book Bridge".

Then came December, and my life passed before me—along with visions of Henry VIII wrestling Francis I, John of Gaunt playing around with Katherine, and Peisistratus invading Athens again. I tried to set up schedules for studying: two days Greek, two days medieval, three days Tudor. It didn't work. It took forever to wade through three graduate years of notes—looking assiduously for tidbits I thought the professors might not know—while reading books and taking yet *more* notes.

January delivered a new year, no classes and an extra ten pounds. I have always been a basically non-fat person. Suddenly I noticed, while sitting on the floor amidst notes, papers and old tuna fish sandwiches, that something was sitting on my lap. It was my stomach.

To say I was nervous is an understatement. And I used my nervous energy digestively as I studied and reviewed, my wife now joining me at feedings as well as at tooth-brushings. And all this time the butterflies in my stomach began to increase and multiply.

It was soon determined that on February 6, from 1 to 3 P.M., the "Four Horsemen of the Apocalypse" would join the head of British history for my Exam. I had been taking the Orals in my head nightly since December; by January, I was reciting it. Barbi couldn't even fix a skirt without a comment from her hebephrenic husband. ("Did you know that worsteds like that skirt didn't really get going commercially until the sixteenth century? Why, in the West Riding of Yorkshire . . . !")

The Sunday night before my last week of preparation I soaked in a tub reading notes on Henry VI when the phone rang. It was the professor of my major field.

Barbi held the phone while I grabbed a towel and listened to my heart rev up. What could be wrong? I concluded that the five professors had decided to call it off—for a year or two—so that I could read a new unpublished nine-volume history of mustard-making in Bedfordshire. I picked up the phone while my stomach churned and groaned.

"Be of good cheer!" He had called to cheer me up five days before the Exam. I slowly sank to the floor as he attempted to calm me down. He failed miserably. I thanked him and slithered back to the tub; I wanted to follow the water down the drain.

Thursday night: the night before the Exam. Now any student knows that after months of reviewing, the "night before" will add little in new material. But at 6 P.M. after Walter Cronkite told me "That's the way it is," I was suddenly transformed from "any student" into "the student taking the Oral Exam!" For months I had awakened my wife at night searching through dictionary and history book for a term to satisfy a bad dream. Now the fear of forgetting dates, terms and people totally occupied my mind the night before the Exam, and for two hours I reviewed trivial points that would have given a computer migraines.

At 8 P.M., I decided I knew nothing and that failing was imminent. I watched a movie until ten, played a game of *Careers* with Barbi (I entered the "Space" career three times—a premonition, I thought!) and went to bed. Four hours and endless mental Exams later, I dozed off . . .

And I dreamed that I showed up at the Exam in cutoffs, that the head of British history wore a football jersey—everything was going wrong. When I awoke, it was nine o'clock and the real nightmare began. I went into the kitchen and found a "give 'em hell" note from Barbi. Then my parents phoned to say good luck. It made matters worse: I had others to disappoint besides myself.

I showered, peeked at a few notes and donned my rarely-worn suit and tie. Then I said good-bye to our cat (she yawned) and drove to school. My English muffin and tea wouldn't leave me alone.

The Taking of the Oral Exam

At noon, I returned some books to the library and sat in a chair day-dreaming about the Great Ordeal of a graduate student. By 12:30 I was up, pacing here and there, speaking to no one and totally lost in an inner world of fear and wonder. All those years for a two-hour exam. All the hundreds of books, thousands of notes, millions of words and facts for three fields at 40 minutes a throw. How did my five professors feel at their exams? Would they see themselves in me today?

At 12:45, I entered the office where it all was to take place. The Tudor examiner greeted me and continued to read a book. Soon the Greek examiner appeared, then the head of British history, the medieval examiner and finally the fourth. It began at 1:05 and ended at 3:54. I know—my left eye was glued to my watch between questions, answers and a lot of heavy breathing.

I cannot relate the questions or the discussions that took place, not because they are strictly confidential, but because most are rather esoteric (the sources for the sixth century B.C. and their problems), and the general ones rather long and involved (the various developments from Henry II to Richard II). It must be said, however, that it was a psychological exam: I knew the stuff; they knew I knew it—it was a question of how I related it and even *if* I could relate it. This is where people pass or fail.

At 3:54, I was asked to leave the room while the professors decided my fate. I walked around the empty hall, staring at my watch, counting the seconds as they slowly ticked away. The Exam had been a total letdown for me: of the one hundred percent I had learned, it seemed I was only tested on *one percent*!

After thirty seconds, someone from inside the room let out a belly laugh.

"That's it. I failed!" I found myself talking out loud. After five minutes had passed I knew, truly knew, that I had blown it and that they were deciding how to tell me that grammar schools need people to talk about George Washington and King George III.

Soon, all the answers I *wanted* to give came to me! At 4:02, I walked around the corner of the office, sat down on a chair and closed my eyes, pondering my situation. I knew I had failed and that there would be one other chance a year later to retake the Oral Exam. But I also knew there was no way that I would wait for that chance—it was now or good-bye PhD.

At 4:04, the door opened and the medieval examiner called out my name. I jumped up preparing to answer another question until I realized there would be no further questions. So startled was I that my feet refused to move, and the professor could not see me.

"It appears the gentleman has gone home," he told the others, and I finally managed to walk into the office. He then said "Congratulations, you passed." This strangely anticlimactical revelation was followed by pats on the back and cheers from the others. I could not believe it, and yet the word "pass" was the only one I expected to hear—perhaps because it was the only word I could have accepted.

Two of the professors took me for a drink, and not until 4:30 did I realize that my wife and numerous friends, relatives and thrillseekers were unaware of my victory. I left the professors and ran to the gym to call Barbi, saying I would be late. She asked if I passed, and a deep breath helped me announce a strangely subdued "Yes."

*

What remains now is losing ten pounds and writing a dissertation—the latter being a book based on researching a problem in British history pertaining to my field and interests. (Henry VII is the candidate.) It will require tedious work, numerous documents and primary material, a trip to England . . . and then the successful oral defense of the dissertation in order to receive the PhD. Another *oral exam*? Not really.

I will be defending *my* work, and I will be as familiar with my research as my examiners. The defense is a minor future event compared to the Oral Exam. And yet to pass the Oral Exam simply means, "We professors allow you to research as an historian, to write a dissertation and, if successful, to pursue a career as an historian." As in a fraternity, I am now accepted, working toward the rewards of teaching, writing and researching: personal achievement and a desire to excite others about my interests.

The fear of failing has left mental scars, but a different, knowledgeable person remains. "You're a better man than I am, Gunga Din," Kipling wrote. Perhaps Gunga was a graduate student.

Mark R. Horowitz is a doctoral candidate in British history.

INDEX